D1428838

PLATO
THE REPUBLIC

*

PENGUIN BOOKS

Penguin Books Ltd, Harmondsworth, Middlesex, England
Penguin Books Inc., 3300 Clipper Mill Road, Baltimore 11, Md, U.S.A.
Penguin Books Pty Ltd, Ringwood, Victoria, Australia

—

First published in this translation 1955
Reprinted 1956, 1958, 1959, 1960, 1961, 1962, 1963, 1964, 1965, 1966

—

Copyright © H. D. P. Lee, 1955

—

Made and printed in Great Britain
by The Whitefriars Press Ltd
London and Tonbridge
Set in Monotype Garamond

TABLE OF CONTENTS

＊

CONTENTS

6

CONTENTS

TRANSLATOR'S INTRODUCTION

*

1. PLATO'S LIFE AND TIMES

PLATO was born in 427 B.C., some three years after the out-break of the Peloponnesian War and just over a year after the death of Pericles. His father, Ariston, who died when he was a few years old, was a member of an old and distinguished Athenian family, as was also his mother Perictione. Ariston and Perictione had two other sons, both older than Plato, Adeimantus and Glaucon, who are two of the main characters in the *Republic*. After Ariston's death Perictione married again, as was the normal Greek custom, her second husband being Pyrilampes, a close friend and supporter of Pericles and himself prominent in public life.

Plato thus came of a distinguished family with many political connexions. Through his stepfather he had a link with Pericles, who gave his name to the great age of Athenian history, and to whom Athenian democracy, as Plato knew it, owed many of its characteristic features; for though Pericles is remembered chiefly for the personal ascendancy which dominated Athenian affairs for thirty years, he was none the less, in domestic politics, a democrat. On the other hand two of Perictione's relations, her uncle Charmides, after whom one of Plato's early dialogues is called, and her cousin Critias, were prominent in the oligarchic movements at the end of the century.

Of Plato's early years we know little. He presumably received the normal education of a Greek boy, learning to read and write and study the poets (cf. p. 113). More important, he grew up in a city at war. The Peloponnesian war, which began just before his birth, lasted until he was twenty-three and ended in defeat and humiliation for Athens, and in the break-up of the confederation which she had led since the Persian wars, and which Pericles had consolidated and turned into

9

something more like an empire than a confederation. Pericles himself died in 425 B.C., a victim of the plague which visited Athens in the early years of the war and brought death and demoralization with it, a demoralization described with vivid terseness by Thucydides. After Pericles' death the more radical democrats were the most influential force in Athenian politics. They were men of a very different kind. Their origins were comparatively humble – Cleon was a tanner, Hyperbolus a lamp-seller; they relied for their power, as Pericles had done, on their ability to sway the popular assembly. But whereas he never sacrificed his independence of judgement, they felt themselves to be dependent on popular favour, and their policies were too often those which they thought the people would like rather than those which the situation demanded. Such at any rate is the judgement of Thucydides;[1] and though he had little cause to love them, and though they certainly did not lack energy or courage or ability, the judgement is not unfounded, and it was under their leadership that Athens finally lost the war. Their external policy is commonly called imperialist. They recognized more clearly than Pericles the element of force in the Athenian confederation, and they were prepared to use it more ruthlessly; they were ready to act on the belief which Thrasymachus expresses in Book I of the *Republic*,[2] that it is natural and right for the strong to exploit the weak.

The first stage of the war ended in a stale-mate in 421 B.C. A few years later Athens embarked on a great expedition against Syracuse in Sicily, another step in the policy of expansion. The expedition was a disastrous failure and by 412 B.C. the men, ships, and money devoted to it were irretrievably lost. The strain of external disaster can sharpen internal conflict. There was constant opposition to the policies of the democratic leaders; to the better-off their external policy seemed folly and their internal policy exploitation of the rich for the benefit of the irresponsible masses. The shock of the Sicilian disaster gave the opposition, the 'oligarchs', their

1. Bk II, 65. Plato echoes it in the *Republic* (p. 248 ff, p. 254).
2. P. 26 ff.

chance, and in 411 B.C. there was a revolution in which control passed to a Council of Four Hundred. This was succeeded a year later by the so-called Government of the Five Thousand, a constitution of which many moderates approved,[1] and which consisted, essentially, in limiting active citizen rights to those able to equip themselves with arms (the Athenian hoplite or infantryman was expected to provide his own arms), who proved to number about nine thousand, about a quarter to a third of the adult male population. The object was to keep political control in the hands of the more responsible elements in the population; but Athens depended on her sea-power, and could not deprive her poorer citizens, who served in the fleet, of a say in her affairs. The Government of the Five Thousand only lasted a year; the democratic constitution was then restored, and savage measures taken by the democrats against their oligarchic opponents, so that the following six years have been described as a 'democratic terror'. It was in this atmosphere of party bitterness that Plato reached his eighteenth year.

The final downfall of Athens came in 404 B.C. It was again followed by an oligarchic revolution, this time carried through with the help of victorious Spartan arms. A commission of thirty was set up; in theory they were to frame a new constitution, but in practice they retained power in their own hands and used it to settle old scores, and any good they may have done initially in 'purging the city of wrongdoers' was forgotten in the savage tyranny that followed. It was a tyranny that lasted only eight months; the Thirty were driven out and subsequently killed, and the democratic constitution, in all essentials the same, restored. Athens was tired of extremists, and on the whole the restored democracy acted with sense and moderation. But it did one thing which Plato could never forgive: in 399 B.C. it put Socrates to death on a charge of impiety and corrupting the young. We have Plato's own account, in his Seventh Letter, written when he was an old man, of his experiences during these years when he was a young man of about twenty-three to twenty-eight. 'I had much

1. Thucydides and Aristotle thought it the best Athens ever had.

the same experience as many other young men. I expected, when I came of age, to go into politics. The political situation gave me an opportunity. The existing constitution, which was subject to widespread criticism, was overthrown....and a committee of Thirty given supreme power. As it happened some of them were friends and relations of mine, and they at once invited me to join them, as if it were the natural thing for me to do. My feelings were what were to be expected in a young man: I thought they were going to reform society and rule justly, and so I watched their proceedings with deep interest. I found that they soon made the earlier regime look like a golden age. Among other things they tried to incriminate my old friend Socrates, whom I should not hesitate to call the most upright man then living, by sending him, with others, to arrest a fellow-citizen and bring him forcibly to execution; Socrates refused, and risked everything rather than make himself party to their wickedness. When I saw all this, and other things as bad, I was disgusted and drew back from the wickedness of the times.

'Not long afterwards the Thirty fell, and the constitution was changed. And again, though less keenly, I felt the desire to enter politics. They were troublous times, and many things were done to which one could object; nor was it surprising that vengeance should sometimes be excessive in a revolution. None the less the returned democrats behaved, on the whole, with moderation. Unfortunately, however, some of those in power brought my friend Socrates to trial on a monstrous charge, the last that could be made against him, the charge of impiety; and he was condemned and executed.'

Plato was probably quite young when he first met Socrates – at any rate, he represents him in his dialogues as being well known to members of his family, for example Adeimantus and Glaucon in the *Republic*. But whenever the meeting took place, it was a turning-point in Plato's life. Socrates' position in European thought is unique. He wrote nothing; yet through his followers, of whom others besides Plato wrote dialogues in which he figured, he has influenced subsequent thought as much as any other single person. In his later years, when Plato knew him, he devoted himself entirely to discussing ethical questions. The oracle at Delphi, in response to an enquiry by one of his admirers, had said that he was the wisest man in Greece. Socrates was sure that he was not, and set out to prove the oracle wrong. His method of doing so was to cross-question people he met about their beliefs, and about their ethical beliefs in particular, since for a Greek 'wisdom' had a strongly ethical meaning. And his questions would commonly take the form of asking people what they meant when they referred to common ethical qualities like self-control, or justice, or fairness. He found that they did not really know, or at any rate could give no satisfactory account of what they meant; and to that extent he was wiser than they – he was aware of his ignorance, they were not. But the cure of ignorance is knowledge, and so, in addition to showing that conventional moral notions were frequently confused and contradictory, Socrates insisted on the importance in morals of knowledge. If only we *knew* what was right, then, he argued, the problems of morality would be comparatively simple; and in quest of that knowledge he never ceased his constant examination of himself and of others.

But being cross-examined with the penetrating thoroughness of Socrates was not an experience which everyone enjoyed; and with all his uncompromising honesty and his essential piety, Socrates was hardly an orthodox character, and Athens had had enough of unorthodoxy. Socrates was linked in the minds of many Athenians with the scepticism and 'modern nonsense' which they blamed for their many misfortunes; what was needed, they felt, was a greater respect for the truths of conventional morality, not a questioning of them. And whatever the immediate occasion of Socrates' trial or the details of his indictment, it was this feeling that led them to condemn him.[1]

But to Plato his condemnation meant a final disillusionment with contemporary politics. The passage from the Seventh Letter, already quoted, continues: 'When I considered all this, the more closely I studied the politicians and the laws and

1. See *The Last Days of Socrates*, H. Tredennick (Penguin Classics).

customs of the day, and the older I grew, the more difficult it seemed to me to govern rightly. Nothing could be done without trustworthy friends and supporters; and these were not easy to come by in an age which had abandoned its traditional moral code but found it impossibly difficult to create a new one. At the same time law and morality were deteriorating at an alarming rate, with the result that though I had been full of eagerness for a political career, the sight of all this chaos made me giddy, and though I never stopped thinking how things might be improved and the constitution reformed, I postponed action, waiting for a favourable opportunity. Finally I came to the conclusion that all existing states were badly governed, and that their constitutions were incapable of reform without drastic treatment and a great deal of good luck. I was forced, in fact, to the belief that the only hope of finding justice for society or for the individual lay in true philosophy, and that mankind will have no respite from trouble until either real philosophers gain political power or politicians become by some miracle true philosophers.'

This, in a few words, is the theme of the *Republic*, from which the concluding sentence is borrowed with some verbal alteration. Plato's decision to abandon a political career was finally taken during the ten years or so after Socrates' death. During those years he is said to have travelled, to Cyrene, to Egypt, and perhaps to Phoenicia; but much of his time must have been spent in Athens, as we are told that he served in the Athenian army in three campaigns. He also wrote his first dialogues, beginning with a defence of Socrates, continuing with others in which he explored the implications of Socrates' life and thought, and ending, probably, with the *Gorgias*, in which the life of philosophy and the life of politics are confronted and politics rejected; and the peculiar bitterness and emotional tension of this last dialogue show how difficult the decision had been.

In 388–7 B.C. Plato visited South Italy, perhaps in order to make the acquaintance of some of the Pythagorean philosophers living there. The Orphic-Pythagorean belief in the after-life and the Pythagorean emphasis on mathematics as a philosophic discipline certainly influenced him strongly, as can be seen in the *Republic*. From Italy he crossed to Sicily and visited the court of Dionysius I of Syracuse, where he learned something of tyranny at first hand. He also made the acquaintance of the tyrant's brother-in-law Dion, who was deeply impressed with Plato's ideas about politics, and was later to try with him to turn the younger Dionysius into a philosopher-ruler. But this visit to Syracuse did not last long. Plato is said to have offended Dionysius, who, according to one version of the story, sold him into slavery, from which he was redeemed by a friend.

He returned to Athens and there in 386 B.C. founded the Academy, where he taught for the rest of his life. The Academy was founded as a school for statesmen. Plato had decided that nothing could be done with contemporary politics and contemporary politicians. He therefore decided to set up a school where a new type of politician could be trained, and where the would-be politician might learn to be a philosopher-ruler. He probably did not expect any very immediate results; but he continued to hope, in his own phrase, that he might turn some statesmen into philosophers, and the Academy was always, under Plato, 'primarily a school of philosophic statesmen'.[1] It was not without a rival. A few years before, Isocrates had also founded a school at Athens. He was continuing the tradition started by the Sophists in the previous century. They were travelling teachers and lecturers, who appeared in the middle of the century in response to the demand for an education that went beyond the grounding in the works of the poets which formed the traditional Greek curriculum. They taught most things; but since success in life is what most men want, and since the ability to persuade your neighbour is always an important element in success, and was particularly important in the Greek democracies, they all taught rhetoric, the art of self-expression and persuasion. From this purely practical political interest many of them proceeded to political and moral theory; Thrasymachus in Book I of the *Republic* is typical of this side of their activity.

1. Cornford, *The Republic of Plato*, p. xxiv.

Isocrates himself criticized the Sophists of his day for triviality and pretentiousness. None the less the rhetorical training which he offered was a continuation of the educational tradition which they started. He believed that a training in the art of self-expression, in the art of composing and setting out a coherent and persuasive argument, provided in itself an educational discipline that was, together with the literary studies on which it was based, the best preparation for life. If it did not teach morality directly, yet by inculcating standards of good taste, and by the intellectual discipline which it involved, it should give what was in effect a moral training. Isocrates therefore claimed that his methods turned out better men and better statesmen than Plato's. And in fact a training in rhetoric remained the standard form of higher education in the ancient world.

Plato's conception of higher education was quite different. Briefly, he thought rhetoric superficial because it gave you the means of expression without telling you what to express. The statesman must first know how society is to be run; exposition and persuasion come afterwards. For detail, we must turn to the *Republic*, the product of Plato's early years in the Academy. We cannot be certain of its exact date; but if we think of it as having been written by about 380 B.C. we shall not be far wrong. And the section on the education of the philosopher (Part VIII in this edition) gives in substance the kind of study that Plato thought suitable for the philosopher-ruler, and the kind of study – mathematics with an increasing stress on astronomy, and 'dialectic', comprising what we should to-day call logic and metaphysics – that was in fact pursued in the Academy. The *Republic*, in short, is a statement of the aims which the Academy set itself to achieve.

The rest of Plato's life is only relevant to the reader of the *Republic* in so far as it illustrates further the attitude to politics already described. He never lost the hope of being able to turn a statesman into a philosopher. When Dionysius I died in 367 B.C. Plato's friend Dion, now chief minister in Syracuse, invited him to come and train Dionysius II, who was then twenty-eight, as a philosopher-statesman. Plato went with hesitation and can have had few illusions about the difficulty of his task. His visit was not a success. Dionysius did not trust Dion, was old to enter on any course of training, and detested the mathematics Plato expected him to do. Dion was banished, and shortly afterwards Plato left. He had been there about a year. He returned in 361, on the invitation of Dionysius, who, in spite of his dislike of mathematics, seems to have liked Plato, or perhaps wanted to impress him. Plato hoped to reconcile Dion and Dionysius, but he failed, and returned again to Athens after about a year. Dion resorted to force, and after various vicissitudes, during which he tried to set up a government of an authoritarian kind, was assassinated in 354 B.C. Plato did nothing to encourage him in these last years, though he continued to regard him with affection, felt his loss deeply, and regarded it as a disaster for Sicily.[1] Dion was undoubtedly sincere, and a man of courage and enterprise; but he was something of a prig, and, like many political idealists, inclined to resort to force when the world refused to accept his ideals.

Rather happier is the story of Plato's dealings with Hermias of Atarneus, of which we learn something in the Sixth Letter. Atarneus is in north-west Asia Minor, and Hermias had made himself a kingdom in that area. He had probably visited Athens, and been impressed by the teaching in the Academy. And when two members of the Academy, Erastus and Coriscus, returned to their native city of Scepsis, in his kingdom, he got in touch with them, and seems to have associated them in some way with him as advisers in his government. This is the situation assumed by the sixth letter, of which Hermias, Erastus, and Coriscus are joint addressees, and it illustrates well 'what in Plato's view was the educational purpose of the Academy; it was to be a training-ground for rulers, not only maintaining a particular political theory, but also furnishing practical guidance to such of its members who had attained to political power'.[2] Hermias is said to have

1. The Seventh and Eighth Letters were both written after Dion's death, and make various practical suggestions to Dion's followers.

2. Wormell, *Literary Tradition concerning Hermias of Atarneus*: Yale Classical Studies, vol. v, 1935.

turned his tyranny into a milder form of government on the advice of the philosophers, and to have handed over Assos to them to rule in gratitude for what they had done. It was at Assos that Aristotle joined them after Plato's death, and when he in turn left to become tutor of Alexander the Great he was carrying on the Platonic tradition.

All this took place during the last ten years of Plato's life and shows his continued hope of finding the philosopher-statesman. And if he looked for him, at Syracuse and Atarneus, in the courts of a tyrant, that was because he believed that political control must always be in the hands of a minority, and where it was concentrated in the hands of one man his conversion was all that was necessary to bring philosophy to bear on the conduct of affairs. With the continued hope of practical intervention went the continued interest in theory; and Plato's last and longest work, the *Laws*, is again about politics. It is the work of his old age, said to have been barely completed before his death in 347 B.C. And though it makes more concessions to common sense and practical possibilities than the *Republic*, it remains closely akin to it in its basic principles: those who have read the *Republic* have read all the essential things Plato has to say on the subject. Which is fortunate; because though the *Laws* contains much of interest, it lacks the inspiration of the *Republic*, and much of it is wearisome reading. But it serves to remind us that for Plato the purpose of the Academy remained unchanged, to train the philosopher-ruler.

2. PLATO ON CONTEMPORARY SOCIETY

A good way to approach the *Republic* itself is to consider the actual types of Greek constitution of which Plato took account when he wrote it. These he deals with in Book VIII (Part IX in this edition), where he lists them as Timarchy, Oligarchy, Democracy, and Tyranny. The type of society which Plato calls Timarchy is one which has no real parallel in modern experience, because it is, as he explicitly tells us, a sketch of the essential features of Spartan society. But for

Plato Sparta was very important indeed, and some of the features of his own ideal society are borrowed from it. The Spartans were, briefly, a military aristocracy living among a subject population, the 'helots'. These helots were peasant serfs, cultivating the land for their Spartan masters; they could be called on to serve as light-armed troops in war, and might occasionally win their freedom, but in general they had neither rights nor privileges. Each year the magistrates declared war on them, so that to kill a Helot was an act of war and not of murder; and the Spartan secret police watched constantly for disaffection and killed mercilessly when they found it.

It was largely because they were a minority living thus in a subject population, which they always feared would revolt and which on several occasions did, that the Spartans followed their peculiar way of life. They were a military caste, in which the individual was rigidly subordinated to the community. Each citizen was a soldier, and education, marriage, and the details of daily life were all strictly regulated with a view to the maintenance of perfect military efficiency. 'When a child was born it was submitted to the inspection of the heads of the tribe, and if they judged it to be unhealthy or weak, it was exposed to die on the slopes of Mount Taygetos. At the age of seven years, the boy was consigned to the care of a state-officer, and the course of his education was entirely determined by the purpose of inuring him to bear hardships, training him to endure an exacting discipline, and instilling into his heart a sentiment of devotion to the State. The boys, up to the age of twenty, were marshalled in a huge school formed in the model of an army.'[1] Here they were under the instruction of young men aged twenty to thirty, who were not yet of age to be admitted to full citizenship. At twenty they entered on military service and were permitted to marry; but they must still live in barracks, and could only pay fugitive and stolen visits to their wives. At thirty they became full citizens, but though they might live at home, they must still dine together in common messes, to which each made a fixed contribution

1. Bury, *History of Greece*, p. 132.

from the 'lot' which each Spartan owned, which he might not alienate, and which was cultivated for him by his helot serfs. 'Spartan discipline extended itself to women too ... The girls, in common with the boys, went through a gymnastic training; and it was not considered immodest for them to practise their exercises almost nude. They enjoyed a freedom which was in marked contrast with the seclusion of women in other Greek states. They had a high repute for chastity; but if the government directed them to breed children for the state, they had no scruples in obeying the command, though it should involve a violation of the sanctity of the marriage-tie.'[1]

No Spartan was allowed to possess wealth in the form of gold or silver, and they continued to use a clumsy iron coinage. Private luxury was forbidden, and Spartan simplicity was proverbial. The individual was entirely lost in the State; he had no life, no problems of his own. He lived in a camp, under military discipline, ready at any moment to fight for his country. It was not surprising that the Spartans were the most efficient soldiers in Greece, though they were not an aggressive people, but notoriously difficult to provoke to war.

These are the features of the Spartan system most relevant to a reader of the *Republic*. Its constitutional arrangements – a unique combination of hereditary kingship, popular election and magistrates, and council of elders – are comparatively unimportant, save perhaps in the respect paid to age and experience; membership of the Council was restricted to those over sixty, and in the *Republic* the status of full Guardianship cannot be reached till fifty. The Spartan system had many admirers in Greece; it had a completeness and aesthetic simplicity which appealed to the Greek mind, and made many Greeks admire it, though few would have wished to live under it. But if they admired they also criticized, and the criticisms Plato makes of Timarchy are typical. He criticizes its exploitation of the lowest class as a wrong relation between ruler and ruled, liable to lead to serious disunity. He criticizes its intellectual limitations; Spartans thought little, and were

1. Bury, *op. cit.*, p. 133.

proverbially thick-headed. They were also, in spite of their system, notoriously avaricious; and so Timarchy is criticized for the institution of private property, forbidden in the ideal state, and the consequent growth of private greed. The Spartan and the Timarchic society, in short, have the merits of discipline, respect for law, and courage, but are stupid, greedy, and brutal to their less privileged classes.

The Spartan system was without parallel, except in Crete. But the other three types of social system which Plato mentions were common; indeed, one may generalize and say that in the fifth and fourth centuries the Greek cities were either democracies or oligarchies, interspersed here and there with tyrannies. During the Peloponnesian war the oligarchies had, on the whole, sided with Sparta, the democracies with Athens. And party differences, always acute in Greece, had been exacerbated by the suspicion that the other party was in league with the enemy. The suspicion was often justified, for both democrat and oligarch habitually put party first; and Plato's references to a party getting help against its opponents from outside (cf. p. 332) and his deep horror of faction and disunity, are a reflection of the bitterness of party-strife, of which Thucydides has left the classic description. 'Both sides claimed to have the good of the community at heart, while both in fact aimed at political control, and in their struggle for ascendancy indulged in the worst excesses.'[1]

To Plato an oligarchy was a society in which power and prestige went with wealth; and since the wealthy are normally few, where power goes with wealth political control is in the hands of a minority. The days of hereditary aristocracy were long over, and though there were of course old families in most states (like Plato's own at Athens), birth had had to come to terms with wealth and, by itself, was, at the most, of limited political influence. So though Plato's characterization of oligarchy may be an over-simplification, it is not an unfair generalization to say that oligarchy in his day meant control by a wealthy minority. It was the controlling influence given

1. Thucydides, III, 82. See *Thucydides, Peloponnesian War* : trans. *Rex Warner* (Penguin Classics).

to wealth that Plato particularly disliked. He had the deepest distrust of what would to-day be called the profit-motive and of the political influence of private wealth; and he thought that in an oligarchy (an 'acquisitive society') you were bound to get increasing exploitation of poor by rich, and an increasing degree of social maladjustment and disunity in consequence. He draws a picture of growing oppression met by growing bitterness and ending in revolution.

In his account of democracy Plato is drawing on his own experiences at Athens. And it is important to remember what a democracy in fifth and fourth century Greece was like. The Greeks lived in city-states, small communities consisting of a 'city' nucleus, with an area of agricultural land attached, from which the urban population drew all or most of its food-supply. The populations varied in size, but were all small by the standards of a modern city. The population of Athens when Plato was born was perhaps 250-300,000, including men, women, and slaves; and Athens was by Greek standards large. In a democracy the vote was confined to the adult male citizen population. At Athens slaves may have numbered some 80-100,000,[1] and there were perhaps 35-40,000 'metics', that is, residents who because they had been born elsewhere did not qualify for citizenship. The total voting population was about 45-50,000. But within this body of voting citizens popular control was complete; for the Greeks never invented representative government, and the sovereign body at Athens was the Assembly, a mass meeting of all adult male citizens. Of course not all citizens bothered to attend regularly, and some whose homes were outside Athens itself found it difficult to do so. But in theory all could attend, and both in theory and in practice the Assembly was the sovereign body by which all political decisions must be taken. It was not practicable for it to meet too often (in theory it met ten times a year; in practice a good deal more often, though probably never more than once a week); and to carry on the business of state between meetings, to deal with much routine and financial business, and above all to draft business for meetings of

1. The number is uncertain, and may have been considerably less.

the Assembly there was a Council of Five Hundred. This further subdivided itself into Committees of fifty, each of which was responsible for carrying on public business during one-tenth of the year. But important as the Council's functions were, its powers were in practice limited by the rule that it should be chosen by lot from the citizen body, that membership was limited to one year, and that no citizen might hold membership more than twice. The Council thus never became a continuing body with a policy of its own: the Assembly remained supreme. Finally, the law-courts also were in popular control. Nearly all cases were tried before panels of jurors drawn by a system of lot and election from the citizen body; and before these panels the magistrates could be tried for any irregularities committed during their year of office.

Such a complete system of popular control has never been known before or since. And it is important to remember that this, and not any form of modern representative government, is the background to Plato's comments on democracy. Its shortcomings in fifth-century Athens and the criticisms then made of it have already been mentioned.[1] It involved, said Thucydides, 'committing the conduct of state affairs to the whims of the multitude',[2] and it has been described by a modern writer as government by perpetual plebiscite. But wide as the differences of background are, it would be quite wrong to dismiss Plato's criticisms of democracy as having no relevance to-day. If we are tempted to do so, we may perhaps remind ourselves that this is the first generation since his when a political leader can address the whole electorate, and, now that television is so widespread, be seen by most of it at the same time. What the ultimate effects of wireless and television will be we cannot yet say. But they have certainly brought political leaders far closer to the ordinary citizen, and opened up opportunities of a direct approach to the whole electorate that did not exist before in modern society.

What then are Plato's criticisms in the *Republic*? If we look

1. P. 10.
2. Bk II, 65.

first at the similes of the ship's captain (p. 249) and the large and powerful animal (p. 254), they seem to contain two criticisms. First, that the people are bad judges in many political matters. The common man has no experience or expert knowledge of such things as foreign policy or economics, and to expect any very sensible judgement from him on such matters is to expect the impossible. He will judge on impulse, sentiment, or prejudice, and though his heart may be sound (and Plato would have doubted whether even this was always true) his head will be muddled. This drawback might perhaps be overcome by good leadership. But here we come to the second criticism, that democracy encourages bad leadership. The people's judgement of their leaders is not always good, and they can't be trusted to make the best choice. But quite apart from that, the popular leader, dependent as he is for his position (and perhaps his income) on popular favour, will constantly be tempted to retain that favour by the easiest possible means. He will play on the likes and dislikes, the weaknesses and foibles of the public, will never tell them an unpleasant truth or advocate a policy that might make them uncomfortable. Like the modern advertiser and salesman, he is dependent on his public, and his position depends on selling them comfort and not telling them the truth. Sophist, salesman, and popular politician are on a par, and the people care little who their leaders are provided they 'profess themselves the people's friends' (p. 330).

But that is not the whole story. The salient characteristic of democracy, we learn in Book VIII, is liberty – 'every individual is free to do as he likes' (p. 329). This gives democratic society a diversity and variety that are very attractive, but its effect is extremely disintegrating. There is a growing dislike of any authority, political or moral; fathers pander to their sons, teachers to their pupils, 'and the minds of the citizens become so sensitive that the least vestige of restraint is resented as intolerable' (p. 337). Where there is so little social cohesion dissension inevitably grows; it takes the form of a struggle between rich and poor which finally degenerates into class-war. The poor have no use for the rich except to squeeze taxes out of them; the rich retaliate, and 'the freedom which the democrat claims will be a freedom of the *two nations*, the rich and the poor, to fight it out between themselves who shall have the larger slice of the cake.'[1]

There remains Tyranny. Plato describes it as arising out of the chaos and dissension into which democracy degenerates; and though he would probably not have wished to maintain that this was an invariable rule, yet some tyrants, ancient and modern, have certainly started as popular leaders, and extreme social disunity may by reaction produce an extreme authoritarianism. Of Plato's treatment of tyranny three things may be said. (1) For him tyranny is essentially a personal rule. The tyrant needs followers, of course, and at a fairly early stage in his career he secures a 'personal bodyguard', a private army bound to him by ties of common interest and guilt. But the basis of his power is a personal one; he is the Leader, and his rule is essentially the exercise of his own personal preferences, the arbitrary rule of an individual. (2) Tyranny has a peculiar self-destructiveness. The tyrant can brook no rival, which means that prominent personalities among his followers must be eliminated; anyone who can or will stand up to him will be swept away. And he needs constant wars, external crises, to distract attention from his internal misrule; which is another source of strain. (3) The tyrant is essentially what we should call a criminal type: the beginning of Book IX (p. 344) is an analysis of the similarity of the tyrant and the criminal, who are said to combine the characteristics of drunkard, sex-maniac, and madman. The tyrant, with his 'master passion', is barely sane, and his life is one of criminal indulgence. Fielding had the same thought in *Jonathan Wild*.

There is little need to comment on this analysis. The dominance of a dictator's personality, his private army, the purges among his followers are familiar. We might comment that his private life need not always be as wildly dissolute as Plato suggests; he is more formidable, though not less criminal if it is not. But the element of criminal violence seems no less in modern tyrannies than in ancient.

1. Crossman, *Plato To-day*, p. 152.

The purpose of this section has been to show, by reviewing Plato's analysis of contemporary forms of society, what he thought the major social evils of his time were; for it was to combat those evils that his own proposals were put forward. We may summarize as follows. In timarchy (Sparta) Plato saw two major evils. The evil of a split community in which one section holds down the remainder by force; and the evil of stupidity – the Spartan might in many ways be a good fellow but he simply had not the intellectual capacity to know what he was doing; indeed he mistrusted the intellect and everything to do with it. In oligarchy the cardinal fault is desire for wealth (a fault which was already apparent in timarchy). Wealth as a social motive is to be mistrusted, and a ruling class which is devoted to its wealth, and which owes its position and power to wealth, will substitute exploitation for government. In democracy there is a radical lack of cohesion, because there is no proper respect for authority moral or political. Democratic government is weak government, which plays on the weaknesses of the common man instead of giving him the leadership he needs; and it is liable to degenerate into a bitter class-struggle between haves and have-nots. Finally, in tyranny we see the danger that the criminal instincts, normally kept under control, will get out of hand. The criminal is present in all societies (certainly in oligarchy and democracy); but in tyranny he has come into his own, and society is run by its criminal elements with the arch-criminal in charge.

3. THE MAIN IDEAS OF THE REPUBLIC

The title *Republic* is doubly misleading to a modern reader. In the first place it suggests that Plato might be writing about a 'republic' in the modern sense, that is, about a particular form of government. In fact the title in Greek can mean indifferently constitution, state, or society; the Latin translation is *respublica*, a word bearing originally the same sort of meanings, and only coming later to bear the narrower meaning of a particular kind of constitution, the meaning it now bears in the English transliteration. Plato, in fact, was writing about society or the state, and that is what his title means. The mistranslation is now hallowed by time, and it would be pedantic to change it; but a word of explanation is required.

But when that explanation has been given, the modern reader may still find something rather different from what it leads him to expect. He will expect, in a work on politics, some references to morals or education; they are topics which recur constantly both in political practice and theory. But he will also expect a great deal of discussion of constitutional and legal matters. What is to be the sovereign body? How is its sovereignty to be exercised? What are to be the relations of legislature, executive and judiciary? How is executive power to be exercised? What subordinate bodies or organizations are there to be, and what powers are they to have? These are the sort of questions which he will expect to find examined. In fact, when he turns to the *Republic*, he will hardly find them mentioned at all. There is of course a good deal of discussion of social and political matters; for example the discussion of contemporary forms of society with which section 2 of this Introduction has been concerned, and which occupies most of Books VIII and IX (Part IX). And Parts II, IV and VI deal largely with political and social topics. But even in these parts of the book Plato is more interested in principles than in details, and we find moral considerations constantly coming in. And the rest of the work is largely devoted to what we should regard as morals (Parts I and V), education (Parts III and VIII), philosophy (Parts VII and X), and religion (Part XI). For this there are several reasons. The Greek city-state, as we have seen, was a comparatively simple affair; there was less constitutional machinery to talk about. And just because the political community was smaller and more intimate the Greeks distinguished less sharply than we do between morals and politics. We tend to think that there is a sphere of private conduct where the state is not concerned, where, as we should say, it is a matter for the individual conscience; but, on the whole, that way of thinking is foreign to the Greeks. The 'ancient Greek view' was 'that the law of the state is the source of all standards of human life, and that the virtue of

27

the individual is the same as the virtue of the citizen.'[1] That is perhaps an over-statement; but it serves to bring out the difference of the Greek approach, an approach which did not prevent the Greeks from being violently individualistic in practice, but which did make them link politics and morals more closely then we do. But there are further more particular reasons. The *Republic*, as we have seen, was written in the years after the founding of the Academy: the Academy's aim was to train philosopher-statesmen, and the *Republic*, as a statement of that aim, was bound to deal at length with education. Plato had decided that the world's ills would not be cured till philosophers ruled; the education of philosophers therefore becomes the most important of political activities. If they can be educated rightly, and given power, the details of administration can safely be left in their hands – this Plato explicitly says.[2] For all these reasons the *Republic* was bound to deal at length with education, and with the moral principles underlying the organization of society, as well as with the general lines on which it should, ideally, be organized; which leaves little room for more practical details, much as we should often like to have them. We have therefore a book which is as much about morals and education and philosophy as about politics in the strict sense. To some of Plato's ideas in these fields we now turn.

(1) *Morals*

The *Republic* starts with a moral question: what is the meaning of Justice or Right? The Greek word is a wide one and covers both individual righteousness and social morality, and from the start therefore the enquiry is concerned with both individual and community, both morals and politics. It soon becomes clear that the question that is being asked is, What is the basis of social and moral obligation? Why should I be either law-abiding or moral if I don't feel like it? More simply still, Why should I be good? The problem is stated in three stages. First Socrates shows that the conventional view that

1. Jaeger, *Paideia*, vol. II, p. 157.
2. P. 171.

justice is 'giving a man his due' is inadequate. Then Thrasymachus comes in with what is, in effect, a flat denial of the conventional view. He is, as we have seen, a typical Sophist and is meant to stand as the representative of a line of thought, not uncommon at the end of the fifth century, which rejected conventional morality as a sham, and substituted self-interest. Enough is said about this section of the argument (which is often rather complicated) in the section headings. Its purpose is to advance the argument a stage by showing that though conventional morality may be muddled and inadequate, it is equally unsatisfactory to reject it as a sham. After Thrasymachus has been reduced to silence, Glaucon and Adeimantus, who remain the chief respondents throughout the rest of the dialogue, say that they are still unsatisfied and that they are going to restate his case for him. And what they in effect ask Socrates to do is to show them that morality is more than a matter of enlightened self-interest. Glaucon puts forward a form of what was later to be known as the Social Contract theory, arguing that we are only moral because it pays us or we have to be, and that given the chance we should all behave extremely badly: Adeimantus reinforces him by stressing the comparatively mercenary motives normally advanced for good behaviour. The problem they put to Socrates is to show that, quite apart from motives of self-interest or social approval, morality is preferable in itself to immorality, right to wrong.

Socrates' immediate reply is to say that the problem is too difficult to solve in the individual; he must look at it 'in larger letters' in society. And so there follows in Parts II, III, and IV the first sketch of the ideal society. But when he returns to the individual in Part V he tries to answer the question in the way that he has been asked; he tries, that is, to show, by an analysis of the elements in the human mind, that its well-being, full development and happiness are to be secured by doing right and not by doing wrong, to prove, in the old saying, that virtue is its own reward. And though other rewards, including rewards and punishments in the life after death, are brought in in Book x, they are a merely secondary consideration.

The elements in the mind which the moralist has to take into account are according to Plato threefold (see p. 183); and it has been suggested that this threefold division is a more or less arbitrary reflection into the individual of the three classes into which the state is organized. The matter is hardly as simple as that. The three elements in the mind and the three classes in society may spring from the same origin (perhaps in Pythagoreanism); but one is hardly likely to have produced the other directly. But the criticism, though an over-simplification, does bring out a feature of Plato's thought – his tendency to argue from the state or community to the individual rather than vice-versa. He is inclined to decide first what he thinks would socially be desirable, and then to cut the individual to fit it, rather than to think of the individual first and then consider how his needs can be met. Though, therefore, it is unlikely that the three elements in the mind were invented to fit the three classes in the state, the movement of thought, from society to individual, is significant.

That the threefold division is not, however, without foundation in experience is suggested in the heading to Part v, §2 (p. 183). But it must be regarded as an attempt to classify the elements involved in moral conflict and decision, and not as a full account of human psychology. There are large parts of human experience (such as sensation and perception) which it does not attempt to touch, and it is better treated as a classification of motives for action, as which it has some merits, than as an exhaustive or scientific analysis of the mind. The main criticism that can be made of it from this point of view is that it omits any consideration of what we call the will. But we are often extremely hazy about what we mean by the will; it is, to the ordinary man, little more than a label for the fact that we often have to make an *effort* to make ourselves do things. And Plato would probably claim to have sufficiently recognized that fact in his element of Reason, which clearly includes not only the faculty of deliberation, but also the ability to decide and to act on our decisions however much effort that calls for. We all know the difference between acting from deliberate choice, acting from a generous impulse, and acting on animal appetite; and that is the difference which Plato is trying to express.

His answer to the question 'What is justice?' is that, in the individual, it consists in keeping a proper balance between the three types of impulse; each will then be 'doing its own job' (cf. p. 181). True morality consists, in fact, in giving due satisfaction to the different impulses in us, and preventing any of them dominating at the expense of the others. Physical desire, ambition, and intellect must all have their due and proper fulfilment, and find their proper place in the good life.

That, in short, is Plato's solution of the problem of individual morality. And there are two questions, at any rate, which it may prompt us to ask. (1) Is the threefold classification of impulses really adequate? It has been suggested that it is not without foundation, and that the criticism that it ignores the will can to some extent be met. But how adequate and how useful is it all the same? How far does it do justice to the complexities of moral choice? (2) The formula as it stands, though it tells us a great deal, leaves a good many blanks. What is the 'proper' place of intellect and appetite? What is the satisfaction 'due' to each? How is the balance to be struck? Plato's own answer the reader must glean from the text. But one is left with the impression that it would be a good deal more ascetic than the ordinary man would find comfortable. The Guardians' life is austere, to say the least of it; and little as we know of the life of the third class, what we do know does not suggest that it will be luxurious (cf. p. 166). Clearly we can fill in the formula in different ways; but Plato, though he has no wish to eradicate physical appetite, took on the whole a low view of physical pleasures (cf. p. 354 ff), and his own interpretation would have been an austere one. He was, perhaps, always a bit of a Puritan.

Of the meaning of justice in society as opposed to the individual little need be said. Justice is defined as 'minding your own business', that is, fulfilling your proper function in society. When all are doing that there is no room for the most dreaded of all evils, disunity. And there are few who would quarrel with the view that social justice has been achieved when each class and element in society is fulfilling its proper function. But again the formula leaves many blanks. What are the different classes or elements in society? What is their proper function, and what is their due? But these are questions that are largely political, and the discussion of Plato's answers to them must for the moment be postponed.

(2) *Education*

Plato's views of education can largely be left to speak for themselves. He thought it of paramount importance, and, since commentaries on him have nearly all been written by dons or schoolmasters, he has been much praised for so thinking. Without in any way questioning the general contention, one may perhaps ask whether education really has quite the power to transform society that Plato and others have thought. There are so many other influences that determine both society and the individual; and anyone engaged in the business of teaching who keeps his sense of proportion will perhaps view his work with a little greater scepticism and a little more saving humility.

But there are one or two other points, besides the conviction of its importance, which are noteworthy in what Plato has to say on the subject.

He was the first person to formulate what we should to-day call a university course. For that is what his course of further education is (Part VIII), even though it is spread out over a far longer period; and the Academy, though it may have had a rival in the school of Isocrates and predecessors in the Sophists, was the first university in Europe. The literary education which precedes it (Part III) is the equivalent of our secondary, and the earlier stage of learning to read and write which that implies the equivalent of our primary education. So that we may say that our three stages are all, explicitly or implicitly, already recognized in the *Republic*.

As far as its curriculum is concerned, we may say that after the primary stage, in which reading and writing are the important elements, the main subjects studied in school are literary and humanistic. The Greek boy who studied Homer and the other poets, and the citizen of the *Republic* who studied Plato's specially prepared books, was studying the literature and history of his country, and the equivalent of our Bible. And in the course of that study he would expect to learn something of the culture, history, and traditions of his own and of neighbouring peoples, as well as the accepted moral and religious beliefs. At the university stage Plato's citizens transferred their attention to mathematics, science, and philosophy. For that is what is meant in modern terms by the study of mathematics and 'dialectic' which Plato outlines. The natural sciences were little developed in his day, and though what he says about astronomy (p. 297) reads oddly to-day, it was the insistence in the Academy on the application of mathematical methods to astronomy which created it as a science; and the exact sciences[1] would almost certainly feature in Plato's curriculum if he were drawing it up to-day. While 'dialectic' simply means philosophy.

So much for intellectual content. But Plato was as concerned to train the character as the mind, and throughout the account of the secondary stage of education he is insistent that its object is moral training as much as intellectual; the section on physical education ends (p. 153f) with an emphatic assertion that physical and intellectual education are not concerned to deal one with the mind and one with the body, but are jointly directed to the training of character. And in so far as the training of character has been a distinctive feature in English education, Plato would approve and perhaps claim to have had some influence on it.

But in all he does the educator should remember that his aim is not to 'put into the mind knowledge that was not there before' – though he may do that within limits – but to turn the mind's eye to the light so that it can see for itself (p. 283); his business, in other words, is not to stick thoughts into his pupils' heads but to make them think for themselves. This is perhaps the best-known passage on education in the *Republic*,

1. But the joke in the comic poet Epicrates about pupils in the Academy trying to decide whether a pumpkin should be classified as a grass is evidence for an interest in classification (logic) rather than botany.

no doubt because of the importance and truth of the principle which it states.

We turn to the actual provision of education. It must be provided exclusively by the state. Anything of such crucial importance cannot be left to private initiative. And because of its crucial importance in forming the minds of the young, the curriculum must also be controlled and defined by the state. Plato thought, for reasons which he explains at length in Part III, that most current Greek literature was highly unsuitable as a medium of education. He therefore proposed a rigid censorship which should apply not only to school text-books, but to all literature.[1] There is to be no expression of opinion other than what the State allows. That is what the long sections on literature and art amount to.

We disagree at once. Our own habit of thought regards freedom of expression as an essential liberty, and freedom to teach what one likes as no less essential. We should agree with Plato that it is for the state to provide education; but many would not wish it to be the sole provider, and few would wish it to censor text-books and determine the content of teaching. Mill has stated the classic arguments for liberty. It is enough to point to the disagreement.

But we may note two things. First, that Plato is so far right that most people would agree that not all books are suitable as school text-books, though there would be wide disagreement about which books.

Second, that Plato himself, with his strong poetic sense, was obviously uneasy about his treatment of the poets, and adds in Book x a kind of justificatory appendix. There is no space to discuss the aesthetic theory he there puts forward. But it is worth asking whether the evil effects which he fears do not sometimes follow. Has not Plato confused art in which bad characters appear with bad art? And if we avoid that confusion can we deny that the effects may follow? Does not constant exposure to the second-rate have a demoralizing effect?

1. Cf. p. 137 and the opening of Bk x, p. 370 ff., from which it is clear that the same principles apply not only to literature used in school but to all literature.

(3) *Philosophy and Religion*

Because the ideal state is to be governed by philosophers, philosophy inevitably plays a large part in the *Republic*; it is the central theme of Parts VII and VIII. But the treatment of it is always rather allusive. Plato is concerned rather with the place of philosophy in the educational curriculum, the kind of studies which lead to it, its usefulness and its effects on the character, than with a detailed exposition of his philosophic beliefs. Their relevant features are brought out in a series of similes – the Sun, the Divided Line, and the Cave; but the *Republic* does not attempt to expound the Platonic philosophy in detail.

The most important feature of that philosophy, for the purpose of the *Republic*, is the belief in two worlds. The world of change and appearance, the everyday, physical world in which we live; and the world of the Forms, the world of eternals and absolutes. For further explanation the reader must be referred to the sections in question (especially Part VII, §5, 6, 7, and Part VIII, §3) and the introductory headings to them. But the following more general comments may be made.

Though the training described in Part VIII is one of rigorous intellectual discipline, a training, as we might say, in the technique of exact thinking, the object at which it is aimed is a matter of personal experience. The teacher, as we have seen, turns the pupil's eye to the light; the pupil is not a passive recipient of knowledge, but must grasp the truth for himself. This applies particularly to the truths of philosophy, about which Plato writes in the Seventh Letter: 'the truths of philosophy are not expressible as are those of other subjects; after long study and discussion under the guidance of an experienced teacher, a spark may suddenly leap, as it were, from mind to mind, and the light of understanding so kindled will then feed itself.'[1]

This is partly the expression of an educational truth and an educational method. But it goes further. For the ultimate

1. 341C.

objective of the philosophic training is religious, and the language of the Seventh Letter and of the *Republic* is the language of religious experience. The vision of the Form of the Good is what others have called the vision of God. That is not to say that the Form of the Good and God are to be identified; they probably should not be, though scholars have disputed the point. But the experience is religious; it has the characteristics that William James noted in all mystical experience,[1] it is a state of knowledge and yet incommunicable in ordinary language. And it is therefore appropriate that the *Republic* should end with a religious myth. For whatever Plato may have thought about the details of the myth, it is clear that it is intended to express in pictorial and poetic form the general philosophic and religious conviction of the *Republic* that the temporal is only the shadow of the eternal, and that the human soul is responsible not simply to itself but to God.

(4) *Society and Politics*

What Plato has to say on these topics can conveniently be considered under three headings: the Class System, Property and the Family, and the Philosopher Ruler.

The Class System. Plato arrives at this from the principle that in any society men will group themselves according to their occupations. In the economic sphere you will get producers, merchants, traders, and so on. The economic structure of the society of which he was thinking, and in which he lived, is elementary; and he is thinking of occupations and not income-groups. But the principle is clear enough. He goes on to apply it in the sphere of war and government. The armies of Greece in the fifth century were citizen-armies; but the fourth century saw the rise of the professional soldier, and that may, in part, have suggested to Plato that his Guardians, who first appear as a military group, should be specialists in war. But it soon appears that they are to perform the functions not only of soldiering but also of government, and they are subdivided into Rulers proper and Auxiliaries, who correspond, roughly,

1. James, *Varieties of Religious Experience*, ch. XVI.

to Government and Army, as opposed to the rest of the population, who make up the third class. Plato's three classes in fact are not so much three as two, one of which is further subdivided.

Many object at once to this division of society into three distinct classes, with a definite order of subordination between them. The words hierarchic society or caste system are used to describe it disapprovingly. Plato might reply that the quarrel is to some extent about words. Any society, he might say, is bound to show economic groupings; few societies can do without their professional army; and in all societies someone has to give orders and someone obey, which means that in practice there will be a minority of people issuing orders (the government) and a majority obeying them (the rest). What people differ about is whether and to what extent these primary groupings should be complicated by further class-divisions based on birth or wealth, and how the governmental minority should in fact be chosen. To Plato's views on these last two topics, which are what the objectors really dislike, we shall return. Meanwhile it is important to see just what his three classes and their mutual relations are.

About his third class he does not tell us a great deal. They are not in any sense a proletariat or working class. They comprise all those engaged in economic activities – farmers, manufacturers, traders, rich or poor (for they are allowed to own property). Their function is to provide for the material and economic needs of the community. Their virtue is obedience, and it is pretty clear that they will be under strict control. The Guardians will see that there is no excessive wealth and poverty among them (p. 166), and will presumably direct and control all their activities. For they are the body of the governed whom the governing minority administers.

The governing minority, the Guardians, discharge between them, as we have seen, the functions of government and army. But that is perhaps too narrowly imprecise a description. The function of the Rulers is to govern, that is to say to take all those decisions of policy which it is the business of government to take. The Auxiliaries' function is 'to assist the Rulers in the execution of their decisions', or 'to enforce the decisions of the Rulers' (p. 159). We must think of them as combining the functions of civil service, military, and police; as being, that is, charged with the execution and implementation (if necessary by force) of government decisions. And if we think of a society in which there is a government by full-time, trained experts, who are precluded by law from any other function, and who have a body of trained civil servants, together with the necessary police and military forces to assist them, we get some idea in modern terms of this part of Plato's proposals.

The two top classes are, as we have seen, really subdivisions of a single class. They share the same way of life, and are put through the same elaborate system of training and promotion outlined in Part VII. There are a large number of promotion bars to be passed, quite enough to grade the Auxiliaries for their various functions, while leaving a small homogeneous Ruler class to emerge at the top; but all have started with equal opportunities. The Third Class have no say in matters of government; but Plato constantly emphasizes that the Rulers have their interests at heart (the difference between Timarchy and the ideal is that in Timarchy oppression has replaced benevolent government) and the Rulers govern with the willing consent of the governed (p. 179). This relationship is set out in the Foundation Myth (p. 160).

Two further criticisms may be considered here. First, Aristotle's criticism that we are not in fact told nearly enough about the Third Class. And though Plato is deliberate in his avoidance of detail, it is difficult not to agree that the criticism is just. There are too many essential questions left unanswered. The second criticism is that Plato's Guardians are a 'hereditary caste'. The critic, of course, assumes that this, if true, is itself a condemnation. Let us agree with him; but point out that his interpretation is wrong. Plato emphatically asserts (p. 160) that promotion from the third class is not only possible but an important feature of his scheme, just as demotion from the two upper classes is also; and in Book VIII we are told that it is failure in this matter that leads to the change to Timarchy.

It is, of course, extremely hard to see how the scheme is to work: here Aristotle's criticism that we are not told enough again comes in. Cornford[1] suggests that all classes must share a common education up to the age of eighteen, in order that the Rulers can promote and demote; certainly the choice would have to be made by then, and this would be one way of making it, and would be in tune with Plato's views on the importance of education. We cannot speak with certainty; but there is no reason to doubt that Plato means what he says. The real point is that what he wants is an aristocracy of talent. He thinks, as we shall see, that he can get this largely by breeding, as one breeds race-horses; but the breeding process is not infallible, and so there must be provision for both promotion and demotion, there must be both snakes and ladders, even though we don't know exactly what the rules are to be. Belief in an aristocracy of talent may be wicked; but it is not the same as belief in a hereditary caste.

Property and the Family. This brings us to Plato's views on property and the family. And the provisions he makes under this head apply only to the two upper classes, the Guardians. The third class, we presume, live under the normal arrangements. But among the Guardians both private property and the family are to be abolished. Plato's dislike of both has one main cause. He thought that private interests and private affections distracted a man from his duties to the community; and both are centred in the family. As far as the abolition of private property is concerned, we have seen already how deeply he distrusted the desire for wealth as a social motive. He thought that it led to nothing but disunity, that pursuit of riches corrupted government and disrupted society, and that as a criterion of suitability for political power they were worthless. He accordingly proposed to limit the differences of wealth in his Third Class very strictly, and by abolishing property altogether in his Guardian class to eliminate the profit-motive from political influence.

The classic comments on this were made by Aristotle.[2] To

1. *Op. cit.* p. 62.
2. *Politics*, Bk II.

them may perhaps be added a sentence from Professor Hayek. 'What our generation has forgotten is that the system of private property is the most important guarantee of freedom, not only for those that own property, but for those who do not.'[1]

Plato's reasons for abolishing the family are slightly more complex. He dislikes the distraction of family affections, but he has other reasons as well. He starts from the principle of the equality of the sexes. By this he means that, though men and women have different functions in the business of reproduction, they should, apart from that difference, follow the same careers, share the same education, and have the same opportunities. Women may not always be able to do quite such heavy or energetic work as men, as for example in war; but within the limitations imposed by their physique equality is to be absolute.

It follows logically that they must be exempted so far as possible from family responsibilities. For under the family system what stands in the way of the kind of sex equality which Plato wants is the domestic responsibility for running a household and bringing up a family. With complete logic therefore he removes that responsibility by abolishing the family and substituting for it a system of state nurseries. This has the further advantage that it makes possible the breeding of Guardians on scientific lines. The production of children is a matter of such vital importance to the state that it is clearly undesirable to leave it to the unregulated operation of private enterprise and individual affection (this point of view comes out in the *Laws* too); Plato therefore arranges for sexual intercourse to be strictly regulated, and confined to certain regular 'marriage festivals', when suitable partners will be mated, with a view to producing the best type of Guardian, just as one breeds dogs or racehorses.

The details of Plato's arrangements seem to us fantastic. Perhaps the best way to get them into proper perspective is to refer to the more up-to-date scheme to be found in Mr Huxley's *Brave New World*. There child-bearing has been

1. *The Road to Serfdom*, p. 78.

abolished entirely, and babies are produced in laboratories, where they are fitted by heredity and subsequent conditioning for the different types of occupation required by the community. The physical relationship between men and women is reduced to a matter of private pleasure and shorn of its emotional implications. These arrangements would have seemed to Plato admirable. Under them the whole business of the production and education of citizens becomes a matter of exact control and knowledge, men and women can be put on a footing of complete equality, with the necessity for periodic child-bearing, which still remained in the *Republic*, finally removed, and with the tiresome business of the physical relationship reduced to a minimum of importance.

For Plato's attitude to the physical relationship seems to have been one of contempt. He knew the instinct as an unruly one; but he always ranked physical pleasures low and believed that unruly instincts were there to be restrained. And his experience of emotional attachments between people was confined to friendships between men. Of love between the sexes as we know it he had no experience, nor would he have though it desirable. In that he was, to some extent, no doubt, influenced by the lower status which women held in Greek society. But this has been much exaggerated, and Professor Kitto has recently written on the subject with refreshing good sense;[1] nor need we suppose that the kind of attachment between husband and wife to which Aristotle's will bears evidence was uncommon. Plato's attitude was more personal than typically Greek.

His desire for equality between the sexes may again be a protest against the very limited scope women were given in contemporary society. So far most modern opinion would agree with him, and it has been said of his scheme, 'if we subtract from it the regulations which are aimed at building them into Amazons, what remains is essentially the modern programme for the education of women.'[2] Yet one may doubt the desirability or possibility of the extreme equality Plato

1. *The Greeks* (Pelican), p. 219 f.
2. Jaeger, *Paideia*, Pt II, p. 246.

demanded. To sweep aside the physiological differences as unimportant, and ignore the profound psychological differences they entail, is not very sensible. Women have indeed their contribution to make; but if you merely expect them to do the same things as men, they are likely, as Plato in effect said, to end up as inferior men. Is it not better to recognize the difference rather than pretend it does not exist?

From the more eugenic standpoint, neither Plato's nor Mr Huxley's proposals are very much like practical politics. But Plato might well point to our increasing knowledge of heredity as an indication that he was on the right lines, and look forward to the day when greater knowledge would give us greater control. How that control was exercised he would not much care, provided that it was used to breed better citizens, but he would certainly be interested by, and perhaps quote in his own justification, the modern evidence that there is a large hereditary element in talent. In practice, however, he would have to agree that the family is not likely to disappear,[1] and his attitude to it is open to another more general criticism. He assumes that family affections and loyalties can only be a source of weakness: that the good family man must be a worse citizen. Family loyalties can, of course, be distracting. But the assumption is an absurd one, though typical of Plato's love of uniformity. He could not see that the greater loyalty draws strength and force from the lesser which it contains, or that his attempt to diffuse family loyalties and affections through the community (p. 220) could only lead to their dilution and weakening.[2] He was unable, as Aristotle, who again made the classic criticisms of him on this point, said, to distinguish between unity and uniformity.

The Philosopher Ruler. The Philosopher Ruler is the central theme of the *Republic*; it is the aim of its whole educational curriculum to produce him, and much that has already been said has dealt with him directly or by implication. At the end of the long course of training there is left a small class (how large we are not told) of those who have survived all tests and

1. He retains it in the *Laws*, under strict supervision.
2. Like a little sugar in a lot of water, Aristotle remarked.

mastered all knowledge; they are the Philosopher Rulers. They represent the highest talent, given the highest training and put at the disposal of the state. They do not serve the state because they want to, they are philosophers who have seen the supreme vision and would prefer to spend their time in philosophy. But they have a duty to their fellow-men, and that they discharge by doing the work of government for which their training has fitted them; they are a dedicated minority ruling in the interests of all.

There is a perennial attraction in this conception of the highest talent put at the disposal of the community, of the ruler whose heart is in heaven dedicating himself to the service of society. We should respect Plato's vision, and not decry it, as is fashionable to-day. At the same time we must not let it dim our sense of criticism, as older commentators, who sometimes write as if Plato could say nothing wrong, were inclined to do. We may ask first, on the plane of a hum-drum realism, whether the long course of abstract studies which Plato proposes is really the best training for dealing with men and affairs; and whether the method of selection he proposes, based largely on proficiency in abstract subjects – examinations in mathematics, science, and philosophy up to the age of thirty-five – is a sensible one. Is not this one of the fallacies to which educators are prone – the belief that people who do well in their courses will do well at everything, and that the longer they spend on them the better they will do? Is not a wider curriculum and a lot more practical experience more likely to produce a better ruler?

More important is the objection that government by a self-perpetuating minority of experts is in any case undesirable, and in particular 'undemocratic'. We have seen that recruits for the course which begins at the age of twenty are drawn from all the classes, though the vast majority of them come from the top two, because they are bred for the job. They are chosen by the Rulers on their merits: there is no question of democratic election, because, as we have seen, Plato thought that as bad a way of choosing rulers as choosing them by their wealth. And before we dismiss Plato's scheme out of hand, we should remember the methods we use to-day for picking people for administrative and managerial training, the tests of character and ability applied by the Civil Service Commissioners, for example, and reflect that those are the modern parallels to what he proposes. He is concerned to pick people for their competence for the job, and not for characteristics, such as wealth or persuasiveness, that have no necessary connexion with that competence. Indeed he might well, at this point, put some questions to us. He would remind us that society to-day is infinitely more complicated than it was in his day. He would ask us how we think this increasingly complicated structure is to be administered if not by men of character and ability. He could then point out that the amount of ability available in any community is limited, and perhaps quote modern statistics in support of this. And if men are not equal in talent and abilities, surely no society can afford to work on the assumption that they are, least of all modern society. Must we not do our best to ensure that the available talent is most profitably employed, that differences of talent are recognized and the highest talent put to the best use? 'Which brings you back,' he might conclude, 'to the philosopher ruler.' For, as we have seen, what Plato wanted was an aristocracy of talent, and we must see the principles behind his detail. And if we want a modern name for his kind of society, the Managerial Society is perhaps the nearest to it; it emphasizes the necessity for control by ability, though it leaves out many of the other elements in the Platonic solution.

More fatal is the objection that the conception of a philosopher ruler encourages us to look for a degree of knowledge and integrity which are in fact not to be found. The knowledge of all human beings is limited, and for any group of them to think that they have the key to all human problems is presumptuous and absurd. But that is what the philosopher-ruler is supposed to have; and certain types of doctrinaire are liable to a similar illusion. Yet to put the government of human affairs into the hands of any class of supposed experts is to ask from them more than they can possibly give. And quite apart from limitations of knowledge, there is the moral problem. Power is a corrupting influence, a corruption which few can resist; and on the whole political leaders are not men of more than average moral integrity – we are perhaps lucky if they are as good as that. It is better to act on that assumption, and to limit power lest it should be abused, than to look for the perfect ruler who needs no such limitation. The argument against Plato's system, in fact, is not that it trusts the common man too little but that it trusts his rulers too much.

4. FINAL ASSESSMENT

Any final assessment of the *Republic* is very difficult. The older generations of commentators were perhaps too apt to idealize Plato; they partly ignored and partly excused anything with which they disagreed, and it is sometimes not easy to discover from them that Plato was not a good nineteenth-century liberal. Hardly a note of criticism will be found, for example, in such an admirable standard commentary as A. E. Taylor's *Plato*. Lately, however, criticism has been sharper. Mr Crossman, trying to assess how Plato would have looked at the world to-day, sums up against him as a reactionary who encouraged, in practice, the 'dictatorship of the virtuous Right'.[1] Dr Popper's[2] verdict is even harsher. He seems to find in Plato the prototype of almost all political wrong-headedness: a totalitarian, opposed to all liberal or humanitarian ideas. In addition Dr Popper finds him fundamentally Utopian, one of those whose method of approach to political problems is to prepare in advance a 'blue-print of the society at which we aim', and then to be quite ruthless in trying to put it into effect.[3] He criticizes him too for supposing that politics can be reduced to an exact science,[4] a criticism echoed by Mr Weldon, who describes this particular supposition in

1. *Plato To-day*, p. 367 ff.
2. *The Open Society and its Enemies.*
3. *Ibid.*, vol. I, p. 138: ch. 9, perhaps the best in a rather uneven book.
4. *Ibid.*, vol. I, p. 23.

one place as 'the illusion of geometrical method', a phrase which recalls Plato's preoccupation with Mathematics.[1]

There is something in all these criticisms. Plato did undoubtedly try to treat politics too much as if it were a deductive science, in which, once you had settled the principles, everything else follows. And as Mr Weldon points out, that error is still with us. He was also a Utopian in Dr Popper's sense, and probably had something of the ruthlessness which this sort of intellectual approach seems to engender in people. You have only to be sufficiently determined to realize heaven on earth to be sure of raising hell. There are, of course, different kinds of hell. Mr Crossman thinks Plato's would have been a Right-wing one; and no doubt you can start from the *Republic*'s demand for an élite and argue that this must in practice entail what Mr Crossman calls a dictatorship of the virtuous Right. On the other hand, the approach which Dr Popper describes as Utopian is more characteristic of Left than Right, and Platonism could equally well afford a basis for the dictatorship of the virtuous Left.[2]

The *Republic*, in fact, is a long book, covering many topics, and the impression it makes on us depends to some extent on the eyes with which we look at it. Let us be critical: Plato would have wished it. But let us keep a sense of proportion and not ride our own political hobby-horses too hard. Let us remember that a great deal of the *Republic* is not about politics at all. A large part of it is about education, and contains much of permanent value; there is a great deal about individual morality – the balance of impulses under the control of reason, the passionate desire for truth, the underlying religious seriousness. There is literary criticism, there is philosophy, there is a wealth of incidental comment on many things. When we do come to politics we find that Plato has little sympathy with the kind of outlook we should call 'democratic'. He had seen democracy at work in Athens, and

1. *Vocabulary of Politics* (Pelican). There are more references to Plato in the index than to any other author.
2. As Bertrand Russell noted in his *Practice and Theory of Bolshevism*, p. 30.

was too deeply critical of its faults to regard it as a desirable form of government (though he was equally critical of other forms). And if we disagree with him, we should start by trying to understand his criticisms and the problems he was trying to solve. The Philosopher Ruler is a mirage, a product of the kind of idealism which asks too much of human nature and is then disappointed by what it finds; but he does stand for a set of problems which are real, and to which every society must find its answer.

5. FORM AND STYLE

The *Republic* is traditionally divided into ten books. But this division, as has often been pointed out, was dictated rather by the technicalities of book-production in the ancient world, the amount that would go onto a papyrus roll, than by the sequence of the argument. The division into parts and sections in this translation attempts to represent the structure of the argument more nearly. The traditional division into books and numbered paragraphs is given in the margin for purpose of reference.

The *Republic* is in dialogue form and its style is conversational. The dialogue form was used by some of Plato's contemporaries, Xenophon for example, as well as by Plato himself; and many have used it since his day. But in the hands of his successors and imitators it is often more formal than dramatic, more a device for stating different points of view than the representation of a discussion between people. Cicero's dialogues, for example, though they may have their conversational interludes, are in the main speeches explaining different philosophical doctrines; and Berkeley's dialogues have little of the air of a real discussion about them. This is partly because of the particular conditions under which Plato wrote. The Athenians loved an argument; their political life was one of constant discussion in Assembly and law court, and they spent most of their spare time in the public places of Athens gossiping, debating, discussing, or listening to others. The activity of Socrates fitted naturally into this context, and though a discussion with him must surely have been, in reality as well as in Plato's representation, a rather one-sided affair, yet those who took part in it undoubtedly felt that they had taken part in a genuine argument. Socrates was a conversationalist, not a lecturer.

It is this conversational atmosphere that Plato reproduces in his dialogues. Their style, of course, varies with the turns of the argument; it can be light-hearted or serious, philosophical or descriptive or dramatic according to the context. And in a work of the length of the *Republic* the dramatic and conversational element can vary; in much of the argument there is very little of it. But none the less the general impression left is that of a conversation, and the style at which the translator must aim is that of an intelligent discussion; he must use the kind of language that people really do use when they are talking about the sort of topics with which the *Republic* deals. This faces him with two difficulties. First the difficulty of terminology. Plato is the least technical of writers and has no highly specialized vocabulary; but moral and abstract terms, of the kind that occur constantly throughout the *Republic*, are notoriously difficult to translate. They have so often overtones of ambiguity which it is impossible to reproduce in another language, with the result that a translation which keeps fairly closely to the literal meaning may be positively misleading to a modern reader, and even where it is not misleading may be 'tedious, or grotesque and silly, or pompous and verbose'.[1] The translator must go behind what Plato said and discover what he means, and if, for example, he says 'examining the beautiful and the good' must not hesitate to render this as 'discussing moral values' if that is in fact the way in which the same thought would be expressed to-day. There is the further difficulty of preserving the conversational atmosphere of the original dialogue, which never quite disappears even though there are long passages where the respondent says little more than 'yes' or 'no'. Cornford, whose version is far nearer the modern idiom than any other,[2]

1. Cornford, *op. cit*. Preface, p. v.
2. My debt to it will be clear from the references in footnotes.

deals with the difficulty by running together long passages of question and answer into a consecutive series of remarks by one speaker. But this method loses the rapid give and take of the original, and evades rather than solves the problem. The older translators such as Jowett or Davies and Vaughan render the original in full; but their idiom is no longer ours, and it may perhaps be doubted whether anyone really *talked* in quite their style. Yet a translation that fails to give the impression of people talking has failed to convey the really characteristic thing about the Platonic dialogue.

It would be too much to hope that the present translation has entirely succeeded in achieving these objects. But it is perhaps worth while to tell the reader what it is attempting, and so give him a standard by which he can judge it for himself.

H. D. P. L.

Clifton, February 1954

NOTE

The translation is made from the Oxford text, except when noted. I have constantly used Adam's edition (*The Republic of Plato*: C.U.P. 1926), referred to in the footnotes as 'Adam'.

THE REPUBLIC

*

PART ONE
INTRODUCTION

*

§1. PRELUDE

*The scene set and the characters introduced. The subject of the dialogue,
Justice or Right, is introduced in a preliminary discussion with
Cephalus, who defines it, in effect, as telling the truth and paying one's
debts.*

I WENT down yesterday to the Piraeus with Glaucon, son of   327
Ariston. I wanted to say a prayer to the goddess and also to
see what they would make of the festival, as this was the first
time they were holding it. I must say that I thought that the
local contribution to the procession was splendid, though the
Thracian contingent seemed to show up just as well. We had
said our prayers and seen the show and were on our way back
to town when Polemarchus, son of Cephalus, saw us in the
distance making our way home and sent his slave running on
ahead to tell us to wait for him. The slave caught hold of my
coat from behind and said 'Polemarchus says you are to wait.'
I turned and asked where his master was. 'He's coming along
behind you,' he said. 'Do wait.' 'We will,' said Glaucon, and
soon afterwards Polemarchus came up; with him were
Adeimantus, Glaucon's brother, Niceratus, son of Nicias, and
others who had all apparently been to the procession.
'Socrates,' said Polemarchus, 'I believe you are starting off on
your way back to town.' 'You are right,' I replied. 'Do you
see how many of us there are?' he asked. 'I do.' 'Well, you
will either have to get the better of us or stay here.' 'Oh, but

there's another alternative,' said I. 'We might persuade you that you ought to let us go.' 'You can't persuade people who won't listen,' he replied. 'No,' said Glaucon, 'you certainly can't.' 'Well you can assume we shan't listen.' 'And don't you know,' added Adeimantus, 'that there is going to be a torch race in the evening on horseback, in honour of the goddess?' 'On horseback?' said I; 'that's a novelty. Do you mean a relay race, in which they carry torches on horseback and hand them on to each other?' 'Yes,' answered Polemarchus, 'and there's to be an all-night carnival as well, which will be worth seeing. We will go out after dinner and watch it; we shall meet a lot of young men there to talk to. So please do stay.' To which Glaucon replied, 'It looks as if we shall have to.' 'Well, if you think so,' I said, 'stay we must.'

So we went to Polemarchus' house, where we found his brothers Lysias and Euthydemus, and besides them Thrasymachus of Chalcedon, Charmantides of Paeania and Cleitophon, son of Aristonymus. Polemarchus' father, Cephalus, was there too, a very old man he seemed to me, for it was a long time since I had seen him last. He was sitting garlanded on some sort of an easy chair, as he had just been sacrificing in the courtyard. There were some chairs standing round about, so we sat down beside him. As soon as he saw me Cephalus welcomed me and said, 'You don't come down to the Piraeus to see us, Socrates, as often as you should. If I were still strong enough to make the journey to town easily, there would be no reason for you to come here; I would visit you. As it is, you ought to come here more frequently: for I myself find that as age blunts one's enjoyment of physical pleasures, one's desire for intelligent conversation and one's enjoyment of it increase correspondingly. So don't refuse me, but come and talk to the young men here and visit us as if we were old friends.' 'As a matter of fact, Cephalus,' I said, 'I enjoy talking to very old men, for they have gone before us, as it were, on a road that we too must probably tread, and it seems to me that we can find out from them what it is like and whether it is rough and difficult or broad and easy. You are now at an age when you are, as the poets say, about to cross the bar, and

I would like to find out from you what you have to tell us. Is it a difficult time of life, or not?'

'I'll certainly tell you what I think about it, Socrates,' he 329 said. 'For some of us old men often meet together, like the proverbial birds of a feather. And when we do meet, most of them are full of woes; they hanker for the pleasures of their youth, remembering how they used to make love and drink and go to parties and the like, and thinking it a great deprivation that they can't do so any more. Life was good then, they think, whereas now they can hardly be said to live at all. And some of them grumble that their families show no respect for their age, and proceed to harp on the miseries old age brings. But in my opinion, Socrates, they are putting the blame in the wrong place. For if old age were to blame, my experience would be the same as theirs, and so would that of all other old men. But in fact I have met many whose feelings are quite different. For example, I was once present when someone was asking the poet Sophocles about sex, and whether he was still able to make love to a woman; to which he replied, "Don't talk about that; I have left it behind me and escaped from the madness and slavery of passion." A good reply I thought then, and still do. For in old age you become quite free of passions of this sort and they leave you in peace; and when your desires lose their intensity and relax, you get what Sophocles was talking about, a release from slavery to all your many passions. In all this, and in the lack of respect their families show them, there is only one thing to blame; and that is not their old age, Socrates, but their character. For if men are sensible and good-tempered, old age is easy enough to bear: if not, youth as well as age is a burden.'

I was delighted by what he said, and tried to lead him on by saying, 'I'm afraid that most people don't agree with what you say, Cephalus, but think that you carry your years lightly not because of your character but because of your wealth. For they say that the rich have many consolations.'

'Of course they don't agree with me,' he said, 'and there's something in what they say, though not as much as they think. The story about Themistocles is very much to the point.

330 A Seriphian was abusing him and saying that his reputation
was due not to his personal merits but to his being an
Athenian, and Themistocles answered, "I certainly should not
have been famous if I had been a Seriphian, but nor would
you if you had been an Athenian." The same remark applies
to those who are not rich and find old age a burden: a good
man may not find old age easy to bear if he's poor, but a bad
man won't be contented even if he is rich.'

'Did you inherit most of your fortune,' I asked Cephalus,
'or did you make it yourself?'

'Did I make my fortune, Socrates?' he said. 'As a business
man I rank somewhere between my grandfather and my
father. For my grandfather, after whom I am named, inherited
about as much as I now have and multiplied it several times
over, while my father Lysanias reduced it to less than what
it is now: for myself, I shall be pleased enough if I leave these
boys of mine a little more than I inherited.'

'The reason why I asked,' I said, 'was that you did not seem
to me over-fond of money. And this is the way in general
with those who have not made it themselves, while those who
have are twice as fond of it as anyone else. For just as poets
are fond of their own poems, and fathers of their own children,
so money-makers become devoted to money, not only because, like other people, they find it useful, but because it's
their own creation. So they are tiresome company, as they
have no standard but cash value.'

'That's true,' he said.

'It is indeed,' said I. 'But I have another question. What do
you think is the greatest advantage you have gained from
being so rich?'

'One,' he replied, 'which many will perhaps not credit. For
you know, Socrates, when a man faces the thought of death
there come into his mind anxieties that did not trouble him
before. The stories about another world, and about punishment in a future life for wrongs done in this, at which he
once used to laugh, begin to plague his mind with the fear
that they may be true. And either because of the weakness of
old age or because, as he approaches the other world, he has

some clearer perception of it, he is filled with doubts and fears and begins to reckon up and see if there is anyone he has wronged. The man who finds that in the course of his life he has done a lot of wrong often wakes up at night in terror, like a child with nightmare, and his life is full of foreboding: but the man who is conscious of no wrong looks forward 331 with cheerfulness and with hope, "the comfort of old age" as Pindar calls it. For I love that passage where he says of the man who has lived a good and godfearing life,

> Sweet Hope,
> Who guides men's wandering purpose,
> Treads at his side, gladdens his heart,
> And comforts his old age.

Wonderful lines! Now it is chiefly for this that I think wealth is valuable, not perhaps to everyone but to good and sensible men. For wealth contributes very greatly to one's ability to avoid both unintentional cheating or lying and the fear that one has left some sacrifice to God unmade or some debt to man unpaid before one dies. Money has many other uses, but taking one thing with another I reckon that for a reasonable man this is by no means its least.'

'That's fair enough, Cephalus,' I said. 'But are we really to say that doing right consists simply and solely in truthfulness and returning anything we have borrowed? Are those not actions that can be sometimes right and sometimes wrong? For instance, if one borrowed a weapon from a friend who subsequently went out of his mind and then asked for it back, surely it would be generally agreed that one ought not to return it, and that it would not be right to do so, or to consent to tell the strict truth to a madman?'

'That is true,' he replied.

'Well then,' I said, 'telling the truth and returning what we have borrowed is not the definition of doing right.'

'Oh yes it is,' said Polemarchus, interrupting, 'at any rate if we are to believe Simonides.'

'Well,' said Cephalus, 'I will hand the argument over to the two of you, for I must go and see about the sacrifice.'

'While I take over from you?' asked Polemarchus.

'You do,' said Cephalus with a smile, and left for his sacrifice.

§2. THE CONVENTIONAL VIEW OF JUSTICE DEVELOPED

Polemarchus takes up the argument and maintains that justice is giving a man his due. Socrates draws a series of absurd conclusions in order to demonstrate the inadequacy of the conventional view.

'Well then,' said I, 'as heir to this argument, tell me, what is this saying of Simonides that you think tells us the truth about doing right?'

'That it is right to give every man his due,' he replied; 'in that, I think, he puts the matter fairly enough.'

'It is indeed difficult to disagree with Simonides,' I said; 'he had the poet's wisdom and inspiration; but though you may know what he meant by what he said, I'm afraid I don't. For he clearly does not mean what we were talking about just now, that we should return anything entrusted to us even though the person asking for it has gone mad. Yet what one has entrusted to another is due to one, isn't it?'

'Yes.'

'Yet in no circumstances should one return it to a madman.'

'True.'

'So Simonides must mean something different from this when he says that it is right to give every man his due.'

'He certainly must,' he replied; 'for his thought is that one friend owes it as a due to another to do him good, not harm.'

'I see,' I said; 'then as between two friends one is not giving the other his due when he returns a sum of money the other has entrusted to him if the return is going to cause harm – is this what Simonides means?'

'Certainly.'

'Well then, ought we to give our enemies too whatever is due to them?'

'Certainly,' he said, 'what is due to them; and that is, I assume, what is appropriate between enemies, an injury of some sort.'

'It looks,' said I, 'as if Simonides was talking about what is right with a poet's ambiguity. For it appears that he meant that it is right to give everyone what is appropriate to him, but he called this his "due".'

'Of course.'

'Yes, but look here,' I said, 'suppose someone asked him "How then does medicine get its name, Simonides? What does it supply that is due and appropriate and to whom?" How do you suppose he would reply?'

'Obviously that it is the science that supplies the body with remedies and with food and drink.'

'And if he were asked the same question about cookery?'

'That it supplies the flavour to our food.'

'Then what about justice? What does it supply?'

'If we are to be consistent, Socrates, it must be the ability to do good and evil to one's friends and enemies.'

'So Simonides says that justice is to benefit one's friends and harm one's enemies?'

'I think so.'

'Who then is best able to benefit his friends and harm his enemies in matters of health?'

'A doctor.'

'And on a risky sea voyage?'

'A navigator.'

'And what about the just man? When and where will he best be able to help his friends and harm his enemies?'

'In war: he will fight against his enemies and for his friends.'

'Good. Yet people who are healthy have no use for a physician, have they, Polemarchus?'

'True.'

'Nor those that stay on land of a navigator?'

'No.'

'Do you then maintain that those who are not at war have no use for a just man?'

'Certainly not.'

'So justice is useful in peacetime?'

'It is.'

'So too is agriculture, for producing crops; and shoe-making for producing shoes.'

'Yes.'

'Well then, what is the use of justice in peacetime, and what do we get out of it?'

'It's useful in business.'

'And by that you mean some form of transaction between people?'

'Yes.'

'Well, if our transaction is a game of chess, is a just man a good and useful partner, or a chess player?'

'A chess player.'

'And if it's a matter of bricks and mortar, is the just man a better and more useful partner than a bricklayer?'

'No.'

'Well, for what kind of transaction is the just man a better partner than the bricklayer? Where does he excel the musician as the musician excels him in music?'

'Where money is involved, I suppose.'

'Except perhaps,' said I, 'when it's a question of buying or selling; if, for example, we are buying or selling a horse, a trainer would be a better partner, would he not? Or if it's a ship, a shipbuilder or sailor?'

'I suppose so.'

'Then in what financial transactions is the just man a better partner than others?'

'When we want to bank our money, Socrates.'

'In fact when we don't want to make use of it at all, but lay it by?'

'Yes.'

'So when we aren't making any use of our money, we find justice useful?'

'It looks rather like it.'

'And so when you want to store a pruning-knife, justice is useful both to community and to individual; but if you want to use it then you turn to the vine dresser. And if you want to keep your shield or your lyre safe you look to the just man, but if you want to use it to the soldier or musician?'

'That seems to follow.'

'And so in all spheres justice is useless when you are using things, and useful when you are not?'

'Maybe.'

'Justice, then, can't be a very serious thing,' I said, 'if that is all the use it is. But there's a further point. In boxing and other kinds of fighting, skill in attack goes with skill in defence, does it not?'

'Of course.'

'So, too, the ability to save from disease implies the ability to produce it undetected, while ability to bring an army 334 safely through a campaign goes with ability to rob the enemy of his secrets and steal a march on him in action.'

'I certainly think so.'

'So a man who's good at keeping a thing will be good at stealing it?'

'I suppose so.'

'So if the just man is good at keeping money safe he will be good at stealing it too.'

'That at any rate is the conclusion the argument leads to.'

'So the just man turns out to be a kind of thief, a view you have perhaps learned from Homer. For he approves of Odysseus' grandfather Autolycus who, he says, surpassed all men in stealing and lying. Justice, in fact, according to you and Homer and Simonides, is a kind of stealing, though it must be done to help a friend or harm an enemy. Is that your meaning?'

'It certainly isn't,' he replied, 'but I don't really know what I did mean. Yet I still think that justice is to help your friends and harm your enemies.'

'But which do you reckon are a man's friends or enemies? Those he thinks good, honest men and the reverse, or those who really are even though he may not think so?'

'One would expect a man's likes and dislikes to depend on what he thinks.'

'But don't men often make mistakes, and think a man honest when he is not, and vice versa?'

'Yes, they do.'

'In that case their enemies are good and their friends bad, and it's only right that they should help the bad and harm the good.'

'I suppose so.'

'Yet good men are not likely to do wrong.'

'True.'

'So that by your reckoning it is right to injure those who do no wrong.'

'Oh no, Socrates; it looks as if my reckoning were wrong.'

'Well then,' I said, 'it must be right to harm wrongdoers and help those who do right.'

'That seems more reasonable.'

'So when men are mistaken in their judgements it will often be right for them to injure their friends, who are really bad, and help their enemies, who are good. Which is the very opposite of what we said Simonides meant.'

'That is the conclusion that follows, certainly,' he said. 'But let us put the matter differently. For our definitions of friend and enemy were perhaps wrong.'

'How wrong?'

'When we defined a friend as one who *seemed* a good, honest man.'

'And how are we to change our definition?'

335 'By defining a friend as one who both *seems* and *is* an honest man: while the man who seems, but is not an honest man, seems a friend, but really is not. And similarly for an enemy.'

'On this reckoning the good man is a friend and the bad man an enemy, and you want us to add to our previous definition of justice (that justice was to do good to a friend and harm to an enemy) by saying that it is just to do good to one's friend if he is good, and to harm one's enemy if he is evil.'

'Yes,' he said, 'that puts it very fairly.'

'But is it really right to harm any man?'

'It certainly is,' he replied: 'we ought to harm bad men who are our enemies.'

60

'If we harm a horse do we make it better or worse?'

'Worse.'

'Worse, that is, by the standards by which we judge horses?'

'Yes.'

'And a dog if harmed becomes a worse dog by the standards of canine excellence?'

'Surely.'

'But must we not then say of a man that if harmed he becomes worse by the standards of human excellence?'

'Certainly.'

'But is not justice the standard of human excellence?'

'It surely must be.'

'Well, musicians will hardly use their skill to make their pupils unmusical, or riding masters to make their pupils bad horsemen.'

'Hardly.'

'Then will just men use their justice to make others unjust? Or, in short, will good men use their goodness to make others bad?'

'That cannot be so.'

'For it is not the function of heat to cool things, but of its opposite: nor the function of dryness to wet things, but of its opposite.'

'No.'

'Well then, it is not the function of the good man to do harm but of his opposite.'

'Clearly.'

'Then since the just man is good, Polemarchus, it is not the function of the just man to harm either his friends or anyone else, but of his opposite, the unjust man.'

'What you say is perfectly true, Socrates.'

'So it wasn't a wise man who said that justice is to give every man his due, if what he meant by it was that the just man should harm his enemies and help his friends. This simply is not true: for as we have seen, it is never right to harm anyone at any time.'

'I agree.'

'So you and I,' said I, 'will both quarrel with anyone who

says that this view was put forward by either Simonides or Bias or Pittacus or any of the canonical sages.'

'For myself,' he replied, 'I am quite ready to join your side of the quarrel.'

336 'Do you know whose I think this saying is that tells us it is right to help one's friends and harm one's enemies? I think it must be due to Periander or Perdiccas or Xerxes or Ismenias of Thebes, or someone else of wealth and arrogance.'

'Very likely,' he replied.

'Well, well,' said I; 'now we have seen this definition of justice to be wrong, will anyone else suggest another one?'

It will be noticed that throughout the foregoing argument Socrates continually draws analogies from various human occupations, from cookery to horse-breeding. To describe all such occupations the Greeks had a single word, 'Technē', for which there is no equivalent in English that will bring out the variety of its meaning. It includes both the fine arts (music) and the practical arts (cookery); all forms of skilled craftsmanship (ship-building) and various professional activities (navigation and soldiering); besides activities calling for scientific skill (medicine). It may thus be said to cover any skilled activity with its rules of operation, the knowledge of which is acquired by training. But it is a very elusive word to translate, varying between art and craft and science according to the emphasis of the context. I have thought it better to translate to suit the context rather than retain a single word throughout; but behind the group of words I have used (which are sufficiently indicated by what I have said) there lies only the one word 'Technē' in the Greek. Whether or how far the analogy from skilled activity of this kind, from craft or profession or science, to morals and politics is a sound one, is one of the fundamental questions which the reader of Plato must constantly be asking himself.

§3. THRASYMACHUS AND THE REJECTION OF CONVENTIONAL MORALITY

1. *First Statement and Criticisms*

Socrates has shown that conventional morality is muddle-headed: Thrasymachus rejects it altogether and substitutes self-interest. He represents a view that was not uncommon in the fifth century, among

the Sophists in particular, and which has indeed never lacked advo-
cates. His presentation of it is extreme and Plato makes him noisy
and offensive. He starts, after some introductory argumentative
sparring with Socrates, by saying that Right is the 'Interest of the
Stronger'; and explains this to mean that the ruling class in any
state will forcibly exact a certain type of behaviour from its subjects
to suit its own interests. Morality is nothing more or less than the code of
behaviour so exacted. Socrates first asks how this is affected by the
fact that rulers may often be mistaken about their own interests; and
then, when Thrasymachus replies that rulers, qua rulers, are never
mistaken, uses the techné-analogy to show that rulers don't pursue
their own interests. The last argument is very theoretical and doubt-
fully valid, but by talking of rulers who cannot err Thrasymachus
has deserted his own would-be realism, and laid himself open to a
purely theoretical refutation.

While we had been talking Thrasymachus had often tried
to interrupt, but had been prevented by those sitting near
him, who wanted to hear the argument concluded; but when
we paused and I asked my question, he was no longer able to
contain himself and gathered himself together and sprang on
us like a wild beast, as if he wanted to tear us in pieces.
Polemarchus and I were scared stiff, as Thrasymachus burst
out and said, 'What is all this nonsense, Socrates? Why do
you go on in this childish way being so polite about each
other's opinions? If you really want to know what justice is,
stop asking questions and then playing to the gallery by refuting anyone who answers you. You know perfectly well that
it's easier to ask questions than to answer them. Give us an
answer yourself, and tell us what you think justice is. And
don't tell me that it's duty, or expediency, or advantage, or
profit, or interest. I won't put up with nonsense of that sort;
give me a clear and precise definition.'

I was staggered by his attack and looked at him in dismay.
If I had not seen him first I believe I should have been struck
dumb; but I had noticed him when our argument first began
to annoy him, and so I managed to answer him, saying diffi-
dently: 'Don't be hard on us, Thrasymachus. If we have made

any mistake in the course of our argument, I assure you we have not done so on purpose. For if we were looking for gold, you can't suppose that we would willingly let mutual politeness hinder our search and prevent our finding it. Justice is much more valuable than gold, and we aren't likely to cramp our efforts to find it by any idiotic deference to each other. I assure you we are doing our best. It's the ability that we lack, and clever chaps like you ought to be sorry for us and not
337 get annoyed with us.'

Thrasymachus laughed sarcastically, and replied, 'There you go with your old affectation, Socrates. I knew it, and I told the others that you would never let yourself be questioned, but go on shamming ignorance and do anything rather than give a straight answer.'

'That's because you're so clever, Thrasymachus,' I replied, 'and you know it. You ask someone for a definition of twelve, and add "And I don't want to be told that it's twice six, or three times four, or six times two, or four times three; that sort of nonsense won't do." You know perfectly well that no one would answer you on those terms. He would reply "What do you mean Thrasymachus; am I to give none of the answers you mention? If one of them happens to be true, do you want me to give a false one?" And how would you answer him?'

'That's not a fair parallel,' he replied.

'I don't see why not,' I said: 'but even if it is not, we shan't stop anyone else answering like that if he thinks it fair, whether we like it or not.'

'So I suppose that is what you are going to do,' he said; 'you're going to give one of the answers I barred.'

'I would not be surprised,' said I, 'if it seemed to me on reflection to be the right one.'

'What if I give you a quite different and far better definition of justice? What plea will you enter then?'

'The plea of ignorance: for those who don't know must learn from those who do.'

'You must have your joke,' said he, 'but you must pay your costs as well.'

'I will when I have any cash.'

'The money's all right,' said Glaucon; 'we'll pay up for Socrates.[1] So let us have your definition, Thrasymachus.'

'I know,' he replied, 'so that Socrates can play his usual tricks, never giving his own views but always asking others to explain theirs and refuting them.'

'But what am I to do?' I asked. 'I neither know nor profess to know anything about the subject, and even if I did I've been forbidden to say what I think by no mean antagonist. It's much more reasonable for you to say something, because you say you know, and really have something to say. Do please therefore do me a favour and give me an answer, and don't grudge your instruction to Glaucon and the others here.' 338

Glaucon and the others backed up what I had said, and it was obvious that Thrasymachus was anxious to get the credit for the striking answer he thought he could give: but he went on pretending he wanted to win his point and make me reply. In the end, however, he gave in, remarking, 'So this is the wisdom of Socrates: he won't teach anyone anything, but goes round learning from others and is not even grateful.'

To which I replied, 'It's quite true, Thrasymachus, to say I learn from others, but it's not true to say I'm not grateful. I am generous with my praise – the only return I can give, as I have no money. You'll see in a moment how ready I am to praise any view I think well founded, for I'm sure the answer you're going to give me will be that.'

'Listen then,' he replied. 'I define justice or right as what is in the interest of the stronger party. Now where is your praise? I can see you're going to refuse it.'

'You shall have it when I understand what you mean, which at present I don't. You say that what is in the interest of the stronger party is right; but what do you mean by interest? For instance, Polydamas the athlete is *stronger* than us, and it's in his *interest* to eat beef to keep fit; we are *weaker* than he, but you can't mean that the same diet is in our *interest* and so *right* for us.'

1. The sophists charged for their instruction.

'You're being tiresome, Socrates,' he returned, 'and taking my definition in the sense most likely to damage it.'

'I assure you I'm not,' I said; 'you must explain your meaning more clearly.'

'Well then, you know that some states are tyrannies, some democracies, some aristocracies? And that in each city power is in the hands of the ruling class?'

'Yes.'

'Each ruling class makes laws that are in its own interest, a democracy democratic laws, a tyranny tyrannical ones and so on; and in making these laws they define as "right" for their subjects what is in the interest of themselves, the rulers, and if anyone breaks their laws he is punished as a "wrong-doer". That is what I mean when I say that "right" is the same thing in all states, namely the interest of the established ruling class; and this ruling class is the "strongest" element in each state, and so if we argue correctly we see that "right" is always the same, the interest of the stronger party.'

'Now,' I said, 'I understand your meaning, and we must try to find out whether you are right or not. Your answer defines "right" as "interest" (though incidentally this is just what you forbade me to do), but adds the qualification "of the stronger party".'

'An insignificant qualification, I suppose you will say.'

'Its significance is not yet clear; what is clear is that we must consider whether your definition is true. For I quite agree that what is right is an "interest"; but you add that it is the interest "of the stronger party", and that's what I don't know about and want to consider.'

'Let us hear you.'

'You shall,' said I. 'You say that obedience to the ruling power is right and just?'

'I do.'

'And are those in power in the various states infallible or not?'

'They are, of course, liable to make mistakes,' he replied.

'When they proceed to make laws, then, they may do the job well or badly.'

'I suppose so.'

'And if they do it well the laws will be in their interest, and if they do it badly they won't, I take it.'

'I agree.'

'But their subjects must obey the laws they make, for to do so is right.'

'Of course.'

'Then according to your argument it is *right* not only to do what is in the interest of the stronger party but also the opposite.'

'What do you mean?' he asked.

'My meaning is the same as yours, I think. Let us look at it more closely. Did we not agree that when the ruling powers order their subjects to do something they are sometimes mistaken about their own best interest, and yet that it is *right* for the subject to do what his ruler enjoins?'

'I suppose we did.'

'Then you must admit that it is *right* to do things that are *not* in the interest of the rulers, who are the *stronger* party; that is, when the rulers mistakenly give orders that will harm them and yet (so you say) it is right for their subjects to obey those orders. For surely, my dear Thrasymachus, in those circumstances it follows that it is "right" to do the opposite of what you say is right, in that the weaker are *ordered* to do what is against the interest of the stronger.'

'A clear enough conclusion,' exclaimed Polemarchus.   540

'No doubt,' interrupted Cleitophon, 'if we are to take *your* word for it.'

'It's not a question of *my* word,' replied Polemarchus; 'Thrasymachus himself agrees that rulers sometimes give orders harmful to themselves, and that it is right for their subjects to obey them.'

'Yes, Polemarchus, that was because he said that it was right to obey the orders of those in power.'

'*And* that the interest of the stronger was right. And having put forward both views he had to admit that the stronger sometimes give orders which are not in their interest which their weaker subjects obey. From which admission it follows that what is in the interest of the stronger is no more right than the reverse.'

'But,' objected Cleitophon, 'what Thrasymachus meant by the interest of the stronger was what the stronger *thinks* to be in his interest; this is what the subject must do and what was intended by the definition.'

'Well, it was not what he said,' replied Polemarchus.

'It does not matter, Polemarchus,' I said. 'If this is Thrasymachus' meaning let us accept it. Tell me, Thrasymachus, was this how you meant to define what is right, that it is that which seems to the stronger to be his interest, whether it really is or not?'

'Certainly not,' he replied; 'do you think that I call someone who is making a mistake "stronger" just when he is making his mistake?'

'I thought,' I said, 'that that was what you meant when you agreed that rulers are not infallible but sometimes make mistakes.'

'That's because you're so malicious in argument, Socrates. Do you, for instance, call a man who has made a mistaken diagnosis a doctor by virtue of his mistake? Or when a mathematician makes a mistake in his calculations do you call him a mathematician by virtue of his mistake and when he makes it? We use this form of words, of course, and talk of a doctor or a mathematician or a scholar "making a mistake"; but in fact, I think, each of them, in so far as he is what we call him, is infallible. And so to be precise (and precision is what you aim at) no skilled craftsman ever makes a mistake. For he makes his mistake because his skill fails him, and he is then no longer a skilled craftsman. So no craftsman or scientist ever makes a mistake, nor does a ruler so long as he is a ruler; though it's true that in common parlance one may *talk* about the doctor or ruler making a mistake as I did in what I was saying just now. To be really precise one must say that the ruler, in so far as he is a ruler, makes no mistake, and so
341 infallibly enacts what is best for himself, which his subjects must perform. And so, as I said to begin with, "right" means the interest of the stronger party.'

'Well,' said I, 'so you think I'm malicious, do you, Thrasymachus?'

'I certainly do.'

'You think my questions were deliberately framed to distort your argument?'

'I know perfectly well they were. But they won't get you anywhere; you can't fool me, and if you don't you won't be able to crush me in argument'.

'My dear chap, I wouldn't dream of trying,' I said. 'But, to stop this sort of thing happening again, will you make this point clear; when you speak of the ruler and stronger party whose interest it is right that the weaker should serve, do you use the words in their more general sense or in the precise sense which you have just defined?'

'I mean ruler in the precisest sense,' he replied. 'Try your low tricks on that if you can – I ask no mercy. But you are not likely to succeed.'

'Surely,' I said, 'you don't think I'm foolish enough to try to beard the lion and trick Thrasymachus?'

'You tried just now,' he answered, 'but nothing came of it.'

'Well, let us leave it at that,' I said; 'but tell me, this doctor in the precise sense you have just been talking about, is he a business-man or a medical practitioner? I mean the man who really is a doctor.'

'A medical practitioner.'

'And a ship's captain? Is he a member of the crew or in command of it?'

'In command.'

'For it would I take it be wrong to take account of his mere presence on board to call him a member of the crew. For he is not captain by virtue of being on board, but because of his professional skill and command of the crew.'

'True.'

'And each group[1] has its own particular interest.'

'Yes.'

'And in each case the object of the profession concerned is to further that interest?'

1. Doctor and patient, captain and crew.

69

'That is its object.'

'Then has any form of professional skill any interest at which it aims over and above its own perfection?'

'What do you mean by that?'

'Suppose, for example,' I replied, 'that you were to ask me whether the body were self-sufficient, with no needs beyond itself, I should answer "It certainly has needs. That is the reason why medicine has been discovered, because the body has its defects and these need curing; medical skill was, in fact, acquired to look after the interests of the body." Would that be a correct answer, do you think?'

'It would.'

342 'Then is the science or art of medicine itself defective? Does it or any other skilled activity need anything to complete it? I mean as the eyes need sight and the ears hearing, so they also need an art to look to their interests and provide them with what they need in this respect. But is it a characteristic of skilled activity as such to be defective, so that each activity needs another to look after its interests, and this one another, and so *ad infinitum*? Or does each look after its own interest? Is it not rather true that each has no need either of its own or another's supervision to check its faults and watch its interests? For there is no fault or flaw in any science or art, nor is it its business to seek the interest of anything but its subject matter; each is faultless and flawless and right, so long as it is entirely and precisely what it is. And it is in your precise sense that I want you to tell me if I am right.'

'You are right,' he said.

'Medicine therefore looks to the interest not of medicine but of the body.'

'Yes.'

'And training to the interest of the horse and not its own. Nor does any art or science seek its own interest (it needs nothing) but that of its subject matter.'

'It looks like it.'

'Yet surely,' I said, 'the arts and sciences rule and control their subject-matter.'

Thrasymachus only agreed to this very reluctantly.

'Then no science studies or enforces the interest of the controlling or stronger party, but rather that of the weaker party subjected to it.'

He agreed to this, too, in the end, though he tried to make a fight of it. Having secured his agreement I proceeded, 'Then it follows that the doctor *qua* doctor prescribes with a view not to his own interest but that of his patient. For we agreed that a doctor in the precise sense controlled the body and was not in business for profit, did we not?'

He assented.

'And did we not also agree that a ship's captain in the precise sense controlled the crew but was not one of them? So that a captain in this sense will not give his orders with his own interest in view, but that of the crew which he controls.'

He agreed reluctantly.

'And therefore, my dear Thrasymachus,' I concluded, 'no ruler of any kind, *qua* ruler, exercises his authority, whatever its sphere, with his own interest in view, but that of the subject of his skill. It is his subject and his subject's proper interest to which he looks in all he says and does.'

2. *Second Statement and Final Refutation*

To avoid a formal defeat in the argument Thrasymachus interrupts it with a reiteration of his main contention. This may be summarized in a sentence from Marx: 'Political power properly so-called is merely the organized power of one class for oppressing another.' Thrasymachus regards conventional morality as a mere by-product of the process of oppression and exploitation: but unlike Marx he regards the class-conflict as a permanent feature of society, and not one that will be resolved in some future ideal state. In addition, he considers that the pursuit of self-interest, in its narrowest and most selfish form, is natural and right for everyone, though only seen in its perfect and uninhibited form in the tyrant.

Socrates deals first with the more strictly political part of Thrasymachus' thesis, and argues that government, like any other form of professional skill, has its own standard of achievement, and is not merely a matter of profit-making or exploitation. The argument that 'money-making' or 'profit-making' is a separate activity may

*seem artificial to modern minds, for do we not exercise our profession
to make our living? But what Plato is trying to say is that government
is a job or profession like others, with specific tasks to perform, which
it may perform well or ill, and that what the individual 'makes out
of it' (as we should say) is to that extent irrelevant.*

343   At this stage of the argument it was obvious to everyone
that the definition of justice had been reversed, and Thrasymachus, instead of replying, remarked, 'Tell me, Socrates,
have you a nurse?'

'What do you mean?' I returned. 'Why not answer my
question, instead of asking that sort of thing?'

'Well, she lets you go round snivelling and drivelling, and
you can't even tell her the difference between sheep and
shepherd.'

'And why exactly should you say that?' I asked.

'Because you suppose that shepherds and herdsmen study
the good of their flocks and herds and fatten and take care of
them with some other object in view than the good of their
masters and themselves; and don't realize that the rulers of
states, if they are truly such, feel towards their subjects as one
might towards sheep, and think about nothing all the time
but how they can make a profit out of them. Your view of
right and wrong is indeed wide of the mark. You are not
aware that justice or right is really what is good for someone
else, namely the interest of the stronger party or ruler, exacted
at the expense of the subject who obeys him. Injustice or
wrong is just the opposite of this, and dictates to the simple
and the just, while they serve its interests because it is stronger
than they, and as subjects promote not their own but their
ruler's happiness. I'm afraid you're very simple-minded,
Socrates; but you ought to consider how the just man always
comes off worse than the unjust. For instance, in any business
relations between them, you won't find the just man better
off at the end of the deal than the unjust. Again, in their
relations with the state, when there are taxes to be paid the unjust man will pay less on the same income, and when there's
anything to be got he'll get it all. Thus if it's a question of

office, if the just man loses nothing else he will suffer from neglecting his private affairs; his honesty will prevent him appropriating public funds, and his relations and friends will detest him because his principles will not allow him to push their interests. But quite the reverse is true of the unjust man. I'm thinking of the man I referred to just now who can make profits in a big way: he's the man to study if you want to find 344 how much more private profit there is in wrong than in right. You can see it most easily if you take the extreme of injustice and wrongdoing, which brings the highest happiness to its practitioners and plunges its victims and their honesty in misery – I mean, of course, tyranny. Tyranny is not a matter of minor theft and violence, but of wholesale plunder, sacred or profane, private or public. If you are caught committing such crimes in detail you are punished and disgraced: sacrilege, kidnapping, burglary, fraud, theft are the names we give to such petty forms of wrongdoing. But when a man succeeds in robbing the whole body of citizens and reducing them to slavery, they forget these ugly names and call him happy and fortunate, as do all others who hear of his unmitigated wrongdoing. For, of course, those who abuse wrongdoing and injustice do so because they are afraid of suffering from it, not of doing it. So we see that injustice, given scope, has greater strength and freedom and power than justice; which proves what I started by saying, that justice is the interest of the stronger party, injustice the interest and profit of oneself.'

After deluging us with this oratorical shower-bath, Thrasymachus intended to leave; the others, however, would not let him, but compelled him to stay and be cross-examined. I supported their pleas, saying, 'My dear Thrasymachus, you can't mean to throw a theory like that at us and then leave us without explaining it or examining its truth. Surely it's no small matter to define the course we must follow if we're to live our lives to the best advantage?'

'I never said it was,' he countered.

'You seemed to say so,' I replied; 'or perhaps it is that you have no consideration for us, and don't care what sort of lives our ignorance of what you claim to know makes us lead.

Come on, let us know your secret – it won't be a bad invest-
ment to give so many of us the benefit of your knowledge.
For as far as I am concerned, you have not convinced me, and
I don't think that injustice pays better than justice even if it
has a clear field to do what it wants. No, my dear Thrasymachus; I grant you your unjust man and I grant him
the ability to continue his wrongdoing by fraud or force, yet
he still does not persuade me that injustice pays better than
justice. And there may be others who feel the same as I do.
It is for you, therefore, to persuade us that we are wrong in
valuing justice more highly than injustice.'

'And how am I to persuade you?' he retorted. 'If you don't
believe what I have just said, what more can I do? Do you
want ideas spoon-fed to you?'

'Not by you at any rate,' I replied. 'But to begin with, do
stick to what you say, or if you modify it, do so openly and
above board. For instance, in what you have just been saying,
you started by defining what a true doctor is: yet when you
came to the true shepherd you abandoned your standard of
accuracy, and now suppose that the shepherd's business is to
fatten his flock, not with a view to its own good, but in the
hope either of a good meal, like a prospective guest at a feast,
or of making a sale, as if he were a business man, not a shepherd. Yet the shepherd's only care is the welfare of the flock
of which he is in charge; for (as we have said) so long as his
art does not fall short in any way of what it should be, all its
needs are sufficiently provided for. And so I thought just now
that we agreed that it followed that any kind of authority,
public or private, pursued only the welfare of the subjects
under its care. But tell me, do you think that the rulers of
states (rulers in the true sense, that is) really like ruling?'

'I don't think it, I know it,' he replied.

'Very well, Thrasymachus,' I said; 'but have you not noticed that no one really wants to exercise other forms of
authority? At any rate, they expect to be paid for them, which
shows that they don't expect any benefit for themselves but
only for their subjects. For tell me, don't we differentiate between one art or profession and another by their ability to

74

produce different results? And please tell me what you really think, so that we can get somewhere.'

'That is how we differentiate them,' he replied.

'And so each one benefits us in a distinct and particular way; the doctor brings us health, the pilot a safe voyage, and so on.'

'True.'

'So wage-earning brings us wages; for that is its function. For you don't identify medicine and navigation, do you? Nor, if you are going to use words precisely, as you proposed, do you call navigation medicine just because a ship's captain recovers his health on a voyage because the sea suits him.'

'No.'

'Nor do you call wage-earning medicine if someone recovers his health while earning money.'

'No.'

'Well then, can you call medicine money-making, if a doctor earns a fee when he is curing his patient?'

'No,' he said.

'We are agreed then that each profession brings its own peculiar benefit?'

'I grant that.'

'Any common benefit, therefore, that all the professions enjoy, must clearly be procured by the exercise of some additional function common to all.'

'It looks like it.'

'And further, if they earn wages it is a benefit they get from exercising the profession of wage-earning in addition to their own.'

He agreed reluctantly.

'This benefit of receiving wages does not therefore come to a man as a result of the exercise of his own particular profession; if we are to be precise, medicine produces health and wage-earning wages, and building produces a house while wage-earning, following in its train, produces wages. Similarly all other arts and professions each perform their own function to the benefit of the subject of which they are in charge; and no man will benefit from his profession, unless he is paid as well.'

'It seems not,' he said.

'But if he works for nothing, does no one benefit?'

'I suppose someone does.'

'In fact it is clear enough, Thrasymachus, that no profession or art or authority provides for its own benefit but, as we said before, for that of the subject of which it is in charge, thus studying the interest of the weaker party and not the stronger. That was why I said just now that no one really wants authority and with it the job of righting other people's wrongs, unless he is paid for it; because in the exercise of his professional skill, if he does his job properly, he never does or orders what is best for himself but only what is best for his subject. That is why, if a man is to consent to exercise authority, you must pay him, either in cash or honours, or alternatively by punishing him if he refuses.'

'What's that, Socrates?' said Glaucon; 'I recognize your two kinds of reward, but I don't know what the punishment is or why you talk of it as pay.'

'Then you don't understand how the best men must be paid if they are to be willing to govern. You know that to be over-ambitious or mercenary is reckoned, and indeed is, something discreditable?'

'Yes.'

'So good men will not consent to govern for cash or honours. They do not want to be called profiteers for demanding a cash payment for the work of government, or thieves for making money on the side; and they will not work for honours, for they aren't ambitious. We must therefore compel them to consent and punish them if they refuse – perhaps that's why it's commonly considered improper to accept authority except with reluctance or under pressure; and the worst penalty for refusal is to be governed by someone worse than themselves. That is what frightens honest men into accepting power, and they approach it not as if it were something desirable out of which they were going to do well, but as if it were something unavoidable, which they cannot find anyone better or equally qualified to undertake. For in a city of good men there might well be as much competition to avoid power as there now is to get it, and it would be quite clear that the true ruler pursues his subjects' interest and not his own; consequently all wise men would prefer the benefit of this service at the hands of others rather than the labour of affording it to others themselves.'

Socrates now turns to the other part of Thrasymachus' argument, that the pursuit of self-interest or injustice is preferable to justice. He deals with it in three stages.

(A) In the first he makes considerable play with ambiguities in the Greek language which it is difficult to render in English. The basis of the argument is again the Techné analogy. No two craftsmen or professional men are in disagreement about the standards of correctness in their own particular craft or profession, and in that sense are not in competition with each other; and since just men also do not compete with each other in this way, they are analogous to the skilled craftsman, and so the just man is 'wise and good', which is what Thrasymachus had denied.

'You see, then, that I entirely disagree with Thrasymachus' view that justice is the interest of the stronger; but the point is one that we can examine again later, and far more important is his recent assertion that the unjust man has a better life than the just. Which side are you on, Glaucon? and which of us seems to be telling the truth?'

'I think the just man's life pays the better.'

'Did you hear the list of good things in the unjust man's 348 life which Thrasymachus has just gone through?' I asked.

'I heard them,' he replied, 'but I'm not persuaded.'

'Shall we then try and persuade him, if we can find any flaw in his argument?'

'By all means,' he said.

'We might, then, answer his speech by one of our own, setting out the advantages of justice, to which he would make a rejoinder, to which we again would reply; but we shall then have to count and measure up the advantages put forward by either side, and shall soon be wanting a jury to decide between them. But if we proceed by mutual agreement, as we have done so far, we can ourselves be both counsel and jury. Which course do you prefer?'

'The latter,' he replied.

'Well then,' said I, turning to Thrasymachus, 'let us begin at the beginning. You say that perfect injustice pays better than perfect justice.'

'That's what I say,' he replied, 'and I've given you my reasons.'

'Then what do you say about this: is one of them a good quality and one a bad?'

'Of course.'

'Justice a good quality, I suppose, and injustice a bad?'

'My dear man,' he replied, 'is that likely? When I am telling you that injustice pays and justice doesn't.'

'Then what do you think?'

'The opposite,' he answered.

'You mean that justice is a bad quality?'

'No; it's merely supreme simplicity.'

'And so injustice is duplicity, I suppose.'

'No; it's common sense.'

'So you think that the unjust are better men and more sensible?'

'If they can win political supremacy, and their wrong-doing have full scope. You perhaps think I'm talking of bag-snatching; even things like that pay, if you aren't found out, but they are quite trivial by comparison.'

'I see what you mean about that,' I said; 'but what surprised me was that you should rank injustice with intelligence and other good qualities, and justice with their opposites.'

'Yet that is just what I do.'

'That is a much tougher proposition,' I answered, 'and it's not easy to know what to say to it. For if you were maintaining that injustice pays, but were prepared to admit that it is a bad and vicious quality, we could base our argument on generally accepted grounds. As it is, having boldly ranked injustice with intelligence and other good qualities, you will obviously attribute to it all the strength of character that we normally attribute to justice.'

349

'You've guessed my meaning correctly,' he said.

'Still, there must be no shirking,' I rejoined, 'and I must pursue the argument as long as I'm sure you are saying what you think. For I think you are really in earnest now, Thrasymachus, and saying what you think to be the truth.'

'What's it matter what I think?' he retorted. 'Stick to the point.'

'It doesn't matter at all,' was my reply; 'but see if you can answer me this further question. Will one just man compete with another and want more than his fair share of an act of justice?'

'Certainly not; otherwise he would not be the simple, agreeable man we supposed him to be.'

'And will he think it right and proper to compete with the unjust man or not?'

'He'll think it right and proper enough, but he'll not be able to.'

'That's not what I'm asking,' I said, 'but whether one just man thinks it improper to compete with another and refuses to do so, but will compete with an unjust man?'

'Yes, that is so,' he replied.

'Then what about the unjust man? Will he compete with the just and want more than his share in an act of justice?'

'Of course he will; he wants more than his share in everything.'

'Will one unjust man, then, compete with another in an unjust action and fight to get the largest share in everything?'

'Yes.'

'Then let us put it this way,' I said. 'The just man does not compete with his like, but only his unlike, while the unjust man competes with both like and unlike.'

'That puts it very well.'

'And the unjust man is a man of good sense, the just man not?'

'Well said again.'

'And so the unjust man is like the man of good sense, while the just man is not?'

'Of course he must *be like* what he *is*, and the just man unlike.'

'Good. So each of them resembles what he is like.'

'Well, what next?'

'So far, so good, Thrasymachus. Do you recognize the distinction between being musical and unmusical?'

'Yes.'

'And which of the two involves knowledge?'

'Being musical; and being unmusical does not.'

'And knowledge is good, ignorance bad.'

'Yes.'

'And the same argument applies to medicine.'

'It does.'

'Then does one musician who is tuning a lyre try to compete with another, or think that he ought to improve on the correct tuning of the instrument?'

'I think not.'

'But he does try to do better than an unmusical layman?'

'He must try to do that.'

350 'What about a doctor then? Does he want to go beyond what is correct in his prescriptions in competition with his fellow-doctors?'

'No.'

'But he tries to do better than the layman?'

'Yes.'

'Then do you think that over the whole range of professional skill, anyone who has such skill aims at anything more in word or deed than anyone with similar skill? Don't they both aim at the same result in similar circumstances?'

'I suppose there's no denying that.'

'But the man who has no skill will try to compete both with the man who has and with the man who has not.'

'Maybe.'

'And the man with professional knowledge is wise and the wise man is good.'

'I agree.'

'So the good man, who has knowledge, will not try to compete with his like, but only with his opposite.'

'So it seems.'

'While the bad and ignorant man will try to compete both with his like and with his opposite.'

'So it appears.'

'But it was surely the unjust man, Thrasymachus, who, we found, competes both with his like and his unlike? That was what you said, wasn't it?'

'It was,' he admitted.

'While the just man will not compete with his like, but with his unlike.'

'True.'

'The just man, then,' I said, 'resembles the good man who has knowledge, the unjust the man who is ignorant and bad.'

'That may be.'

'But we agreed that a thing *is* what it is *like*.'

'We did.'

'Then,' I concluded, 'we have shown that the just man is wise and good and the unjust bad and ignorant.'

Thrasymachus' agreement to all these points did not come as easily as I have described, but had to be dragged from him with difficulty, and with a great deal of sweat – for it was a hot day. And I saw something then I had never seen before, Thrasymachus blushing. So when we had agreed that justice meant good character and knowledge and injustice their opposites, I said, 'Well, we have settled that point, Thrasymachus; but you will remember that we also said that injustice was strength.'

'I remember well enough,' he replied; 'but I still don't accept your last arguments, and have more to say about them. Yet if I were to say it, I know you would accuse me of making speeches. Either therefore let me say all I have to say, or else, if you prefer it, continue your cross-questioning; and I will answer "Very good", "Yes", and "No", like someone listening to old women's gossip.'

'But please answer as you really think,' I replied.

'I will, to please you,' he said, 'since you won't let me speak at length. Does that satisfy you?'

'It does indeed,' said I, 'and if you will answer like that, I will ask the questions.'

'Ask away then.'

*(B) Thrasymachus had claimed that injustice is a source of strength.
On the contrary, says Socrates, it is a source of disunity and therefore
of weakness. There must be honour among thieves if they are to
achieve any common action.*

'Well then, to proceed with the argument, my next question
351 is about the relation of justice and injustice. We said, I think,
that injustice was stronger and more effective than justice,
whereas if, as we have now agreed, justice implies good
character and knowledge it will not, I think, be difficult to
show that it is stronger than injustice, which, as must be
obvious to anyone, implies ignorance. But I don't want to
argue in general terms like this, Thrasymachus, but rather as
follows. Would you say that a state might be unjust and
wrongly try to reduce others to subjection, and having succeeded in so doing continue to hold them in subjection?'

'Of course,' he replied. 'And the most efficient state, whose
injustice is most complete, will be the first to do so.'

'I understood that that was your argument,' said I. 'But do
you think that the more powerful state needs justice to exercise this power over its neighbour or not?'

'If you are right and justice implies knowledge, it will need
justice; but if I am right, injustice.'

'I am delighted that you are not just saying "yes" and "no",
but are giving me a fair answer, Thrasymachus.'

'I'm doing it to please you.'

'Thank you,' said I. 'Then will you be kind enough to tell
me too whether you think that any group of men, be it a
state or an army or a set of gangsters or thieves, can undertake any sort of wrongdoing together if they wrong each
other?'

'No.'

'Their prospect of success is greater if they don't wrong
each other?'

'Yes, it is.'

'Because, of course, if they wrong each other that will breed hatred and dissension among them; but if they treat each other fairly, there will be unity of purpose among them.'

'Yes – I won't contradict you.'

'That's very good of you,' I said. 'Now tell me this. If it is the function of injustice to produce hatred wherever it is, won't it cause men to hate each other and quarrel and be incapable of any joint undertaking whether they are free men or slaves?'

'It will.'

'And so with any two individuals. Injustice will make them quarrel and hate each other, and they will be at enmity with themselves and with just men as well.'

'They will.'

'And in a single individual it will not lose its power, will it, or produce any different result?'

'I grant you that.'

'Injustice, then, seems to have the following results, whether it occurs in a state or family or army or in anything else: it renders it incapable of any common action because of factions and quarrels, and sets it at variance with itself and with its opponents and with all just men.' 352

'Yes.'

'And it produces its natural effects also in the individual. It renders him incapable of action because of internal conflicts and division of purpose, and sets him at variance with himself and with all just men.'

'Yes.'

'And the gods, of course, are just.'

'Granted.'

'So the unjust man is an enemy of the gods, and the just man their friend.'

'Go on, make the most of it,' he retorted. 'I won't annoy the company by contradicting you.'

'If you will go on answering my questions in the same way,' I replied, 'you will complete my entertainment. We have shown that just men are more intelligent and more truly effective in action, and that unjust men are incapable of any joint action at all. Indeed, when we presumed to speak of unjust men effecting any joint action between them, we were quite wrong. For had they been completely unjust they would never have kept their hands off each other, and there must have been some element of justice among them which prevented them wronging each other as well as their victims, and brought them what success they had; they were in fact only half corrupted when they set about their misdeeds, for had their corruption been complete, their complete injustice would have made them incapable of achieving anything. All this seems to me to be established against your original contention.'

(C) Finally, Socrates shows that the just man is happier than the unjust. Using the idea of 'function', he argues that man needs justice to enable him to perform his own particular function. Justice, however, remains undefined. 'Happiness depends on conformity to our nature as active beings. What active principles that nature comprises, and how they are organized into a system we learn in the immediately following books' (Taylor, Plato, p. 270).

'We must now proceed to the further question, which we postponed, whether the just or the unjust live the better or happier lives. The answer is, in fact, already clear, I think, from what we have said; but we must look at it more closely. For the question is not a trivial one; it is our whole way of life that is at issue. So tell me, do you think a horse has a function?'

'Yes.'

'And would you define it as something that only the horse (or whatever it may be) can do, or, at any rate, that the horse does best?'

'I don't understand.'

'Look at it this way. We can see only with our eyes, and hear only with our ears?'

'True.'

'So we can rightly call these the functions of eye and ear.'

'Yes.'

'So again, though you could cut off a vine-shoot with a

carving-knife or a chisel or other tool, you would do the job best if you used a pruning-knife made for the purpose, which, surely, we may call its "function"?'

'We may.'

'And I think you may see now what I meant by asking if the "function" of a thing was not that which only it can do or that which it does best.'

'Yes, I understand,' he replied, 'and I think that is what we mean by a thing's function.'

'Good,' said I. 'And has not everything which has a function its own particular virtue or excellence? Let me take the same examples again. The eyes have a function; have they not also their own particular excellence?'

'They have.'

'The ears too have a function, and therefore their own excellence. And so with all other things?'

'Yes, that is so.'

'Come, then; could the eyes properly perform their function if instead of their own peculiar virtue or excellence they had the corresponding defect?'

'How could they? For you mean, I suppose, blindness instead of sight?'

'I mean whatever their virtue may be. For I am not concerned with that yet, but only to find out whether a thing's characteristic virtue enables it to perform its function well, while its characteristic defect makes it perform it badly.'

'Yes, that is true certainly,' he replied.

'So we can say that the ears if deprived of their own peculiar virtue perform their function badly; and the same argument applies in all other cases.'

'I agree.'

'Then the next point is this. Is there any function that it is impossible to perform except with the mind? For example, paying attention, controlling, deliberating and so on: can we divorce any of these from the conscious mind of which we should say they were characteristic?'

'No.'

'And life – is not that a function of mind?'

'Certainly.'

'And the mind therefore will have its peculiar virtue?'

'It will.'

'And if deprived of its peculiar virtue it will be incapable of performing its function well, will it not?'

'Quite incapable.'

'It follows therefore that goodness enables the mind to perform its functions of control and attention well, and badness the reverse.'

'It follows.'

'And we agreed,[1] did we not, that justice was the peculiar virtue of the mind and injustice its defect?'

'We did.'

'So the just-minded man will have a good life, and the unjust a bad life?'

'So it appears from your argument.'

554 'But the man who has a good life is prosperous and happy, and his opposite the reverse?'

'Of course.'

'So the just man is happy, and the unjust man miserable?'

'I grant that.'

'And so, since it never pays to be miserable, but to be happy, we can say, my dear Thrasymachus, that justice pays better than injustice.'

'Well it's a holiday today,' he replied, 'so have a good time.'

'It is you who are giving me a good time, Thrasymachus,' I replied, 'for you have been most agreeable since you stopped being cross with me. But I'm not having a good time all the same; and it's my own fault, not yours. I'm like a greedy guest who hurries on to the next course before he has properly finished the last. For we started off to enquire what justice is, but before we had found the answer we were asking whether it was a virtue and involved knowledge, or not; and then when we came across the question whether injustice pays better than justice, instead of letting it alone and sticking to the problem in hand, off we went in pursuit, so that I'm still none the wiser after all our discussion. For until I know what

1. Above, p. 81.

justice is I'm hardly likely to find out whether it is a virtu
not, or whether it makes a man happy or unhappy.'

Note on Some Terms Used in Translation

*One of the standing difficulties of translation is that words do not
bear the same range of meaning and association in different languages;
and so a word that is a satisfactory translation of another in one context is not satisfactory in another. This is particularly true of moral
terms, and the reader may have noticed in Book I a certain indecisive-
ness in the use of some words, as if the writer could not make up his
mind which to use and kept shifting between them: in particular, such
words as right, wrong, justice, injustice, good, bad, benefit, harm,
injury. This reflects ambiguities in the Greek. The Republic is
concerned with 'Justice', as we traditionally translate it. But the Greek
group of words (noun, adjective, verb) cover a field which no single
English word does. Thus 'justice' is a very wide term covering right
conduct or morality in general; and the verb from the same root can
mean to act 'rightly' or 'justly', while the converse can mean to act
'wrongly' or 'unjustly' but also to 'wrong' or 'injure'. The most that a
translator can do is to pick the word which he thinks conveys the most
relevant meaning, and to give some idea of the ambiguities involved by
varying the word used. But the English reader when he meets the word
'justice' in particular should remember the wider overtones which the
Greek word conveys.*

§4. ADEIMANTUS AND GLAUCON RESTATE THE CASE FOR INJUSTICE

*There has been a touch of broad caricature about the picture of
Thrasymachus, and Plato evidently thinks that the view which he
represents needs a clearer statement and fairer treatment. Accordingly, Glaucon says that he is not content with the way in which Socrates
has dealt with Thrasymachus and proceeds to restate his argument in
a different form; he is followed by Adeimantus, who supplements what
he has said.*

1. Glaucon *maintains that justice, or morality, is merely a matter
of convenience. It is natural for men to pursue their own interests
regardless of others; but it would be impossible to run an orderly*

society on that basis, and the system of morality is arrived at as a compromise. But it is only a compromise and has no other authority, as can be seen easily enough by considering how a man would behave if its sanctions were removed. And a contrast between the perfectly 'just' and perfectly 'unjust' man shows conclusively that 'injustice' is the more paying proposition.

I thought, as I said this, that there would be no more argument; but in fact we had little more than begun. For Glaucon, who never lacked initiative, would not let Thrasymachus' withdrawal pass unchallenged, but asked: 'Do you really want to convince us that right is in all circumstances better than wrong or not?'

'If I were given the choice,' I replied, 'I should want to convince you.'

'Well then, you are not making much progress,' he returned. 'Tell me, do you agree that there is one kind of good which we want to have simply for its own sake and without regard for its consequences? For example, happiness or pleasure, so long as pleasure brings no harm and its results don't make us unhappy.'

'Yes, that is one kind of good.'

'And is there not another kind of good which we desire both for itself and its consequences? Wisdom and sight and health, for example, we welcome on both grounds.'

'We do,' I said.

'And there is a third category of good which includes exercise and medical treatment and earning one's living as a doctor or otherwise. All these we should regard as painful but good for us; we should not choose them for their own sakes but for what we get out of them, wages or what not.'

'There is this third category. But what is your point?'

'In which category do you place justice and right?'

558 'In the highest category, which anyone who is to be happy welcomes both for its own sake and for its consequences.'

'That is not the common opinion,' Glaucon replied. 'It is normally put into the painful category, of goods which we pursue for the rewards they bring and in the hope of a good reputation, but which in themselves are to be avoided as unpleasant.'

'I know that is the common opinion,' I answered; 'which is why Thrasymachus has been criticizing it and praising injustice. But I'm not easy to convince.'

'Listen to me then, and see if I can change your mind,' he said. 'For you seem to have fascinated Thrasymachus into a premature submission, like a snake charmer; but I am not satisfied yet about justice and injustice. I want to be told what exactly each of them is and what its effects are on the mind of its possessor, quite apart from any question of rewards or consequences. So what I propose to do, if you agree, is this. I shall re-state Thrasymachus' argument under three heads: first, I shall state the common opinion on the nature and origin of justice; second, I shall show that those who practise it do so under compulsion and not because they think it good in itself; third, I shall argue that this conduct is reasonable because the unjust man has, by common reckoning, a better time than the just man. I don't believe all this myself, Socrates, but Thrasymachus and hundreds of others have dinned it into my ears till I don't know what to think; and I've never heard the case in favour of justice as against injustice argued to my satisfaction, that is, I've never heard justice recommended on its own merits apart from its consequences. That is what I want to hear you do. I therefore propose to state, forcibly, the argument in favour of injustice, and thus give you a model which I want you to follow when your turn comes to argue in favour of justice. Do you agree to this suggestion?'

'Nothing could please me better,' I replied, 'for it's a subject which all sensible men should be glad to discuss.'

'Splendid,' said Glaucon. 'And now for my first heading, the nature and origin of justice. What they say is that our natural instinct is to inflict wrong or injury, and to avoid suffering it, but that the disadvantages of suffering it exceed the advantages of inflicting it; after a taste of both, therefore, men decide that, as they can't have the ha'pence without the 359 kicks, they had better make a compact with each other and avoid both. They accordingly proceed to make laws and mutual agreements, and what the law lays down they call lawful and right. This is the origin and nature of justice. It lies between what is most desirable, to do wrong and avoid punishment, and what is most undesirable, to suffer wrong without redress; justice and right lie between these two and are accepted not as being good in themselves, but as having a relative value due to our inability to do wrong. For anyone who had the power to do wrong and called himself a man would never make any such agreement with anyone – he would be mad if he did.[1]

'This then is the account they give of the nature and the origins of justice; the next point is that men practise it against their will and only because they are unable to do wrong. This we can most easily see if we imagine that a just man and an unjust man have each been given liberty to do what they like, and then follow their subsequent careers. We shall catch the just man in exactly the same pursuits as the unjust, led by self-interest, the motive which all men naturally follow if they are not forcibly restrained by the law and made to respect each other's claims.

'The best illustration of the liberty I am talking about would be if we supposed them to be possessed of the power which Gyges, the ancestor of the famous Lydian, had in the story. He was a shepherd in the service of the then king of Lydia, and one day there was a great storm and an earthquake in the district where he was pasturing his flock and a chasm opened in the earth. He was much amazed, and descended into the chasm and saw many astonishing things there, among them, so the story goes, a bronze horse, which was hollow and fitted with doors, through which he peeped and saw a corpse of more than human size. He took nothing from it save a gold ring it had on its finger, and then made his way out. He was wearing this ring when he attended the usual meeting of shepherds which reported monthly to the king on the state of his flocks; and as he was sitting there with the others he happened to twist the bezel of the ring towards the inside of

1. This is the first occurrence of what was later called the Social Contract theory.

his hand. Thereupon he became invisible to his companions, 360
and they began to refer to him as if he had left them. He was
astonished, and began fingering the ring again, and turned the
bezel outwards; whereupon he became visible again. When he
saw this he started experimenting with the ring to see if it
really had this power, and found that every time he turned
the bezel inwards he became invisible, and when he turned it
outwards he became visible. Having made his discovery he
managed to get himself included in the party that was to
report to the king, and when he arrived seduced the queen and
with her help attacked and murdered the king and seized the
throne.

'Let us now imagine there to be two such rings, one for the
just man and one for the unjust. There is no one, it would
commonly be supposed, who would have such iron strength
of will as to stick to what is right and keep his hands off other
people's property. For he would be able to steal from the
shops whatever he wanted without fear of detection, to go
into any man's house and seduce his wife, to murder or to
release from prison anyone he felt inclined, and generally
behave as if he had supernatural powers. And in all this the
just man would differ in no way from the unjust, but both
would follow the same course. This, it would be claimed, is
strong evidence that no man is just save under compulsion,
and that no man thinks justice pays him personally, since he
will always do wrong when he gets the chance. Indeed, the
supporter of this view will continue, men are right in thinking
that injustice pays the individual better than justice; and if
anyone who had the liberty of which we have been speaking
neither wronged nor robbed his neighbour, men would think
him a most miserable idiot, though of course they would
pretend to admire him in public because of their own fear
of being wronged.

'So much for that. Finally, we come to the decision between
the two lives, and we shall best be able to make this decision
if we contrast extreme examples of just and unjust men. By
that I mean if we make each of them perfect in his own line,
and do not in any way mitigate the injustice of the one or the

justice of the other. To begin with the unjust man. He must have a professional skill like that of the most capable pilot or doctor, for example, who know just what they can or can't do, never attempt the impossible, and are able to retrieve any errors they make. The unjust man must, similarly, if he is to be thoroughly unjust, be able to avoid detection in his wrongdoing; for the man who is found out is a poor specimen, and the most accomplished form of injustice is to seem just when you are not. So our completely unjust man must be perfect in his wickedness; he must be able to commit the greatest crimes and at the same time get himself an unblemished reputation, while, if he makes a mistake he must be able to retrieve it, and, if any of his wrong-doing comes to light, be ready with a convincing defence, or when force is needed be prepared to use force, relying on his own courage and energy or making use of his friends or his wealth.

'Beside our picture of the unjust man let us set one of the just man, the man of true simplicity of character who, as Aeschylus says, wants 'to be and not to seem good'. We must, indeed, not allow him to seem good, for if he does he will have all the rewards and honours paid to the man who has a reputation for justice, and we shall not be able to tell whether his motive is love of justice or love of the rewards and honours. No, we must strip him of everything except his justice, and our picture of him must be drawn in the opposite way to our picture of the unjust man; for our just man must have the worst of reputations even though he has done no wrong. So we shall be able to test his justice and see if it can stand up to unpopularity and all that goes with it; we shall give him an undeserved and lifelong reputation for wickedness, and make him stick to his chosen course until death. In this way, when we have pushed the life of justice and of injustice each to its extreme, we shall be able to judge which of the two is the happier.'

'I say, Glaucon,' I put in, 'you're putting the finishing touches to your two portraits as energetically as if you were getting them ready for a show.'

'I'm doing my best,' he said. 'And these being our two

characters, it is not, I think, difficult to describe the sort of life that awaits each. And if the description is somewhat crude, remember that it's not I that am responsible for it, Socrates, but those who think more of injustice than justice. It is their account that I must now repeat.

'The just man, then, as we have pictured him, will be scourged, tortured, and imprisoned, his eyes will be put out, 362 and after enduring every humiliation he will be crucified, and learn at last that we should want not to be, but to seem just. And so that remark which I quoted from Aeschylus could be more appropriately applied to the unjust man; for he, because he deals with realities and not appearances, wants not to *seem* but to *be* unjust. He

> Reaps thought's deep furrow, for therefrom
> Spring goodly schemes

– schemes which bring him respectability and office, and which enable him to marry into any family he likes, to make good matches for his children, and to pick his partners in business, while all the time, because he has no scruples, he is on the make. In all kinds of competition public or private he always comes off best and does down his rivals, and so becomes rich and can help his friends and harm his enemies. His sacrifices and offerings to the gods are on a magnificent scale, and his services to the gods, and to any man he wishes to serve, are far better than those of the just man, so that it is reasonable to suppose that the gods care more for him. And so the conclusion, Socrates, is that a better time awaits the unjust man than the just at the hands both of gods and men.'

2. Adeimantus, *supplementing what Glaucon has said, stresses the unworthy motives commonly given for right conduct. Men only do right for what they can get out of it, in this life and the next. They much prefer to do wrong, because in general it pays better; and they are encouraged to do wrong by contemporary religious beliefs which tell them that they can avoid punishment in this world if they sacrifice to the gods lavishly enough, and in the next if they go through the*

appropriate initiation ceremonies. Adeimantus and Glaucon ask Socrates to show that just or right conduct is preferable in itself and without reference to any external rewards or punishments.

When Glaucon had finished speaking I had it in mind again to make some reply to him, but his brother Adeimantus forestalled me, saying, 'You don't suppose that is a complete statement of the argument, do you, Socrates?'

'But why not?' I replied.

'The most essential point has not been stated.'

'Well,' said I, 'they say blood is thicker than water; so if your brother has left anything out, lend him a hand. Though as far as I am concerned, he has said quite enough to floor me and make me quite incapable of rescuing justice.'

'That's nonsense,' he answered. 'But listen to what I have to say. In order to make clearer what I take to be Glaucon's meaning, we ought to examine the converse of the view he stated, that is, the arguments normally used in favour of justice and against injustice. For fathers tell their sons, and pastors and masters of all kinds urge their charges to be just not because they value justice for itself, but for the social prestige it brings; they want them to secure by a show of justice the power and family connexions and other things which Glaucon enumerated, all of which are procured for the just man by a good reputation. And they go on to enlarge on the importance of reputation, and add that if a man stands well with heaven there is a whole list of benefits available for the pious, citing the authority of Hesiod and Homer. For Hesiod says that for the just the gods make the oaks bear "acorns at the top, bees in the middle", while his sheep "are heavy with fleeces". And Homer speaks in similar terms of "some perfect king, ruling with the fear of god in his heart, and upholding the right, so that the dark soil yields its wheat and barley, the trees are laden with ripe fruit, the sheep never fail to bring forth their lambs, nor the sea to provide its fish".

'The rewards which Musaeus and his son provide for the just are still gayer, for after they have got them to the other world they sit them down to a banquet of the Blest and leave

363

94

them drinking for all time in full evening dress, as if they thought that the supreme reward of virtue was to be drunk for eternity. And some extend the rewards of heaven still further and say that the pious and honest leave children's children and a long posterity to follow them. That is the sort of recommendation they produce for justice. The unjust and the irreligious they plunge into some sort of mud in the underworld or make them carry water in sieves, while in this world they give them a bad name and inflict on them all the punishments which Glaucon described as falling on the just man who seemed to be wicked – they can think of no others.

'So much for the way in which justice is recommended and injustice blamed. But there is another line of argument about them which one meets in the poets as well as in ordinary conversation. People are unanimous about the merits of self-control or justice, but think they are difficult to practise and call for hard work, while self-indulgence and injustice are easy enough to acquire, and regarded as disgraceful only by convention; wrong on the whole pays better than right, they say, and they are ready enough to call a bad man happy and respect him both in public and private provided he is rich and powerful, while they have no respect for the poor and powerless, and despise him, even though they agree that he is the better man. But most surprising of all are the stories about the gods and virtue, which tell how they often allot misfortune and a hard life to the good and the reverse to the wicked. There are itinerant evangelists and prophets who knock at the door of the rich man's house, and persuade him that they have some kind of divine power, and that any wrong that either he or his ancestors have done can be expiated by means of charms and sacrifices and the pleasures of the accompanying feasts; while if he has any enemy he wants to injure they can for a small fee damage him (whether he is a good man or not) with their spells and incantations, by which they profess to be able to persuade the gods to do their will. In support of all this they cite the evidence of the poets. Some, in support of the easiness of vice, quote Hesiod: "Evil can men attain easily and in companies: the road is smooth and her dwelling near. But the gods have decreed much sweat before a man reaches virtue" and a road that is long and hard and steep. Others quote Homer on turning aside the gods –

The very gods are capable of being swayed. Even they are turned from their course by sacrifice and humble prayers, libations and burnt offerings, when the miscreant and sinner bend the knee to them in supplication.

Or they produce a whole collection of books of ritual instructions written by Musaeus and Orpheus, whom they call descendants of the Moon and the Muses; and they persuade not only individuals but whole communities that, both for living and dead, remission and absolution of sins may be had by sacrifices and childish performances, which they are pleased to call initiations, and which they allege deliver us from all ills in the next world, where terrible things await the uninitiated.

'Now what do you think, Socrates, is likely to be the effect of this sort of talk about virtue and vice, and how far gods and men think them worth while, on the minds of young men who have enough natural intelligence to gather the implications of what they hear for their own lives, the sort of person they ought to be and the sort of ends they ought to pursue? Such a young man may well ask himself, in Pindar's words,

> Shall I by justice mount the higher, or by deceit,

and there dig in for life? For it is clear from what they tell me that if I am just, it will bring me no advantage but only trouble and loss, unless I also have a reputation for justice; whereas if I am unjust, but can contrive to get a reputation for justice, I shall have a marvellous time. Well then, since the sages tell me that "appearance counts for more than reality" and determines our happiness, I had better think entirely of appearances; I must put up a facade that has all the outward appearance of virtue, but I must always have at my back the "cunning, wily fox" of which Archilochus so shrewdly speaks. You may object that it is not easy to be wicked and never be found out; I reply, that nothing worth while is easy, and that all we have been told points to this as the road to happiness. To help us avoid being found out we shall form clubs and secret societies, and we can always learn the art of public speaking, political or forensic; and so we shall get our way by persuasion or force and avoid the penalty for doing our neighbour down. "Yet neither deceit nor force is effective against the gods." But if there are no gods or if they care nothing for human affairs, why should we bother to deceive them? And if there are gods and they do care, our only knowledge of them is derived from tradition and the poets who have written about their genesis, and they tell us that they can be persuaded to change their minds by sacrifices and "humble prayers" and offerings. We must believe both statements or neither; and if we believe them then the thing to do is to sin first and sacrifice afterwards from the proceeds. For if we do right we shall merely avoid the wrath of heaven, but lose the profits of wrong-doing; but if we do wrong we shall get the profits and, provided that we accompany our sins and wickednesses with prayer, be able to persuade the gods to let us go unpunished. "But we shall pay in the next world for the sins we commit in this, either ourselves or our descendants." To which the answer is that ritual and the absolution of heaven are very powerful, as we are told by the most advanced human societies, and by children of the gods who have been poets and prophets with a divine message and have said the same thing. 366

'What argument, then, remains for preferring justice to the worst injustice, when both common men and great men agree that, provided it has a veneer of respectability, injustice will enable us, in this world and the next, to do as we like with gods and men? And how can anyone, when he has heard all we have said, possibly avoid laughing when he hears justice being praised, if he has any force of character at all, any advantages of person, wealth, or rank? For indeed if there is anyone capable of disproving what we have said, with a sure knowledge of the superiority of justice, his feeling for the wicked will be forgiveness rather than anger; he will know that unless a man is born with some heaven-sent aversion to wrong-doing, or unless he acquires the knowledge to refrain from it, he will never do right, of his own free will, but will censure wrong doing only if cowardice or age or weakness make him powerless to practise it himself. That is all too obvious: give him the power, and he will be the first to use it to the full.

'The root of the whole matter is the assertion from which this whole discussion between the three of us started, and which we may put as follows. "All you professed partisans of goodness, from the heroes of old whose tales have survived to our own contemporaries, have never blamed injustice or praised justice except for the reputation and honours and rewards they bring; no one, poet or layman, has ever sufficiently enquired what the effect of each is on the mind of the individual (an effect that may be unobserved by either gods or men), and no one has explained how it is that injustice has the worst possible effect on the character and justice the reverse. Had you adopted that method from the beginning and set about convincing us when we were young, there would be no need for us to guard against our neighbours wronging us; each man would be his own policeman, because he would be afraid that by doing wrong he was doing himself a grave and permanent injury."

'This, more or less, is the view Thrasymachus and others would put forward about right and wrong. It is, in my opinion, a gross misrepresentation of the truth; but (to be candid) I have stated it as forcibly as I can because I want to hear you argue against it. What we want from you is not only a demonstration that justice is better than injustice, but a description of the essential effects, harmful or otherwise, which each produces on its possessor. And follow Glaucon's instructions and leave out the common estimation in which they are held. Indeed, if you do not assign to each the reputation the other bears, we shall consider that you are concerned to praise or blame the appearance of right or wrong and not the reality, and that your advice is the same as Thrasymachus's, that we should do wrong and avoid being found out, and that you agree with him that justice is what is good for someone else, the interest of the stronger party, while injustice is what pays oneself, and is to be pursued at the expense of the weaker party. You have agreed that justice falls into the highest category of goods, of goods, that is, which we choose not only for their consequences but also, and far more, for themselves, such things as sight, hearing, intelligence, health, and all other qualities which bring us a real and not merely an apparent benefit. Let us therefore hear you commending justice for the real benefits it brings its possessor, compared with the damage injustice does him, and let us hear no more of rewards and reputation. I am prepared to listen to other people commending or condemning justice and injustice in this way by an assessment of their consequences; but you have spent your life studying the matter, and from you, if I may say so, we won't put up with it. Prove to us therefore, not only that justice is superior to injustice, but that, irrespective of whether gods or men know it or not, one is good and the other evil because of what it inevitably does to its possessor.'

PART TWO

PRELIMINARIES

*

§I. FIRST PRINCIPLES OF SOCIAL ORGANIZATION

So far the discussion has been about Justice (or right conduct or morality) in the individual. But Socrates now says that it is easier to study things on a large scale than on a small, and proposes accordingly to discuss justice in the State or community first, and then see how the conclusions so reached apply to the individual. This method of argument, from the State or community to the individual, runs throughout the dialogue.

Socrates starts by asking how society is made up. His account, though historical in form, is not seriously so meant; he is concerned to find out what are the underlying principles of any society, even the simplest. He finds them to be two. First, mutual need. Men are not self-sufficient, they need to live together in society: and so any theory, like that of Thrasymachus, which regards society and social regulations as 'unnatural' is false. Second, difference of aptitude. Different people are good at different things, and it is best for all that each should concentrate on developing his particular aptitudes.

Starting from these two principles Socrates deals first with what we should call the economic structure of society, though in a very simple form. He finds five main economic classes or functions: (1) Producers, agricultural or industrial, (2) Merchants, (3) Sailors and Shipowners, etc., (4) Retail traders, (5) Wage-earners or manual labourers. (Slaves are not mentioned, but their existence, it is clear from elsewhere, is assumed. Plato would regard them as appendages to the classes he has defined rather than a separate class on their own.)

Socrates finally sketches the life that the simplest form of society, organized on these lines, would lead. Though he professes to regard this primitive society as the ideal, the description is commonly regarded as an ironic parody of the 'simple life' theories of Plato's day.

MUCH as I had always admired the abilities of Glaucon and Adeimantus, I was delighted by what they had said. 'Glaucon's admirer was right,' I began in reply, 'to open his poem on your achievements at the battle of Megara with the words,

> Sons of Ariston, pair divine
> Sprung from a famous sire.

The words are apt; you must indeed have something divine about you, if you can put the case for injustice so strongly, and yet still believe that right is better than wrong. And I am sure that you genuinely believe it; I can tell that from your character and bearing – though the speeches you have made would have left me in doubt. But the surer I feel the more doubtful I am what to do. I don't see how I'm to help you; I don't think I've got the ability – witness my failure to convince you just now, when I thought I had demonstrated the superiority of justice in my discussion with Thrasymachus. Yet I don't see how I can refuse; for I am afraid it would be very wrong, while I've life and breath in me, to hear justice slandered as I have done and then refuse to come to the rescue. So I must do my best not to let her down.'

Glaucon and the rest of them begged me to proceed and not let the argument drop, but try to find out what justice and injustice are and what is their real usefulness. So I began by saying, quite frankly, 'This is a very obscure subject we're enquiring into, and I think it needs very keen sight. We aren't very clever, and so I think we had better proceed as follows. Let us suppose we are rather short-sighted men and are set to read a distant notice written in small letters; we then discover that the same notice is up elsewhere on a larger scale and in larger lettering: won't it be a godsend to us to be able to read the larger notice first and then compare it with the smaller, to see if they are the same?'

'Certainly,' replied Adeimantus; 'but what bearing has this on our enquiry?'

'I will tell you. Justice can be a characteristic of an individual or of a community, can it not?'

'Yes.'

'And a community is larger than an individual?'

'It is.'

'We may therefore find that the amount of justice in the larger entity is greater, and so easier to recognize. I accordingly propose that we start our enquiry with the community, and then proceed to the individual and see if we can find in the smaller entity anything corresponding to what we have found in the larger.'

'That seems a good idea,' he agreed.

'Well then,' said I, 'if we were to look at a community coming into existence, we might be able to see how justice and injustice originate in it, which would, we may hope, make it easier to find what we are looking for.'

'Much easier.'

'Do you think, then, that we should attempt such a survey? For it's not, I assure you, a thing to undertake without thought.'

'My mind is made up,' returned Adeimantus; 'go on.'

'Society originates, then,' said I, 'so far as I can see, because the individual is not self-sufficient, but has many needs which he can't supply himself. Or can you suggest any other origin for it?'

'No, I can't,' he said.

'And when we have got hold of enough people to satisfy our many varied needs, we have assembled quite a large number of partners and helpers together to live in one place; and we give the resultant settlement the name of a community or state?' [1]

'Yes, I agree.'

'And in the community all mutual exchanges are made with the benefit of the partners in view?'

'Certainly.'

'Come then,' I said, 'let us proceed with our imaginary sketch of the origin of the state. It springs, as we have seen, from our needs.'

'Yes.'

'And our first and greatest need is clearly the provision of food to keep us alive.'

1. πόλις, the Greek 'city-state', translated here as 'state', 'community', or 'society'.

'Clearly.'

'Our second need is shelter, and our third clothing of various kinds.'

'Yes.'

'Well then, how will our state supply these needs? It will need a farmer, a builder, and a weaver, and also, I think, a shoemaker and one or two others to provide for our bodily needs. So that the minimum state would consist of four or five men.'

'Evidently.'

'Then should each of these men contribute the product of his labour to a common stock? For instance, should the farmer provide enough food for all four of them, and devote enough time and labour to food production to provide for all their common needs? Or, alternatively, should he disregard the others, and devote a quarter of his time to producing a quarter the amount of food, and the other three quarters one to building himself a house, one to making clothes, and another to making shoes? Should he, in other words, avoid the trouble of sharing with others and devote himself to providing for his own needs only?'

To which Adeimantus replied, 'The first alternative is perhaps the simpler.'

'Nor need that surprise us,' I rejoined. 'For as you were speaking, it occurred to me that, in the first place, no two of us are born exactly alike. We have different aptitudes, which fit us for different jobs.'

'We have indeed.'

'So do we do better to stick to one trade or to try to practise several?'

'To stick to one,' he said.

'And there is a further point. It is fatal in any job to miss the right moment for action. The workman must be at the call of his job; his job will not wait till he has leisure to spare for it. Quantity and quality are therefore more easily produced when a man specializes appropriately on a single job for which he is naturally fitted.'

'That's certainly true.'

'We shall need more than four citizens, then, Adeimantus, to supply the needs we mentioned. For the farmer, it seems, will not make his own plough or hoe, or any of his other agricultural implements, if they are to be well made. The same is true of the builder and the many tools he needs, and of the weaver and shoemaker. And so smiths and other craftsmen must share the work and swell the numbers of our small community.'

'They must.'

'And it will still not be unduly large, if we add cowherds and shepherds and stockmen of various kinds, to provide oxen for the plough and draught-animals for builder and farmer, as well as hides and wool for shoemaker and weaver.'

'No,' he answered; 'but it will no longer be so very small.'

'And yet it is almost impossible to found a state in a place where it will not need imports.'

'Quite impossible.'

'So we shall need another class in our community to fetch for it what it needs from abroad.'

'Yes.'

371 'And if our agent goes empty-handed, and takes with him nothing of which those from whom he is to get what we want are in need, he will return empty-handed. So we must produce at home not only enough for our own needs but also enough goods of the right kind for the foreigners who supply us. Which means an increase in the number of farmers and other workers in our state.'

'The increase will be necessary.'

'And it will of course include agents to handle the export and import of goods, whom we call merchants. We shall need them too.'

'We shall.'

'And if our trade is to be overseas, we shall need a whole lot of experts on ships and seafaring.'

'Yes, a whole lot of them.'

'Then within our state, how are its citizens to exchange the products of their labour? For such mutual exchange was the reason for its foundation.'

'They will buy and sell.'

'And that will require a market, and a currency as the medium of exchange.'

'Certainly.'

'And if a farmer or any other producer brings his goods to market at a time when no one who wants to exchange with him is there, will he sit about in the market and neglect his own job?'

'Certainly not,' he replied. 'There is a class who see here a chance of doing a service. It consists, in a well-run community, of those who are least fit physically, and unsuitable for other work. For their job ties them to the market place, where they buy goods from those who want to sell and sell goods to those who want to buy.'

'And so this requirement produces a class of retailers in our state. For that is what we call those whose business is to trade with the public at home, as opposed to merchants who travel abroad.'

'Agreed.'

'There is another class whose services we need – those who have no great powers of mind to contribute, but whose physical strength makes them suitable for manual labour. They market their strength and call the return they get for it their wages, and in consequence are usually called wage-earners. And with them our population is complete.'

'Yes, I think it is.'

'Then can we say that our state is now full grown?'

'Perhaps we can.'

'If so, where are we to find justice and injustice in it? With which of the elements we have examined does it originate?'

'I don't know, Socrates,' he replied, 'unless it be in some 372 relationship between them.'

'You may be right,' said I; 'we must press on with our enquiry. So let us first consider how our citizens, so equipped, will live. They will produce corn, wine, clothes, and shoes, and will build themselves houses. In the summer they will for the most part work unclothed and unshod, in the winter they will be clothed and shod suitably. For food they will prepare wheat-meal or barley-meal for baking or kneading. They will serve splendid cakes and loaves on rushes or fresh leaves, and will sit down to feast with their children on couches of myrtle and bryony; and afterwards they will drink wine and pray to the gods with garlands on their heads, and enjoy each other's company. And fear of poverty and war will make them keep the numbers of their families within their means.'

'I say,' interrupted Glaucon, 'that's pretty plain fare for a feast, isn't it?'

'You're quite right,' said I. 'I had forgotten; they will have a few luxuries. Salt, of course, and olive oil and cheese, and different kinds of vegetables from which to make various country dishes. And we must give them some dessert, figs and peas and beans, and myrtle-berries and acorns to roast at the fire as they sip their wine. So they will lead a peaceful and healthy life, and expect to die at a ripe old age, leaving their children to do the same in their turn.'

§2. CIVILIZED SOCIETY

Glaucon protests at the uncivilized nature of the life of this primitive society. Socrates proceeds to add to it the refinements of civilization, and so to multiply the number of trades and occupations and increase the population. The increase in wealth and population will lead to war, which means that we shall need a new class of soldiers to fight for us (the principle of specialization demands that they should be a separate class). These soldiers or 'Guardians' Plato will develop into the ruling class of his state: they retain their military function but their function as governors soon overshadows it.

Plato's profession to regard the civilized society of this chapter (which would have seemed quite normal to the ordinary Athenian) as unhealthy is not merely ironic; the rest of the Republic *contains, in effect, the reforms he proposes in order to reduce it to health: cf. p. 140 below (399e).*

'Really, Socrates,' Glaucon commented, 'you might be catering for a community of pigs!'

'And how would you do it, Glaucon?' I asked.

'Give them the ordinary comforts,' he replied. 'Let them sit on chairs and eat off tables, and have normal civilized food.'

'All right,' I said, 'I understand. We are to study not only the origins of society, but also society when it enjoys the luxuries of civilization. Not a bad idea, perhaps, for in the process we may discover how justice and injustice are bred in a community. For though the society we have described seems to me to be the true norm, just as a man in health is the norm, there's nothing to prevent us, if you wish, studying one whose temperature luxury has raised. Such a society will not be satisfied with the standard of living we have described. It will want chairs and tables and other furniture, and a variety of delicacies, scents, cosmetics, sweets, and mistresses. And we must no longer confine ourselves to the bare necessities of our earlier description, houses, clothing, and shoes, but must add the fine arts of painting and embroidery, and introduce materials like gold and ivory. Do you agree?' 373

'Yes,' he said.

'We shall have to enlarge our state again. Our healthy state is no longer big enough; its size must be enlarged to make room for a multitude of occupations none of which is concerned with necessaries. There will be hunters and fishermen, and there will be artists, sculptors, painters, and musicians; there will be poets and playwrights with their following of reciters, actors, chorus-trainers, and producers; there will be manufacturers of domestic furniture of all sorts, and fashion-experts for the women. And we shall need a lot more servants – tutors, nurses, ladies' maids, barbers, confectioners, and cooks. And we shall need swineherds too: there were none in our former state, as we had no need of them, but now we need pigs, and cattle in quantities too, if we are to eat meat. Agreed?'

'There's no denying it.'

'We shall need doctors too, far more than we did before.'

'With our new luxuries we certainly shall.'

'And the territory which was formerly enough to support us will now be too small. If we are to have enough for pasture and plough, we shall have to cut a slice off our neighbours' territory. And if they too are no longer confining themselves to necessities and have embarked on the pursuit of unlimited material possessions, they will want a slice of ours too.'

'The consequence is inevitable!'

'And that will lead to war, Glaucon, will it not?'

'It will.'

'For the moment,' I said, 'we are not concerned with the effects of war, good or bad; let us merely note that we have found its origin to be the same as that of most evil, individual or social.'[1]

'Yes, I agree.'

574 'But it means a considerable addition to our state, the addition of an army, which will go out and fight for its interests and defend its citizens against all comers.'

'But can't the citizens fight for themselves?'

'Not if the principle, on which we all, yourself included, agreed when we started constructing our state, is sound. And that was, if you remember, that one man could not do more than one job or profession well.'

'Yes, that is true.'

'Well, soldiering is a profession, is it not?'

'Very much so.'

'And is it of any less consequence to us than shoe-making?'

'Certainly not.'

'Well, we forbade our shoemaker to try his hand at farming or weaving or building and told him to stick to his last, in order that our shoemaking should be well done. Similarly with other trades, we assigned each man to the one for which he was naturally suited, and which he was to practise throughout his life to the exclusion of all others, and so become good at his job and never miss the right moment for action. Now it is surely of the greatest importance that the business of war should be efficiently run. For soldiering is not so easy a job that a man can be a soldier at the same time as he is a farmer or shoemaker or follows some other trade; why you can't even become a competent draughts or dice player if you don't practise seriously from childhood, but only do it in your spare

1. i.e. acquisitiveness.

time. Does a man become competent as an infantryman, or in any other branch of military service, the moment he picks up a shield or any of the other tools of the soldier's trade? Merely to pick up the tools of any other trade does not turn a man into a craftsman or games-player: the tool is useful only to the man who knows how to use it and has had enough practice in the use of it.'

'True; otherwise tools would indeed be precious.'

'And so the business of defence, just because it is the most important of all, requires a correspondingly complete freedom from other affairs and a correspondingly high degree of skill and practice.'

'I suppose it does,' he said.

'It will need also natural aptitude.'

'Of course.'

'And so it would seem to be our business, if we can, to choose men with suitable aptitudes for the defence of our state. And let me say,' I added, 'that it's no mean task to undertake. Still, we must not shrink from it, but do it to the best of our ability.'

'We must.'

375

§3. QUALITIES REQUIRED IN THE GUARDIANS

From this point onwards Plato's main preoccupation is with the Guardian class (later to be subdivided into two); the producers, merchants, and others, who carry on the day-to-day economic life of society, are hardly mentioned again. Plato is concerned with government, and his interest therefore is almost entirely confined to the governing class.

The Guardians are now compared to watchdogs, and shown to need physical strength, courage, and a philosophic temperament. Courage requires 'high spirits'. The Greek word which this phrase translates is used by Plato to cover a group of characteristics such as pugnacity, enterprise, ambition, indignation, which he will later regard as one of the three main elements of the mind or personality. In traditional English 'mettle' or 'spirit' (as e.g. in 'a man of mettle', 'a man of spirit') is a fair translation, and the slang term 'guts' and the politer 'vitality' have a somewhat similar meaning; compare also the distinction made in common parlance between qualities of the 'heart' and 'head', and see below, p. 183.

'There is,' said I, 'a certain similarity between the qualities needed in a good watchdog and those needed in our guardians. I mean that each must have keen perceptions and speed in pursuit, and also strength to fight if he catches his quarry.'

'Yes, he will need all these qualities.'

'And also courage, if he is to fight well.'

'Of course.'

'And no horse or dog or any other creature will have courage unless it has mettle and spirit. For have you not noticed what an irrepressible and unbeatable thing high spirits are, making their possessor quite fearless and indomitable in the face of danger?'

'I have indeed.'

'We know therefore what the physical qualities of our guardians must be, and that they must have high spirits as a quality of character.'

'Yes.'

'But if they have these qualities, Glaucon,' I said, 'won't they be aggressive in their behaviour to each other and to the rest of the community?'

'It won't be easy to prevent it.'

'And yet they ought to be gentle towards their fellow-citizens, and dangerous only to their enemies; otherwise they will destroy each other before others can destroy them.'

'True.'

'What are we to do, then?' I said. 'Where are we to find the gentle and generous disposition which will counteract their high spirits? If we deprive them of either quality, they won't make good guardians; yet we seem to be asking the impossible, and if so a good guardian is an impossibility.'

'I am afraid it is.'

I felt myself in a difficulty, but I thought over what we had just been saying, and then exclaimed: 'You know, we really deserve to be in a difficulty. For we have failed to press our analogy far enough.'

'In what way?'

'We have not noticed that there are natures which combine the qualities we thought incompatible.'

'And where are they to be found?'

'In different kinds of animal, but particularly in the watch-dog which we have used as our analogy. For have you not observed that it is characteristic of a well-bred dog to behave with the utmost gentleness to those it is used to and knows, but to be savage to strangers?'

'Yes, I've noticed that.'

'The kind of guardian we were looking for is therefore quite a possibility and not at all unnatural.'

'So it appears.'

'Would you agree then that our prospective guardian needs in addition to his high spirits something of the disposition of a philosopher?'

'I don't understand what you mean,' he said.   376

'It is a remarkable characteristic which you will find in the dog. It is annoyed when it sees a stranger, even though he has done it no harm: but it welcomes anyone it knows, even though it has never had a kindness from him. Haven't you ever thought how remarkable this is?'

'I can't say I ever thought about it before,' he replied. 'But of course it's quite true.'

'And yet it is a trait that shows real discrimination and a truly philosophic nature,' I said, 'for the dog distinguishes the sight of friend and foe simply by knowing one and not know-ing the other. And a creature that distinguishes between the familiar and the unfamiliar on the grounds of knowledge or ignorance must be gifted with a real love of know-ledge.'

'There is no denying it,' he said.

'But is not philosophy the same thing as the love of know-ledge?'

'It is.'

'And so for man too we may venture to lay it down that

gentleness towards his own fellows and neighbours requires a philosophic disposition and a love of learning.'

'We may.'

'Then our perfect guardian must have the following characteristics: a philosophic disposition, high spirits, speed, and strength.'

'I entirely agree.'

PART THREE

EDUCATION: THE FIRST STAGE

In reading what follows it is important to have in mind one or two of the main features of Greek education. It was, normally, a matter for the private individual: and in making it the concern of the state, Plato was doing something that to the Athenian (though not to the Spartan; and Plato was to some extent influenced by Sparta) was an innovation. Education had three principal subdivisions. Reading and writing physical education, and what we may call secondary or literary education. This last consisted mainly in a study of the works of the poets, which were learnt to be recited and, where necessary, sung to the lyre, so that it included a knowledge of music; it corresponded, broadly, to the 'secondary' stage of our own system, and was followed by two years military training which began at eighteen. It must also be remembered that the Greeks had no Bible, and what the Bible has been to us as a source of theology and morals, the poets were to the Greeks. And if Plato seems very preoccupied with the moral and theological aspect of the poets it is because it was from them that the ordinary Greek was expected to acquire his moral and theological notions.

*

§1. SECONDARY OR LITERARY EDUCATION

Since the minds of the young are very impressionable we must, if we are to educate them properly, make sure that the poetry on which they are brought up is suitable for the purpose. Most existing poetry is unsuitable: (a) Theologically, because it misrepresents God. God is perfectly good, and therefore changeless and incapable of deceit, and must never be otherwise represented.

'WE may assume then that our guardians need these qualities. But how are they to be brought up and educated? If we try to answer this question, I wonder whether it will help us at all in our main enquiry into the origin of justice and injustice? We do not want to leave out anything relevant, but we don't want to embark on a long digression.'

To which Adeimantus replied, 'I expect it will help us all right.'

'Then, my dear Adeimantus, we must certainly pursue the question,' I rejoined, 'even though it proves a long business. So let us set about educating our guardians as if we had as much time on our hands as the traditional story-teller.'

'Let us by all means.'

'What kind of education shall we give them then? We shall find it difficult to improve on the time-honoured distinction between the training we give to the body and the training we give to the mind and character.'

'True.'

'And we shall begin with the mind and character, shall we not?'

'Of course.'

'In this type of education you would include stories, would you not?'

'Yes.'

377 'These are of two kinds, true stories and fiction.[1] Our education must use both, and start with fiction.'

'I don't understand you.'

'But you know that we begin by telling children stories. These are, in general, fiction, though they contain some truth. And we tell children stories before we start them on physical training.'

'That is so.'

'That is what I meant by saying that we start to train the mind before the body. And the first step, as you know, is always what matters most, particularly when we are dealing with those who are young and tender. That is the time when they are taking shape and when any impression we choose to make leaves a permanent mark.'

'That is certainly true.'

'Shall we therefore allow our children to listen to any

---

1. The Greek word PSEUDOS and its corresponding verb meant not only 'fiction' – stories, tales – but also 'lies' – fraud and deceit: and this ambiguity should be borne in mind.

stories written by anyone, and to form opinions the opposite of those we think they should have when they grow up?'

'We certainly shall not.'

'Then it seems that our first business is to supervise the production of stories, and choose only those we think suitable, and reject the rest. We shall persuade mothers and nurses to tell our chosen stories to their children and so mould their minds and characters rather than their bodies. The greater part of the stories current to-day we shall have to reject.'

'Which are you thinking of?'

'We can take some of the major legends as typical. For all are cast in the same mould and have the same effect. Do you agree?'

'Yes: but I'm not sure which you refer to as major.'

'The stories in Homer and Hesiod and the poets. For it is the poets who have always made up stories to tell to men.'

'Which stories do you mean and what fault do you find in them?'

'The worst fault possible,' I replied, 'especially if the story is an ugly one.'

'And what is that?'

'Misrepresenting gods and heroes, like a portrait painter who fails to catch a likeness.'

'That is a fault which certainly deserves censure. But give me more details.'

'Well, on the most important of subjects, there is first and foremost the foul story about Ouranos and the things Hesiod says he did, and the revenge Cronos took on him. While the 378 story of what Cronos did, and what he suffered at the hands of his son, is not fit to be repeated as it is to the young and innocent, even if it were true; it would be best to say nothing about it, or if it must be told, tell it to a select few under oath of secrecy, at a rite which required, to restrict it still further, the sacrifice not of a mere pig but of something large and expensive.'

'These certainly are awkward stories.'

'And they shall not be repeated in our state, Adeimantus,' I said. 'Nor shall any young audience be told that anyone who commits horrible crimes, or punishes his father unmercifully, is doing nothing out of the ordinary but merely what the first and greatest of the gods have done before.'

'I entirely agree,' said Adeimantus, 'that these stories are unsuitable.'

'Nor can we permit stories of wars and plots and battles among the gods; they are quite untrue, and if we want our prospective guardians to believe that quarrelsomeness is one of the worst of evils, we must certainly not let them embroider robes with the story of the Battle of the Giants,[1] or tell them the tales about the many and various quarrels between gods and heroes and their friends and relations. On the contrary, if we are to persuade them that no citizen has ever quarrelled with any other, because it is sinful, our old men and women must tell children stories with this end in view from the first, and we must compel our poets to tell them similar stories when they grow up. But we can permit no stories about Hera being tied up by her son, or Hephaestus being flung out of Heaven by his father for trying to help his mother when she was getting a beating, or any of Homer's Battles of the Gods, whether their intention is allegorical or not. Children cannot distinguish between what is allegory and what isn't, and opinions formed at that age are usually difficult to eradicate or change; it is therefore of the utmost importance that the first stories they hear shall aim at producing the right moral effect.'

'Your case is a good one,' he agreed, 'but if someone wanted details, and asked what stories we were thinking of, what should we say?'

To which I replied, 'My dear Adeimantus, you and I are not writing stories but founding a state. And the founders of a state, though they must know the type of story the poet must produce, and reject any that do not conform to that type, need not write them themselves.'

'True: but what are the lines on which our poets must work when they deal with the gods?'[2]

1. Such a robe was woven by Athenian maidens for presentation to Athene.
2. Plato uses gods (plural) or god (singular) indifferently: when he uses god we must not interpret him in terms of monotheism.

'Roughly as follows,' I said. 'God[1] must surely always be represented as he is, whether the poet is writing epic, lyric, or drama.'

'He must.'

'And the truth is that God is good, and he must be so described.'

'True.'

'But nothing good is harmful or can do harm. And what does no harm does no evil. Nor can a thing which does no evil be the cause of any evil.'

'That is true.'

'And what is good is of service and a cause of well-being.'

'Yes.'

'So the good cannot be the cause of everything. It can only account for the presence of good and not for evil.'

'Most certainly,' he agreed.

'Then God, being good, cannot be responsible for everything, as is commonly said, but only for a small part of human life, for the greater part of which he has no responsibility. For we have a far smaller share of good than of evil, and while we can attribute the good to God, we must find something else to account for the evil.'

'I think that's very true,' he said.

'So we cannot allow Homer or any other poet to make this stupid mistake about the gods, or say that

Zeus has two jars standing on the floor of his palace, full of fates, good in one and evil in the other;

and that the man to whom Zeus allots a mixture of both has "varying fortunes sometimes good and sometimes bad", while the man to whom he allots unmixed evil is "chased by the gadfly of despair over the face of the earth".[2] Nor can we allow references to Zeus as "dispenser of good and evil". And we cannot approve if it is said that Athene and Zeus prompted the breach of solemn promises by Pandarus, or that the strife

1. See note 2, page 116.
2. *Iliad*, xxiv, 527. Quotations from Homer are made, with his permission, from the translations by Dr Rieu in the *Penguin* series. In this particular passage the version quoted by Plato differs slightly from the accepted text.

of the goddesses and the judgement of Paris was due to
580 Themis and Zeus. Nor again can we let our children hear from
Aeschylus that

God implants guilt in man, when he wishes to destroy a house
utterly.

No: we must forbid anyone who writes a play about the
sufferings of Niobe (the subject of the play from which these
last lines are quoted), or the woes of the house of Pelops, or
the Trojan war, or any similar topic, to say they are acts of
God; or if he does he must give the sort of reason we are now
demanding, and say that God's acts were good and just, and
that the sufferers were benefited by being punished. What the
poet must not be allowed to say is that those who were
punished were made wretched through God's action. He may
refer to the wicked as wretched because they needed punishment, provided he makes it clear that in punishing them God
did them good. But if our state is to be run on the right lines,
we must take every possible step to prevent anyone, young or
old, either saying or being told, whether in poetry or prose,
that God, being good, can cause harm or evil to any man. To
say so would be sinful, inexpedient, and inconsistent.'

'I should approve of a law for this purpose and you have
my vote for it,' he said.

'Then of our laws laying down the principles which those
who write or speak about the gods must follow, one would
be this: *God is the source of good only*.'

'I am quite content with that,' he said.

'And what about our second law? Do you think God is a
kind of magician who can appear at will in different forms at
different times, sometimes turning into them himself and
appearing in many different shapes, at other times misleading
us into the belief that he has done so? Or is he without deceit
and least likely of all things to change his proper form?'

'I don't, at the moment, know what the answer to that is.'

'Well, if he does change his proper form, must not the
change be due either to himself or to another?'

'It must.'

'And is not the best always least liable to change or alteration by an external cause? For instance, the healthiest and
strongest animals are least liable to change owing to diet
and exercise, or plants owing to sun and wind and the like.'   381

'That is so.'

'And characters which have most courage and sense are
least liable to be upset and changed by external influences.
And similarly any composite object, a piece of furniture or a
house or a garment, is least subject to wear if it is well made
and in good condition.'

'That is true.'

'So in general, whether a thing is natural or artificial or
both, it is least subject to change from outside if its condition
is good.'

'So it seems.'

'But the state of God and the Divine is perfect; and therefore God is least liable of all things to be changed into other
forms.'

'That is so.'

'Then will God change or alter himself of his own will?'

'If he changes at all,' he replied, 'that must be how he does.'

'Will the change be for the better or for the worse?'

'Any change must be for the worse. For God's goodness is
perfect.'

'You are absolutely right,' I said. 'And, that being so, do
you think that any man or god would deliberately make himself worse in any respect? If you agree that this is impossible,
then it must also be impossible for a god to wish to change
himself. Every god is as perfect and as good as possible, and
remains in his own form without variation for ever.'

'The conclusion is unavoidable.'

'So we cannot have any poet saying that the gods "disguise
themselves as strangers from abroad, and wander round our
towns in every kind of shape"[1]; we cannot have stories about
the transformations of Proteus and Thetis, or poets bringing
Hera on the stage disguised as a priestess begging alms for
"the lifegiving children of Inachus river of Argos". We must

1. *Odyssey*, xvii, 485.

stop all stories of this kind, and stop mothers being misled by them and scaring their children by perversions of the myths, and telling tales about a host of fantastic spirits that prowl about at night; they are merely blaspheming the gods and making cowards of their children.'

'None of these things should be allowed.'

'Then if the gods are themselves unchangeable, will they use their power to deceive us into thinking that they appear in all sorts of disguises?'

'They might, I suppose.'

382 'Come,' said I, 'can God want to disguise himself and deceive us, either in word or action?'

'I don't know,' he replied.

'But,' I asked, 'don't you know that gods and men all detest true falsehood, if I may so describe it?'

'I don't understand.'

'I mean that in things which touch most nearly the most important part of him no man really wants to be deceived, but is terrified of it.'

'I still don't understand.'

'Because you think I'm talking about something mysterious,' I answered. 'But all I mean is that no one wants to be deceived in his own mind about things and not to know the truth; that's where men are least ready to put up with falsehood and detest it most.'

'Yes, I agree with that.'

'But surely when a man is deceived in his own mind about something, we can fairly call his ignorance of the truth "true falsehood". For a false statement is merely some kind of representation of a state of mind, an expression consequent on it, and not the original unadulterated falsehood. Don't you agree?'

'Yes.'

'So real falsehood is detested by gods and men.'

'I agree.'

'But what about spoken falsehood? Is it not sometimes and on some occasions useful, and so not utterly detestable? We can use it, for example, as a kind of preventive medicine against our enemies, or when one of our own friends tries to do something wrong from madness or folly. And we can make use of it in the myths we are engaged in discussing; we don't know the truth about the past but we can invent a fiction as like it as may be.'

'That's perfectly true.'

'In which of these ways is falsehood of use to God? Does he need to make up fictions because he does not know the past?'

'That is absurd.'

'So God is not the author of poetic fictions.'

'No.'

'Does he tell lies because he is afraid of his enemies, then?'

'Certainly not.'

'Or because of the folly or madness of any of his friends?'

'God loves neither the foolish or the mad,' he replied.

'God has, then, no reason to tell lies; and we conclude that there is no falsehood at all in the realm of the spiritual and divine?'

'Most certainly.'

'God is therefore without deceit or falsehood in action or word, he does not change himself, nor deceive others, awake or dreaming, with visions or signs or words.'

'I agree entirely with what you say.'

'Do you agree then that the second principle to be followed in all that is said or written about the gods is that they shall not be represented as using magic disguises or fraud to deceive us in any way?'

'I agree.'

'And so among the many things we admire in Homer we shall not include the dream Zeus sent to Agamemnon. Nor shall we admire Aeschylus when he makes Thetis say that Apollo sang at her wedding in praise of her child

> Promising him long life, from sickness free,
> And every blessing: his triumphant praise
> Rejoiced my heart. Those lips, I thought, divine,
> Flowing with prophecy, must God's promise speak.
> Yet he the speaker, he our wedding guest,
> Phoebus Apollo, prophet, slew my son.

If a poet says this sort of thing about the gods we shall be angry and refuse to let him produce his play; nor shall we allow it to be used to educate our children – that is if our guardians are to grow up godfearing and holy, so far as that is humanly possible.'

'I agree entirely with your principles,' he said, 'and we can treat them as law.'

(b) *Morally, most existing poetry is unsuitable because in its repre-sentations of gods and heroes it describes, and so encourages, various forms of moral weaknesses.*

'As far as religion is concerned, then, we have now out-lined the sort of stories men ought and ought not to be brought up on, if they are to honour the gods and their parents, and know how important it is to love one another.'

'And I think we are quite right,' he said.

'But what if they are to be brave? Must we not add some-thing that will give them the least possible fear of death? Will anyone who fears death ever be brave?'

'Certainly not.'

'And will anyone who believes in terrors in the after-life be without fear of death, and prefer death in battle to defeat and slavery?'

'No.'

'It looks, then, as if we shall have to control those who write on this topic too. We must ask the poets to stop giving their present gloomy account of the after-life, which is both untrue and unsuitable to produce a fighting spirit, and make them speak more favourably of it.'

'I agree,' he said.

'We must begin, then,' I said, 'by cutting out all passages such as the following –

I would rather be a serf in the house of some landless man, with little enough for himself to live on, than king of all dead men that have done with life; [1]

1. *Odyssey*, XI, 489.

or

and expose to mortal and immortal eyes the hateful chambers of decay that fill the gods themselves with horror; [1]

or again

Ah then, it is true that something of us does survive even in the Halls of Hades, but with no intellect at all, only the ghost and semblance of a man; [2]

and

he alone has a mind to reason with: the rest are mere shadows flitting to and fro; [3]

and

his disembodied soul took wing for the House of Hades, bewailing its lot and the youth and manhood that it left; [4]

and

the spirit vanished like a wisp of smoke and went gibbering under ground; [5]

and finally

gibbering like bats that squeak and flutter in the depths of some mysterious cave when one of them has fallen from the rocky roof, losing his hold on his clustered friends, with shrill discord the company set out. [6]

We must ask Homer and the other poets to excuse us if we delete all passages of this kind. It is not that they are bad poetry or are not popular; indeed the better they are as poetry the more unsuitable they are for the ears of children or grownups, if they are to prefer death to slavery as free men should.'

'I absolutely agree.'

'We must get rid, too, of all those horrifying and frightening names in the underworld – the Rivers of Wailing and Gloom, and the ghosts and corpses, and all other things of this kind

1. *Iliad*, xx, 64. 2. *Iliad*, xxiii, 103. 3. *Odyssey*, x, 495.
4. *Iliad*, xvi, 856. 5. *Iliad*, xxiii, 100. 6. *Odyssey*, xxiv, 6.

whose very names are enough to scare everyone who hears them. They may be useful for other purposes; but we are afraid they will scare our guardians and make them jumpy and nervous.'

'And our anxiety is justified.'

'We must get rid of them, then, and require our poets to give us an account on the opposite lines.'

'Clearly.'

'We must also, I suppose, cut out pitiful laments by famous men.'

'We must,' he replied, 'if we are to be consistent.'

'Let us see if we shall be justified. We agree, surely, that one good man does not think death holds any terror for another who is a friend of his, and so would hardly mourn for him as if he had suffered something terrible.'

'That is true.'

'And what is more, we reckon that the good man's life is the most complete in itself and least dependent on others. So the loss of son or brother, or of property or what not, will hold the least terrors for the good man, who, when some such catastrophe overtakes him, will mourn it less and bear it more calmly than others.'

'He will.'

388 'So we should be quite right to cut out from our poetry lamentations by famous men. We can give them to the less reputable women characters or to the bad men, whom those we are bringing up as guardians of our state will be ashamed to imitate.'

'You are quite right.'

'We shall therefore again request Homer and the poets not to describe Achilles, the son of a goddess as

sometimes lying on his side, sometimes on his back, and then again on his face,

and then standing up and

wandering aimlessly along the salt sea beach,[1]

1. *Iliad*, XXIV, 10.

or

picking up the dark dust in both hands and pouring it on his head,[1]

with all the weeping and wailing the poet describes. Nor can we allow a Priam, who was closely related to the gods, to

grovel in the dung and implore them all, calling on each man by his name.[2]

Still more emphatically shall we forbid the poets to represent the gods lamenting with words like

Ah misery me, the unhappy mother of the best of men.[3]

And least of all can we have them presuming to misrepresent the greatest of all gods by making him say

I have a warm place in my heart for this man who is being chased before my eyes round the walls of Troy.[4]

and

Fate is unkind to me – Sarpedon whom I dearly love is destined to be killed by Patroclus son of Menoetius.[5]

For, my dear Adeimantus, if our young men take passages like these seriously and don't laugh at their absurdity, they are hardly likely to think this sort of thing unworthy of them as men, or to try to control the temptation to similar words and actions. They will feel no shame and show no endurance, but break into complaints and laments at the slightest provocation.'

'That is quite true.'

'But that is not the behaviour our argument has just required; and we must trust it till someone produces a better one.'

'Yes, we must.'

'And surely we don't want our guardians to be too fond of laughter either. A disposition to violent laughter commonly 389 means instability; and we must not therefore allow descrip-

1. *Iliad.*, XVIII, 23.　　2. *Iliad.*, XXII, 414.　　3. *Iliad.*, XVIII, 54.
4. *Iliad.*, XXII, 168.　　　5. *Iliad*, XVI, 433.

tions of reputable characters being overcome by laughter. And similar descriptions of gods are far less allowable.'

'Far less, I agree.'

'So we can't have Homer saying of the gods

and a fit of helpless laughter seized the happy gods as they watched Hephaestus bustling up and down the hall.[1]

Your argument won't allow that.'

'Call it my argument if you like,' he replied; 'in any event we can't allow it.'

'And surely we must value truthfulness highly. For if we were right when we said just now that falsehood is no use to the gods and only useful to men as a kind of medicine, it's clearly a medicine that should be entrusted to doctors and not to laymen.'

'Yes.'

'It will be for the rulers of our city, then, if anyone, to deceive citizen or enemy for the good of the State; no one else must do so. And if any citizen lies to our rulers, we shall regard it as a still graver offence than it is for a patient to lie to his doctor, or for an athlete to lie to his trainer about his physical condition, or a sailor to his captain on any matter concerning the state of the ship or crew. And so if you find anyone else in our state telling lies, "whether he be craftsman, prophet, physician or shipwright",[2] you will punish him for introducing a practice likely to capsize and wreck the ship of state.'

'We must punish him if we are to be as good as our word.'

'Then again we shall want our young men to be self-controlled; and for the mass of men does not self-control largely consist in obedience to their rulers, and controlling their own desire for the pleasures of eating, drinking, and sex?'

'I agree.'

'We shall approve therefore the sort of thing that Homer makes Diomede say,

Be quiet, man, and take your cue from me;[3]

1. *Iliad*, I, 599.   2. *Odyssey*, XVII, 383.   3. *Iliad*, IV, 412.

and verses like those which follow it,

The Achaeans moved forward, breathing valour, in silent obedience to their officers.[1]'

'We shall indeed.'
'But what about

You drunken sot, with the eyes of a dog and the courage of a doe,[2]

and the lines that follow? Can we approve of them and other 390 impertinences of the rank and file against their commanders, in prose or verse?'

'We cannot.'

'For they are hardly likely to encourage the young to self-control, though we need not be surprised if they give pleasure in other ways. What do you think?'

'I agree.'

'Then is it likely to encourage self-restraint in the young, if the poets represent the wisest of men saying that he thinks the best moment of all is when

the tables are laden with bread and meat, and a steward carries round the wine he has drawn from the bowl and fills their cups[3]?

And what about lines like

death by starvation is the most miserable end that one can meet[4]?

And then there is the story of how Zeus stayed awake, when all the other gods and men were asleep, with some plan in mind, but forgot it easily enough when his desire was roused; he was indeed so struck by Hera's appearance that he wanted to make love to her on the spot, without going indoors, saying that he had never wanted her so much since the days when they first used to make love "without their parents' knowledge".[5] And there's the story of Hephaestus trapping Ares and Aphrodite in similar proceedings.'

'All these are most unsuitable,' he commented emphatically.

'But when a poet tells or a dramatist presents tales of heroic

1. *Iliad*, III, 8; and IV, 431.   2. *Iliad*, I, 225.
3. *Odyssey*, IX, 8.   4. *Odyssey*, XII, 342.   5. *Iliad*, XIV, 294 ff.

endurance against odds, then we must give him an audience. For instance, when Homer makes Odysseus strike himself on the chest, and "call his heart to order", saying,

Patience my heart! You have put up with fouler than this.[1]'

'We must certainly listen to him then.'

'But we must not let him make his characters mercenary or grasping. We cannot let a poet say,

The gods can be won with gifts, and so can the king's majesty.[2]

We cannot agree that Achilles' tutor Phoenix advised him properly when he told him not to stop being angry and help the Achaeans unless they brought him presents. Nor can we consent to regard Achilles as so grasping that he took Agamemnon's presents and refused to give up Hector's body unless he was paid a ransom.'[3]

'It would be quite wrong,' he said, 'to approve of things of this sort.'

'I say it with hesitation, because of Homer's authority,' I said, 'but it is really wicked to say these things about Achilles or believe them when we hear them said. There are other examples. Achilles says to Apollo,

You have made a fool of me, Archer-king, and are the most mischievous of gods: how much I should like to pay you out if I had the power.[4]

He refuses to trust the River Scamander, who is a god, and is ready to fight him, and he parts with the lock of his hair that he had dedicated to the River Spercheius and gives it to "the dead Lord Patroclus".[5] We can believe none of this, and we shall regard as untrue also the whole story of the dragging of the body of Hector round the tomb of Patroclus and the slaughter of prisoners at his pyre.[6] We cannot, in fact, have our citizens believe that Achilles, whose mother was a goddess, and whose father, Peleus, was a man of the utmost self-

---

1. *Odyssey*, XX, 17.   2. Proverbial.   3. *Iliad*, IX, 515; XIX, 278.
4. *Iliad*, XXII, 15, 20.   5. *Iliad*, XXI, 130; XXIII, 140.
6. *Iliad*, XXIV, 14; XXIII, 175.

control and a grandson of Zeus, and who had in Chiron the wisest of schoolmasters, was so lacking in discipline that he combined in himself the two contrary and pestilential faults of grasping meanness about money and excessive arrogance to gods and men.'

'You are right,' he said.

'We must therefore neither believe nor allow the story of the dreadful ravages of Theseus, son of Poseidon, and Peirithous, son of Zeus, or any of the other lies now told about the terrible and wicked things done by other sons of gods and by heroes. We must compel our poets to say either that they never did these things or that they are not the sons of gods; we cannot allow them to assert both. And they must not try to persuade our young men that the gods are the source of evil, and that heroes are no better than ordinary mortals; that, as we have said, is a wicked lie, for we proved that no evil can originate with the gods.'

'Of course.'

'Moreover such lies are positively harmful. For those who hear them will be lenient towards their own shortcomings if they believe that this sort of thing is and was always done by the relations of the gods,

> kindred of Zeus, to whom belongs
> the ancestral altar high in heaven
> on Ida's mount,

and in whose veins

> still runs the blood of Gods.[1]

We must put a stop to stories of this kind before they breed vicious habits in our young men.'   392

'We certainly must.'

So far the argument has been confined to the poets' treatment of gods and heroes: similar rules cannot be laid down for the treatment of men until justice has been defined.

1. Aeschylus *Niobe.*

'We have now dealt with the kind of things that should and should not be said about gods and demi-gods, heroes and the life after death. If we ask what kind of literature still remains, the answer is, presumably, that which deals with human beings.'

'Clearly.'

'But we cannot deal with that topic at present.'

'Why not?'

'Because I am afraid that we shall find that poets and story-tellers have expressed the most erroneous opinions about it. They have said that unjust men are often happy, and just men wretched, that wrong-doing pays if you can avoid being found out, and that justice is what suits someone else but is to your own disadvantage. We must forbid them to say this sort of thing, and require their poems and stories to have quite the opposite moral. Do you agree?'

'I'm quite sure you're right,' he replied.

'But if you agree with me there, can I not already claim your agreement about the subject we are discussing?'

'Yes, that is a fair claim.'

'We must not agree, therefore, about the kind of thing that ought to be said about human life, until we have defined justice, and the advantages it brings to its possessor irrespective of appearances.'

'Quite true.'

(c) Formal requirements

Plato turns from content to form. He classes poetry according to the degree to which it employs what we should call 'direct speech' as opposed to indirect speech and narrative. Direct speech involves what he calls 'representation'; that is, it requires the poet or narrator to put himself in the position of the character speaking, think his thoughts and feel his feelings. Plato objects to this on the grounds that he does not want his Guardians to deviate from their own character by representing other characters, especially bad characters. If the discussion seems at times, to us, academic, we should remember that the Greek schoolboy, when reciting Homer, was 'expected to throw himself into the story and deliver the speeches with the tones and gestures of an actor', and that it is to such 'imaginative identification',[1] *and to any use of the drama in education that Plato, rightly or wrongly, objects.*

'So much then for the subject-matter of literature. We must next deal with its presentation, and so cover both content and form.'

To this Adeimantus replied that he did not understand what I meant. 'Then I must explain,' I said; 'perhaps you will see if I put it this way. Any story or poem deals with things past, present, or future, does it not?'

'It must.'

'And for the purpose it employs either simple narrative or representation, or a mixture of both.'

'I'm still not quite clear what you mean.'

'I'm afraid you are laughing at my obscurity,' I said. 'So let me try to explain my meaning by confining myself to a particular example, like an incompetent lecturer. You know the beginning of the *Iliad*, where the poet says that Chryses begs Agamemnon to release his daughter; and when Agamemnon gets angry and refuses, Chryses calls down the wrath of the 393 gods on the Greeks?'

'Yes.'

'Well, up to the words

He appealed to the whole Achaean army, and most of all to its two commanders, the sons of Atreus,[2]

the poet is speaking in his own person, and does not attempt to persuade us that the speaker is anyone but himself. But afterwards he speaks in the person of Chryses, and does his best to make us think that it is not Homer but an aged priest who is talking. This is the way in which he constructs his narrative right through the *Iliad* and *Odyssey*.'

'That is true enough,' he said.

'So his narrative includes both speeches and passages between speeches, does it not?'

'It does.'

'And when he speaks in the person of someone else, may

1. Cornford.   2. *Iliad*, 1, 15.

we not say that he is imitating as nearly as he can the manner of speech of the character concerned?'

'And to imitate another person in speech or manner is to "*represent*" the person one is imitating?'

'It is.'

'This then is the way in which Homer and the other poets use representation in the course of their narrative.'

'Yes, I understand.'

'If, of course, the poet never pretended to be anyone but himself, his poetic narrative would be wholly devoid of representation. But to prevent any possibility of misunderstanding, I will explain how this could be done. Suppose that Homer, after telling how Chryses came with his daughter's ransom to beg her back from the Achaeans, or rather their kings, had gone on not as if it were Chryses speaking but Homer, there would have been no representation but only narrative. The passage would have run as follows (I'm not a poet, so I shall give it in prose) – The priest came and prayed that the gods would allow the Achaeans to capture Troy and return in safety, and begged the Achaeans to show their respect for the gods by releasing his daughter in exchange for the ransom. The others respected his request and agreed, but Agamemnon was angry and told him to go away now and never return; otherwise his sceptre and priestly garlands might afford him no protection. And he said that he would not release his daughter before she grew old with him in Argos, and that if he wanted to get home safely he had better go, and not annoy him any more. The old man was afraid when he heard what Agamemnon said, and departed without a word, but when he had left the camp he prayed earnestly to Apollo, calling on him by all his titles and reminding him of all the services he had rendered him in building temples and paying sacrifices; and he begged him in his prayer that, in return, he would avenge his tears on the Achaeans with his arrows. That,' I concluded, 'is how the passage would run in simple narrative without representation.'

'I see,' he replied.

'And so you will see,' I went on, 'that the opposite of this is when a poet omits the sections between the speeches and relies entirely on dialogiue.'

'Yes, I understand,' he answered; 'that is what happens in tragedy, for example.'

'Exactly,' I said. 'And I think I have now made clear what I failed to explain before, that poetry and fiction fall into three classes. First, that which employs representation only, tragedy and comedy, as you say. Secondly, that in which the poet speaks in his own person; the best example is lyric poetry. Thirdly, that which employs both methods, epic and various other kinds of poetry. Is that clear?'

'Yes: I understand now what you were trying to say,' he said.

'And you will remember that just before that I said that we had settled the question of subject-matter and must now deal with that of form.'

'Yes, I remember.'

'What I meant, then,' I said, 'was that we must decide whether we should allow our poets to use representation in their narrative, and if so to what extent and for what purpose, or whether we should forbid it entirely.'

'I suspect,' he replied, 'that you are wondering whether we should allow tragedy and comedy in our state or not.'

'Maybe,' I replied, 'or maybe the question is more far-reaching. I don't know yet; we must follow the argument and see where it leads us.'

'Fair enough,' he said.

'Do you think, then, Adeimantus, that we want our guardians to be capable of playing many characters, or not? Does it not follow, from the principles we adopted earlier, that one man does one job well, and that if he tries to take on a number of jobs, the division of effort will mean that he will fail to make his mark at any of them?'

'The conclusion is unavoidable.'

'And it will also apply to representation; a man cannot play many characters as well as he can one.'

'He cannot.'

'He will therefore be unable to do anything worth while at 395 all well if he is to be a versatile character actor. For the same writers are incapable of equally good work even in two such closely allied forms of representation as comedy and tragedy. You did say they were forms of representation, did you not?'

'Yes; and it's true that a man can't write both.'

'Nor can the same people be reciters and actors, or actors in tragedy and comedy – all these being forms of representation.'

'True.'

'And we can subdivide human nature still further, and show that it is impossible to play many roles well, whether in real life or in representations of it on the stage.'

'That's very true.'

'But we argued originally that our guardians were to be freed from all forms of manual work; their life's work was to be the provision of perfect freedom for our state, a task to which they were to devote all their energies. That, therefore, is the only role they must play in life or literature; and with this end in view the only characters on which they must model themselves from their earliest years must be men of courage, self-control, independence, and religious principle. They must no more act a mean part than do a mean action or any other kind of wrong. For we soon reap the fruits of literature in life, and prolonged indulgence in any form of literature leaves its mark on the moral nature of a man, affecting not only the mind but physical poise and intonation.'[1]

'That is very true,' he replied.

'Since then we care for the moral welfare of our guardians,' I said, 'we will not allow them to take the parts of women, young or old (for they are men), nor to represent them abusing their husbands or presumptuously quarrelling with heaven, when they imagine themselves happy, or crying and

1. Plato is thinking of the dramatic recitation – 'representation' – which was, as we have seen, an essential part of Greek education, and it is with this that the Greek of this passage is in its literal sense concerned. I have diverged a little more than usual from the literal sense in order to bring out the meaning of the passage in modern terms. For it must be remembered that Plato thought these effects were also produced by merely *watching* drama; cf. p. 425f.

complaining in misfortune. Far less can we permit representation of women in sickness or love or child-birth.'

'We must forbid this sort of thing entirely.'

'And the same is true of slaves – male or female – when they are behaving like slaves.'

'Agreed.'

'And of bad and cowardly characters whose behaviour is just the opposite of what we demand. They indulge in comic 396 abuse and back-chat, drunk or sober, and say and do things that are an offence against themselves and their neighbours. Nor do I suppose we shall tolerate representations of the actions or words of madmen. We must recognize that there are men and women who are mad and bad, but we cannot have them represented in poetry or drama.'

'You are quite right,' he said.

'Then can we tolerate representations of smiths or craftsmen at work, or men rowing triremes or in command of them?'

'No: because none of these are occupations to which our guardians should pay any attention.'

'And what about horses neighing and bulls bellowing, and rivers splashing and the sea roaring, and thunders rolling, and so on?'

'We have already forbidden madness and the representation of madness,' he replied.

'What you mean, I suppose, is that there is one style of narrative which the good man will employ when he has anything to say, and a different style in which the man of opposite character and upbringing will always choose to express him self.'

'Describe them,' he said.

'I think,' I replied, 'that the decent man, when he comes in the course of a narrative to a speech or action by a good man, will be willing to impersonate him and feel no shame at so doing. This will be especially true if he is representing the good man behaving with steadiness and determination, and only failing in a few respects and to a limited degree, owing to illness or love or drink or some other misfortune. But if he comes across an unworthy character, he will be ashamed to imitate it seriously, except perhaps for its short periods of good behaviour, because it falls below his standards. He has no practice in such representation, and will not consent to model himself on characters which his judgement despises as lower than his own, except perhaps for the purpose of amusement.'

'Very likely.'

'He will, in fact, make use of the form of narrative which we mentioned when we were talking of Homer's epics a few minutes ago, and will combine both representation and narrative, but the proportion of representation will be small. Or am I wrong?'

'No, that's just the kind of way in which he will express himself.'

397 'And other types of man will be all the readier to vary their style the worse they are, and will think nothing beneath them. They will seriously try to represent in public all the things we were talking about. We shall have the noises of thunder and wind and hail, and of axles and wheels, the notes of trumpets, pipes, whistles, and every possible instrument, the barking of dogs, the baaing of sheep, and twittering of birds. All these will be represented with voice and gesture, and narrative will play but a small part.'

'That follows too.'

'These then are the two styles of expression to which I referred,' I said.

'Yes, I see,' he replied.

'And of these two styles, one is pretty uniform, needing merely music of appropriate mode and rhythm to accompany it. In fact if one handles it rightly one and the same mode can be employed throughout, because of the uniformity of the style, and the same is true of rhythm.'

'That is certainly true,' he said.

'The other style, on the other hand, will have the opposite requirements. It will need every kind of mode, and every kind of rhythm, if it is to find suitable expression. For its variety is unlimited.'

'That is true too.'

'But must not all poets and writers go in for one or other of these two styles or some combination of them?'

'They must.'

'Then what are we to do?' I asked. 'Are we to admit both styles and their combination into our city, or pick on one of them?'

'My own vote,' he replied, 'would go to the style which represents the good man.'

'And yet, Adeimantus,' I reminded him, 'the combination of the two styles is very pleasant, and the opposite style to the one you have chosen gives most pleasure of all to children and nurses and the general public.'

'Yes, if pleasure's what they're after.'

'But perhaps you will say that it is unsuitable for our state, because there one man does one job and does not play a multiplicity of roles.'

'It certainly is unsuitable.'

'And so ours is the only state in which we shall find (for example) the shoemaker sticking to his shoemaking and not turning pilot as well, the farmer sticking to his farming and not taking on court work into the bargain, and the soldier sticking to his soldiering and not running a business on the side?'

'Yes.'

'So if we are visited in our state by someone who has the 398 skill to transform himself into all sorts of characters and represent all sorts of things, and he wants to show off himself and his poems to us, we shall treat him with all the reverence due to a priest and giver of rare pleasure, but shall tell him that he and his kind have no place in our city, being forbidden by our code, and send him elsewhere, after anointing him with myrrh and crowning him. For ourselves, we shall for our own good employ story tellers and poets who are severe rather than amusing, who follow the style of the good man and in all their works abide by the principles we laid down for them when we started out on this attempt to educate our military class.' [1]

1. The Guardians – their military function is still to the fore. The paragraph makes it clear that, though he is dealing primarily with education, Plato would have excluded from his state all poetry of the type to which he objects.

'That undoubtedly is what we should do,' he said, 'if we had the choice.'

'And I think,' said I, 'that that probably completes our survey of the literature to be employed in our education. Because we have dealt both with subject-matter and with form.'

'I agree,' he replied.

(d) Musical requirements

Music is dealt with on a similar basis. Greek music was employed largely as an accompaniment to song, and what this section is concerned to say is that, having laid down rules governing the content and form of poetry, we must now require their musical accompaniment to be appropriate. As appears from the text, the Greeks were more inclined than we are to associate certain types of music with certain types of feeling and sentiment. But the technicalities of Greek music are still not fully understood.

'Then we are left with the varieties of music and song to discuss,' I went on; 'and I suppose that it's pretty obvious to everyone what requirements we shall have to make about them, if we are to be consistent.'

Glaucon laughed. 'I'm afraid I'm not included in your "everyone",' he said; 'for at the moment I can't really suggest what we ought to say – though I'm not without my suspicions.'

'Well at any rate you can agree easily enough that song consists of three elements, words, mode, and rhythm.'

'Yes, I agree to that.'

'As far as the words are concerned, then, the same rules will apply as those we laid down for words not set to music, both for their content and form.'

'True.'

'And surely the mode and rhythm should suit the words.'

'Certainly.'

'But we agreed to ban dirges and laments, did we not?'

'We did.'

'Tell me then – you are a musician – which are the modes suitable for dirges?'

'The Mixed Lydian and the Extreme Lydian.'

'Then we can reject them,' I said: 'even women, if they are respectable, have no use for them, let alone men.'

'Quite right.'

'But drunkenness, softness, or idleness are also qualities most unsuitable in a Guardian?'

'Of course.'

'What, then, are the relaxing modes and the ones we use for drinking songs?'

'The Ionian and certain Lydian modes, commonly described as "languid".'

'Will they then,' I asked, 'be of any use for training 399 soldiers?'

'None at all,' he replied. 'You seem to be left with the Dorian and Phrygian.'

'I'm no expert on modes,' said I; 'but I want one that will represent appropriately the voice and accent of a brave man on military service or any dangerous undertaking, who faces injury, defeat, or death, or any other misfortune with the same steadfast endurance. And I want another mode to represent him in the ordinary voluntary occupations of peace-time: for instance, persuading someone to grant a request, praying to God or instructing or admonishing his neighbour, or again submitting himself to the requests or instruction or persuasion of others, and in all showing no conceit, but moderation and common sense and willingness to accept the outcome. Give me these two modes, one stern, one pleasant, to express courage and moderation in good fortune or in bad.'

'The two modes you are asking for,' he rejoined, 'are the two I have just mentioned.'

'And so,' I went on, 'we shan't need for our music and song instruments of many strings with a wide harmonic range. We shan't keep craftsmen to make instruments of this kind, such as harps and harpsichords.'

'I suppose not.'

'Then shall we allow flutes and flute-makers in our city? Has not the flute the widest range of all, being in fact the original which other instruments of wide range imitate?'

'That's plain enough,' he said.

'We are left, then, with the lyre and the cithara for use in our city. Though the shepherds in the country might have some sort of pipe.'

'That seems to be the conclusion of our argument.'

'We aren't really doing anything revolutionary, you know,' I said, 'in preferring Apollo and his instruments to Marsyas and his.'

'No, I quite agree,' he replied.

'And what is more, ' I pointed out, 'we are insensibly getting rid of the luxury from which we said our state suffered.'

'Quite right too,' he replied.

'Well, let us continue the process,' said I. 'After mode we should presumably deal next with rhythm. We shan't want very elaborate or varied combinations, but merely need to find which rhythms suit a life of courage and discipline. We shall then adapt the metre and tune to the appropriate words, and not the words to the metre and tune. But it's your business to say what these rhythms are, as you did with the modes.'

'I'm afraid I really can't do that,' he replied. 'There are three basic types of rhythm, from which the various combinations are built up, just as there are four elements which go to build up the modes. So much I know and can tell you. But which are suited to represent which kind of life, I cannot say.'

'Well, we'll consult Damon [1] about it,' I said, 'and ask him what combinations are suitable to express meanness, insolence, madness, and other evil characteristics, and which rhythms we must keep to express their opposites. I seem to remember hearing him talking about "march rhythms" and "composite rhythms", "dactyls", and "heroics", arranging them in various ways and marking the stresses; he talked also, I think, about "iambics and trochees", and assigned them longs and shorts. And I believe that he praised or blamed the composition of the foot as well as the rhythm as a whole, or perhaps it was the combination of the two: I really can't remember. In any

1. A well-known fifth-century musician.

case, as I said, we can refer to Damon. For it would need a lot of argument to settle the details, don't you think?'

'It would indeed.'

Summary

Plato proceeds to sum up the general purpose of this stage of education – to train both character and moral and aesthetic judgement, these last two being closely allied. The influence of environment on growing minds is again emphasized: it is because of this that so rigid a censorship of the music and poetry to be used in education is required. If we miss a reference to any kind of scientific training, it should be remembered that mathematical and (so far as it then existed) scientific training is reserved for a later stage of the Guardians' education: see p. 308 f.

'But there is one thing we can decide at once, that beauty and ugliness result from good rhythm and bad.'

'That is undeniable.'

'And good rhythm is the consequence of music that suits good poetry, bad rhythm of the opposite; and the same is true of mode and tune, if, as we said a moment ago, both the rhythm and mode should be suited to the words and not vice versa.'

'The words must of course determine the music,' he said.

'But what about the style and content of the poetry themselves?' I asked. 'Don't they depend on character, just as the other things depend on them?'

'They must.'

'Good literature, therefore, and good music and beauty of form generally all depend on goodness of character; I don't mean that lack of awareness of the world which we politely call "goodness", but a character of real judgement and principle.'

'I quite agree.'

'And are not these things which our young men must try to acquire, if they are to perform their function in life properly?'

'They must.'

401   'And they are to be seen in painting and similar arts, in weaving and embroidery, in architecture and furniture, and in living things, animals and plants. For in all of these we find beauty and ugliness. And ugliness of form and disharmony are akin to bad art and bad character, and their opposites are akin to and represent good character and discipline.'

'That is perfectly true.'

'It is not only to the poets therefore that we must issue orders requiring them to represent good character in their poems or not to write at all; we must issue similar orders to all artists and prevent them portraying bad character, ill-discipline, meanness, or ugliness in painting, sculpture, architecture, or any work of art, and if they are unable to comply they must be forbidden to practise their art. We shall thus prevent our guardians being brought up among representations of what is evil, and so day by day and little by little, by feeding as it were in an unhealthy pasture, insensibly doing themselves grave psychological damage. Our artists and craftsmen must be capable of perceiving the real nature of what is beautiful, and then our young men, living as it were in a good climate, will benefit because all the works of art they see and hear influence them for good, like the breezes from some healthy country, insensibly moulding them into sympathy and conformity with what is rational and right.'

'That would indeed be the best way to bring them up.'

'And that, my dear Glaucon,' I said, 'is why this stage of education is crucial. For rhythm and harmony penetrate deeply into the mind and have a most powerful effect on it, and if education is good, bring balance and fairness, if it is bad, the reverse. And moreover the proper training we propose to give will make a man quick to perceive the shortcomings of works of art or nature, whose ugliness he will rightly dislike; anything beautiful he will welcome, and will

402 accept and assimilate it for his own good, anything ugly he will rightly condemn and dislike, even when he is still young and cannot understand the reason for so doing, while when reason comes he will recognize and welcome her as a familiar friend because of his education.'

'In my view,' he said, 'that is the purpose of this stage of education.'

'Well then,' I went on, 'when we were learning to read we were not satisfied until we could recognize the letters of the alphabet wherever they occurred; we did not think them beneath our notice in large words or small, but tried to recognize them everywhere on the grounds that we should not have learned to read till we could.'

'That is true.'

'And we can't recognize reflections of the letters in water or in a mirror till we know the letters themselves. The same process of learning gives us skill to recognize both.'

'Yes, it does.'

'Then I must surely be right in saying that we shall not be properly educated ourselves, nor will the guardians whom we are training, until we can recognize the qualities of discipline, courage, generosity, greatness of mind, and others akin to them, as well as their opposites, in all their many manifestations. We must be able to perceive both the qualities themselves and representations of them wherever they occur, and must not despise instances great or small, but reckon that the same process of learning gives us skill to recognize both.'[1]

'You are most certainly right,' he agreed.

'And is not the fairest sight of all,' I asked, 'for him who has eyes to see it, the combination in the same person of good character and good looks to match them, each bearing the same stamp?'

'It is indeed.'

'And such a combination will also be most attractive, will it not?'

'Certainly.'

'It is, then, with people of this sort that the educated man will fall in love; where the combination is imperfect he will not be attracted.'

'Not if the defect is one of character,' he replied; 'if it's a physical defect, he will not let it be a bar to his affection.'

1. There may be a reference here to Plato's 'Theory of Ideas': see p. 234.

'I know,' I said; 'you've got, or once had, a boy friend like that. And I agree with you. But tell me: does excessive pleasure go with self-control and moderation?'

'Certainly not; excessive pleasure breaks down one's control just as much as excessive pain.'

'Does it go with other kinds of goodness?'

'No.'

403 'Then does it go with excess and indiscipline?'

'Certainly.'

'And is there any greater or keener pleasure than that of sex?'

'No: nor any more frenzied.'

'But to love rightly is to love what is beautiful and good with discipline and intelligence.'

'I entirely agree.'

'Then can true love have any contact with frenzy or excess of any kind?'

'It can have none.'

'It can therefore have no contact with this sexual pleasure, and lovers whose love is true must neither of them indulge in it.'

'They certainly must not, Socrates,' he replied emphatically.

'And so I suppose that you will lay down laws in the state we are founding which will allow a lover to associate with his boy-friend and kiss him and touch him, if he permits it, as a father does his son, if his motives are good; but require that his association with anyone he's fond of must never give rise to the least suspicion of anything beyond this, otherwise he will be thought a man of no taste or education.'

'That is how I should legislate.'

'And that, I think,' said I, 'concludes what we have to say about this stage of education, and a very appropriate conclusion too – for the object of education is to teach us to love beauty.'

'I agree.'

§2. PHYSICAL EDUCATION

Plato does not go into detail but makes it clear that he is thinking of a military rather than an athletic training: which is why, perhaps, he tends to regard it, as appears later, as a stage of education, lasting approximately from the eighteenth to the twentieth year, rather than as something which accompanies the secondary education which he has just finished describing. Young men at Athens, in fact, spent two years, from eighteen to twenty, doing a course of compulsory military training, and it is of military training as much as of physical education in our sense that Plato is thinking.

The passage proceeds to criticize certain developments of contemporary medicine of which Plato disapproved (criticisms which read oddly to us), and to condemn litigiousness (Plato undoubtedly has contemporary Athens in mind); it ends by emphasizing that physical, as much as literary, education is aimed primarily at the development of character.

'The next stage in the training of our young men will be physical education. And here again they must be carefully trained from childhood onwards. I have my own opinions about it: let me see if you agree. In my view physical excellence does not of itself produce good character: on the other hand, excellency of mind and character *will* make the best of the physique it is given. What do you think?'

'I agree.'

'We should do well then to leave the elaboration of rules for physical training to minds that have been thoroughly educated: all we need do, for brevity's sake, is to give a rough outline.'

'Yes.'

'We have already forbidden drink. A guardian is the last person in the world to get drunk and not know where he is.'

'It would be absurd,' he replied, 'for a guardian to need someone to look after him.'

'What about diet? Our guardians, you will agree, are competing in the most important of all contests. Should they train like ordinary athletes?' 404

'Perhaps so.'

'But the athlete in training is a sleepy creature and his health delicately balanced. Haven't you noticed how they sleep most of their time, and how the smallest deviation from their routine leads to serious illness?'

'Yes, I've noticed that.'

'So we shall need a better adjusted form of training for our soldier-athletes. They must be as wakeful as watchdogs, their sight and hearing must be of the keenest, and their health must not be too delicate to endure the many changes of food and drink, and the varieties of temperature that campaigning entails.'

'I agree.'

'And do you not also agree that the best form of physical training would be one akin to the simple education we have just been describing?'

'What do you mean?'

'I mean a suitably simple physical training, concentrating particularly on training for war.'

'In what way?'

'Even Homer can tell you that,' I replied. 'For you know that when his heroes are on campaign he does not give them fish to eat, although they are on the shore of the Hellespont, nor boiled meat, but only roast. That is what suits soldiers best, because it is, generally speaking, easier to cook something direct on the fire than carry round pots and pans for the purpose.'

'Much easier.'

'And Homer, I think, never mentions seasonings. Indeed, even the ordinary athlete knows that if he is to be fit he must keep off them.'

'And he is quite right to do so.'

'In that case I assume that you don't approve of the luxury of Syracusan and Sicilian cooking.'

'I should think not.'

'And what about Corinthian girl-friends? Do you disapprove of them for men who want to keep fit?'

'I certainly do.'

'And Attic confectionery, which is supposed to be so good, must go too?'

'It must.'

'We might, I think, with justice compare these luxurious ways of living and eating with the music and song which used a wide range of harmony and rhythm. Elaborate music, we found, produces indiscipline, and elaborate food produces disease. But simplicity in music produces discipline of character, and simplicity in physical education health of body.'

'Very true.'

'And the prevalence of indiscipline and disease in a com- 405 munity leads, does it not, to the opening of law courts and surgeries in large numbers, and law and medicine begin to give themselves airs, especially when they are paid so much attention even by free men.'

'That is bound to happen.'

'And when not only the lower classes and workers, but also those who have some pretensions to education, need skilled doctors and lawyers, that is a pretty conclusive proof that the education in a state is thoroughly bad. For is it not a scandalous sign of a bad education if one's sense of right and wrong is so deficient that one has to seek justice at the hands of others as one's masters and judges?'

'I can't think of anything worse,' he said.

'Yet it's worse still, don't you think,' I replied, 'when a man not only spends most of his life in court as plaintiff or defendant, but is even ignorant enough to be proud of it; when he is convinced that he is an expert law-breaker, up to every kind of twist, and that he knows all the tricks to wriggle out of a conviction? And all this for mean and unworthy ends, without any idea how far better it is to arrange one's life so that one has no need of a judge dozing on the bench.'

'Yes,' he agreed, 'that's still worse.'

'And it's disgraceful too to need a doctor not only for injury or regular disease, but because by leading the kind of life we have described we have filled our bodies with gases and discharges, like a stagnant pool, and driven the medical profession to invent names for our diseases, like flatulence and catarrh. Don't you agree?'

'I do indeed,' he replied, 'these new-fangled names for diseases are very far-fetched.'

'And I don't think you would have found them in the days of Asclepius,'[1] I added. 'Or so I should judge from the fact that when Eurypylus was wounded at Troy, and given Pramnian wine mixed with barley-meal and grated cheese to drink – a mixture you would have thought would have given him a fever – the sons of Asclepius had no fault to find with the women who gave him the drink, or with Patroclus who prescribed it.'

'And yet it was an odd prescription for a wounded man,' he said.

'I don't think so,' I replied, 'for it was not till the days of Herodicus, so they say, that doctors made use of modern methods of nursing disease. Herodicus was an athletic trainer, whose health failed, and he proceeded to make first and foremost himself, and then many others after him, miserable by a combination of medicine and physical training.'

'How did he do that?'

'By dying a lingering death. His whole attention was devoted to a disease that was mortal; he could not cure himself of it, but spent the rest of his life busy doctoring himself and being made wretched by any departure from his routine treatment. And his skill prolonged the struggle till he was an old man.'

'What a reward to win!'

'And quite a suitable one for a man who did not know that it was not from ignorance or lack of skill that Asclepius did not reveal this method of treatment to his successors, but because he knew that in a well-run society each man has a job which he must do, and has no time to spend his life being ill and undergoing cures. We see that this applies to the working class, and it is absurd not to see that it also applies to the wealthy and privileged, as we think them.'

'Explain,' he said.

1. Mythical patron of doctors.

'If a carpenter is ill,' I replied, 'and goes to a doctor he expects to be given an emetic or purge and be cured, or to get rid of the trouble by an operation. If he is ordered to undergo a long cure, wrapping his head up and all that sort of thing, he will probably say that he's no time to be ill and that a life in which one must give all one's attention to one's ailments and none to one's proper job simply is not worth living. Then he will dismiss the doctor who has given the advice, go back to his normal routine, and either regain his health and get on with his job, or, if his constitution won't stand it, die and be rid of his troubles.'

'That's the right way for that sort of man to treat medical advice,' he agreed.

'The reason being,' I said, 'that he has a job to do, and if he 407 does not do it, life is not worth while.'

'Yes, clearly.'

'But hasn't the rich man a job to do, which will make his life not worth living if he can't do it?'

'He isn't usually reckoned to have.'

'You haven't listened to Phocylides,' was my reply, 'who said that when a man no longer has to work for his living, he should "practise excellence".'

'I should have thought he might start even earlier,' he said.

'Don't let's quarrel with him about that,' I returned, 'but let us ask ourselves whether the rich man should make this his job, and whether his life is worth living if he can't carry on with it. Valetudinarianism prevents a man giving his attention to carpentry and similar occupations: is it also a hindrance to obeying Phocylides' orders?'

'It certainly is a hindrance. There's nothing worse than this fussiness about one's health, in excess of normal healthy exercise. It's tiresome in the home, as well as in the army, or in any civilian office.'

'Worst of all, it makes any kind of study or thought or meditation difficult. If you are always wondering if you've got a headache or are feeling giddy, and blaming your studies for it, you will never be able to exercise your mind or test your abilities. You'll always think you're ill, and never stop worrying about your health.'

'That's what's likely to happen.'

'Let us say, then, that Asclepius too knew all this, and therefore introduced medical treatment for those who have a good constitution and lead a healthy life. If they get some specific disease, he gets rid of it by drugs or surgery, but tells them to go on leading their normal life so as not to make them less useful to the community. But he makes no attempt to cure those whose constitution is basically diseased; the result of treating them with all the refinements of dosing and diet can only be an unhappy prolongation of life, and the production of children as unhealthy as themselves. No, he thought that no treatment should be given to the man who cannot survive the routine of his ordinary job, and who is therefore of no use either to himself or society.'

'You talk as if Asclepius was a real political scientist!'

'Of course he was,' said I, 'and that is why we find that his 408 sons are good soldiers at Troy, and doctor people in the way I am describing. You will remember how, when Menelaus was wounded by Pandarus, they "sucked out the blood and skillfully applied soothing ointments".[1] But they gave him no further orders about diet, any more than they did to Eurypylus; for they thought that "ointments" were enough to cure a man who had lived a normal healthy life, whatever he drank after treatment. The life of a man whose constitution was bad and undermined by loose living was, they thought, of no use to them or to anyone else; it was not their business to use their skill on such cases or cure them, even if they were richer than Midas.'

'Discerning men, these sons of Asclepius.'

'Which is as it should be,' I said. 'But Pindar and the tragedians don't believe us, and say that Asclepius was a son of Apollo, that he was bribed by a large fee to cure a rich man who was at death's door, and blasted by a thunderbolt in consequence. But we cannot, if we are to be consistent, agree

1. *Iliad*, IV, 218.

with them on both counts: if he was a god he was not out for profit, and if he was out for profit he was not a god.'

'All that is very true. But tell me, Socrates,' he asked, 'surely we shall need good doctors in our state. And good doctors are those who have the widest experience in treating patients both in health and sickness, just as good judges are those who have mixed with all sorts of people.'

'We certainly need good doctors,' I answered, 'but do you know what I mean by good?'

'I shall if you tell me.'

'I will try. But your question does not admit of a single answer.'

'What do you mean?'

'The best way for a doctor to acquire skill is to have, in addition to his knowledge of medical science, as wide and as early an acquaintance as possible with serious illness; in addition he should have experienced all kinds of disease in his own person and not be of an altogether healthy constitution. For doctors don't use their bodies to cure other people – if so, they could not allow their health to be bad – they use their minds; and if they're defective mentally their treatment can't be good.'

'True.'

'But with a judge it's a matter of mind controlling mind. 409 And the mind must not be brought up from its youth to associate with wickedness, or to run through a whole range of crimes in order to get first-hand experience on which to judge them in other people, as the doctor did with diseases of the body: on the contrary, the mind must, while it is still young, remain quite without experience or contact with bad characters, if its moral development is to be good and its moral judgement sound. That is why people of good character seem simple when they are young, and are easily taken in by dishonesty – because they have in themselves nothing to give them a sympathetic understanding of vice.'

'That's a common experience,' he agreed.

'Which is why a good judge must not be a young man,' I replied, 'but an old one to whom knowledge of wickedness has come late in life, not as a feature he perceives in his own character, but as an evil whose effects he has learned after long practice to discern in other people, something about which he knows but of which he has no personal experience.'

'A man like that would be a real judge indeed.'

'And a good one, which is what you asked,' I pointed out; 'for he has the qualities of mind that are needed. But your wily, knowing type, who has been up to all sorts of tricks and has a reputation for super-smartness, looks pretty formidable so long as he is dealing with men like himself, against whom his own bad principles put him on his guard; but when he comes up against men of good character he looks very silly with his untimely suspicions and the unawareness of what honesty is that he owes to his own bad principles. But he meets more rogues than honest men, and so appears a clever fellow and not a silly one, both to himself and others.'

'That's perfectly true,' he said.

'We must not look to this type, then, for our good and wise judge, but to the other. Vice can never know either itself or virtue, but virtue, when instruction is added to natural endowment, can in course of time acquire knowledge of vice as well as of itself. It is the good man, therefore, and not the bad man who will, in my opinion, make our wise judge.'

'I agree with you.'

'These then are the kind of doctors and judges for whom 410 you will legislate in your state. They will treat those of your citizens whose physical and psychological constitution is good; as for the others, they will leave the unhealthy to die, and those whose psychological constitution is incurably warped they will put to death.'

'That seems to be the best thing both for the individuals concerned and for society.'

'And so,' I said, 'your young men, so long as they maintain their simple form of education, which, as we have said, breeds discipline, will take care not to need judicial treatment.'

'True.'

'And if they successfully follow on the same track in their physical training, they will never need a doctor except in cases of necessity.'

'I agree.'

'It is, of course, to stimulate their energy and initiative that they undergo these severities in their training, not merely to make themselves tough, which is the object of the diet and exercises of the ordinary athlete. And that, my dear Glaucon,' I went on, 'is why I say that the purpose of the two established types of education (literary and physical) is not, as some suppose, to deal one with the mind and the other with the body.'

'What is it then?' he asked.

'I think that perhaps in the main both aim at training the mind.'

'And how do they do that?'

'Have you noticed,' I asked, 'how a lifelong devotion to physical exercise, to the exclusion of anything else, produces a certain type of mind? Just as a neglect of it produces another type? One type tends to be tough and uncivilized, the other soft and over-sensitive, and ...'.

'Yes, I have noticed that,' he broke in; 'excessive emphasis on athletics produces a pretty uncivilized type, while a purely literary and academic training leaves a man with less backbone than is decent.'

'It is the energy and initiative in their nature that may make them uncivilized,' I said; 'if you treat it properly it should make them brave, but if you overstrain it it turns them tough and uncouth, as you would expect.'

'I agree,' he said.

'The philosophic temperament, on the other hand, is gentle; too much relaxation may produce an excessive softness, but if it is treated properly the result should be civilized and humane.'

'That is so.'

'Now we agreed that our Guardians must have both these elements in their nature, did we not?'

'Yes.'

'And must not the two elements be combined to produce a 411 mind that is civilized and brave, as opposed to cowardly and uncivilized?'

'That is so.'

'So when a man surrenders to the charms of music and lets the sound of the sweet, soft, mournful strains we have described flood into his soul, and gives up all his time to the pleasures of song, the effect at first on his energy and initiative of mind, if he has any, is to soften it as iron is softened in a furnace, and made workable instead of hard and unworkable: but if he does not break the enchantment, the next stage is that it melts and runs, till the spirit has quite run out of him and his mental guts (if I may so put it) are entirely removed, and he has become what Homer calls "a feeble fighter".'

'That is all very true.'

'This result is one that follows quickly if he is naturally spiritless in the first place. But if he is a man of spirit, the effect is, by weakening his spirit, to make him unstable, a man who flies into a rage at a trifle and calms down as quickly. His energy has degenerated into peevishness and ill-temper and constant irritability.'

'Exactly.'

'On the other hand, there is the man who takes a lot of strenuous physical exercise and lives well, but has little acquaintance with literature or philosophy. The physical health that results from such a course first fills him with confidence and energy, and increases his courage. But if he devotes himself exclusively to it, and never opens a book, any capacity he may have for learning is weakened by being starved of instruction or enquiry and by never taking part in any intelligent discussion, and becomes deaf and blind, because its perceptions are never cleared and strengthened by use.'

'That is what happens.'

'And so he becomes an unintelligent philistine, with no use for reasoned conviction, and an animal addiction to settle everything by brute force. His life is one of clumsy ignorance, unrelieved by grace or beauty.'

'That describes him exactly.'

'What I should say therefore is that these two methods of education seem to have been given by god to men to train our initiative and our reason. They are not intended, one to train body, the other mind, except incidentally, but to ensure a proper harmony between energy and initiative on the one 412 hand and reason on the other, by tuning each to the right pitch. And so we may venture to assert that anyone who can produce the best blend of the physical and intellectual sides of education and apply them to the training of character, is producing harmony in a far more important sense than any mere musician.'

'A very reasonable assertion.'

'We must therefore ensure, my dear Glaucon,' I said, 'that there is always someone like this in charge of education in our state, if its constitution is to be preserved.'

'We most certainly must.'

PART FOUR

GUARDIANS AND AUXILIARIES

*

§1. THE THREE CLASSES AND THEIR MUTUAL RELATIONS

The Guardian class is subdivided into Guardians proper, or Rulers, and Auxiliaries. The Rulers exercise supreme authority in the state, and are selected by exacting tests (the educational aspect of these is dealt with later, p. 287). The Auxiliaries (I retain the traditional translation: there is no single term which describes their function completely) discharge Military, Police, and Executive duties under the orders of the Rulers. Everything which the Rulers do is done for the good of the community. Plato sketches a Foundation Myth and stringently requires that children are to be moved from class to class according to merit and capability; he does not give details, which would have been difficult to work out, but there is no reason to doubt his seriousness.

Plato has been criticized for his Foundation Myth as if it were a calculated lie. That is partly because the phrase here translated 'magnificent myth' (p. 159) has been conventionally mistranslated 'noble lie'; and this has given rise to the idea that Plato countenances political propaganda of the most unscrupulous kind. In fact, as Cornford points out, the myth is accepted by all three classes, Guardians included. It is meant to replace the national traditions which any community has, which are intended to express the kind of community it is, or wishes to be, its ideals, rather than to state matters of fact. And one of Plato's criticisms of democracy was, in effect, that it was government by propaganda, telling the right lie to the people (cf. pp. 253-4).

'THAT, then, is an outline of the way in which we should educate and bring up our Guardians. For we need not go into detail about their dramatic performances, field sports of various kinds, and athletic competitions on foot or horseback.

The details follow naturally from what we have said, and should give no particular difficulty.'

'Yes, I dare say they won't be particularly difficult,' he agreed.

'Well,' I continued, 'what comes next? We shall have to decide, I suppose, which of our Guardians are to govern, and which to be governed.'

'I suppose so.'

'Well, it is obvious that the elder must have authority over the younger.'

'That is obvious.'

'And again that those who govern must be the best.'

'That's equally obvious.'

'And the best farmers are those who have the greatest skill at farming, are they not?'

'Yes.'

'And so if we want to pick the best guardians, we must pick those who have the greatest skill in watching over the interests of the community.'

'Yes.'

'For that shan't we need men who, besides being intelligent and capable, really care for those interests?'

'True.'

'But we care most for what we love.'

'Inevitably.'

'And the deepest affection is based on community of interest, when we feel that our own good and ill fortune is completely bound up with that of someone else.'

'That is so.'

'So we must choose from among our guardians those who appear to us, when we scrutinize their whole career, to be most completely devoted to what they judge to be the interests of the community, and never prepared to act against them.'

'They are the men for our purpose.'

'A close watch must be kept on them, then, at all ages, to see if they stick to this principle, and do not forget or throw overboard, under the influence of force or propaganda, the conviction that they must always do what is best for the community.'

'What do you mean by throwing overboard?' he asked.

'I will explain,' I said. 'It seems to me that when any belief leaves us, the loss is either voluntary or involuntary. Voluntary when the belief is false and we learn better, involuntary whenever the belief is true.'

413

'I understand what you mean by a voluntary loss, but I don't see how it happens involuntarily.'

'But why? Surely you agree that men are always unwilling to lose a good thing, but willing enough to be rid of a bad one. And isn't it a bad thing to be deceived about the truth, and a good thing to know what the truth is? For I assume that by knowing the truth you mean knowing things as they really are.'

'Yes, you are quite right,' he conceded, 'and I agree that men are unwilling to lose a belief that is true.'

'So when it happens it must be due to theft or propaganda or force.'

'Now I don't understand again,' he said.

'I'm afraid I'm talking too theatrically,' I answered. 'By "theft" I simply mean the insensible process by which we are argued out of our beliefs, or else simply forget them in course of time. Now perhaps you understand.'

'Yes.'

'By "force" I mean what happens when we change our beliefs under the influence of pain or suffering.'

'This too I understand,' he said.

'And I think that you too would call it "propaganda" when people are enticed into a change of opinion by promises of pleasure, or terrified into it by threats.'

'Yes, propaganda and deceit always go together.'

'To go back to what I was saying, then,' I continued, 'we must look for the Guardians who will stick most firmly to the principle that they must always do what they think best for the community. We must watch them closely from their earliest years, and set them tasks in doing which they are most likely to forget or be led astray from this principle; and we must choose only those who don't forget and are not easily misled. Do you agree?'

'Yes.'

'And with the same end in view we must see how they stand up to pain and suffering.'

'We must.'

'We must also watch their reactions to the third kind of test, propaganda. If we want to find out if a colt is nervous we expose him to alarming noises: so we must introduce our Guardians when they are young to fear and, by contrast, give them opportunities for pleasure, proving them far more rigorously than we prove gold in the furnace. If they bear themselves well and are not easily bamboozled, if they show themselves self-reliant and maintain in all circumstances the principles of balance and harmony they learned in their education, then they may be expected to be of the greatest service to the community as well as to themselves. And any Guardian who survives these continuous trials in childhood, youth, and manhood unscathed, shall be given authority in our state; he shall be honoured during his lifetime and when he is dead shall have the tribute of a public funeral and appropriate memorial.

'That in brief, and without going into details,' I concluded, 'is the way in which I would select the Guardians who are to be given authority as Rulers.'

'And that's the way I think it should be done,' he replied.

'Strictly speaking, then, it is for them that we should reserve the term Guardian in its fullest sense, their function being to see that friends at home shall not wish, nor foes abroad be able, to harm our state: while the young men whom we have been describing as Guardians should more strictly be called Auxiliaries, their function being to assist the Rulers in the execution of their decisions.' [1]

'I agree,' he said.

'Now I wonder if we could contrive one of those convenient stories we were talking about a few minutes ago,' I asked, 'some magnificent myth that would in itself carry conviction to our whole community, including, if possible, the Guardians themselves?'

1. Or 'enforce the decisions of the Rulers' (Cornford).

'What sort of story?'

'Nothing new – a fairy story like those the poets tell about the sort of thing that often happened "once upon a time", but never does now: indeed, if it did, I doubt if people would believe it without a lot of persuasion, though they believed the poets.'

'You seem to be hesitating to tell us more,' he said.

'And when I do you will understand my hesitation,' I assured him.

'Never mind,' he replied, 'tell us.'

'I will,' I said, 'though I don't know how I'm to find the courage or the words to do so. I shall try to persuade first the Rulers and Soldiers,[1] and then the rest of the community that the upbringing and education we have given them was all something that happened only in a dream. In reality they were fashioned and reared, and their arms and equipment manufactured, in the depths of the earth, and Earth herself, their mother, brought them up, when they were complete, into the light of day; so now they must think of the land in which they live as their mother and protect her if she is attacked, while their fellow-citizens they must regard as brothers born of the same mother earth.'

'No wonder you were ashamed to tell your story,' he
415 commented. I agreed that it was indeed no wonder, but asked him to listen to the rest of the story.

'We shall,' I said, 'address our citizens as follows:

"You are, all of you in this land, brothers. But when God fashioned you, he added gold in the composition of those of you who are qualified to be Rulers (which is why their prestige is greatest); he put silver in the Auxiliaries, and iron and bronze in the farmers and the rest. Now since you are all of the same stock, though children will commonly resemble their parents, occasionally a silver child will be born of golden parents, or a golden child of silver parents, and so on. Therefore the first and most important of God's commandments to the Rulers is that they must exercise their function as Guardians with particular care in watching the mixture of metals in the characters of the children. If one of

---

1. i.e. the Auxiliaries.

their own children has bronze or iron in its make-up, they must harden their hearts, and degrade it to the ranks of the industrial and agricultural class where it properly belongs: similarly, if a child of this class is born with gold or silver in its nature, they will promote it appropriately to be a Guardian or an Auxiliary. For they know that there is a prophecy that the State will be ruined when it has Guardians of silver or bronze."

That is the story. Do you think there is any way of making them believe it?'

'Not in the first generation,' he said, 'but you might succeed with the second and later generations.'

'Even so it should serve to increase their loyalty to the state and to each other. For I think that's what you mean.'

§2. THE RULERS' AND AUXILIARIES' WAY OF LIFE

The Rulers and Auxiliaries are to live a life of austere simplicity, without private property or (as will appear more clearly later, p. 211) family life; for private property was, Plato thought, the chief temptation that led men to sacrifice public to personal interests (cf. p. 219). The happiness of both will lie in their service of the community; for it is the happiness of the community as a whole, and not of any particular class, that is the objective.

'But let us leave that to public opinion to decide, and arm our earthborn citizens and conduct them to their city, under the leadership of the Rulers. On arrival the Rulers [1] must pick a site for a camp which will best enable them to control any internal disaffection or to repel any attack by an external enemy, descending like a wolf on the fold. When they have

---

1. The Myth was addressed to all three classes, and the previous sentence appears, again, to refer to all three. In this sentence there is no change of subject in the Greek, yet in it and in all that follows Plato is clearly speaking of the Guardians (or Rulers) only – an interesting unconscious indication of his real preoccupation, throughout, with the ruling class.

made their camp, they will sacrifice to the appropriate gods, and then arrange sleeping quarters. Do you agree?'

'Yes.'

'And these quarters must provide adequate shelter both in summer and winter, mustn't they?'

'Yes; for I take it you mean them to live there.'

'I do; but as soldiers and not as men of means.'

'What is the difference?'

416 'I will try to explain. It would be the most dreadful disgrace for a shepherd to keep sheep dogs so badly bred and trained, that disobedience or hunger or some bad trait or other led them to worry the sheep and behave more like wolves than dogs.'

'It would of course be dreadful.'

'We must therefore take every possible precaution to prevent our Auxiliaries treating our citizens like that because of their superior strength, and behaving more like savage tyrants than partners and friends.'

'We must certainly try to prevent that.'

'And the greatest possible care will have been taken, will it not, if they have been properly educated?'

'As in fact they have been,' he said.

To which I replied, 'We oughtn't to be too positive about that, my dear Glaucon; what we can be positive about is what we have just said, namely that they must be given the right education, whatever that may be, as the surest way to make them behave humanely to each other and the subjects in their charge.'

'That is true.'

'It would therefore be reasonable to say that, besides being so educated, they should be housed and their material needs provided for in a way that will not prevent them being efficient Guardians, yet will not tempt them to prey upon the rest of the community.'

'There is truth in that.'

'Well then,' I said, 'if that is our object, I suggest that they should live and be housed as follows. First, they shall have no private property beyond the barest essentials. Second, none of them shall possess a dwelling-house or other property to which all have not the right of entry. Next, their food shall be provided by the other citizens in payment for the duties they perform as Guardians; it shall be suitable for men living under the rigours of military training and discipline, and in quantity enough to ensure that there is neither a surplus nor a deficit over the year. They shall eat together in messes and live together like soldiers in camp. They must be told that they have no need of mortal and material gold and silver, because they have in their hearts the heavenly gold and silver given them by the gods as a permanent possession, and it would be wicked to pollute the heavenly gold in their possession by mixing it with earthly, for theirs is without impurity, while 417 that in currency among men is a common source of wickedness. They alone, therefore, of all the citizens are forbidden to touch or handle silver or gold; they must not come under the same roof as them, nor wear them as ornaments, nor drink from vessels made of them. Upon this their safety and that of the state depends. If they acquire private property in land, houses, or money, they will become farmers and men of business instead of Guardians, and harsh tyrants instead of partners in their dealings with their fellow citizens, with whom they will live on terms of mutual hatred and suspicion; they will be more afraid of internal revolt than external attack, and be heading fast for destruction that will overwhelm the whole community.

'These are the reasons why we should provide for the housing and other material needs of the Guardians in the way I have described. So shall we legislate accordingly?'

'Let us do so by all means,' answered Glaucon.

'But look here, Socrates,' interrupted Adeimantus, 'how BK would you answer the objection that you aren't making your IV Guardians particularly happy? It's their own fault, of course, 419 because the state is in their control, but they don't seem to get any good out of it. Other rulers possess lands and build themselves large houses and furnish them magnificently; they offer sacrifices to the gods at their own expense, they entertain visitors from abroad, and have plenty of the gold and silver you were just talking about, and everything else which is commonly thought to make a man happy. But one might almost describe your Guardians as a set of hired mercenaries with nothing to do in the city but perpetual guard-duty.'

'Yes,' I replied, 'and what is more, they do it for their keep only, and get no pay over and above it like other men, so that they can't go for a holiday abroad on their own if they want to; they have nothing to spend on women or on all those other things which those who are commonly reckoned well-off spend their money on. And there are a whole lot of other complaints you have omitted.'

'Let us take them as read then,' he said.

'And you want to know how we should reply?'

'Yes.'

'I think,' I said, 'that we shall find our reply if we stick to the path we have been pursuing, and say that, though it would not in fact be in the least surprising if our Guardians were very happy indeed, our purpose in founding our state was not to promote the happiness of a single class, but, so far as possible, of the whole community. Our idea was that we were most likely to find justice in such a community, and similarly injustice in a really badly run community, and so be able to decide the question we are trying to answer. We are therefore at the moment trying to construct what we think is a happy community by securing the happiness not of a select minority, but of the whole. The opposite kind of community we will examine presently. Now if we were painting a statue and were met with the criticism that we were not using the most beautiful colours for the most beautiful parts of the body – for we had not coloured the eyes, the body's most precious feature, red, but black – we could, I think, reasonably reply as follows: "It is absurd to expect us to represent the beauty of the eye in a way which does not make it look like an eye at all, and the same is true of the other parts of the body; you should look rather to see whether we have made the whole beautiful by giving each part its due. So, in the present case, don't make us give our Guardians the kind of happiness that will make them anything but Guardians. We could perfectly well clothe our farmers in royal robes and put crowns on their heads and tell them to cultivate the land at their pleasure, and we could sit our potters round the fire, and let them drink and enjoy themselves, putting their wheel at their side for them to work as they feel inclined; indeed, we could try to make the whole community happy by giving everyone else similar comforts. But you must not ask us to do so; for the result of such advice will be that our farmers are no longer farmers nor our potters potters, and that all the classes that make up our community lose their characteristic form. In some cases this does not matter much – the community suffers nothing very terrible if its cobblers are bad and become degenerate and pretentious; but if the Guardians of its laws and constitution, who alone have the opportunity to bring it good government and prosperity, become a mere sham, then clearly it is completely ruined."

'So if we are making genuine guardians, who will never harm the community, while our critic prefers idlers [1] enjoying themselves in something more like a fun-fair than a city, then he is not thinking of a community at all. We must therefore decide whether our object in setting up the Guardian class is to make it as happy as we can, or whether happiness is a thing we should look for in the community as a whole. If it is, our Guardians and Auxiliaries must be compelled to act accordingly and be persuaded, as indeed must everyone else, that it is their business to perfect themselves in their own particular job; then our city will be built on the right basis, and, as it grows, we can leave each class to enjoy the degree of happiness its nature permits.'

'That,' he said, 'seems to put it very fairly.'

§3. FINAL PROVISIONS FOR UNITY

The Guardians must see that in the Third Class, which is alone allowed to possess property, extremes of wealth and poverty are excluded. Their military training will ensure success in war, but they must maintain unity by not allowing the state to grow too large, and

1. Reading ἀργούς for γεωργούς in 421b2.

by ensuring that the measures for promotion and demotion from one class to another are carried out. Above all they must maintain the educational system unchanged; for on education everything else depends, and it is an illusion to imagine that mere legislation without it can effect anything of consequence.

Religious arrangements are to be left to the Oracle at Delphi, 'which was normally consulted before the foundation of a new city'.[1]

'I wonder,' I asked, 'whether you will think a very similar view of mine as reasonable?'

'What exactly is it?'

'That there are two things that can ruin and corrupt the rest of our workers.'

'What are they?'

'Riches and poverty,' I said.

'And how do they do it?'

'Well, do you think that a potter who has become rich will want to ply his trade any longer?'

'No.'

'He will become more idle and careless than he was, won't he?'

'Much more.'

'And so a worse potter.'

'Yes, much worse.'

'And again, if he is prevented by poverty from providing himself with tools and other necessities of his trade the quality of his work will deteriorate, and his sons and anyone else studying the trade under his instruction will be taught it worse.'

'Inevitably.'

'Both poverty and wealth, therefore, have a bad effect on the quality of the work and on the workman himself.'

'So it appears.'

'So we have found two further things,' I said, 'which our Guardians must at all costs prevent from slipping unobserved into our state.'

'What are they?'

1. Cornford.

'Wealth and poverty,' I answered. 'One produces luxury 422 and idleness and a passion for novelty, the other meanness and bad workmanship and revolution into the bargain.'

'I agree,' he replied. 'But how do you think our state will be able to fight a war, Socrates, if it has no wealth, especially if it is compelled to fight against an enemy that is both large and wealthy?'

'It would be more difficult to fight a single enemy of this sort than two,' I said.

'What do you mean?' he asked.

'In the first place,' I said, 'if they have to fight, our Guardians will fight as trained soldiers against their rich antagonists.'

'Yes, I grant that.'

'But come, Adeimantus,' I said, 'don't you think that one fully-trained boxer is easily a match for two men who are not boxers, but rich and fat?'

'Not if they both set on him at once, perhaps.'

'Not even if he is able to retreat a little, and then turn on the leader and hit him, and repeat the process often in the hot sun? Surely in this way he could get the better of more than two?'

'Yes, of course: there would be nothing surprising in that.'

'And don't you agree that rich men are likely to have more knowledge and experience of boxing than of war?'

'Yes.'

'Well then, it would appear that our trained soldiers should easily be a match for two or three times their number.'

'I will grant that,' he said; 'I think you are right.'

'So suppose we send envoys to one of the two states to say, truly enough, that, unlike them, we have no use for silver or gold, which are forbidden us, and to propose that if they will fight on our side they shall have all the other state has got. Do you think that any state hearing these terms will prefer to fight against our tough and wiry watchdogs, rather than with them and against fat and tender sheep?'

'I should think not. But don't you think that our state might be in some danger because of its lack of wealth, if the others pooled all their resources?' he asked. To which I replied:

'You're lucky to be able to think of any community as worth the name of "state" which differs from the one we are building.'

'But what should I call the others?' he asked.

'We ought to find some grander name for them,' I replied. 'Each of them is, as we might say, not so much a single state as a collection of states. For it always contains at least two states, the rich and the poor, at enmity with each other; each of these in turn has many subdivisions, and it is a complete mistake to treat them all as a unity. Treat them as a plurality, offer to hand over the property or the power or the persons of one section to another, and you will have allies in plenty and very few enemies. As long as your state maintains the discipline we have laid down, it will remain supreme, I don't mean in common estimation, but in real truth, even though it has only a thousand defenders. You won't easily find a single state so great anywhere among the Greeks or barbarians, though you'll find many that are thought much greater. Or do you disagree?'

'No, certainly not.'

'I suggest, therefore,' I said, 'that our Rulers might use this as the best standard for determining the size of our state and the maximum amount of territory it needs.'

'What standard?'

'The state should, I think,' I replied, 'be allowed to grow so long as growth is compatible with unity, but no further.'

'A fair limit,' he said.

'So we can add to the instructions we shall give our Guardians one to the effect that they are to avoid at all costs either making the state too small or relying on mere bulk, but keep it adequate in size and a unity.'

'A nice easy job for them!' he remarked ironically.

'And here's an easier one,' I continued in the same vein; 'we mentioned it before when we said that if any child of a guardian is a poor specimen, it must be degraded to the other classes, while any child in the other classes who is worth it, must be promoted to the rank of Guardian. By this it was implied that all citizens ought to devote their full energy to the particular job for which they are naturally suited. In that way the integrity and unity both of the individual and of the city will be preserved.'

'Yes, a still easier job!' he replied.

'But seriously, Adeimantus,' I said, 'there's nothing very much in all these things we are asking them to do, provided they take care of the main feature, or rather the sufficient condition of the whole system.'

'And what is that?'

'The educational system. If they are well brought up, and become reasonable men, they can easily see to all we have asked them to, and indeed a good many things we have omitted, such as the position of women, marriage, and the production of children, all of which ought so far as possible to be dealt with on the proverbial basis of "all things in common between friends".' [1]

'Yes, they can deal with all these problems.'

'And once we have given our community a good start,' I pointed out, 'the process will be cumulative. By maintaining a sound system of education you produce citizens of good character, and citizens of sound character, with the advantage of a good education, produce in turn children better than themselves and better able to produce still better children in their turn, as can be seen with animals.'

'That is likely enough.'

'In a word therefore, those in charge of our state must stick to the system of education and see that no deterioration creeps in; they must maintain it as a first priority and avoid at all costs any innovation in the established physical or literary curriculum. When they hear someone saying

it is always the latest song men care for most,

they must be afraid that people will think that the poet means not new songs, but a new *kind* of song, and that that is what he is recommending. But such innovation should not be recommended, nor should the poet be so understood. You should hesitate to change the style of your literature, because you

1. The first mention of the so-called 'community of wives and children' in the *Republic*; see p. 202.

risk everything if you do; the music and literature of a country cannot be altered without major political changes – we have Damon's word for it and I believe him.'

'And you can count on my agreement too,' said Adeimantus.

'And so it is here, in education, that our Guardians must build their strong-point.'

'It is in education that bad discipline [1] can most easily creep in unobserved,' he replied.

'Yes,' I agreed, 'because people don't treat it seriously there, and think no harm can come of it.'

'It only does harm,' he said, 'because it makes itself at home and gradually undermines morals and manners; from them it invades business dealings generally, and then spreads into the laws and constitution without any restraint, until it has made complete havoc of private and public life.'

'Is it really as bad as that?' I said.

'Yes, I think it is.'

'Then doesn't it follow, as we said to begin with, that our children's amusements must be more strictly controlled; because once they and the children lose their discipline, it becomes impossible to produce good, orderly citizens?'

425 'Yes, it follows.'

'But if children play on the right lines from the beginning and learn orderly habits from their education, it produces quite the opposite results and corrects any previous flaws there may have been in the society.'

'True enough.'

'And people so brought up discover rules which seem quite trivial, but which their predecessors had entirely neglected.'

'What sort of rules?'

'Things like when to be silent in the presence of your elders, when to sit down and stand up, and one's duty to look after one's parents; besides the whole business of one's dress and bearing, keeping one's hair and clothes and shoes tidy, and so on. Do you agree?'

'Yes.'

1. The Greek word means, literally, 'transgression of law, decency, order', and so the spirit that leads to such transgression.

'But I think it would be silly to try and legislate for such things. Laws and regulations won't either produce them or maintain them.'

'No, they won't.'

'No, Adeimantus,' I said; 'for it's the bent given by education that is likely to determine all that follows – birds of a feather, you know.'

'Yes, of course.'

'And the final consequence is a grand result that is good or bad accordingly.'

'Inevitably,' he agreed.

'And that,' I concluded, 'is why I should not try to legislate for such minor matters.'

'And you are quite right,' he said.

'Then are we to embark on a whole lot of market regulations and the like? For instance, there are commercial contracts, and industrial relations, questions of slander and assault, legal actions and empanelling of juries, exaction and payment of taxes agricultural or commercial, and the general business of regulating business and police and trade and other affairs. What about all this?'

'Good men need no orders,' he said. 'They will find out easily enough what legislation is in general necessary.'

'They will,' I agreed, 'if God enables them to preserve the laws we have already described.'

'Otherwise,' he said, 'they will spend their whole time making and correcting detailed regulations of the sort you've described, under the illusion that they are reforming society.' [1]

'You mean,' said I, 'that they will lead lives like invalids who are too vicious to give up their unhealthy habits.'

'Exactly.'

'And a fine time they have of it! For all their cures and medicines have no effect – except to make their ailments still more complicated – yet they live in hope that every new medicine they are recommended will cure them.'

'Exactly,' he said; 'that's just what happens to that sort of invalid.'

1. In what follows Plato has Athens in mind.

'Then,' I replied, 'is it not amusing they should detest anyone who tells them the truth – that until they put an end to their eating and drinking and womanizing and idleness, they will get no good out of drugs or operations, or out of patent medicines or anything else of the kind?'

'Not so very amusing,' he said, 'there's nothing attractive in unwillingness to take good advice.'

'It looks as if you don't approve of this sort of people.'

'I certainly don't.'

'And you won't approve if a whole city follows the course we have described, I suppose. For I think you will agree that this is what cities are doing which forbid on pain of death any alteration in the established constitution, but are badly governed and will honour as a great and good man anyone who leaves things as they are, but flatters them agreeably and gives them pleasure by running their errands, or is clever at anticipating their wishes.'

'I agree that that's what they're doing,' he said, 'and I don't approve in the least.'

'And what about those who are willing and eager to apply the flattery? Aren't you surprised at their boldness and irresponsibility?'

'Yes, except when they are deceived by popular applause into thinking that they really are statesmen.'

'Oh come,' I said, 'won't you forgive them? Surely a man who doesn't know how to use a foot-rule can hardly avoid thinking himself a six-footer if lots of people like himself tell him he is?'

'Hardly.'

'Then don't be hard on them. You can really get quite a lot of amusement out of them. They legislate for all the affairs we described, and then improve on their own legislation, under the impression that they can put an end to breaches of contract and all the other things I was talking about, and not knowing that the operation's about as hopeful as cutting off a Hydra's head.'

427   'Yet that's all they're doing,' he said.

'I shouldn't have thought therefore,' I concluded, 'that a

real legislator ought to bother about making laws and institutions of this sort either in a good state or a bad one: in one they are no use and nothing comes of them, in the other they are partly obvious and partly the automatic result of earlier training.'

'Then what have we left to do in the way of legislation?' he asked. I replied that there was nothing indeed for us to do ourselves, 'But,' I said, 'there remain for Apollo and the Delphic oracle laws of the first importance and significance to make.'

'What about?' he asked.

'The founding of temples and the institution of sacrifices, and other services to the gods and spirits and heroes, besides the arrangements for the burial of the dead and the rites we must pay to the powers of the other world to secure their goodwill. We know nothing about all these things ourselves, and when we found our state we won't entrust them, if we have any sense, to any one but their traditional interpreter. And it is Apollo who by tradition interprets them to all men from his shrine at the earth's centre.'

'You are right; we must act accordingly.'

PART FIVE

JUSTICE IN STATE AND INDIVIDUAL

*

§1. JUSTICE IN THE STATE

The State which we have founded must possess the four cardinal virtues of wisdom, courage, discipline, and justice. It will have wisdom because of the knowledge possessed by the Rulers, courage because of the courage of the Auxiliaries, and discipline because of the harmony between all three Classes and their common agreement 'about who ought to rule'. Finally, Justice is the principle which has in fact been followed throughout, the principle of one man one job, of 'minding one's own business', in the sense of doing the job for which one is naturally fitted and not interfering with other people.

'WELL, we seem to have got your city founded for you, Adeimantus,' I said. 'Now you must get your brother and Polemarchus and the rest of them to see if they can help you throw any light on the problem where we shall find justice and injustice in it, how they differ from each other, and which of them anyone who is to be happy needs, irrespective of whether gods or men think he has it or not.'

'Nonsense, Socrates,' said Glaucon. 'You promised to deal with the problem yourself, because you said it would be wrong for you not to support justice for all you were worth.'

'That's true,' I said; 'I remember. I must do as I said, but you must all help.'

'Yes, we will,' he said.

'I think we shall probably find what we want as follows. If we have founded it properly, our state is presumably perfect.'

'It must be.'

'Then it will obviously have the virtues of wisdom, courage, discipline, and justice.'[1]

'Obviously.'

1. 'This is apparently the first passage in Greek literature where the doctrine of four cardinal virtues ... is expressly enunciated.' Adam.

'Then if we can identify some of these qualities in it, the ones that are left will be the ones we are still looking for.'

'Yes.'

428

'So suppose us to be looking for one of any four things. If we can find it at once, well and good. But if we find the other three first, by so doing we have in effect identified the object of our search, which must obviously be the one left over.'

'That's true.'

'Should we not therefore follow this method in the present case, where again there are four things at issue?'

'Obviously.'

'The first of the four that is apparent is wisdom, and there is one odd feature about it.'

'What?' he asked.

'The state we have described seems to me to be genuinely wise. For its judgement is good, isn't it?'

'Yes.'

'And the quality of good judgement is clearly a form of knowledge or skill, as it is because of knowledge and not because of ignorance that we judge well.'

'Clearly.'

'But there are many different kinds of skill in our city.'

'Of course there are.'

'And do we say it has wisdom and judgement because of the skill of its carpenters?'

'Certainly not – that merely makes it good at carpentry.'

'So it's not called wise because it has the highest degree of skill in woodwork?'

'No.'

'The same is presumably true of bronze and other materials. And I expect you would agree that skill in farming merely makes it good at agriculture.'

'Yes.'

'Well then,' I said, 'is there any form of skill to be found among any of the citizens in the state we've just founded which is exercised not on behalf of any particular interest but on behalf of the city as a whole, in such a way as to benefit the state both internally and externally?'

'There is.'

'What is it, and where shall we find it?' I asked.

'It is the Guardians' skill,' he answered, 'and is to be found with those we called Guardians in the full sense.'

'And how do you describe the state because of it?'

'I say it has judgement and wisdom.'

'And which do you think that there will be more of in our state, metal-workers or Guardians in this sense?'

'Many more metal-workers,' he said.

'Won't the Guardians, in fact, be far fewer in number than those in any other skilled trade you can name?'

'Yes.'

'So the state founded on natural principles is wise as a whole in virtue of the knowledge inherent in its smallest constituent class, which exercises authority over the rest. And the smallest class is the one which naturally possesses that form of knowledge which alone of all others deserves the title of wisdom.'

'That is all perfectly true,' he agreed.

'Well, then we have somehow or other managed to find this one of our four virtues and where it belongs.'

'And as far as I'm concerned I'm quite satisfied with our findings,' he said.

'And it's not very difficult,' I went on, 'to see where the virtue of courage lies, which makes us call our state brave. We shall say it's brave or cowardly with sole reference to the part which does its fighting and campaigning.'

'That is all that need be considered.'

'Because I don't think that members of other classes are competent, by being cowardly or brave, to make the state one or the other.'

'No, they aren't.'

'Our city is therefore brave too in virtue of a part of itself. That part retains in all circumstances the ability to judge rightly about the nature and extent of dangers in accordance with the standards laid down by law in its education. For that, I take it, is what you mean by courage.'

'I didn't quite understand what you said,' he answered; 'say it again.'

'I say,' I replied, 'that courage is a sort of retentiveness.'

'What sort?'

'The sort that will retain the opinion inculcated by the established education about what is dangerous and why. And by retaining it in "all circumstances" I meant retaining it steadfastly in pleasure and pain, desire and fear. If you like, I'll give you an analogy.'

'Yes, do.'

'Well, take dyeing,' I said. 'You know that, when they want to dye wool purple, they are very particular about the colour of the material, which must be white; they then subject it to an elaborate process to prepare it to take the dye before they actually dip it. And the colour of anything dyed by this process remains fast, and the dye won't come out if you wash the material, whether you use soap or not; but if they start with wool of any other colour or don't give it this treatment – well, you know what happens to it.'

'Yes – the colour washes out and it looks absurd' he said.

'Assume, then,' I said, 'that this was the sort of result we were doing our best to achieve in choosing our soldier-class, and in educating them physically and mentally. Our whole object was to steep them in the spirit of our laws like a dye, so that nature and nurture might combine to fix in them indelibly their convictions about what is dangerous, and about all other topics, and prevent them being washed out by those most powerful solvents, pleasure, so much more effective than soap and chemicals, and pain and fear and desire, the most effective of all. This kind of ability to retain in all circumstances a judgement about danger which is correct by established standards is what I propose to call courage, unless you have any alternative to suggest.' 430

'No,' he replied, 'I haven't. For I imagine that you would not regard mere uninstructed judgement, such as an animal or slave might have on these matters, as being in accordance with tradition, even if right, and that you would use some other name for it.'

'You are quite right,' I said.

'Then I accept your definition of courage.'

'Accept it as a definition of the ordinary citizen's courage, and you won't be far wrong,' I replied; 'we will go into it more fully later, if you like.[1] For the moment it's justice not courage we are looking for, and for this purpose I think the definition's adequate.'

'That is fair enough.'

'Well, we are left with two virtues to look for in our state,' I said, 'discipline and the real object of our whole inquiry, justice.'

'Yes, we are.'

'I wonder if we could find justice without having to bother further about discipline.'

'Personally,' he said, 'I don't know, and I shouldn't want to find it, if it meant we were to give up looking for discipline. What I should like you to do is to look for discipline first.'

'And I should not like to refuse you,' I said.

'Then carry on,' he said.

'I will,' I replied. 'At first sight, discipline looks more like some sort of harmony or concord than the other virtues did.'

'In what way?'

'Discipline,' I said, 'is surely a kind of order, a control of certain desires and appetites. So people use " being master of oneself" (whatever that means) and similar phrases as indications of it. Isn't that so?'

'Certainly.'

'But "master of oneself" is an absurd phrase. For if you're master *of* yourself you're presumably also subject *to* yourself, and so *both* master *and* subject. For there is only one person in question throughout.'

'Undoubtedly.'

'What the expression is intended to mean, I think, is that

1. Strictly speaking, only the Rulers can have true courage, because true courage must be based on full knowledge, which only they have. This will appear more fully later.

there is a better and a worse element in the character of each individual, and that when the naturally better element controls the worse then the man is said to be "master of himself", as a term of praise. But when (as a result of bad upbringing or bad company) one's better element is overpowered by the numerical superiority of one's worse impulses, then one is criticized for not being master of oneself and for lack of self-control.'

'Which is quite reasonable.'

'Then look at our newly founded state,' I said, 'and you will find the first of these descriptions applies to it. For you will admit that it is right to call it master of itself, if we speak of discipline and self-mastery where the better part rules the worse.'

'Yes, I see; that's quite true.'

'And, what is more, the greatest variety of desires and pleasures and pains is generally to be found in children and women and slaves, and in the less reputable majority of so-called free men.'

'Certainly.'

'While the simple and moderate desires, guided by reason and judgement and reflection, you will find in a minority who have the advantages of natural gifts and good education.'

'True.'

'This feature too you can see in our state, where the desires of the less reputable majority are controlled by the desires and the wisdom of the superior minority. And so if any city is to be said to be master of its pleasures and desires, and of itself, ours must be.'

'That is certainly true.'

'Then on all these counts we can surely say it has discipline.'

'We can indeed,' he said.

'And of our state, if of any, it will be true that government and subjects will agree about who ought to rule. Or don't you think so?'

'I'm quite sure of it,' he said.

'In these circumstances, of which class do you think discipline is characteristic, rulers or subjects?'

'Of both, I suppose,' he replied.

'So you can see how right we were to guess just now that discipline was like a kind of harmony.'

'Why?'

'Because, unlike courage and wisdom, which made our state 432 brave and wise by being present in a particular part of it, discipline operates by being diffused throughout the whole of it. It produces a concord between its strongest and weakest and middle elements, whether you define them by the standard of good sense, or of strength, or of numbers or money or the like. And so we are quite justified in regarding discipline as this sort of natural harmony and agreement between higher and lower about which of them is to rule in state and individual.'

'I entirely agree.'

'Good,' said I; 'it looks as if we had spotted three of the qualities we are looking for in our state. What about the fourth element in its goodness? It must obviously be justice.'

'Obviously.'

'Then we must stand like hunters round a covert and make sure that justice does not escape us and disappear from view. It must be somewhere about. Try and see if you can catch sight of it before I can, and tell me where it is.'

'I wish I could,' he said. 'It's about as much as I can manage to follow your lead and see things when you point them out.'

'Then follow me and hope for the best.'

'I will,' he said; 'lead on.'

'It looks to me,' I said, 'as if we were in a pretty difficult and obscure spot; it's dark and I can't see my way through it. But we must push on all the same.'

'Yes, we must,' he agreed.

I cast about a bit and then cried, 'Tally ho, Glaucon! I think we are on the track, and our quarry won't altogether escape us.'

'That's good news.'

'We really are being a bit slow.'

'In what way?'

'Our quarry is right under our noses all the time, and we haven't seen it but have been making perfect fools of ourselves. We are like people looking for something they have in their hands all the time; we're looking in all directions except at the thing we want, which is probably why we haven't found it.'

'How do you mean?'

'I mean that it seems to me that we have failed to understand that we have in a sort of way been talking about it all through our discussion.'

'You are a long time leading up to what you've got to say; I'm getting impatient.'

'Well, then listen, and see if you think I'm talking sense. I believe justice is the principle we laid down at the beginning and have consistently followed in founding our state, or else some variant of it. We laid down, if you remember, and have often repeated, that in our state one man was to do one job, the job he was naturally most suited for.'   433

'Yes, we did.'

'And further, we have often heard and often said that justice consists in minding your own business and not interfering with other people.' [1]

'Yes.'

'So perhaps justice is, in a certain sense, just this minding one's own business. Do you know why I think so?'

'No; why?'

'Because I think that the virtue left over, now that we have discussed discipline, courage and wisdom, must be what makes their existence possible and preserves them by its presence. [2] And we agreed that it would be justice that was left over if we found the other three.'

'It must be.'

'Now, if we were asked to judge which of these virtues by its presence contributed most to the goodness of our state, we should find it a difficult decision to make. Is it the agreement

---

1. The reference is to ordinary conversation, and not to any earlier passage in the dialogue.

2. Reading παρέχει with Adam.

between rulers and subjects? Is it the retention by our soldiers of a proper judgement about what is and is not dangerous? Is it the Guardians' ability to govern wisely? Or is it the ability of the individual – child or woman, slave, free man or artisan, ruler or subject – to get on with his own job and not interfere with other people?'

'A difficult decision, I agree.'

'At any rate, wisdom, discipline, courage, and the ability to mind one's own business are all comparable in this respect; and we can regard justice as making a contribution to the goodness of our city comparable with that of the rest.'

'Yes, certainly.'

'Look at it again this way. I assume that you will make it the duty of our rulers to administer justice?'

'Of course.'

'And won't they try to follow the principle that men should not take other people's belongings or be deprived of their own?'

'Yes, they're bound to.'

'Their reason presumably being that it is *just.*'

'Yes.'

'So we reach again by another route the conclusion that justice is keeping to what belongs to one and doing one's own job.'

434

'That is true.'

'There's another point on which I should like your agreement. Suppose a builder and a shoemaker tried to exchange jobs, each taking on the tools and the prestige of the other's trade, or suppose alternatively the same man tried to do both jobs, would this and other exchanges of the kind do great harm to the state?'

'Not much.'

'But if someone who belongs by nature to the class of artisans and business men is puffed up by wealth or popular support or physical strength or any similar quality, and tries to do an Auxiliary's job; or if an Auxiliary who is not up to it tries to take on the functions and decisions of a Ruler and exchange tools and prestige with him; or if a single individual tries to do all these jobs at the same time – well, I think you'll agree that this sort of mutual interchange and interference spells destruction to our state.'

'Certainly.'

'Interference by the three classes with each other's jobs, and interchange of jobs between them, therefore, does the greatest harm to our state, and we are entirely justified in calling it the worst of evils.'

'Absolutely justified.'

'But will you not agree that the worst of evils for a state is injustice?'

'Of course.'

'Then that gives us a definition of injustice. And conversely, when each of our three classes (businessmen, Auxiliaries, and Guardians) does its own job and minds its own business, that, by contrast, is justice and makes our city just.'

'I entirely agree with what you say,' he said.

'Don't let's be too emphatic about it yet,' I replied. 'If we find that the same definition of justice applies to the individual, we can finally agree to it – there will be nothing to prevent us; if not, we shall have to think again. For the moment let us finish our investigation.'

§2. THE ELEMENTS IN MENTAL CONFLICT

Plato starts by reasserting the parallel between state (society) and individual; 'since the qualities of a community are those of the component individuals, we may expect to find three corresponding elements in the individual soul. All three will be present in every soul; but the structure of society is based on the fact that they are developed to different degrees in different types of character' (Cornford, p. 126). After a warning that in what follows we must not expect too much philosophic precision, Plato proceeds to examine the conflict of motives in the individual, and concludes that we cannot, without contradiction, assume the existence of less than three types of motive or impulse in the mind. First there is reason, the faculty that calculates and decides: second there is desire or appetite, in the sense of bare physical and instinctive craving. There is also a third type of motive, covering, as noted above (p. 109), such characteristics as pugnacity, enterprise, ambition, indignation, which are often found in conflict with unthinking impulse.

This is often referred to as Plato's doctrine of 'the three parts of the soul'. Two main questions arise in understanding it: (1) To what extent and in what sense does Plato think of separate 'parts' of the soul or mind? In the present passage the words he uses most commonly (eidos, genos) mean 'kinds', 'types', 'forms', though he does on occasion use the Greek word for part (meros); the word 'element' used in the translation is deliberately indeterminate. Elsewhere Plato sometimes speaks as if the soul or mind had three distinct parts, as in the Phaedrus and Timaeus, sometimes as if there were a single stream of mental energy manifesting itself in different activities, as in the Symposium. We perhaps do well, first, to remember that he has warned us that he is not speaking with scientific precision, but rather on the level of ordinary conversation; and, second, to bear in mind that he is concerned with morals and not with psychology, with a general classification of the main motives or impulses to action, rather than a scientific analysis of the mind. He is, in fact, probably always conscious that in speaking of 'parts' ('elements' or what not) of the soul he is using a metaphor. (2) What exactly are the three 'elements' that Plato describes? There is little difficulty with two of them. By 'appetite' Plato means the purely instinctive desires in their simplest form; it is easy enough, on a common-sense level, to recognize them. 'Reason' includes not only the ability to understand and to think before we act, the faculty of calculation and foresight, but also the ability to make up one's mind, the faculty of decision. The third element at first appears more miscellaneous, including, as we have seen, such qualities as indignation, courage, determination, spirit, and so on. Two illustrations may help us to understand it. First the distinction, still commonly made, between 'heart' and 'head'. When we make that distinction we do not include under 'heart' the mere animal instincts; we perhaps include more of the 'feelings' than Plato, but our meaning is not far from his second 'part of the soul'. (In the Timaeus reason is located in the head, 'spirit' in the breast, i.e. heart, and appetite in the belly.) Second, when Butler analysed the motives of moral action he found them threefold. Conscience, a rational faculty capable of judgement and having authority: particular passions, like hunger and thirst: and 'self-love', or, as we

*should call it to-day, the 'self-regarding instinct'.[1] Each of these two
analyses recognizes a rational, controlling, authoritative part of the
mind; each recognizes animal instinct; but each also recognizes a third
element, one which is not easy to define, but which is perhaps most com-
prehensively described as self-regard, and which ranges from self-asser-
tion, through self-respect, to our relations with others (Butler coupled
'self-love' and 'benevolence') and our concern for our reputation and
good name.*

*Plato uses two words, thumos and thumoeides, for this element in
the mind. Neither is easy to translate. I have used 'anger', 'indignation', 'spirit' as seemed to suit the context best. Plato, in any case,
never developed a precise terminology.*

'We thought it would be easier to see justice in the individual if we looked for it first in a larger field. We thought the
state provided this, and so we set about founding an ideal
state, being sure we should find justice in it. Let us therefore
transfer our findings to the individual, and if they fit him, well
and good; on the other hand, if we find justice in the individual is something different, we will return to the state and
test our new definition. So by a process of comparison we may
strike a spark which will illuminate justice for us, and once we
see it clearly we can establish it among ourselves.'

'That is the right method; let us follow it,' he said.

'Then when we apply the same epithet to two things, one
large and the other small, will they not be similar in respect of
that to which the common epithet is applied?'

'Yes.'

'So there will be no difference between a just man and a just
city, so far as the characteristic of justice goes.'

'None.'

'But we agreed that a city was just when its three natural
constituents were each doing their job, and that it was disciplined and brave and wise in virtue of certain other states and
dispositions of those constituents.'

'That is so,' he said.

1. Cf. Field, *Plato* (H.U.L.), p. 96; for Butler see Duncan-Jones,
Butler's Moral Philosophy (Pelican).

'Well, then,' I continued, 'we shall expect the individual to have the same three constituents in his character and to be affected similarly, if we are to be justified in attributing the same virtues to him.'

'That must follow.'

'Another nice little inquiry we've tumbled into!' I exclaimed. 'Has the character these three constituents or not?'

'I shouldn't call it a little inquiry,' he said; 'but it's probably true enough that, as the saying goes, anything that's worth-while is difficult.'

'So it seems. And I assure you that in my opinion we shall never find an exact answer by the method of argument we are using now – to get one we should have to go much further afield[1]; but we can probably find one that will satisfy the standards of our present discussion.'

'That's good enough,' he replied; 'at any rate, it would suit me for the present.'

'And it will be quite enough for me.'

'Then press on with the investigation.'

'Well, we are bound to admit that the qualities that characterize a state must also exist in the individuals that compose it. There is nowhere else for them to come from. It would be absurd to suppose that the vigour and energy for which northern people like the Thracians and Scythians have a reputation aren't due to their individual citizens; and similarly with intelligence, which is characteristic of our own part of the world, or with the commercial instinct which one attributes particularly to the Phoenicians and Egyptians.'

'That's perfectly true.'

'Here, then, we have a fact which is not particularly difficult to recognize. What is difficult is to see whether we perform all our functions with the same part of us, or each with a different part. Do we learn with one part of us, feel angry with another, and desire the pleasures of eating and sex with another? Or do we employ our mind as a whole when our energies are em-

1. Plato refers to this longer treatment again in Bk VI (p. 267), and, in fact, gives it in Bks VI–VII.

ployed in any of these ways? These are questions it's difficult to answer satisfactorily.'

'I agree,' he said.

'Then let us try to decide whether the faculties concerned are the same or different.'

'How are we to do it?'

'Clearly one and the same thing cannot act or be affected in opposite ways at the same time in the same part of it and in relation to the same object; so if we meet these contradictions, we shall know we are dealing with more than one faculty.'

'Granted.'

'Then look – can a thing be at rest and in motion at the same time and in the same part of itself?'

'No.'

'Let us be even more precise, to avoid ambiguities later on. If we were told that a man, who was standing still but moving his hands and his head, was both at rest and in motion, we should not accept that as a proper statement of the case, but say that part of him was standing still and part of him in motion. Isn't that so?'

'Yes.'

'We might have a still more ingenious case put to us. It might plausibly be argued that a top, spinning round a fixed axis, is both at rest and in motion as a whole, as indeed is any body in circular motion on the same spot. We should not agree, but argue that it is not the same *parts* of such bodies that are at rest and in motion; they have both an axis and a circumference, and their axis, as it has no inclination in any direction, is at rest, but their circumference is in motion. And further, if their axis inclines in any direction, right or left, up or down, while they are still spinning, then they are not at rest at all.'

'That is quite correct,' he agreed.

'We shan't, then, be shaken by instances of this kind into believing that the same thing can act or be affected in opposite ways, or have opposite qualities, at the same time in the same part of itself and in relation to the same thing.'

437

'*I* certainly shan't.'

'Anyway,' I said, 'we don't want to have to examine all such

187

objections and prove at length they aren't true, so let us proceed on the assumption we are right, it being understood that if we see reason to change our minds all the consequences of our assumption will fall to the ground.'

'Yes, that's the thing to do.'

'Then would you not class assent and dissent, impulse and aversion, attraction and repulsion and the like as *opposite* actions or states – no matter which?'

'Yes,' he said, 'I should.'

'And what about hunger and thirst and the desires generally,' I went on, 'or, again, willing and wishing, don't they all fall into one of the two groups of opposites just mentioned? When a man's mind desires anything, has he not an *impulse* towards it? If he wishes to get anything, does he not feel *attraction* for it? And if he wills to have a want satisfied, is it not as a result of *assent* given to an inward question prompted by his longing for it?'

'I agree.'

'And what about disinclination, unwillingness and dislike? Shouldn't we put them in the opposite group, with repulsion and rejection?'

'Of course.'

'That being so, we can say that the desires form a class, of which those we call thirst and hunger are the clearest examples.'

'Yes.'

'And thirst is the desire for drink, hunger for food?'

'Yes.'

'Then is thirst, in so far as it is thirst, the desire for anything more than simply drink? Is it thirst for hot drink or cold, for a lot to drink or a little, or for any particular kind of drink at all? Isn't it rather that if you are hot as well as thirsty you want a cold drink, while if you're cold you want a hot one; and if your thirst is great you want a lot to drink, if it's small you only want a little? Simple thirst, on the other hand, is the desire for its natural object, drink, without qualification: and the same is true of hunger and food.'

'In that case,' he said, 'each desire is directed simply towards its own natural object, and any qualification is an addition.'

'And we must beware,' I went on, 'of letting ourselves be 438 upset by the objection that no one simply desires drink, but drink that is good for him, and similarly food that is good for him. For – so runs the argument – all men desire what is good for them, and therefore, if thirst is a desire, it will be the desire for drink (or what not) that is good for one; and the same is true of the other desires.' [1]

'It's an argument which perhaps has some force,' he said.

'Yes,' I answered, 'but among correlative terms either both must be qualified or both unqualified.'

'I don't understand.'

'Well, you can understand that "greater" must always mean greater than something which is *smaller*.'

'Yes.'

'And *much* greater means *much* greater than something *much* smaller. Agreed?'

'Yes.'

'And the same is true of greater and smaller *in the past* or *in the future*.'

'Of course. What then?'

'And is not the same also true of more and less, double and half and the like, of heavier and lighter, quicker and slower, of hot and cold, and indeed of all relative terms?'

'Yes, it is.'

'But what about knowledge? Isn't the same thing true again? Knowledge unqualified is knowledge of an object (or whatever you like to call it); knowledge of a particular kind and type is knowledge of a particular kind and type of object. For example, when men discovered how to make houses, this was a form of knowledge differing from others, and was called building. And wasn't it so called because it is knowledge

---

1. The object here, and in the following argument is 'to distinguish thirst as a mere blind craving for drink, from a more complex desire whose object includes the pleasure or health expected to result from drinking' (Cornford, p. 131). In particular, there is the Socratic argument, referred to in this passage, that all desire is directed towards 'the good'. 'It is necessary to insist that we do experience blind cravings which can be isolated from any judgement about the goodness of their object' (Cornford, *loc. cit.*).

of a certain *type,* different from all other kinds of knowledge?'

'Yes.'

'And isn't it knowledge of a certain type because it has a certain type of object? And is not the same true of all forms of knowledge and technique?'

'Yes, that is so.'

'I hope you can see now,' I said, 'that that is what I meant when I said that among correlative terms both must be unqualified or both qualified. And I don't mean that you can transfer the epithet simply from one term to the other, saying for example that the knowledge of health and disease is healthy and diseased, or that the knowledge of good and evil is itself good and evil. What I mean is that when the object of knowledge is of a particular kind, for example health or disease, then the knowledge itself must also be of a particular kind and is in consequence no longer called knowledge simply, but medical knowledge, which has a particular kind of object.'

'I understand; and I think you are right.'

439 'Then isn't thirst a relative term?' I asked. 'For it is, of course, the desire –'

'– for drink; I agree,' he said.

'And for a particular *kind* of drink there will be a particular kind of thirst. But thirst in itself is the desire not for a lot or a little to drink, or for good drink or bad, or, in a word, for any *kind* of drink at all, but for drink pure and simple.'

'Exactly.'

'The mind of the thirsty man, therefore, in so far as he is thirsty, simply wants to drink, and it is to that end that its energies are directed.'

'Clearly.'

'If therefore there is something in it that resists its thirst, it must be some part of it other than the thirsty impulse which is dragging it like a wild animal to drink. For we have agreed that the same thing cannot act in opposite ways with the same part of itself towards the same object.'

'That is impossible.'

'For instance, it is not fair to say that an archer's hands are pulling and pushing the bow at the same time, but that one hand is pushing it, the other pulling.'

'Certainly.'

'Now, can we say that men are sometimes unwilling to drink even though they are thirsty?'

'Oh yes; that is often true,' he said.

'Then how are we to describe such cases?' I asked. 'Must we not say that there is one element in their minds which bids them drink, and a second which prevents them and masters the first?'

'I suppose so.'

'And isn't the element of control, when present, due to our reason, while the urges and impulses are due to our feelings and unhealthy cravings?'

'Clearly so.'

'Then we shan't be without justification if we recognize these two elements as distinct. We can call the reflective element in the mind the reason, and the element with which it feels hunger and thirst, and the agitations of sex and other desires, the irrational appetite – an element closely connected with pleasure and satisfaction.'

'That is a perfectly reasonable distinction,' he agreed.

'Well, we've defined two elements in the mind, then,' I said. 'Now, is indignation, and the part in which we feel it, a third element, or is it of the same nature as one of the two we have defined?'

'Maybe it's the same as appetite,' he said.

'I rely on a story I once heard,' I answered. 'It's about Leontion, son of Aglaion, who was on his way up from the Peiraeus, outside the north wall, when he noticed some corpses lying on the ground with the executioner standing by them. He wanted to go and look at them, and yet at the same time held himself back in disgust. For a time he struggled with himself and averted his eyes, but in the end his desire got the 440 better of him and he ran up to the corpses, opening his eyes wide and saying to them, "There you are, curse you – a lovely sight! Have a real good look!"'

'I've heard the story too.'

'And it shows,' I said 'that anger is different from desire and sometimes opposes it.'

'Yes, it does.'

'And don't we often see a man whose desires are trying to force him to do something his reason disapproves of cursing himself and getting indignant with them? It's like a struggle between political factions, with indignation fighting on the side of reason. But I don't suppose you've ever observed indignation, either in yourself or in anyone else, taking the side of the desires once reason has decided a course is wrong.'[1]

'No, certainly not.'

'And what about a man who feels he's in the wrong? The more honest he is, the less angry he feels at hunger or thirst or any similar suffering which he thinks is inflicted on him with justification. He simply refuses to feel indignant about it.'

'Quite true.'

'But it's quite different if he thinks he's being wronged. Then his heart boils with indignation and fights obstinately for what he thinks right, persevering and winning through hunger and cold and all similar trials. It won't give up the struggle till death or victory, or till reason calls it back to heel like a shepherd calls his dog.'

'That describes it exactly,' he agreed; 'and,' he went on, 'in our state we said the Auxiliaries were to be like watchdogs

---

1. As it stands this sentence overstates the case. A few sentences below Plato makes the proviso that the second element is reason's 'natural auxiliary, unless corrupted by bad upbringing'. It is an essential feature of his moral theory that different elements predominate to different degrees in different types of character (see Books VIII–IX), and that the control of reason is not always perfect. Reason's 'natural auxiliary' may be 'corrupted', and the three elements in the mind may 'interfere with each other' and try to 'do each other's business'. Perhaps in such cases reason is 'corrupted' too; it is not easy to define Plato's meaning precisely. But this should not prevent us from seeing the simple moral fact that he is trying to describe; and moralists have commonly insisted that 'self-love', 'self-regard', and 'self-interest', if 'enlightened', will lead to moral conduct – self-love, said Butler, in general 'coincides with virtue'. Unfortunately 'self-love' is all too often not enlightened; the fact is clear, though it may be difficult to say why and how.

obeying the Rulers, who were the shepherds of the community.'

'I see you quite understand what I mean. But there's another point.'

'What?'

'That we've changed our mind about this third element in the mind. We were wondering if it was something like appetite; now we have gone to the other extreme and are saying that, when there's a conflict in the mind, it's more likely to fight for reason.'

'That's quite true.'

'Then is it different from reason? Or is it a species of reason, and are there not three, but only two elements in the mind, reason and appetite? The state was made up of three classes, 441 businessmen, auxiliaries, and governors; is the mind like it in having spirit as a third element, which, unless corrupted by bad upbringing, is reason's natural auxiliary?'

'There must be a third element.'

'Yes there must,' I said, 'if spirit can be shown to be distinct from reason, as it is from appetite.'

'But that's not difficult to prove,' he answered. 'You can see it in children, who are full of spirit as soon as they're born; but some never seem to become reasonable, and most of them only at a late stage.'

'That puts it very well,' I agreed; 'and you can see the same thing in animals. There is further evidence in the passage from Homer we quoted before,[1] where Odysseus "strikes himself on the chest and calls his heart to order". It is clear enough that Homer here makes one element rebuke another, distinguishing the power to reflect about good and evil from unreasoning passion.'

'You are absolutely right.'

§3. JUSTICE IN THE INDIVIDUAL

Justice in the individual is now defined analogously to justice in the state. The individual is wise and brave in virtue of his reason and

1. 390 d: *Odyssey*, xx, 17.

'spirit' respectively: he is disciplined when 'spirit' and appetite are in proper subordination to reason. He is just in virtue of the harmony which exists when all three elements of the mind perform their proper function and so achieve their proper fulfilment; he is unjust when no such harmony exists.

'Well, it's been a rough passage, but we've got there all right and are pretty well agreed that there are the same three elements in the individual as in the state.'

'True.'

'Must it not follow, then, that the individual is wise in the same way and with the same part of himself as the state? And similarly with courage and with all the other virtues?'

'It must.'

'And so, my dear Glaucon,' I went on, 'we shall also say that the individual man is just in the same way that the state is just.'

'That must follow too.'

'And I suppose we have not forgotten that the state was just when the three elements within it each minded their own business.'

'No, I don't think we've forgotten that.'

'Then we must remember that each of us will be just, and do his duty, only if each part of him is performing its proper function.'

'Yes, we must certainly remember that.'

'So the reason ought to rule, having the ability and foresight to act for the whole, and the spirit ought to obey and support it. And this concord between them is effected, as we said, by a combination of intellectual and physical training, which tunes up the reason by intellectual training and tones down the crudeness of natural high spirits by harmony and rhythm.'

'Certainly.'

'When these two elements have been brought up and trained to their proper function, they must be put in charge of appetite, which forms the greater part of each man's make-up and is naturally insatiable. They must prevent it taking its fill of the so-called physical pleasures, for otherwise it will get too large and strong to mind its own business and will try to subject and control the other elements, which it has no right to do, and so wreck life entirely.'

'True.'

'At the same time,' I went on, 'won't these two elements be the best defence that mind and body have against external enemies? One of them will do the thinking, the other will fight under the orders of its superior and provide the courage to carry its decisions into effect.'

'Yes, I agree.'

'And we call an individual brave, I think, when he has the spirit to obey reason in danger, in spite of pleasure and pain?'

'That is quite right.'

'And we call him wise in virtue of that small part of him which is in control and issues the orders, knowing as it does what is best for each of the three elements and for the whole.'

'Yes, I agree.'

'Then don't we call him self-controlled when all these three elements are in harmonious agreement, when reason and its subordinates are all agreed that reason should rule and there is no dissension?'

'That is exactly what we mean by self-control or discipline in a city or in an individual.'

'And a man will be just in virtue of the principle we have referred to so often.'

'That must be so.'

'Well, then,' I said, 'is our picture in any way indistinct? Does it look as if justice in the individual were different from what we found it to be in the state?'

'I can't see any difference,' he answered.

'If there are still any doubts in anyone's mind,' I said, 'a few elementary examples should finally convince them.'

'What sort of examples?'

'Well, suppose for instance we were asked whether our state or a man of corresponding nature and training would

embezzle money. Do you think we should reckon him more
443 likely to do it than other people?'

'He would be the last person to do such a thing.'

'And wouldn't it be out of the question for him to commit
sacrilege or theft, or to betray his friends or his country?'

'Out of the question.'

'And he would never break any promise or agreement, and
be most unlikely to commit adultery, dishonour his parents or
be irreligious.'

'Most unlikely.'

'And is not the reason for all this that each element within
him is performing its proper function, whether it is giving or
obeying orders?'

'Yes, that is the reason.'

'Are you now convinced, then, that justice is the quality
that produces men and states of this character?'

'Yes, I am quite convinced,' he said.

'So our dream has come true, and, as we guessed, we have
been lucky enough to run across an elementary type of
justice right at the beginning of the foundation of our
state.'

'Yes, we have.'

'In fact the provision that the man naturally fitted to be a
shoemaker, or carpenter, or anything else, should stick to his
own trade has turned out to be a kind of image of justice –
hence its usefulness.'

'So it seems.'

'Justice, therefore, we may say, is a principle of this kind;
but its real concern is not with external actions, but with a
man's inward self. The just man will not allow the three elements which make up his inward self to trespass on each
other's functions or interfere with each other, but, by keeping
all three in tune, like the notes of a scale (high, middle, and low,
or whatever they be), will in the truest sense set his house in
order, and be his own lord and master and at peace with himself. When he has bound these elements into a single controlled
and orderly whole, and so unified himself, he will be ready for
action of any kind, whether personal, financial, political or

commercial; and whenever he calls any course of action just and fair, he will mean that it contributes to and helps to maintain this disposition of mind, and will call the knowledge which controls such action wisdom. Similarly, by injustice he will mean any action destructive of this disposition, and by ignorance the ideas which control such action.'

444

'That is all absolutely true, Socrates.'

'Good,' I said. 'So we shan't be very far wrong if we claim to have discerned what the just man and the just state are, and in what their justice consists.'

'Certainly not.'

'Shall we make the claim, then?'

'Yes.'

'So much for that,' I said. 'And next, I suppose, we ought to consider injustice.'

'Obviously.'

'It must be some kind of internal quarrel between these same three elements, when they interfere with each other and trespass on each other's functions, or when one of them sets itself up to control the whole when it has no business to do so, because its natural role is one of subordination to the control of its superior. This sort of situation, when the elements of the mind are in confusion, is what produces injustice, indiscipline, cowardice, ignorance and vice of all kinds.'

'Yes, that's so.'

'And if we know what injustice and justice are, it's clear enough, isn't it, what is meant by acting unjustly and doing wrong or, again, by acting justly?'

'How do you mean?'

'Well,' I said, 'there is an analogy here with physical health and sickness.'

'How?'

'Healthy activities produce health, and unhealthy activities produce sickness.'

'True.'

'Well, then, don't just actions produce justice, and unjust actions injustice?'

'They must.'

'And as health is produced by establishing a natural order of control and subordination among the constituents of the body, disease by the opposite process, so justice is produced by establishing in the mind a similar order of control and subordination among its constituents, and injustice by the opposite process.'

'Certainly.'

'It seems, then, that virtue is a kind of mental health or beauty or fitness, and vice a kind of illness or deformity or weakness.'

'That is so.'

'And virtue and vice are in turn the result of one's practice, good or bad.'

'They must be.'

§4. CONCLUSION

The definition of justice has now been given; but Socrates has been asked (p. 99 above) not only to define it, but to show that it pays better in all circumstances than injustice. This, says Glaucon, is now as self-evident as that health is preferable to disease. But Socrates objects that it cannot be fully seen until our study of the good state and the good man, now complete, is supplemented by a study of the different forms of bad state and corresponding bad character. Of these there are four, and Socrates is about to describe them, when he is interrupted. He does not return to the description until Book VIII.

'We are left, then, I suppose, with the question whether it pays to act justly and do right and be just irrespective of appearances, or to do wrong and be unjust provided you escape punishment and consequent improvement.'

'I think we have already shown the question to be an absurd one, Socrates,' he replied. 'Men don't reckon that life is worth living when their physical health breaks down, even though they have all the food and drink and wealth and power in the world. So we can hardly reckon it worth living when the principle of life itself breaks down in confusion, and a man wilfully avoids the one thing that will rid him of vice and crime, the acquisition of justice and virtue in the sense which we have shown them to bear.'

'Yes, it is an absurd question,' I agreed. 'But I don't think we ought to give up just when we've got to a point from which we can get a really clear view of the facts.'

'The last thing in the world we want to do is to give up,' he returned.

'Follow me, then,' I said, 'and we will see how many different kinds of wickedness there are – a thing which, incidentally, is well worth seeing.'

'Go on. I'm waiting your lead.'

'You know, we seem to me to have climbed in our argument to a kind of peak, from which we can see that there is only one kind of goodness, but many kinds of wickedness, though there are four in particular that are worth our attention.'

'Explain.'

'We shall probably find that there are as many types of character as there are kinds of political constitution.'

'And how many is that?'

'Five of each,' I replied.

'And what are they?'

'The first kind of political constitution is the one we have been describing. It can be called by either of two names. If there is a single outstanding man among the Rulers, it is called a Monarchy; if not, it is called an Aristocracy.'

'Agreed.'

'This, then, I regard as one of my five kinds. For, whether control is in the hands of a single man or of a larger number, they won't make any change of importance in the constitution of our State so long as they have been brought up and educated as we have described.'

'They aren't likely to,' he said.

'This, then, is my standard of a good state and a good constitution, and of a good man. And by that standard all other

BK
V
449

forms of social organization and of individual character are bad or defective, and we can classify their faults under four headings.'

'What are they?' he asked.

PART SIX

WOMEN AND THE FAMILY

*

The next three books, V–VII (Parts VI–VIII in this translation) are in form a digression; but in fact Plato is dealing with two features of his State which he can hardly pass over without further explanation. (1) He has, for the Rulers and Auxiliaries, abolished the family and private property (p. 161 f.); he now deals more fully with the reasons for and consequences of this, under two main headings, the Status of Women and the Abolition of the Family. (2) He has also (p. 156–7) sub-divided Guardians into Rulers and Auxiliaries; and the long sections on the Philosopher Ruler and Further Education of the Guardians describe how this is to be done.

§1. THE STATUS OF WOMEN

Socrates is interrupted and asked to explain in greater detail his references to the 'community of wives and children'. In reading his explanation it is important to distinguish principle and detail. No one to-day will be very shocked by the suggestion that women should take part in athletics; but in most Greek states, other than Sparta, it would have seemed preposterous, and so Plato introduces it with a good deal of explanation and apology. But all this is detail. The principles are more important. First, the interest of the state or society counts for everything, that of the individual for nothing. Second, the only difference between men and women is one of physical function – one begets, the other bears children. Apart from that, they both can and should perform the same functions (though men will, on the whole, perform them better), and should receive the same education to enable them to do so; for in this way society will get the best value from both.

Though Plato's ideas would have seemed revolutionary to the ordinary Greek, the status of women had been a topic of discussion before he wrote, and ideas similar to those which he puts forward were in the air.

I WAS going on to describe these forms of wickedness in order, and show how they seemed to me to derive from each other, when Polemarchus, who was sitting a little way from Adeimantus, stretched out a hand and took hold of his coat by the shoulder. He pulled him towards him and, leaning forward, whispered something in his ear, of which I only caught the words 'What shall we do? Shall we let it go?'

'Certainly not,' replied Adeimantus aloud; and when I asked what it was they weren't going to let go, he answered, 'You.'

'And why me?' I said.

'We think you are being lazy,' he answered, 'and trying to avoid dealing with a most important part of the subject. You think you are going to get away with a passing reference to it, as if it was perfectly obvious that the rule "all things in common between friends" should apply to women and children.' [1]

'But wasn't I quite right?' I asked.

'Yes, but here, as so often, what is right needs explanation. What do you mean by "in common"? It might be used in many senses; so let us be told the one you mean. We have been waiting for you to give us some idea of how the Guardians are to produce children, and look after them when they are born, and how this whole business of community of wives and children is to work; for it seems to us that this is a matter in which it is vital to society that the right arrangements should be made. You were just going on to other forms of constitution before dealing adequately with it, but, as you heard just now, we decided that we would not let you do so till you had discussed it as fully as everything else.'

450

'This resolution has my vote too,' added Glaucon.

'In fact, Socrates,' said Thrasymachus, 'you can take it we're unanimous.'

'You don't know what you're doing, holding me up like this,' I said. 'It's an enormous subject, and you're starting again from the beginning just as I was congratulating myself on having finished, and was feeling glad that no one had questioned what I had said. You don't know what a hornet's nest you're stirring up by challenging me. I deliberately avoided the subject before, because of all the trouble it would cause.'

1. See p. 169 above.

'But what do you think we are here for?' asked Thrasymachus; 'a treasure-hunt or a discussion?'

'But a discussion must have some limit,' I said.

'My dear Socrates,' said Glaucon, 'anyone with any sense knows there's no limit short of a lifetime when one's discussing this sort of thing. Don't worry about us, but get along and answer our questions. Tell us how you think our Guardians are to have wives and children in common, and how the children are to be looked after between their birth and the beginning of their education, which everyone agrees is a most difficult stage. Do explain to us how it's all to be managed.'

'I can assure you it won't be easy to explain,' I said. 'There's so much that is doubtful, far more than there is in anything we've so far discussed. It may indeed be doubted whether what I describe is possible at all, and granted it's possible, it may well be doubted if it's for the best. Hence my hesitation; I'm afraid you will think I'm merely day-dreaming.'

'You really needn't hesitate. We've a sympathetic audience, and not unduly unreceptive or sceptical,' he said. To which I replied, 'It's good of you to say so; I suppose you are trying to encourage me.'

'Yes,' he said.

'Well, you're having just the opposite effect,' said I. 'If I was sure I knew what I was talking about, encouragement would be in place; when one's talking among sensible friends about issues which touch them nearly, and knows one is telling the truth, one can speak with certainty and confidence. But when one is doing what I am doing now, and trying to discuss things about which one is far from certain, it's a frightening and tricky business; not because I may make a fool of myself – it would be childish to worry about that – but because if I slip up I shall drag my friends down with me just where it's most important to be sure of the truth. I only hope Fate won't punish me for what I am going to say. For it's better to be guilty of manslaughter, than of fraud in matters of right and wrong. It's a risk better run with enemies than friends, and so your encouragement is cold comfort.'

Glaucon laughed. 'My dear Socrates,' he said, 'if we are led

451

into error by this discussion, we'll acquit you of manslaughter or fraud, and discharge you without a stain on your character. So cheer up.'

'Well,' I said, 'the law says that a discharge from the courts leaves one's character clean, and so I suppose the same holds good here.'

'Then proceed on that assumption,' he said.

'Well, then,' I began, 'we must go back and pick the subject up again. We ought perhaps to have dealt with it in its proper place, but maybe it's a good plan to let the women come on the stage now, after the men have played their part, especially in view of your challenge. We can, I think, only make satisfactory arrangements for the possession and treatment of women and children, by men born and educated as we have described, if we stick to the principle we started with; and our object was, you remember, to make them like watchdogs guarding a flock.'

'Yes.'

'Let us, then, arrange for their birth and upbringing accordingly. We can then see if it suits our purpose.'

'How do you mean?'

'What I mean is this. Ought female watchdogs to perform the same duties as male, and watch and hunt and so on with them? Or ought they to stay at home on the grounds that the bearing and rearing of their puppies incapacitates them from other duties, so that the whole burden of the care of the flocks falls on the males?'

'They should share duties, though we shouldn't expect the females to be quite so strong.'

'And can you use any animal for the same purpose as another,' I asked, 'unless you bring it up and train it in the same way?'

'No.'

'So if we are going to use men and women for the same purposes, we must teach them the same things.'

452 'Yes.'

'We educated the men both physically and intellectually; we shall have to do the same for women, and train them for war as well, and treat them in the same way.'

'It seems to follow from what you said,' he agreed.

'I dare say,' I rejoined, 'that their novelty would make many of our proposals seem ridiculous if they were put into practice.'

'There's no doubt about that,' he said.

'And won't the most ridiculous thing of all be to see the women taking exercise naked [1] with the men in the gymnasium? It won't only be the young women; there will be old women too, just as there are old men who go on with their exercises when they are wrinkled and ugly to look at.'

'Gosh!' he said, 'that's going to be a funny sight by present standards.'

'Still,' I said, 'now we've launched our women on this career we must not be afraid of the clever jokes that are bound to be made about all the changes involved, about their physical training and education, and above all about them being trained to carry arms and ride.'

'You are quite right.'

'So having started off, we must go on to legislate for the real difficulties. We will ask the critics [2] to be serious for once, and remind them that it was not so long ago that the Greeks thought – as most of the barbarians still think – that it was shocking and ridiculous for men to be seen naked. When the Cretans, and later the Spartans, first began to take exercise naked, wasn't there plenty of material for the wit of the comedians of the day?'

'There was indeed.'

'But when experience showed them that it was better to strip than wrap themselves up, what reason had proved best

1. The Greeks always exercised naked, and the nakedness is merely a consequence of the proposal that women should take part in athletics at all.

2. Aristophanes in the *Ecclesiazusae* ('Women in Parliament') had already made fun of ideas similar to those which Plato expresses in this section, and Plato may have him in mind.

ceased to look absurd to the eye. Which shows how idle it is to think anything ridiculous except what is wrong. Indeed, anyone who tries to raise a laugh at the sight of anything but what is foolish and wrong will never, when he is serious, make goodness the object of his ambition.'

'That is certainly true,' he said.

'The first thing we have to decide, then, is whether these proposals are feasible or not. For, whether it's asked in joke or 453 in earnest, we must admit the question, Is the female of the human species capable of taking part in all the occupations of the male, or in none, or in some only? And if in some, is military service one of them? That's the best way to begin, and the way in which we are most likely to reach a fair conclusion.'

'Yes, I agree.'

'Then shall we ask ourselves the question on behalf of our imaginary critic, so that his position does not go undefended?'

'Go ahead.'

'Let us then suppose him to say: "My dear Socrates and Glaucon, there's really no need for others to criticize you. You have yourselves, at the beginning of the process of founding your state, agreed on the principle that each man was naturally fitted for a particular job."'

'Yes, we must certainly admit that.'

'"Well," he will continue, " isn't there a very great natural difference between men and women?" And when we admit that too, he will ask us whether we ought not to give them different roles to match these natural differences. When we say yes, he will ask, "Then aren't you making a mistake, and contradicting yourselves, when you go on to say that men and women should follow the same occupations, in spite of the great natural difference between them?" What about that? Can you see how to answer him?'

'It's not easy to answer on the spur of the moment,' he replied. 'I can only turn to you and ask you to state our case in reply, whatever it is.'

'Now that's just what I was afraid of,' I protested; 'I saw all this coming – that's why I was so unwilling to start legislating about the possession of wives and rearing of children.'

'It doesn't look an easy job,' he admitted.

'It certainly isn't easy,' I replied. 'But you've got to swim whether you're thrown into a swimming bath or into the middle of the sea; so we must try and keep our heads above water in this argument, and swim on in the hope of being rescued by Arion's dolphin [1] or some other miracle.'

'Yes, I suppose we must.'

'Well, let's see if we can find a way out. We admit that different natures need different kinds of occupation, and that men and women have different natures; and yet we go on to give the same occupations to these admittedly different natures. That is the charge we have to meet, isn't it?'

'That is it.'

'You know, Glaucon, it's extraordinary the effect that being 454 a critic can have.'

'In what way?'

'I think a lot of critics fall quite unconsciously into a confusion between scoring points in debate and arguing seriously. They fail to make the distinctions necessary for the discussion of a subject, and so get side-tracked into purely verbal contradictions; they aren't really arguing, but only scoring off each other.'

'That does often happen,' he agreed. 'But does it apply to us now?'

'It certainly does. At any rate, I'm afraid we're unconsciously starting to dispute about words.'

'How?'

'We are sticking obstinately to the verbal debating point that different natures should not be given the same occupations; but we haven't considered what we mean by natures being the same or different, and what our intention was when we laid down the principle that different natures should have different jobs, similar natures similar jobs.'

'No, we've not taken that into consideration.'

'Yet we might just as well, on this principle, ask ourselves

1. 'The musician Arion, to escape the treachery of Corinthian sailors leapt into the sea and was carried ashore at Taenarum by a dolphin, Herod. i, 24' (Cornford).

whether bald men and long-haired men are not naturally opposite types, and, having agreed that they are, allow bald men to be cobblers and forbid long-haired men to be, or vice versa.'

'That would be absurd.'

'But the reason why it is absurd,' I pointed out, 'is simply that we were not assuming that natures are the same or different in an unqualified sense, but only with reference to their suitability for the same or different kinds of employment. For instance, we should regard a man and a woman with medical ability as having the same nature. Do you agree?'

'Yes.'

'But a doctor and a carpenter we should reckon as having different natures.'

'Yes, entirely.'

'Then if men or women as a class appear to be qualified for different occupations,' I said, 'we shall assign them different occupations accordingly; but if the only difference apparent between them is that the female bears and the male begets, we shall not admit that this is a difference relevant for our purpose, but shall still maintain that our male and female guardians ought to follow the same occupations.'

'And rightly so,' he agreed.

'Then let us proceed to ask our opponent to tell us for what professions or occupations in society men and women are differently suited by nature.'

'A fair question.'

'But he may well reply, as you did just now, that it's not easy to answer on the spur of the moment, though there would be no great difficulty if he were given time to think.'

'He may.'

'So shall we ask him to follow us and see if we can show him convincingly that there is no social function peculiar to woman?'

'Go ahead.'

455   'Then let us ask him to answer this question. When you say a man has a natural ability for a subject, don't you mean that he learns it easily and can pick it up himself after a little instruction; whereas a man who has no natural ability learns with

difficulty, and can't remember what he's learnt even after long instruction and practice? And if he has natural ability aren't his mind and body well co-ordinated, otherwise not? Aren't these the sort of criteria by which you distinguish natural ability?'

'No one will deny that.'

'Then is there anything men do at which they aren't far better in all these respects than women? We need not waste time over exceptions like weaving and cooking, at which women are thought to be experts, and get badly laughed at if men do them better.'

'It's quite true,' he replied, 'that in general the one sex is much better at everything than the other. A good many women are better than a good many men at a good many things. But the general rule is as you stated it.'

'There is therefore no function in society which is peculiar to woman as woman or man as man; natural abilities are similarly distributed in each sex, and it is natural for women to share all occupations with men, though in all women will be the weaker partners.'

'Agreed.'

'Are we therefore to confine all occupations to men only?'

'How can we?'

'Obviously we can't; for we are agreed, I think, that one woman may have a natural ability for medicine or music, another not.'

'Yes.'

'And one may be athletic, another not; one be good at sol-   456
diering, another not.'

'I think so.'

'Then may a woman not be philosophic or unphilosophic, high-spirited or spiritless?'

'She may.'

'Then there will also be some women fitted to be Guardians: for these qualities, you will remember, were those for which we picked our men [1] Guardians.'

'Yes, they were.'

1. P. 109 ff.

'So men and women have the same natural capacity for Guardianship, save in so far as woman is the weaker of the two.'

'That is clear.'

'We must therefore pick suitable women to share the life and duties of Guardian with men; they are capable of it and the natures of both are alike.'

'Yes.'

'And like natures should have like employment, shouldn't they?'

'Yes.'

'We come back again, then, to our former agreement that it is natural that our Guardians' wives should share their intellectual and physical training.'

'There's no doubt about it.'

'So what we proposed was no impossible day-dream; it was entirely natural, and it is our present practice which now seems unnatural.'

'It looks like it.'

'Well, set out to discover whether our proposals were possible, but also whether they were the best that could be made. We have shown them to be possible; we must go on to satisfy ourselves that they are best.'

'Yes, we clearly must.'

'To turn a woman into a Guardian we presumably need the same education as we need to turn a man into one, as it will operate on the same nature in both.'

'True.'

'There's another point I'd like your opinion on.'

'What is it?'

'Do you think some men are better than others? Or are all equally good?'

'They certainly aren't all equally good!'

'Then in our imaginary state which will produce the better men – the education which we have prescribed for the Guardians or the training our shoemakers get?'

'It's absurd to ask.'

'All right. So the Guardians will be the best citizens?'

'Far the best.'

'Then won't the women Guardians be the best women?'

'Much the best again.'

'And is there anything better for a state than to produce men and women of the best possible kind?'

'No.'

'But that is the result of the education we have described.'   457

'Of course it is.'

'So the arrangements we proposed are not only possible but also the best our state could have.'

'Yes.'

'Our women Guardians must strip for exercise, then – their character will be all the clothes they need. They must play their part in war and in all other duties of a Guardian, which will be their sole occupation; only, as they are the weaker sex, we must give them a lighter share of these duties than men. And any man who laughs at women who, for these excellent reasons, exercise themselves naked is, as Pindar says, "picking the unripe fruit of laughter" [1] – he does not know what he is laughing at or what he is doing. For it will always be the best of sayings that what benefits us is good, what harms us bad.'

'I agree entirely.'

§2. MARRIAGE AND THE FAMILY

If men and women are to lead the same lives, the family must be abolished. But the sex instinct has to be satisfied and controlled, and new citizens produced. Plato therefore substitutes for the family a system of eugenic breeding analogous to that used in breeding domestic animals. There will be mating festivals at which the Rulers will contrive that the couples from whom they wish to breed shall mate; the children will be looked after in state nurseries. The advantages of the system are, first, that it makes it possible to breed good citizens, and, second, that it gets rid of the distracting loyalties, affections and interests of the family system, and diverts them to the service of the community – the Guardians will become one family. Here, again, community

1. Omit σοφίας with Adam.

is more important than individual, and the women Guardians 'bear children for the state' (*p.* 216).[1]

'Well, then, we're through one wave without drowning. We've dealt with the position of women, and shown that our men and women Guardians should both follow the same occupations; and we've proved without inconsistency that our proposals are both practical and advantageous.'

'Yes, and a pretty big wave it was.'

'You won't say that,' I said, 'when you see the next one.'

'Go on then; let me see it.'

'It follows from what we've said, and from our whole previous argument, that our men and women Guardians should be forbidden by law to live together in separate households, and that wives should be held in common by all; similarly, children should be held in common, and no parent should know his child, or child his parent.'

'That's a much bigger wave,' he said. 'And we shall meet much more scepticism about the possibility or advantages of such a thing.'

'I don't think there can be much doubt about the advantages of women and children being held in common, or about it being the ideal arrangement,' I said; 'but there are likely to be grave doubts about its possibility.'

'Both points will surely be disputed,' he answered.

'You mean I'm to be attacked on both issues,' I said. 'I had hoped you would agree about the advantages of the proposal, and that I should evade that issue and only have to discuss its possibility.'

'I know,' he replied; 'but you didn't get away with it, and are charged on both counts.'

'I must stand my trial, then,' I said. 'But grant me one favour. 458 Let me indulge my fancy like a day-dreamer out for a solitary walk. To save himself the trouble of thinking whether what he wants is possible, he gives up all thought of ways and means and imagines his wish fulfilled; he then goes on to amuse him-

1. Compare the *Laws*, 804d, where Plato says that children 'belong to the state rather than to their parents'.

self with a description of all he intends to do next, thus encouraging his habit of mental laziness. I'm not feeling very strong myself, and I want to put off any discussion of the possibility of my proposals till later, and assuming them, if I may for the moment, to be possible, to consider how the Guardians would put them into practice, and to show how they would in fact be the best possible both for the Guardians and for the state as a whole. I will try to go into these questions with you first, and leave the question of possibility till later, if you will allow me to.'

'I will certainly agree to that. Continue.'

'Well, I suppose,' I began, 'that if our Rulers and their Auxiliaries are each to be worthy of their name, the Auxiliaries must be willing to obey orders, and the Rulers to issue them, either in direct obedience to the laws, or in obedience to their spirit when we have left them discretion.'

'I suppose so.'

'As law-giver, you have already picked your men Guardians. You must now pick women of as nearly similar natural capacities as possible to go with them. They will live and feed together, and have no private home or property, and in the course of their common life and all through their training they are bound to meet constantly for exercise, and so naturally and necessarily be led to mate with each other. Or perhaps you don't think this a necessity?'

'A necessity of instinct rather than logic,' he said; 'but instinct is rather more effective than logic when it comes to getting the common man to do anything.'

'Much more,' I agreed. 'But to continue – it would be a sin either for mating or for anything else in our ideal society to take place without regulation. The Rulers would not allow it.'

'No, it wouldn't be right.'

'It follows that we must arrange for marriage, and make it as sacred an affair as we can. And a sacred marriage is one that produces the best results.'

'Yes, certainly.'

'How, then, are we to get the best results? Tell me,' I said 459 to Glaucon, 'haven't I seen a lot of hunting dogs and game birds at your house? And there's something about their breeding and mating you must have noticed.'

'What?'

'In the first place, though they are all well bred, don't some of them prove superior to the rest?'

'Yes.'

'Then do you breed from all indifferently? Or do you take care to breed so far as possible from the best of them?'

'From the best of them.'

'And does that mean from the youngest, or the oldest, or those in their prime?'

'Those in their prime.'

'And you reckon that any dog or bird bred otherwise is likely to turn out an inferior specimen?'

'I do.'

'What about horses and other animals? Does the same apply to them?'

'It would be surprising if it didn't.'

'My goodness,' I exclaimed, 'what skill our Rulers will need, if the same thing is true of human beings!'

'It's true enough,' he replied. 'But how does the skill come in?'

'Because they will need to use a lot of medicine; and we commonly consider that a comparatively unqualified doctor can treat a patient who is prepared to diet and does not need medicine, but that when medicine is required someone better qualified is called for.'

'That's true; but what is its bearing?'

'This – that our Rulers will have to employ a great deal of fiction and deceit for the benefit of their subjects; and you will remember that we agreed that they might be used as a kind of medicine.'[1]

'It is the right way to use them.'

'And they will have to be used a lot in this matter of marriage and child-bearing.'

'How?'

'We must, if we are to be consistent, and if we're to have a

1. P. 126.

real pedigree herd,[1] mate the best of our men with the best of our women as often as possible, and the inferior men with the inferior women as seldom as possible, and keep only the off-spring of the best.[2] And no one but the Rulers must know what is happening, if we are to avoid dissension in our Guardian breed.'

'That is very true.'

'So we must arrange festivals in which our brides and bride-grooms will be brought together. There will be religious rites and our poets will write songs suitable to the occasion. The number of unions we will leave to the Rulers to settle. Their aim will be to keep the number of inhabitants[3] constant, allowing for wastage by war and disease, and, so far as they can, to prevent our state becoming too large or too small.' 460

'Quite right.'

'And we shall have to arrange an ingenious system of draw-ing lots, so that our inferior Guardian can, at each mating festival, blame the lot and not the Rulers.'

'That will certainly be necessary.'

'And among the other honours and rewards our young men can win for distinguished service in war and in other activities, will be more frequent opportunities to sleep with a woman[4]; this will give us a pretext for ensuring that most of our children are born of that kind of parent.'

'Good.'

1. This goes, perhaps, a little beyond the Greek: but Plato deliberately uses words to recall the analogy with stock-breeding.

2. This phrase (with that about 'getting rid of' children just below) has been used, e.g. by Adam, to show that Plato sanctioned infanticide. There would be nothing very shocking to Greek sentiment in this, but, as Cornford points out, Plato has provided at 415c (p. 161) for the rele-gation of inferior offspring of Guardians to the third class, and makes the same provision again in the *Timaeus* 19A. Yet in the phrase below he mentions children who are born physically defective, and infanticide of such children was practised at Sparta. Probably he intended both methods, relegation and infanticide, to be used as appropriate.

3. Plato speaks loosely as if these regulations applied to all classes and not to the Guardians only.

4. i.e. at the marriage festivals.

'Each generation of children will be taken by officers appointed for the purpose, who may be men or women or both – for men and women will of course be equally eligible for office –'

'Yes, of course.'

'These officers will take the children of the better Guardians to a nursery and put them in charge of nurses living in a separate part of the city: the children of the inferior Guardians, and any defective offspring of the others, will be quietly got rid of.' [1]

'They must be if we are to keep our Guardian stock pure,' he agreed.

'They will arrange for the suckling of the children by bringing their mothers to the nursery when their breasts are still full, taking every precaution to see that no mother recognizes her child; if the mothers have not enough milk they will provide wet-nurses. They will see that the mothers do not suckle children for more than a reasonable length of time, and will hand over all the sitting up at night and hard work to nurses and attendants.'

'Child-bearing will be an easy job for the Guardians' wives on those conditions,' he commented.

'Which is as it should be,' I replied. 'But to continue. We said that one should breed from creatures in their prime. Would you agree that a woman is in her prime for about twenty, a man for about thirty years?'

'Which twenty and which thirty?'

'A woman,' I replied, 'should bear children for the state from her twentieth to her fortieth year; a man should beget them from the time he passes his prime as a runner [2] until he is fifty-five.'

461 'That is the period of their prime, both physically and mentally.'

'If any man or woman above or below these ages takes any part in the begetting of children for the community, we shall

1. See note 2 p. 215.
2. Perhaps a quotation from a victory ode, referring to a race-horse put to stud after its racing career was over.

regard it as a sin and a crime. If they escape detection, the child they beget will be begotten in secrecy and fear and incontinence, without the rites celebrated by priests and priestesses and by the whole state at each marriage festival, and without the prayers they offer that the children may be better and more useful citizens than the parents.'

'That is true.'

'The same rule will apply if any man still in his mating years lays hands on a woman of child-bearing age without the Rulers' sanction; we shall regard the child as a bastard by civil and religious law.'

'Quite rightly.'

'But when our men and women get past the age for breeding, then we can leave them free to mate as they please, provided that no man mates with his daughter or granddaughter, or with his mother or any of her forbears, and no woman with her son or father or their descendants or forbears. But we shall order them to make every effort to prevent any child conceived in these unions from being born, and if they fail to prevent its birth, to dispose of it as a creature that must not be reared.'[1]

'That is all quite reasonable. But how,' he asked, 'can they know which are fathers and daughters, as you require?'

'They can't,' I answered. 'But a man will call all males and females born in the tenth or the seventh month[2] after he has been a bridegroom sons and daughters, and they will call him father; he will call their children grandchildren, and they will in turn call his marriage-group grandfathers and grandmothers, while all who are born during the period when their mothers and fathers were producing children will call each others brothers and sisters. This will enable them to observe the prohibitions we mentioned. There will be no rule to pre-

1. i.e. the alternatives are abortion (not uncommon in the ancient world) or infanticide.

2. 'The majority of ancient writers ... denied that children were born in the eighth month of pregnancy' (Adam). Plato's months here are, of course, lunar months.

vent brothers and sisters cohabiting, if the lot so falls out and Delphi approves.'[1]

'I quite agree.'

'Well, that completes the description of the sort of community of women and children there will be in your state, Glaucon. And our next business,' I went on, 'is, I take it, to argue that it fits into our general plan and is indeed much the best arrangement.'

462

1. The details of this sentence are a little difficult to disentangle. Plato is dealing with the unions of the over-age; but the rules he lays down for them will, *a fortiori*, apply to the Guardians generally, and the last sentence has this wider application.

He first explains what is meant by father, mother, son, daughter, etc., under his system. What he does is to substitute relationships between *groups* for those between individuals; the basic group comprises all those mated at a particular marriage festival, who will be related collectively as fathers and mothers to all children born as a result of that festival. (We must suppose these festivals to take place at regular intervals, say annually or biennially, and to last for a definite time, say a week or fortnight.) Other relationships are worked out on the same principle and Plato adds, for completeness, a definition of brother and sister. Granted these definitions, it should, as he points out, be easy enough to avoid the relationships he wishes to prevent.

It will be noticed that it is the father-daughter, son-mother type of relationship which he forbids. It was this type of incest about which the Greeks felt particularly strongly. Brother-sister unions were, they knew, practised in Egypt, and their own custom allowed marriage between uncle and niece, aunt and nephew, and half-brother and half-sister. In the last sentence, as the reference to the lot makes clear, Plato is thinking of his marriage festivals, and 'brother' and 'sister' are probably used primarily in his special sense. It would, indeed, restrict the possibilities of mating unduly if brothers and sisters in that sense could not marry – parents are producing children for thirty (men) and twenty (women) years. But he has not precluded unions between brother and sister in the normal sense, and here probably allows them as a special case of brother and sister in his own sense. Children of the same parents would not, in his state, know that they were blood relations, as he has explained above, and such relationship would in any event, under his scheme, have no significance. The reference to Delphi has no special importance. The sanction of Delphi is needed because marriage is a religious institution; it might be asked 'once for all to approve the whole scheme of marriage laws, or it might be formally invoked at each festival' (Cornford, p. 159).

'Yes, certainly.'

'The best way to set about that will be to ask ourselves what we regard as the greatest social good, the objective of the law-giver's activity, and what as the greatest social evil; and then to consider whether the proposals we have just outlined are leading us towards the good and away from the evil.'

'Yes, that is the way.'

'Is there anything worse for a state than to be split and dis-united? or anything better than cohesion and unity?'

'No.'

'And is not cohesion the result of the common feeling you get when all members of a society are glad or sorry at the same successes and failures?'

'Certainly.'

'But cohesion is dissolved when feelings differ between indi-viduals, and the same events, whether of public or private con-cern, delight some and dismay others.'

'Of course.'

'And doesn't this happen when people no longer agree in their use of the words "mine" and "not mine", "somebody else's" and "not somebody else's"?'

'That is very true.'

'So the best-run state is one in which as many people as pos-sible use the words "mine" and "not mine" in the same sense of the same things. What is more, such a state most nearly re-sembles an individual. For example, when one of us hurts his finger, the sensation is transmitted to our central conscious-ness in such a way that the whole organism is aware of the pain suffered in a part of it, and so we say that the man in ques-tion has a pain in *his* finger. And the same is true of pain or pleasure a man feels in any other part of himself.'

'Yes,' he agreed, 'and, as you said, the same thing is most nearly true of the best-run communities.'

'That is because such a community will regard the indi-vidual who experiences gain or loss as a part of itself, and be glad or sorry as a whole accordingly.'

'That's bound to be so in a good society.'

'It's time for us to return to our own state and see whether it has these features we've agreed on, or whether we must look elsewhere for them.'

'Let us do so.'

463 'Well, our state, like others, contains both rulers and common people, all of whom will call each other fellow-citizens.'

'True.'

'And in states other than our own, what do the common people call their rulers, in addition to calling them fellow-citizens?'

'In most states they call them masters[1]; in a democracy they call them simply the government.'

'But what will the common people say the rulers in our state are besides fellow-citizens?'

'Protectors and defenders.'

'And what will the rulers say about the common people?'

'That they provide their livelihood.'

'And what do the rulers in other states call the common people?'

'Slaves.'

'And what do they call each other?'

'Fellow-rulers.'

'And in our state?'

'Fellow-Guardians.'

'And in other states, is there not a certain friendship and community of interest between some of the rulers, and not between others?'

'There certainly is.'

'And don't they regard themselves as sharing the interests of their friends, but not those of other people?'

'Yes.'

'And what about our Guardians? Could any of them seriously say he had nothing to do with his fellows?'

'Certainly not,' he replied. 'For he's bound to regard any of them he meets as related to him, as brother or sister, father or mother, son or daughter, grandparent or grandchild.'

'You are quite right. And here is a further point. They won't

---

1. Perhaps 'bosses'. The Greek word is the normal one for a master of slaves or an employer of labour.

be allowed to treat these relationships as merely nominal, but will be required to behave accordingly. They will be expected to show their fathers all the customary honour, love and obedience; any other behaviour will be considered a sin and a crime and subject both to divine and human disapproval. Isn't this the sort of thing you'll expect your citizens to din into the ears of the children about their conduct towards those they are to call their fathers and other relations?'

'Yes. It would be absurd for them merely to use the words without acting accordingly.'

'In our society of all societies, then, the citizens will agree in their use of that phrase we were talking about just now, and will refer to the successes and misfortunes of their fellows as *their own*. And didn't we say that this way of talking and think- 464 ing led to common feeling?'

'Yes, quite rightly.'

'Our citizens, then, are devoted to a common interest, which they call *their own*; and in consequence entirely share each other's feelings of joy and sorrow.'

'Yes.'

'And the element in our constitution to which this is due is the community of women and children in the Guardian Class.'

'Yes, that is the chief reason for it.'

'But we agreed that this unanimity was the greatest good a society can enjoy – we compared, you remember, a well-run society to the human body, in which the whole is aware of the feelings of the part. And so we may say that the community of women and children among its protectors confers the greatest of all benefits on our state.'

'Yes, we may.'

'And what is more, we are being quite consistent, because we said earlier that our Guardians, if they were to do their job properly, should have no houses or land or any other possessions of their own, but get their daily bread from others in payment for their services, and consume it together in common.'

'Yes, we said that.'

'Then don't you agree that, as I say, these last arrangements will make them even better Guardians than before? They will prevent the dissension that starts when different people call different things their own, carting off to their private houses anything they can lay hands on for themselves, and when each has his own wife and children, and his own private joys and sorrows; for our citizens, whose interests are identical and whose efforts are all directed towards the same end, feel almost all their joys and sorrows together.'

'Yes, I entirely agree.'

'And besides, since they have no private property except their own persons, won't litigation virtually disappear? There won't in fact be any of the quarrels which are caused by having money or children or family.'

'They will inevitably be rid of all that sort of thing.'

'And there will be no justification for actions for violence and assault; for we shall decree that it is both right and lawful for one man to defend himself against another of the same age. This will make them keep themselves fit, and have the additional advantage that if one man is angry with another, he can take it out of him on the spot, and will be less likely to pursue the quarrel further.'

'True enough.'

'But we shall lay it down that older men are to have authority over all younger men, and power to punish them; and that, as is only right, no younger man shall attempt to do violence to or strike his elders, unless ordered to do so by the Rulers. Indeed I don't think that the young will behave badly to their elders in any way, because they will be prevented by fear and respect. Respect will stop them laying hands on their parents, and they will fear the assistance the victim would get from his sons and brothers and parents.'

'Yes, that follows.'

'Our laws in fact will mean that the Guardians will live at peace with each other; and if they don't quarrel among themselves, there will be no danger of rebellion or faction in the rest of the community.'

'None whatever.'

'There are other minor evils they will get rid of, which are really so insignificant that I hesitate to mention them. The poor won't have to flatter the rich, and there will be none of the difficulties and anxieties of raising a family and earning what is necessary to feed a household of servants – borrowing, not paying one's debts, and scraping enough together somehow for one's wife and servants to spend. All these vexations are, I think you will agree, too obvious and too sordid to be worth talking about.'

'They're painfully obvious.'

'Well, they will be rid of them all, and will lead a far more enviable life than any Olympic victor.'

'How?'

'They will have far more to make them happy. Their success is more worth while, and their material rewards are greater. Their success brings security to the whole community, and their reward is that they and their children are maintained and have all their needs supplied at public cost, that they are held in universal honour while they live, and given a worthy burial when they die.'

'These are indeed great rewards.'

'And yet do you remember,' I asked, 'how earlier on someone or other objected that we weren't making our Guardians happy, because they were to have nothing of their own in spite of being in control of everything? And you will remember that we answered that we would return to the question later, if convenient; but that for the moment we were concerned to define the Guardians' duties and to ensure the happiness of the community as a whole and not of any particular section of it.'

466

'Yes, I remember.'

'Well, if the life our Guardians are to lead is better and more splendid than an Olympic victor's, we can't really compare it with a cobbler's or farmer's or any other manual worker's.'

'I should think not.'

'None the less, let me repeat again what I said then: if any Guardian looks for happiness in a way unworthy of his status, if he tires of the restraint and security of the ideal life we have drawn for him, and is misled by some extravagant idea of happiness into using his power to appropriate the community's wealth – well, he will learn the wisdom of Hesiods' saying that the half is more than the whole.' [1]

'My advice to him would be to stick to his own way of life.'

'Do you agree, then, that the best arrangement is for our men and women to share a common education, to bring up their children in common and to have a common responsibility, as Guardians, for their fellow-citizens, as we have described? That women should in fact, so far as possible, take part in all the same occupations as men, in peace and in war, watching and hunting with them like watchdogs, and that there is nothing unwomanly in this natural partnership of the sexes?'

'I agree,' he said.

§3. THE RULES OF WAR

Socrates has promised to show next that his proposals are not only desirable but possible. But he digresses to discuss the conduct of war. He deals first with military rewards and punishments, and then with the rules of warfare and treatment of enemies. He deprecates war between Greek States and lays down rules to regulate and humanize it. He clearly regards war as a permanent feature of human affairs; but, equally clearly, he hopes for a measure of Greek unity.

'It remains, then,' I said, 'to decide whether and how this sharing of functions is possible among human beings, as it is among animals.'

'You've taken the words out of my mouth,' he replied.

'I suppose the arrangements they will make for the conduct of war are fairly obvious?' I asked.

'What will they be?' he said.

'Men and women will serve together, and take the children to war with them when they are old enough, to let them see, as
467 they do in other trades, the job they will have to do when they grow up. And besides seeing what goes on, they will fetch and carry and make themselves useful to their mothers and fathers

1. Proverbial, of making the best of what you have.

during the campaign. Haven't you noticed how, in a trade like the potters', children serve a long apprenticeship, watching how things are done, before they take a hand in the work themselves?'

'Yes, I have.'

'Oughtn't the Guardians to take just as much care, when they are training their children, to let them see what their duties are and get used to them?'

'It would be absurd if they didn't.'

'And besides, any animal fights better in the presence of its young.'

'That's true. But isn't there a considerable risk, Socrates, that if they are defeated, as may well happen in war, their children will be killed as well as themselves, and the country be unable to recover?'

'That's perfectly true,' I replied. 'But in the first place do you think they should avoid risks altogether?'

'No.'

'Then, if they are to take risks, ought they not to do so when they will really profit from success?'

'Obviously.'

'But won't it make all the difference to children who are to be fighting men when they grow up if they see something of war when they are young? Isn't it a risk worth taking?'

'Yes, well worth it.'

'We must therefore make it possible for our children to be spectators of war, but arrange for their safety, and all will be well.'

'Yes.'

'Then, to begin with, their fathers will be as knowledgeable as men can be in these matters, and be able to tell whether a campaign is dangerous or not, and avoid taking them on it if it is.'

'Good.'

'And they will be put in charge of really trustworthy officers, who are qualified both by age and experience to be in charge as their leaders.'

'That is as it should be.'

'Yes, but things often turn out very differently from what we expect, and I think we ought to give our children wings as an additional precaution, so that they can fly away if necessary.'

'What do you mean?' he asked.

'I mean that we must put them on horseback as young as possible, and when they have learnt to ride take them to see the fighting, on horses that aren't too spirited or fiery, but fast and easy to manage. Then they will get the best view of what goes on and be able to follow their more experienced leaders to safety quite easily, if need be.'

'That seems to me a good arrangement.'

468 ' Then what about the actual fighting? What treatment will your soldiers expect for themselves or give their enemies? I wonder if I'm right about that.'

'Tell us what you think.'

'I think that any of them who deserts or runs away or shows any other signs of cowardice should be relegated to the artisans or farmers; and any of them taken prisoner should be abandoned to his captors to deal with as they wish.'

'I entirely agree.'

'Then what about anyone who has distinguished himself for bravery? Do you agree that he should first be duly crowned in the campaign by all the young men, women and children?'

'Yes.'

'And that they should shake his hand?'

'I agree again.'

'But I'm afraid you won't agree to what I'm going to say next.'

'What is it?'

'That he should exchange kisses with them.'

'I think it's the best idea of all,' said Glaucon. 'And what is more, I should add to your law a clause that would forbid anyone to refuse his kisses for the rest of the campaign, as an encouragement to those in love with a boy or girl to be all the keener to win an award for bravery.'

'A very good clause,' I said. 'For we have already said that the better citizens are to be chosen more often for marriage than others, so that they may have correspondingly more children.'

'So we said.'

'And we have Homer's authority for honouring bravery in the young. For he tells how, when Ajax had distinguished himself in battle, he was "paid the honour" of a helping from the "long chine of the beast",[1] as if it were a suitable honour for a brave man in his prime, both a compliment and something to keep up his strength.'

'And how right Homer was.'

'Then we will follow his advice, this time at any rate. At sacrifices and similar occasions we will reward bravery, according to its degree, not only with song and the other privileges we mentioned, but "with the best seat at the table, the first cut off the joint, and a never empty cup." [2] In this way we shall honour the bravery of our men and women and improve their physique.'

'An excellent suggestion.'

'Good. And then those who die bravely on active service we shall reckon as men of gold –'

'Most certainly.'

'– and believe with Hesiod that when they die they "become 469 holy, Guardian Spirits on earth, protectors to shield mortal men from harm."' [3]

'Yes.'

'And we shall bury them with whatever particular ceremonies Delphi prescribes for men of such heroic mould, and for the rest of time treat their tombs with reverence and worship them as Guardian Spirits.[4] And we shall pay the same honour to all those who are judged to have lived a life of special distinction and who die of old age or otherwise.'

'Very right.'

'And how will our soldiers treat their enemies? First, over

1. *Iliad*, VII, 321.
2. *Iliad*, VIII, 162.
3. Cf. Hesiod, *Works and Days*, 122.
4. The Greek 'daimon' was a spirit intermediate between gods and men.

slavery. Do you think it is right for Greeks to sell Greeks into slavery, or to allow others to do so, so far as they can prevent it? Ought they not rather to make it their custom to spare their fellows, for fear of falling under barbarian domination?'

'It would be infinitely better to spare them.'

'There will then be no Greek slave in our state, and it will advise other Greek states to follow suit.'

'Certainly. That would encourage them to let each other alone and turn against the barbarian.'

'Then is it a good thing to strip the dead, after a victory, of anything but their arms? It gives the cowards an excuse not to pursue the enemy who are still capable of fight, if they can pretend they are doing their duty by poking about among the dead. Indeed, many an army has been lost before now by this habit of plunder. And don't you think there's something low and mean about plundering a corpse, and a kind of feminine small-mindedness in treating the body as an enemy when the fighting spirit which fought in it has flown? It's rather like the dog's habit of snarling at the stones thrown at it, but keeping clear of the person who's throwing them.'

'Yes, it's very like that.'

'So we'll have no stripping of corpses and no refusal to allow burial.'[1]

'I entirely agree,' he said.

'Nor shall we dedicate the arms of our enemies in our temples, particularly if they are the arms of fellow-Greeks and we have any feeling of loyalty towards them. On the contrary, we shall be afraid that we should desecrate a temple by offering them the arms of our own people, unless indeed Apollo rules otherwise.'

'Quite right.'

'Then what about devastating the lands and burning the houses of Greek enemies? What will your soldiers do about that?'

'I'd like to know what you think about it.'

1. Greek custom allowed the recovery and burial of his dead by an enemy after a battle.

'I don't think they ought to do either, but confine themselves to carrying off the year's harvest. Shall I tell you why?'

'Yes.'

'I think that the two words "war" and "civil strife" refer to two different realities. They are used of disputes which arise in two different spheres, the one internal and domestic, the other external and foreign; and we call a domestic quarrel "civil strife", and an external one "war".'

'Quite a suitable definition.'

'Then do you think it equally suitable if I say that all relations between Greek and Greek are internal and domestic, and all relations between Greek and barbarian foreign and external?'

'Yes.'

'Then when Greek fights barbarian or barbarian Greek we shall say they are at war and are natural enemies, and that their quarrel is properly called a "war"; but when Greek fights Greek we shall say that they are naturally friends, but that Greece is torn by faction, and that the quarrel should be called "civil strife".'

'I agree with your view.'

'Consider, then,' I went on, 'what happens in civil strife in its normal sense, that is to say, when there is civil war in a single state. If the two sides ravage each other's land and burn each other's houses, we think it an outrage, and regard two parties who dare to lay waste the country which bore and bred them as lacking in all patriotism. But we think it reasonable, if the victors merely carry off their opponents' crops and remember that they can't go on fighting for ever but must come to terms some time.'

'Yes, because the last frame of mind is the more civilized.'

'Well, then,' I said, 'your city will be Greek, won't it?'

'It must be.'

'And its people brave and civilized?'

'Certainly.'

'Then they will love their fellow-Greeks, and think of Greece as their own land, in whose common religion they share.'

'Yes, certainly.'

471   'And any quarrel with Greeks they will regard as civil strife, because it is with their own people, and so won't call it "war".'

'That's true.'

'They will fight in the hope of coming to terms. And their object will be to correct a friend and bring him to his senses, rather than to enslave and destroy an enemy. It follows that they will not, as Greeks, devastate Greek lands or burn Greek dwellings; nor will they admit that the whole people of a state – men, women, and children – are their enemies, but only the minority who are responsible for the quarrel. They will not therefore devastate the land or destroy the houses of the friendly majority, but press their quarrel only until the guilty minority are brought to justice by the innocent victims.'

'For myself,' he said, 'I agree that our citizens ought to behave in this way to their enemies; though when they are fighting barbarians they should treat them as the Greeks now treat each other.'

'Then let us lay it down as a law for our Guardians, that they are neither to ravage land nor burn houses.'

'We will do so,' he agreed; 'it is a good rule, like all our others.'

PART SEVEN

THE PHILOSOPHER RULER

*

§1. THE IDEAL AND THE REAL

Socrates is again reminded of his promise to demonstrate the practicability of his State. He starts by distinguishing Ideal and Real, and maintaining that even if the ideal he has sketched cannot be realized in every detail, it has still been worth describing as a standard to aim at. He then goes on to assert that the only hope of realizing it, even imperfectly, is for political power to be put in the hands of 'philosophers'.

'BUT it seems to me, Socrates, that if we let you go on like this you will forget all about your promise to prove that the state we have described is a practical possibility, and if so how; all you've just been saying has merely been putting the question off. I'll admit that your state would be ideal if it existed, and I'll fill in the gaps in your description myself. I know that the mutual loyalty the citizens would feel because they know they can call each other brothers, fathers, and sons, would make them most formidable enemies; and that the presence of their women on campaign, whether they fought with them or acted as a reserve, would make them altogether invincible, because of the panic it would cause in their enemies and the support it would give in case of need; and I can see how many domestic advantages they would have. I grant all this, and a thousand other things too, *if* our state existed, and I don't want to hear any more details. Let us now concentrate on the job of proving *that* it can exist and *how* it can exist.'

'This is a very sudden attack,' I countered, 'and you've no sympathy with my delays. I've just escaped two waves; but the third, which you are trying to bring on me now, is the biggest and the most difficult of the three, though you may not know it. When you have seen and heard it, you will forgive me for the very natural hesitation which made me afraid to put forward and examine such a paradoxical theory.'

'The more of these excuses we hear,' he replied, 'the less likely we are to let you off explaining how our state can be realized. Get on and don't waste time.'

'Well,' I said, 'perhaps I ought to remind you first of all that we started our discussion by trying to find a definition of justice and injustice.'

'Yes – what of it?' he asked.

'I was only going to ask whether, when we find out what justice is, we shall require the just man to answer the description exactly, without any modification? Or shall we be content if he approximates to it pretty closely and has more of it about him than other men?'

'That will content us.'

'Then we were looking for an ideal when we tried to define justice and injustice, and to describe what the perfectly just or perfectly unjust man would be like if he ever existed. By looking at these perfect patterns and the measure of happiness or unhappiness they would enjoy, we force ourselves to admit that the nearer we approximate to them the more nearly we share their lot. That was our purpose, rather than to show that they could be realized in practice, was it not?'

'That is quite true.'

'If a painter, then, draws an idealized picture of a man, complete to the last detail, is he any the worse painter because he cannot point to a real original?'

'No, certainly not.'

'But haven't we been painting a word-picture of an ideal state?'

'True.'

'Is our picture any the worse drawn, then, because we can't show how it can be realized in fact?'

'No.'

'That, then, is the truth of the matter. But if I'm to go on, to oblige you, and show how and under what conditions we can get nearest our ideal, you must admit that the same principles apply.'

'What principles?'

473 'Does practice ever square with theory? Is it not in the na-

ture of things that, whatever people think, practice should fall short of the precision of theory? What do you think?'

'I agree.'

'Then don't insist on my showing that every detail of our description can be realized in practice, but grant that we shall have met your demand that the ideal should be realized, if we are able to find the conditions under which a state can approximate most closely to it. Will you be content with that? I would.'

'And so will I.'

'The next thing, I suppose, is to try to show what fault it is in the constitutions of existing states that prevents them from being run like ours, and what is the least change that would bring them into conformity with it – a single change if possible, failing that two, or as few and as small as may be.'

'Certainly.'

'I think we can show that the necessary transformation can be effected by a single change,' I said, 'but it's hardly a small or easy one, though it is possible.'

'Tell us what it is.'

'I'm now facing what we called the biggest wave,' I replied. 'I'll tell you what it is, even if it swamps me in a surge of laughter and I'm drowned in ridicule; so listen to what I'm going to say.'

'Go on.'

'The society we have described can never grow into a reality or see the light of day, and there will be no end to the troubles of states, or indeed, my dear Glaucon, of humanity itself, till philosophers become kings in this world, or till those we now call kings and rulers really and truly become philosophers, and political power and philosophy thus come into the same hands, while the many natures now content to follow either to the exclusion of the other are forcibly debarred from doing so. This is what I have hesitated to say so long, knowing what a paradox it would sound; for it is not easy to see that there is no other road to happiness, either for society or the individual.'

Glaucon's reply to this was to exclaim, 'My dear Socrates, if you produce theories of that sort, you can't be surprised if 474 most decent people take their coats off, pick up the nearest weapon, and come after you in their shirt sleeves to do something terrible to you. If you can't find an argument to hold them off and escape, you'll learn to your cost what it is to be laughed at.'

'But it's all your doing,' said I.

'And I've done very well too,' he retorted. 'But I won't desert you, and will give you what help I can, though it won't amount to more than encouragement, and perhaps a willingness to answer your questions more reasonably than others would. So you must try to convince the sceptics with that amount of help.'

'You're such a powerful ally that I will go ahead,' I replied.

§2. DEFINITION OF THE PHILOSOPHER

The word 'philosopher' was by no means unambiguous in Greek, and Plato proceeds to define what he means by it and to explain the qualities of character he demands in his true philosopher. The philosopher is, briefly, the man who has a passion for the truth. To explain this Plato has to bring in his own philosophic beliefs. For him there are two orders of reality. There is the world of every-day experience, of becoming and change, of visible and sensible things; and there is the unchangeable eternal world, the world of the Platonic 'Forms',[1] apprehended by the intellect, not the senses. The first of these two worlds is in some sense an image or shadow of the other, which contains the patterns which it imperfectly imitates. The first world is the object of what Plato calls doxa, *opinion or belief; it can never be* known *because the object of* knowledge *is the eternal unchanging world of Forms. The Forms are 'absolutes', or 'essential realities', like Goodness or Beauty or Triangularity, which Plato supposes to have an independent existence of their own. The two following quotations may help the modern reader to understand this basic philosophical belief, which is constantly assumed throughout the remainder of Book V and Books VI and VII. The first is from Cornford.[2] After saying that the Forms are objects of knowledge, he goes on, 'in this respect the Forms resemble the laws of nature*

---

1. The older translation, 'Ideas', is now commonly avoided because it suggests things 'in our minds'.

2. *Op. cit.*, p. 176.

sought by modern natural science: a law is an unseen intelligible principle, a unity underlying an unlimited multiplicity of similar phenomena, and supposed to be unalterable. The Forms, however, are not laws of the sequence or co-existence of phenomena, but ideals or patterns, which have a real existence independent of our minds and of which the many individual things called by their names in the world of appearances are like images or reflections.' The second is from Bertrand Russell[1]: 'The way the problem arose for Plato was more or less as follows. Let us consider, say, such a notion as justice. *If we ask ourselves what justice is, it is natural to proceed by considering this, that, and the other just act, with a view to discovering what they have in common. They must all, in some sense, partake of a common nature, which will be found in whatever is just and in nothing else. This common nature, in virtue of which they are all just, will be justice itself, the pure essence the admixture of which with facts of ordinary life produces the multiplicity of just acts. Similarly with any other word which may be applicable to common facts, such as "whiteness", for example. The word will be applicable to a number of particular things because they all participate in a common nature or essence. This pure essence is what Plato calls an "idea" or "form". (It must not be supposed that "ideas" in his sense exist in minds, though they may be apprehended by minds.) The "idea" justice is not identical with anything that is just: it is something other than particular things, which particular things partake of. Not being particular, it cannot itself exist in the world of sense. Moreover, it is not fleeting or changeable like the things of sense: it is eternally itself, immutable and indestructible.*

'Thus Plato is led to a supra-sensible world, more real than the common world of sense, the unchangeable world of ideas, which alone gives to the world of sense whatever pale reflection of reality may belong to it. The truly real world, for Plato, is the world of ideas; for whatever we may attempt to say about things in the world of sense, we can only succeed in saying that they participate in such and such ideas, which, therefore, constitute all their character. Hence it is easy to pass on into a mysticism. We may hope, in a mystic illumination, to see the ideas as we see objects of sense; and we may imagine that the ideas exist in heaven. These mystical developments are very natural, but the basis of the theory is in logic.'

1. *Problems of Philosophy*, p. 143.

1. *The Philosopher and the two Orders of Reality*

The philosopher is in love with truth, that is, not with the changing world of sensation, which is the object of opinion, but with the unchanging reality which is the object of knowledge. In the latter part of this section the argument centres round the Greek word εἶναι *('to be'), which can be used to denote existence, reality, or truth, with consequent ambiguities with which Plato's contemporaries and predecessors were much occupied.*

'If we are to escape the attack with which you threaten us, we must define these philosophers whom we have claimed should be rulers. When that is clear we shall be able to defend ourselves by showing that there are some who are naturally fitted for philosophy and political leadership, while the rest should follow their lead and let philosophy alone.'

'It's time for a definition,' he said.

'Then follow my lead,' I replied, 'and we will see if we can reach a satisfactory explanation somehow or other.'

'Lead on.'

'Well, I hardly need to remind you,' said I, 'that if a man can be properly said to love something, it is the whole he loves and not merely parts of it.'

'I'm afraid I do need reminding,' he replied, 'because I don't understand.'

'I hardly expected that answer from you, Glaucon,' I replied; 'anyone as susceptible as you should surely know that those of your temperament are always getting bitten with a passion for some boy in the bloom of youth, who absorbs all their attention and affection. You know how it is. You praise a snub nose by calling it charming, a Roman nose you call commanding, and one between the two just right; a dark complexion is manly, a fair one angelic. And who do you think invented the description 'honey-pale' but some lover making fond excuses for pallor on the cheek of youth? In fact there's no excuse you won't make and nothing you won't say to defend youth at its flower.'

'If you insist on attributing all the habits of lovers to me, I'll agree for the sake of argument.'

'Oh come,' I said, 'it's just the same with people who are fond of wine. Haven't you noticed how with them any excuse is good enough for any kind of drink?'

'Yes indeed.'

'And I expect you've noticed too how ambitious people, if they can't get command of any army, will take a battalion, and if the more important people don't look up to them, are content if the smaller fry do, so keen are they on having prestige of some sort.'

'That's very true.'

'Then tell me this – when we say someone has a passion for something or other, don't we mean that he wants everything of that particular kind, and not some things only?'

'Yes.'

'And so a philosopher's passion is for wisdom of every kind without distinction?'

'True.'

'Then we shan't regard anyone as fond of knowledge or wisdom who is fussy about what he studies, especially if he is young and has not yet got the judgement to know what is good for him and what is not. Just as we don't say that anyone who is fussy about his food has a good appetite or a passion for eating, but call him a poor eater.'

'And we shall be quite right.'

'But the man who is ready to taste every form of knowledge, is glad to learn and never satisfied – he's the man who deserves to be called a philosopher, isn't he?'

'Your philosophers will be an odd crowd, then,' was Glaucon's reply to this. 'For theatre-fans and music-lovers are anxious enough to learn, and so fall under your description; but they're an odd crew to class as philosophers, because nothing would induce them to spend time on rational argument. They run round the city and country Dionysia, never missing a festival, as if they were under contract to listen to every performance. Shan't we have to call all those who share their enthusiasm, or are devotees of the minor arts, philosophers?'

'Certainly not, though there is some resemblance.'

'Then who are the true philosophers?' he asked.

'Those whose passion is to see the truth.'

'That is clearly right; but what does it mean?'

'It would be difficult to explain to everyone; but you, I think, will agree with me on the following point.'

'What point?'

'That, since beauty and ugliness are opposites, they are two 476 things, each of the pair being a single thing.'

'Yes.'

'The same is true of justice and injustice, good and evil, and all formal characteristics; each is a single thing in itself, but each appears as a multiplicity because it is seen in combination with actions and material objects and other characteristics.'

'That is true.'

'I use this principle to distinguish your theatre-lovers and art-lovers and practical men from the philosophers in the true sense, who are the subject of our discussion.'

'And how do you do it?'

'The music-lovers and theatre-lovers are delighted by the beauty of sound and colour and form, and the works of art which make use of them, but their minds are incapable of seeing and delighting in the essential nature of beauty itself.'

'That is certainly so,' he agreed.

'And those who can reach absolute Beauty and see it as it is in itself are likely to be few.'

'Very few indeed.'

'Then what about the man who recognizes the existence of beautiful things, but does not believe in absolute Beauty, and is incapable of following anyone who wants to lead him to a knowledge of it? Is he awake, or merely dreaming? Look; by dreaming don't we simply mean the confusion between image and the reality of which it is an image, whether the dreamer be asleep or awake?'

'I should certainly say that a man in that state of mind was dreaming.'

'Then what about the man in the opposite state of mind, who believes in absolute Beauty and can see both it and the particular things which share its character, and does not confuse the particular thing and universal character? Do you think he is awake or dreaming?'

'He is very much awake.'

'So we might say that, because he knows, his state of mind is one of knowledge; whereas the other man, who believes only, is in a state of belief.'

'Certainly.'

'And if the man whom we say believes but does not know is annoyed, and objects to our statement, can we soothe him and win him over gently, without letting him know the extent of his disease?'

'We must if we can.'

'Let's think what to say to him. Shall we tell him that we don't in the least grudge him any knowledge he has, and are indeed delighted he has it; and then go on to ask him if he will answer this question, "Does a man who knows, know something or nothing?"? You answer for him.'

'I shall answer that he knows something.'

'Something existent or non-existent?'

'Something existent; how could something that didn't exist 477
be known?'

'Then are we satisfied that, whichever way we look at it, the fully existent is fully knowable, and the completely non-existent entirely unknowable?'

'Quite satisfied.'

'Good. Then if there were anything whose nature was such that it was both existent and non-existent, would it not lie between the fully existent and completely non-existent?'

'Yes.'

'Then since the object of knowledge is existent, and the object of ignorance, necessarily, non-existent, we shall have to see if there is something between knowledge and ignorance to correspond to this intermediate reality.'

'Yes.'

'Isn't there something we call belief?'

'Of course.'

'Is its function the same as that of knowledge or different?'

'Different.'

'So belief and knowledge must have different objects corresponding to their different functions.'

'They must.'

'Then the object of knowledge is what exists, whose reality it is its function to know. – But there's a definition I think I should make before I go on.'

'What is it?'

'Let us class together as "faculties" the powers in us and in other things that enable us to perform our various functions. Thus I call sight and hearing faculties – do you understand the class I mean?'

'Yes, I understand.'

'Then let me tell you what I think about them. A faculty has neither colour, nor shape, nor any of the similar qualities which enable me to distinguish other things one from another; I can only identify a faculty by its object and its function, and say that one faculty has one object and function, and another faculty another. What about you? What do you do?'

'The same as you.'

'Let us go back, then,' I said. 'Tell me, do you think knowledge is a faculty? Could you classify it otherwise?'

'No; it is the most powerful of all faculties.'

'And should belief be classified as a faculty?'

'Yes; it is the power which enables us to believe.'

'But a little while ago you agreed that knowledge and belief were different.'

'Yes,' he replied, 'because no reasonable person would identify the infallible with the fallible.'

'Splendid,' I said; 'we are clearly agreed that opinion and knowledge are different.'

'We are.'

'Each therefore has a different object and a different function.'

'That follows.'

'The object of knowledge is what exists and its function to know about reality.'

'Yes.'

'But the function of belief is to believe, didn't we say?'

'Yes.'

'Is its object the same as the object of knowledge? And are the fields of knowledge and belief the same? Or is that impossible?'

'It's impossible on the principles we've agreed. If different faculties have different objects, and belief and knowledge are two separate faculties, as we maintain, then it follows that the fields of knowledge and belief must be different.'

'Then if the field of knowledge is what exists, the field of belief must be something other than what exists.'

'Yes.'

'Is it the non-existent? or is it impossible even to believe what does not exist? Consider. Belief is surely directed to something. Or is it possible to believe and yet believe in nothing?'

'No, that's impossible.'

'So a man who believes, believes something.'

'Yes.'

'But what does not exist can hardly be called something – it is, properly speaking, nothing.'

'True.'

'Now, we correlated ignorance with the non-existent, knowledge with the existent.'

'Quite right.'

'So belief must be correlated with neither?'

'Agreed.'

'So belief is neither ignorance nor knowledge.'

'So it seems.'

'Then does it lie beyond them? Is it clearer than knowledge or less clear than ignorance?'

'No.'

'Then in that case,' I asked, 'do you think it is obscurer than knowledge, but clearer than ignorance?'

'Very much so.'

'Does it lie between the two?'

'Yes.'

'Belief is in fact an intermediate state.'

'Certainly.'

'Now we said before that if it appeared that there was anything that was both existent and non-existent, this would lie between pure existence and complete non-existence, and would be the object of neither knowledge nor ignorance, but of a faculty to be found between them.'

'True.'

'And we now see that what we call belief occupies that intermediate position.'

'That is so.'

'It remains for us to discover something that has the characteristics both of existence and non-existence, and cannot be said to have the characteristics of either without qualification; if we find it we can fairly say that it is the object of belief, thus correlating extremes to extremes and mean to mean. Do you agree?'

'Yes.'

'Having established these principles, I shall return to our 479 friend who denies that there is any absolute Beauty or any eternally unchanging Form of Beauty, but believes in the existence of many beautiful things, who loves visible beauty but but cannot bear to be told that Beauty is really one, and Justice one, and so on – I shall return to him and ask him, "Is there any of these many beautiful objects of yours that may not also seem ugly? or of your just and righteous acts that may not appear unjust and unrighteous?"'

'No,' replied Glaucon, 'they are all bound to seem in a sense both beautiful and ugly; and the same is true of the other characteristics in question.'

'And what about things which are double something else? If they are double one thing can't they be equally well regarded as half something else?'

'Yes.'

'And things which are large or heavy may equally well, from another point of view, be called small and light.'

'Yes; any such thing will in a sense have both characteristics.'

'Then can we say that such things *are*, any more than they *are not*, any of the many things we say they are?'

'They are ambiguous like the puzzles you hear at parties,' he replied, 'or the children's riddle about the eunuch hitting the bat and what he threw at it and what it was sitting on.[1] They are neither one thing nor the other, and one can't think of them either as being or as not being, or as both, or as neither.'

'Can you think of anything better to do with them, then, than place them between existence and non-existence? They are not so obscure as to be less real than non-existence, or so luminously clear as to be more real than existence.'

'True.'

'Our conclusion, therefore, it seems, is that conventional opinions about beauty and similar terms hover somewhere between the realms of non-existence and full existence.'

'Yes.'

'And we agreed that, if it appeared that there was any such realm of reality, it should be called the object of belief and not of knowledge; the fluctuating intermediate realm being apprehended by the intermediate faculty.'

'Yes, we did.'

'Those, then, who are able to see visible beauty – or justice or the like – in their many manifestations, but are incapable, even with another's help, of reaching absolute Beauty, may be said to *believe,* but cannot be said to *know* what they believe.'

'That follows.'

'And what about those who see the eternal, unchanging absolute realities? They surely have knowledge and not opinion.'

'That follows too.'

'And they set their hearts on the objects of knowledge, while those of the other type are set on the objects of belief – for, as you will remember, we said that their eyes and hearts were 480 fixed on the beauty of sound and colour and so on, and that they could not bear the suggestion that there was such a thing as absolute Beauty.'

'Yes, I remember.'

1. A man who was not a man (a eunuch) threw a stone that was not a stone (a pumice-stone) at a bird that was not a bird (a bat) sitting on a twig that was not a twig (a reed).

'We shan't be far wrong, therefore, to say that they love belief rather than knowledge. Do you think they will be very annoyed with us for saying so?'

'Not if they take my advice,' he replied; 'they ought not to be annoyed at the truth.'

'And those whose hearts are fixed on Reality itself deserve the title of Philosophers.'

'Yes, certainly.'

2. *The Qualities of Character required in the Philosopher*

The philosopher is shown to require, as philosopher, all the qualities that could be asked for in a good ruler.

BK
VI
484

'Well, Glaucon,' I said, 'we can now see, at last, what a philosopher is and what he is not, but we've had to go a long way round to find out.'

'I doubt if we could have done it more shortly,' he replied.

'I don't think we could. Though I think we could have managed better if it had been the only subject we were discussing, and we hadn't so much else to get through before we can see the difference between a good life and a bad.'

'Then where do we go from here?'

'The next question is this. If philosophers have the ability to grasp eternal and immutable truth, and those who are not philosophers are lost in multiplicity and change, which of the two should be in charge of a state?'

'What would be a reasonable line to take?' he asked.

'To say that we will choose as Guardians whichever of them seem able to maintain the laws and customs of society.'

'Right.'

'And isn't it obvious whether it's better for a blind man or a clear-sighted one to keep an eye on anything?'

'There's not much doubt about that,' he agreed.

'But surely "blind" is just how you would describe men who have no true knowledge of reality, and no clear standard in their mind to refer to, as a painter refers to his model, and which they can study closely before they start laying down rules about what is fair or right or good where they are needed, or maintaining, as Guardians, any rules that already exist.'

'Yes, blind is just about what they are.'

'Shall we make them Guardians, then? Or shall we prefer the philosophers, who know the truth, and have no less experience, and can rival them in all qualities of character?'

'It would be absurd not to choose the philosophers, if they are not inferior in all these other qualities; for in the vital quality of knowledge they are clearly superior.'

485

'Then oughtn't we to show how knowledge can be combined with these other qualities in the same person?'

'Yes.'

'As we said at the beginning of our discussion, the first thing is to find out what their natural character is. When we have agreed about that we shall, I think, be ready to agree that they can have those other qualities as well, and that they are the people to put in charge of society.'

'Explain.'

'One trait in the philosopher's character we can assume is his love of the knowledge that reveals eternal reality, the realm unaffected by change and decay. He is in love with the whole of that reality, and will not willingly be deprived even of the most insignificant fragment of it – just like the lovers and men of ambition we described earlier on.'[1]

'Yes, we can take that for granted.'

'Then if the philosopher is to be as we have described him must he not have a further characteristic?'

'What?'

'Truthfulness. He will never willingly tolerate an untruth, but will hate it as much as he loves truth.'

'That seems likely enough.'

'It's not only likely,' I replied, 'it is an absolutely necessary characteristic of the lover that he should be devoted to everything closely connected to the object of his affection.'

'True.'

'And is there anything more closely connected with wisdom than truth?'

1. P. 236–7 above.

'No.'

'So it's hardly possible to combine in the same character a love of wisdom and a love of falsehood.'

'Quite impossible.'

'So the man who has a real love of knowledge will aim at the whole truth from his earliest years.'

'Certainly.'

'And we know that if man's desires set strongly in one direction, they are correspondingly less strong in other directions, like a stream whose water has been diverted into other channels. So when the current of a man's desires flows towards knowledge and the like, his pleasure will be entirely in things of the mind, and physical pleasures will pass him by – that is if he is a genuine philosopher and not a sham.'

'That most certainly follows.'

'And he will be self-controlled and not grasping about money. Other people are more likely to worry about the things which make men so eager to get and spend money.'

486   'True.'

'And of course, when you are distinguishing the philosophic character, you must see it has no touch of meanness; pettiness of mind is quite incompatible with the attempt to grasp things divine or human as a whole and in their entirety.'

'Very true.'

'And if a man has greatness of mind and the breadth of vision to contemplate all time and all reality, can he regard human life as a thing of any great consequence?'

'No, he cannot.'

'So he won't think death anything to be afraid of.'

'No.'

'And so mean and cowardly natures can't really have any dealings with philosophy.'

'No, they can't.'

'And a good man, who is neither mean nor ungenerous nor boastful nor cowardly, can hardly be difficult to get on with or unjust.'

'Hardly.'

'So when you are looking for the your philosophic character

you will look to see whether it has been, from its early days, just and civilized or uncooperative and barbarous.'

'Certainly.'

'And you will also, I think, want to know whether it learns easily or not. For you can't expect anyone to like anything which he does with pain and trouble and little success.'

'No, you can't.'

'And can a man avoid being entirely without knowledge if he can't retain anything he's learnt, and has no memory at all? He will labour in vain and in the end be compelled to hate himself and the whole business of learning.'

'Inevitably.'

'So we can't include forgetfulness as a character that qualifies a man for philosophy; we must demand a good memory.'

'Yes, certainly.'

'Again, a nature that has no refinement or style will tend inevitably to lack a sense of proportion; and a sense of proportion is nearly related to truth.'

'Yes, it is.'

'So we want, in addition to everything else, a character with a grace and sense of proportion that will automatically lead it on to see the truth about things.'

'I agree.'

'Do you agree, then, that we have now been through a list of characteristics, which all go together, and which the mind must have if it is to grasp reality fully and completely?'

'Yes, it must certainly have them all.' 487

'Can you, then, possibly find fault with an occupation for the proper pursuit of which a man must combine in his nature good memory, readiness to learn, breadth of vision and versatility of mind, and be a friend of truth, justice, courage, and discipline?'

'Momus [1] himself could find no fault there.'

'Grant, then, education and maturity to round them off, and aren't they the only people to whom you would entrust your state?'

1. The god of criticism and mockery.

§3. THE PREJUDICE AGAINST PHILOSOPHY AND THE CORRUPTION OF THE PHILOSOPHIC NATURE IN CONTEMPORARY SOCIETY

Adeimantus objects that however well all this sounds in theory, in practice philosophers are either useless or dangerous. Socrates replies that the better type of philosopher is useless because contemporary democratic society has no use for him, and so he has no alternative but to stand aside from the corruption of political life; and that the philosophic character is only dangerous when corrupted. Besides, there are plenty of charlatans to take the place of the true philosopher, though they are no worse than the public they flatter.

Two things should be remembered in this section. First, Plato's distrust of democracy as he had seen it at Athens; there are few more vivid condemnations of democratic politicians than the simile of the 'large and powerful animal' (p. 254). Second, his dislike of the educational tradition represented by the contemporary school of Isocrates. Isocrates continued the tradition, started by the Sophists, of a general education centred upon rhetoric, the art of public speaking and self-expression. Plato, who, it should be remembered, also regarded his Academy as a school for statesmen, insisted on a more rigorous intellectual discipline of the kind to be outlined in Book VII. Isocrates thought Plato unrealistic, Plato thought Isocrates superficial.

Here Adeimantus interrupted. 'Of course no one can deny what you have said, Socrates. But whenever people hear you talking like this they have an uneasy feeling that because they're not very experienced in this procedure of question and answer, you lead them on with your questions bit by bit, until at the end of the argument all their admissions are added up and they are badly caught out and shown to have contradicted themselves; they feel your arguments are like a kind of verbal chess in which the unskilled player is always in the end checkmated and reduced to silence by the expert, though he's really in the right none the less. Look at our present discussion. It might well be said that it was impossible to contradict you at any point of the argument, but yet that it was perfectly plain that people who study philosophy too long, and don't treat it simply as part of their early education and then drop it, become, most of them, very odd birds, not to say thoroughly vicious; while even the best of them are reduced by this study you praise so highly to complete uselessness as members of society.'

When he had finished, I asked him whether he thought these charges untrue, to which he replied, 'I don't know; I'd like to hear what you think.' I answered that they seemed to me perfectly true. 'Then how,' he asked, 'can you possibly say that society's troubles will never cease until it is ruled by philosophers, if you agree that they're useless members of society?'

'To answer that question,' I said, 'I must give you an illustration.'

'A thing which, of course, you never normally do!'

'There you go,' I said, 'pulling my leg when you've landed 488 me with such a difficult point to prove. But just you listen to my illustration, and you'll see what a jam I'm in. For there's really no single thing one can use to illustrate the plight of the better type of philosopher in contemporary society; one must draw on several sources for one's illustrations in defence of him, like a painter combining two or more animals in one.

'Suppose the following to be the state of affairs on board a ship or ships. The captain is larger and stronger than any of the crew, but a bit deaf and short-sighted, and doesn't know much about navigation. The crew are all quarrelling with each other about how to navigate the ship, each thinking he ought to be at the helm; they know no navigation and cannot say that anyone ever taught it them, or that they spent any time studying it; indeed they say it can't be taught and are ready to murder anyone who says it can. They spend all their time milling round the captain and trying to get him to give them the wheel. If one faction is more successful than another, their rivals may kill them and throw them overboard, lay out the honest captain with drugs or drink, take control of the ship, help themselves to what's on board, and behave as if they were on a drunken pleasure-cruise. Finally, they reserve their admiration for the man who knows how to lend a hand in controlling the captain by force or fraud; they praise his seamanship and navigation and knowledge of the sea and condemn everyone else as useless. They have no idea that the true navigator must study the seasons of the year, the sky, the stars, the winds and other professional subjects, if he is to be really fit to control a ship; and they think that it's quite impossible to acquire professional skill in navigation (quite apart from whether they want it exercised) and that there's no such thing as an art of navigation. In these circum-

489 stances aren't the sailors on any such ship bound to regard the true navigator as a gossip and a star-gazer, of no use to them at all?'

'Yes, they are,' Adeimantus agreed.

'I think you probably understand, without any explanation, that my illustration is intended to show the present attitude of society towards the true philosopher.'

'Yes, I understand.'

'Then you must tell it to anyone who is surprised that society does not value its philosophers, and try, first, to convince him that it would be far more surprising if it did.'

'I will,' he said.

'And tell him it's quite true that the best of the philosophers are of no use to their fellows; but that he should blame, not the philosophers, but those who fail to make use of them. For it is not natural for the master to request the crew to be guided by him or for the wise to wait on the rich (the author of that epigram was wrong [1]); the true and natural order is for the sick man, whether rich or poor, to wait on the doctor, and for those in want of guidance to wait on him who can give it, if he's really any use, and not for him to wait on them. And you won't be far wrong if you compare the politicians who at present rule us to the sailors in our illustration, and those whom they call useless visionaries to the true navigators.'

'That is very true.'

'These are the reasons and conditions which make it difficult for the best of all pursuits to get a good reputation from men

1. Simonides, 'being asked on one occasion by Hiero's queen whether it was better to be a man of genius or rich, replied "Rich, for men of genius are found at the court of the rich"' (Adam).

whose practice runs contrary to it. But far the most damaging reproach to philosophy is brought on it by those who pretend to practise it, and whom your critic has in mind when he says that most people who practise it are vicious, and the best of them useless – a criticism with which I agreed, did I not?'

'Yes.'

'Well, we have explained the reason for the uselessness of the best of them.'

'Yes, we have.'

'Shall we go on to explain why the majority of them are necessarily corrupted, and show, if we can, that it's not philosophy's fault?'

'Yes, please do.'

'Let's begin by recalling how we described the character that anyone who is to be a really good man must have. Its 490 first requisite, if you remember, was truthfulness, which he must pursue at all costs on pain of becoming an impostor and being excluded from true philosophy.'

'That was what we said.'

'This alone is a startling paradox in view of common opinion.'

'It certainly is,' he agreed.

'Then may we not fairly plead in reply that our true lover of knowledge naturally strives for truth, and is not content with common opinion, but soars with undimmed and unwearied passion till he grasps the essential nature of things with the mental faculty fitted to do so, that is, with the faculty which is akin to reality, and which approaches and unites with it, and begets intelligence and truth as children, and is only released from travail when it has thus reached knowledge and true life and satisfaction?'

'That is as fair a reply as we can make.'

'Then can such a man love falsehood? Must he not hate it?'

'He must.'

'And where truth gives the lead we shan't expect a company of evils to follow, but a good, sound character and self-discipline as well.'

'Very true.'

'Then I don't think we need insist on a review of the whole array of qualities the philosophic nature must have. You will remember that they included courage, breadth of vision, quickness to learn and a good memory. At that point you interrupted to say that, while everyone would be compelled to agree with what we said, if he turned from words to things and looked at the realities we were talking about, he would say that it was clear that some philosophers were useless and others complete rogues. In our attempt to find the cause of this reproach we are now faced with the question, why are most philosophers rogues? And that is why we have been compelled to bring our definition of the character of the true philosopher in again.'

'That is so,' he agreed.

'This, then, is the philosophic nature whose deterioration we must examine; often it is completely corrupted, but sometimes it survives, and then, as you said, men say it's no use, 491 though quite harmless. After that we must examine the types of character that imitate it and set out on a way of life for which they are quite unsuited and which is quite beyond them, and by their many mistakes bring philosophy into the universal disrepute you have described.'

'Tell me,' he said, 'about this deterioration.'

'I will try to describe it if I can,' I replied. 'I think everyone will agree that the combination of qualities we have required in the character of our ideal philosopher will, in all human likelihood, occur very seldom.'

'Very seldom indeed.'

'Yet think of the many powerful factors that may cause its deterioration in these rare characters.'

'What are they?'

'Most extraordinary of all is that each one of the qualities we praised in it – courage, self-discipline and the rest – corrupts its possessor and distracts him from philosophy.'

'I'm surprised to hear that.'

'What is more,' I went on, 'what we normally consider the good things of life all contribute to ruin and distract him –

good looks, wealth, physical strength, being well connected and all the rest – you know the type of thing I mean.'

'Yes,' he said. 'But I'd like to know more precisely what you're getting at.'

'Take it as a whole,' I replied, 'and it will be clear enough, and you won't think these preliminaries so odd.'

'How do you mean?'

'We know that the growth of any living thing, plant or animal, depends on it getting the right nourishment and climate and country to grow in; and the more robust it is the more it feels the lack of them, as bad and good are more incompatible than bad and indifferent. So it's reasonable to expect that high quality will come off worse in an unfavourable environment than poor quality.'

'Yes, reasonable enough.'

'Well then, Adeimantus,' I said, 'on this principle, must we not say that the most gifted characters become particularly bad if they are badly brought up?'

'That is true.'

'Our ideal philosophic character, therefore, if it is properly taught, must develop to perfection, but if it is sown and grows in unsuitable soil, the very opposite will happen, unless providence intervenes. Or do you share the common view that some of our young men are corrupted by sophists? Can the influence of individual sophists really corrupt them to any extent? Isn't it really the public themselves who are sophists on a grand scale, and give a complete training to young and old, men and women, turning them into just the sort of people they want?' 492

'When do they do that?' he asked.

'When they crowd into the seats in the assembly or law courts or theatre, or get together in camp or any other popular meeting place, and, with a great deal of noise and a great lack of moderation, shout and clap their approval or disapproval of whatever is proposed or done, till the rocks and the whole place re-echo, and redouble the noise of their boos and applause. Can a young man remain unmoved by all this? How can his individual training stand the strain? Won't he be swamped by the flood of popular praise and blame, and carried away before it till he finds himself agreeing with popular ideas of right and wrong, behaving like the crowd and becoming one of them?'

'Yes, that's bound to happen,' he agreed.

'And yet we've still said nothing about the most persuasive force of all.'

'What?' he asked.

'The punishments – disfranchisement, fines, or death – which these educational experts inflict on those who won't listen to them, bringing force to bear where persuasion has failed.'

'Yes, punish they certainly do.'

'Then what effect can the private teaching of any individual sophist have against such pressure?'

'None, I'm afraid,' he said.

'None at all,' I agreed, 'and it's sheer folly to make the attempt. To produce a different type of character, educated on standards different from those of public opinion, never has been possible, and never will be possible – in terms, that is, of human possibility, and short of a miracle as they say. For, make no mistake, to escape harm and grow up on the right lines in our present society is something that can fairly be called miraculous.'

'I agree,' he said.

'Then I hope you will agree to this too. All those individuals who make their living by teaching, and whom the public call "sophists" and envy for their skill, in fact teach nothing but the conventional views held by the mass of the people; and this they call a science. What I mean is this. Suppose a man was in charge of a large and powerful animal, and made a study of its moods and wants; he would learn when to approach and handle it, when and why it was especially savage or gentle, what the different noises it made meant, and what tone of voice to use to soothe or annoy it. All this he might learn by long experience and familiarity, and then call it a science, and reduce it to a system and set up to teach it. But he would not really know which of the creature's tastes and desires was fair or unfair, good or bad, right or wrong; he would simply use the terms on the basis of its reactions, calling what pleased it good, what annoyed it bad. He would have no other standard of judgement, but would call the necessities of the animal's nature right and fair, remaining quite blind to the real difference between necessity and goodness, and quite unable to tell anyone else what it was. He would make a queer sort of teacher, wouldn't he?'

'Very queer.'

'But is there really any difference between him and the man who thinks that the knowledge of the passions and pleasures of the mass of the common people is a science, whether he be painter, musician, or politician? If he keeps such company, and submits his poems or other productions, or his public services, to its judgement, he is going out of his way to make the public his master and to subject himself to the fatal necessity of producing only what it approves. And have you ever heard any serious argument to prove that such productions have any genuine merit?'

'No, and I don't expect I shall.'

'Bearing all this in mind, let us recall our earlier distinction between abstract beauty and particular beauty, between the abstract quality and its many particular examples. Do you 494 think the common man will allow it? Will he ever believe anything of the sort?'

'He certainly won't.'

'So philosophy is impossible among the common people.'

'Quite impossible.'

'And the common people must disapprove of philosophers.'

'Inevitably.'

'So also will all individuals who mix with the crowd and want to be popular with it.'

'That is obvious.'

'What hope can you see in all this that the philosophic nature will remain true to itself and persevere to the end? You will remember that we agreed earlier that it must be quick to learn, have a good memory, and be brave and generous. With such gifts a man is bound from the first to take the lead among his fellows, especially if he is as gifted physically as mentally.'

'Yes, that's bound to happen.'

'And his friends and fellow-citizens will want to use him for their own purposes when he grows up.'

'Of course they will.'

'They will be very submissive when they ask favours or express their admiration, flattering in anticipation the power that will one day be his.'

'That is the way of the world,' he said.

'Then, in the circumstances, how do you expect him to behave?' I asked. 'Especially if his native country is a great one and he is himself a man of wealth and family, and well-set-up and good-looking into the bargain. Isn't he bound to be filled with boundless ambition, and think himself capable of running the affairs of Greece, and of all the world besides; won't he become very high and mighty and full of senseless ostentation and inane pride?'[1]

'Yes, he will.'

'Suppose someone approaches him while he is falling into this state, and gently tells him the truth – that he's completely lacking in understanding, and won't acquire it unless he works for it like a slave; do you think he'll find it easy to listen, beset with so many evil influences?'

'No, he'll find it very difficult.'

'If, however,' I went on, 'his natural gifts and his natural bent for reason make him susceptible to its influence, and draw him towards philosophy, what reaction must we expect from his companions, who think they are going to be deprived of his support and society? There's nothing they won't do or say to prevent him being won over, or to hinder his advisers by private intrigue and public prosecution.'

'That is inevitable.'

'Then how can he possibly be a philosopher?'

'He cannot possibly.'

'Do you see, then,' I concluded, 'that we were quite right to say that the very constituents of the philosophic nature were

1. Plato is commonly supposed to have Alcibiades in mind in this passage.

responsible, when it is badly brought up, for its fall from grace, to which riches and all other so-called worldly goods of the same kind also contribute?'

'Yes,' he agreed, 'we were quite right.'

'These, then, are the many influences that destroy the best natures – which are rare enough in any case, as we said – and spoil them for the highest of all pursuits. And it is men so gifted who inflict the deepest injuries on communities and individuals, and indeed, if inclined that way, do them the greatest good. Small natures never do much good or harm to either.'

'Very true.'

'So Philosophy is deserted by those who should be her true lovers, who leave her for a life that does not really suit them, while she, like an abandoned orphan, suffers at the hands of second-rate interlopers all the shame and abuse which you have said her detractors accuse her of, when they say that half her companions are worthless and the other half downright wicked.'

'That is what is commonly said.'

'And quite rightly,' I replied. 'For when they see so good a piece of territory, with all its titles and dignities, unoccupied, a whole crowd of squatters gladly leave the meaner trades, at which they have acquired a considerable degree of skill, and rush into philosophy, like a crowd of criminals taking refuge in a temple. For philosophy, abused as it is, still retains a far higher reputation than other occupations, a reputation which these stunted natures covet, their minds being as cramped and crushed by their mechanical lives as their bodies are deformed by manual trades. This all follows, doesn't it?'

'Yes.'

'They are for all the world like some bald-headed little tinker who's just got out of prison and come into money, and who dresses himself up in his best new suit, like a bridegroom, and sets off to marry his boss's daughter because her family's fallen on hard times.'

'The comparison is fair enough.'

496

'What sort of children are they likely to produce? A mean and misbegotten lot, I think.'

'Inevitably.'

'And when men who aren't fit to be educated get an education they don't deserve, are not the thoughts and opinions they produce fairly called sophistry, without a legitimate idea or any trace of true wisdom among them?'

'Certainly.'

'So only a very small remnant survives, Adeimantus, of all those worthy to have any dealings with philosophy – perhaps some honest man saved by exile from the influences that would corrupt his natural loyalty for her, or some great mind born in a petty state and so despising politics; and there may be a gifted few who turn to philosophy from other occupations which they rightly despise. I suppose, too, that there are some who are handicapped like our friend Theages, who had every other temptation to desert philosophy, but was prevented by bad health from going into public life. My own divine sign, I think, hardly counts, as hardly anyone before me has had it. This small company, then, when they have tasted the happiness of philosophy and seen the frenzy of the masses, understand that political life has virtually nothing sound about it, and that they'll find no ally to save them in the fight for justice; and if they're not prepared to join in the general wickedness, and yet are unable to fight it single-handed, they are likely to perish like a man thrown among wild beasts, without profit to themselves or others, before they can do any good to their friends or society. When they reckon all this up, they live quietly and keep to themselves, like a man who stands under the shelter of a wall during a driving storm of dust and hail; they see the rest of the world full of wrongdoing, and are content to keep themselves unspotted from wickedness and wrong in this life, and finally leave it with cheerful composure and good hope.'

497 'If they do all that they will have done quite a lot,' he said.

'Yes, but they might do much more in a suitable society, where they could develop more fully, to their own salvation and that of the community.'

§4. THE PHILOSOPHER RULER NOT IMPOSSIBLE

There is nothing inherently impossible in the idea of a philosopher ruler. Philosophers might gain political power, or an existing ruler might become a philosopher; and the public would soon be persuaded of the benefits of philosophic rule. But the philosophic training must be the right one, and the changes in society would have to be radical.

Plato's own attempts to carry his ideal into the world of practical politics on the lines suggested in this section have been referred to in the Introduction, pp. 16 ff.

'But I think we've said enough about the reasons for the bad reputation of philosophy and how unjust it is – or have you anything to add?'

'No, I've nothing more; but I'd like to know which of existing societies you think suits it.'

'There isn't one,' I replied, 'which is just my complaint. There's no existing form of society good enough for the philosophic nature; with the result that it gets warped and altered, like a seed sown in foreign soil whose influence always makes it degenerate into the local growth. In exactly the same way the philosophic type loses its true powers, and falls into habits alien to it. If only it could find the ideal society to match its own excellence, then its truly divine quality would appear clearly, and all other characters and ways of life stand revealed as merely human. But I know you're going to ask what this ideal society is.'

'You're wrong,' he said, 'I'm not. I was going to ask whether it was the state whose foundation we have been describing.'

'It is in all respects but one,' I replied; 'for we said that there must be in our state some authority with the same idea of society as that you embodied in your legislation.'

'Yes, that was what we said,' he agreed.

'But we did not make it clear enough. I was afraid of what your criticisms had already shown to be a long and difficult demonstration; and the hardest part of it is still to come.'

'And what is that?'

'How a state can handle philosophy without destroying itself. All great undertakings are risky, and, as they say, what is worth while is always difficult.'

'None the less,' he said, 'we must clear the point up and so complete our demonstration.'

'It's not the will but the ability that may be lacking,' I rejoined. 'You'll see for yourself how anxious I am to do it. Watch me now, I'm going to be bold enough to risk saying that the state should tackle philosophy in a way quite opposite to the present.'

'Explain.'

498 'At present,' I said, 'those who do take it up are quite young, and study it just before they go on to set up house and earn their living; they start on the most difficult part (I mean abstract argument) and give it up when they've barely touched it, even those who go furthest with it. Later in life, if they are invited to listen to a philosophic discussion, they think it quite an event, the sort of thing one does in one's spare time, and by the time they are old any philosophy they have is extinguished even more finally than Heraclitus' sun [1] – it will never be relit.'

'And what's the right way to approach it?' he asked.

'The exact opposite. When they are young, children should only tackle the amount of philosophic training their age can stand; while they are growing to maturity the chief attention should be devoted to their bodies, if they are to find them a useful tool for philosophy. When they are older and their minds begin to mature, their mental training can be intensified. Finally, when their strength begins to fail, and they are no longer fit for political or military service, they can be given their head, and devote all their main energies to philosophy – that is if their life is to be a happy one and their fate after death to match their life on earth.'

'You certainly speak boldly enough, Socrates,' said Adeimantus; 'but I think that the majority of your audience will be all the bolder to contradict you, and remain quite unconvinced, not least Thrasymachus.'

'Now don't start a quarrel between me and Thrasymachus,

1. Heraclitus said there was 'a new sun every day'.

when we've just become friends – not that we were ever really enemies. I shan't give up till we have convinced him and the rest of them, or at any rate done something to prepare them for a future incarnation when they will meet these arguments again.'

'That's rather a long time ahead.'

'Not so long compared with the whole of time. But there's no reason to be surprised if we can't convince the majority of people. They have never seen our words come true. They are used to carefully balanced periods,[1] not the kind of impromptu argument we are having now; and as to a man who will live up to our ideals and do his best to match them both in practice and precept, and who rules a state as good as himself – that is a thing of which they've never seen a single instance.' 499

'Never indeed.'

'Nor have they heard enough free and fair discussion, which strains every nerve to discover the truth out of sheer desire for knowledge, and gives a wide berth to tricks of argument whose only object is to make an effect or win a point, whether in law-court or lecture-room.'

'No, they've not,' he agreed.

'It was for these reasons and with all this in mind,' I said, 'that we felt bound in all honesty, though with some trepidation, to say that there would never be a perfect state or society or individual until some chance compelled this minority of uncorrupted philosophers, now called useless, to take a hand in politics, willy-nilly, and compelled society to listen to them; or else until providence inspired some of our present rulers and kings, or their sons, with a genuine love of true philosophy. There is no reason to suppose that either or both of these things is impossible; if there were, I think you will agree that there would be some justification for laughing at us for day-dreaming.'

'Yes, there would.'

'We are therefore ready to maintain that, whether it be in the infinity of past time, or in the future, or even at the present in some country beyond our horizons, whenever men skilled in

1. Isocrates again.

philosophy take part in politics, then the society we have described either exists or existed or will exist, and the spirit of philosophy herself gain control. No impossibility is involved. What we have described is admittedly difficult, but it is not impossible.'

'I agree with you.'

'But you don't expect most people to do so?'

'Probably not.'

'You know, you mustn't make accusations like that against the common run of men. They'll change their minds if instead of bullying them you are gentle with them, and try to remove their prejudice against learning and show them what you mean by philosophers, defining their character and habits in the terms you used just now and showing that you don't mean what they think you mean. Or do you think that people who are naturally amiable and good tempered will show spite if you don't show it yourself? Let me say at once that I don't think this sort of perversity is characteristic of the majority of men, but only of comparatively few.'

'And of course I agree with you.'

'Do you agree too that the popular dislike of philosophy is due to that disorderly gang of intruders, their mutual abuse and jealousy, and their unphilosophic preoccupation with personalities?'

'Very much so.'

'Because the true philosopher, as you know, Adeimantus, whose mind is on higher realities, has no time to look at the affairs of man, or to take part in their quarrels with all the jealousy and bitterness they involve. His eyes are turned to contemplate fixed and immutable realities, a realm where there is no injustice but all is reason and order, and which is the model which he imitates. For is there any way to stop a man assimilating himself to the character of anything with which he enjoys dealing?'

'No.'

'So the philosopher whose dealings are with the divine order himself acquires its characteristics so far as a man may, though he will have many detractors.'

'Yes, he will.'

'Then if the philosopher is compelled to try to impose the pattern, which he has seen, not only on himself but also on others, and to mould the habits of individuals and of the community, will he lack the skill to produce discipline and justice and all the other ordinary virtues?'

'Certainly not.'

'And if the public discover that we are telling the truth about philosophers, will they still be angry with them and disbelieve us when we say that no state can find happiness unless the artist drawing it uses a divine pattern?'

501

'If they do make the discovery, they will stop being angry. But what do you mean about a pattern?'

'The first thing our artist must do,' I replied, '– and it's not easy – is to take human society and human habits and wipe them clean out, to give himself a clean canvas. For our philosophic artist differs from all others in being unwilling to start work on an individual or a city, or draw out laws, until he is given, or has made himself, a clean canvas.'

'He is quite right.'

'After that his first step will be to sketch in the outline of his society.'

'Yes, and then?'

'He will, I suppose, as he works, look frequently at his model, the ideals of justice and beauty and discipline and similar qualities, and again at the copy of them he is trying to make in human nature, mixing and blending traits to give the colour of manhood, and taking always as his pattern that quality in men that Homer called godly and godlike. He will sometimes delete and draw again, of course, but will go on till he has made human nature as acceptable to God as may be.'

'It should be a very beautiful picture.'

'Do you think,' I asked, 'we are beginning to persuade our would-be attackers of the skill of the artist whose praises we sang to them, and into whose hands we were going to put human society, which made them so angry? Will they listen to us less impatiently now?'

'Certainly, if they have any sense.'

'What objections have they left to bring? Can they say that the philosopher does not love reality and truth?'

'That would be quite absurd.'

'Can they deny that the character we have described has the highest standards?'

'No.'

'Or that such a character, given suitable scope, will make the perfect philosopher, if any will? Will they prefer the other lot whom we excluded?'

'Certainly not.'

'Will they still be angry when we say that until society is controlled by philosophers there will be no end to the troubles of states or individuals, and no realization in practice of the institutions we have described in theory?'

'Less angry than they were perhaps.'

'Then do you mind if we go further and say that they are altogether reconciled and won over? That should shame them 502 into agreement if anything will.'

'Very well then.'

'Then let us assume that we have convinced them so far,' I said. 'Do you think that any of them will object that kings' or rulers' sons are not likely to have the philosophic character?'

'No; no one would say that.'

'And will anyone be able to argue that anyone so born must inevitably be corrupted? We admit that it is difficult to avoid corruption; but will anyone object that not a single individual could avoid it in the whole of time?'

'Hardly.'

'But one is enough for our purpose,' I said; 'if society obeys him, he can set all our doubts at rest.'

'He can.'

'Because once he has power and institutes all the laws and customs we have described, there's no impossibility in supposing that the citizens will carry them out.'

'None at all.'

'And would it be a miracle if others agreed with us?'

'I think not.'

'As, then, we have already shown at sufficient length that

our proposals, if practicable, are the best that can be devised, the conclusion seems to be that our proposed legislation, if put into effect, would be the ideal, and that to put it into effect, though difficult, would not be impossible.'

'That is our conclusion.'

§5. THE GOOD AS ULTIMATE OBJECT OF KNOWLEDGE

Plato proceeds to the education of the philosopher, with which the rest of this Part is concerned. He begins by laying down that the philosopher must have a true sense of values. These values are absolute, and the ultimate source and standard of them is Absolute Goodness, or the Form of the Good. This stands in a peculiar relation to all other Forms, being the source not only of their value but of their existence. Socrates refuses to describe it directly, but does so by means of a simile, in which the Good is compared to the Sun, and which may be set out in tabular form as follows:

Visible World	Intelligible World
The Sun	*The Good*
Source of $\begin{cases} Growth\ and \\ Light, \end{cases}$	*Source of* $\begin{cases} Reality\ and \\ Truth, \end{cases}$
which gives	*which gives*
Visibility to objects of sense	*Intelligibility to objects of thought* [1]
and	*and*
the power of seeing to the eye.	*the power of knowing to the mind.*
The faculty of sight.	*The faculty of knowledge.*

'Well, then, that part of our job is done – and it's not been easy; we must now go on to the next, and ask about the position and training of these saviours of our society. What are they to learn and at what age are they to learn it?'

'Yes, that's our next question.'

'I didn't really gain anything,' I said, 'by being clever and putting off the difficulties about the possession of women, the production of children and the establishment of Rulers till

1. The Forms.

later. I knew that my true society would give offence and be difficult to realize; but I have had to describe it all the same. I've dealt with the business about women and children, and now I've got to start again on the Rulers. You will remember that we said they must love their country, and be tested both in pleasure and pain, to ensure that their loyalty remained unshaken by pain or fear or any other misfortune; those who failed the test were to be rejected, but those who emerged unscathed, like gold tried in the fire, were to be established as rulers and given honours and rewards both in life and after death.[1] This is roughly what we said, but we were afraid of stirring up the problems we are now facing, and our argument evaded the issue and tried to get by without being seen, as it were.'

'Yes, I remember,' he said.

'You know, I hesitated before to say the rash things I've said,' I replied; 'but now let me be brave and say that our Guardians, in the fullest sense, must be philosophers.'

'So be it.'

'Think how few of them there are likely to be. The elements in the character which we have insisted they must have don't usually combine into a whole, but are normally found separately.'

'What do you mean?'

'Readiness to learn and remember, quickness and keenness of mind and the qualities that go with them, and enterprise and breadth of vision, aren't usually combined with steadiness, discipline, and willingness to lead a quiet life; such keen temperaments are very unstable and quite devoid of steadiness.'

'True.'

'And again steady, trustworthy, reliable characters, who are unmoved by fear in war, are equally unmoved by instruction. Their immobility amounts indeed to numbness and, faced with anything that demands intellectual effort, they yawn and sink into slumber.'

'That's all quite true.'

'But we demand a fair share of both sets of qualities from

1. See p. 157 ff.

anyone who is to be given the highest form of education and any share of office or authority.'

'And rightly.'

'So the character we want will be a rare occurrence.'

'It will.'

'And we must not only test it in the pains and fears and pleasures we have already described, but also try it out in a series of intellectual studies which we omitted before, to see if it has the endurance to pursue the highest forms of knowledge, 504 without flinching as others flinch in physical trials.'

'A fair test; but what,' he asked, 'are these highest forms of knowledge?'

'You remember,' I answered, 'that we distinguished three elements in the mind, and then went on to deal with justice, self-control, courage and wisdom.'

'If I didn't remember that,' he said, 'I shouldn't have any claim to hear the rest of the argument.'

'Then do you remember what we said just before that?' [1]

'What?'

'We said that a really clear view of them could only be got by making a detour for the purpose, though we could get an approximate idea of them on the basis of our earlier argument. You said that was good enough, and so our subsequent description fell short, in my view, of real precision; whether it was precise enough for you, is for you to say.'

'I thought you gave us fair measure, and so, I think, did the others.'

'In matters like this nothing is fair measure that falls short of the truth in any respect,' I replied. 'You can't use the imperfect as a standard – though people are sometimes content with it, and don't want to look further.'

'Yes, but it's usually because they're too lazy.'

'A most undesirable quantity in a Guardian of constitution and laws.'

'A fair comment.'

'Then he must take the longer way round,' I said, 'and must work as hard at his intellectual training as at his physical;

1. P. 186.

otherwise he will never reach the highest form of knowledge, as he certainly should.'

'But is there anything higher than justice and the other qualities we discussed?'

'There is,' I said. 'And we ought not to be content with a mere sketch even of these qualities, or fail to complete the picture. For it would be absurd, would it not, to devote all our energies to securing the greatest possible precision and clarity in matters of little consequence, and not to demand the highest precision in the most important things of all?'

'Quite absurd,' he agreed. 'But you can hardly expect to escape cross-questioning about what you mean by the highest form of knowledge and its object.'

'I don't expect anything of the kind,' I returned; 'ask your questions. Though you've heard about it often enough, and either don't understand for the moment, or else are deliberately giving me trouble by your persistence – I suspect it's the latter, because you have certainly often been told that the highest form of knowledge is knowledge of the essential nature of goodness, from which things that are just and so on derive their usefulness and value. You know pretty well that that's what I have to say, and that I'm going to add that our knowledge of it is inadequate, and that because we are ignorant of it the rest of our knowledge, however perfect, can be of no benefit to us, just as it's no use possessing anything if you can't get any good out of it. Or do you think there's any point in possessing anything if it's no good? Is there any point in having all other forms of knowledge, if you don't know what is right and good?'

'I certainly don't think there is.'

'And you know of course that most people think that pleasure is the Good, while the more sophisticated think it is knowledge.'

'Yes.'

'But those who hold this last view can't tell us what knowledge they mean, but are compelled in the end to say they mean knowledge of the Good.'

'Which is quite absurd.'

'An absurdity they can't avoid, if, after criticizing us for *not* knowing the Good, they then turn round and talk to us as if we *did* know it; for they say it is "knowledge of the good" as if we understood what they meant when they use the word "good".'

'That's perfectly true.'

'Then what about those who define Good as pleasure? Is their confusion any less? Aren't they compelled to admit that there are bad pleasures?'

'Of course they are.'

'And they thus find themselves admitting that the same things are both good and bad, don't they?'

'Yes.'

'So it's obvious that the subject is full of obscurities.'

'It is indeed.'

'Well, then, isn't it obvious too that when it's a matter of justice or fairness many people prefer the appearance to the reality, and are glad to appear to have these qualities even when they haven't; but that no one is satisfied with something that only *appears* good for him, but wants something that *really* is, and has no use here for appearances?'

'Absolutely true.'

'Good, then, is the end of all endeavour, the object on which every heart is set, whose existence it divines, though it finds it difficult to say just what it is; and because it can't grasp it with the same assurance as other things it misses any value those other things have. Can we possibly agree that the best of our 506 citizens, to whom we are going to entrust everything, should be in the dark about so important a subject?'

'It's the last thing we can admit.'

'At any rate a man will not be a very useful Guardian of what is right and fair if he does not know in what their goodness consists; and I suspect that until he knows this no one can understand them.'

'Your suspicions are well founded.'

'So our society will not be properly regulated unless it is in charge of a Guardian who has this knowledge.'

'That must be so,' he said. 'But what about you? Do you

think that the Good is knowledge or pleasure? or do you think it's something else?'

'What a man!' I exclaimed. 'I knew it! It's been obvious for some time that you wouldn't be satisfied with other people's opinions!'

'But I don't think it's right, Socrates,' he protested, 'for you to be able to tell us other people's opinions but not your own, when you've given so much time to the subject.'

'Yes, but do you think it's right for a man to talk as if he knows what he does not?'

'He has no right to talk as if he knew; but he should be prepared to say what his opinion is, so far as it goes.'

'Well,' I said, 'haven't you noticed that opinion without knowledge is always a poor thing? At the best it is blind – isn't anyone with a true but unthinking opinion like a blind man on the right road?'

'Yes.'

'Then do you want a poor, blind, halting display from me, when you can get splendidly clear accounts from other people?'

'Now, for goodness' sake don't give up when you're just at the finish, Socrates,' begged Glaucon. 'We shall be quite satisfied if you give an account of the Good similar to that you gave of justice and self-control and the rest.'

'And so shall I too, my dear chap,' I replied, 'but I'm afraid it's beyond me, and if I try I shall only make a fool of myself. So please let us give up asking for the present what the Good is in itself; I'm afraid a satisfactory answer is beyond the scope of our present inquiry. But I will tell you, if you like, about something which I imagine to be a child of the Good, and to resemble it very closely – or would you rather I didn't?'

'Tell us about the child and you can owe us your account of the parent,' he said.

507 'It's a debt I wish I could pay you in full, instead of only paying interest [1] on the loan,' I replied. 'But for the present you must accept my description of the child of the Good as inter-

1. The Greek for 'interest' (the 'offspring' of a loan) is the same as for 'child'.

est. But take care I don't inadvertently cheat you by paying in bad money.'

'We'll be as careful as we can,' he said. 'Go on.'

'I must first get your agreement to, and remind you of something we have said earlier in our discussion, and indeed on many other occasions.'

'What is it?'

'We distinguish between the many particular things which we call beautiful or good, and absolute beauty and goodness. Similarly with all other collections of things, we say there is corresponding to each set a single, unique Form which we call an "absolute" reality.'

'That is so.'

'And we say that the particulars are objects of sight but not of intelligence, while the Forms are the objects of intelligence but not of sight.'

'Certainly.'

'And with what part of ourselves do we see what we see?'

'With our eyes.'

'And we hear with our ears, and so on with the other senses and their objects.'

'Of course.'

'Then have you noticed,' I asked, 'how extremely lavish the designer of our senses was when he gave us the faculty of sight and made objects visible?'

'I can't say I have.'

'Then look. Do hearing and speech need something else in addition to themselves to enable the ear to hear and the sound to be heard – some third element without which the one cannot hear or the other be heard?'

'No.'

'And the same is true of most, indeed all, the other senses. Or can you think of any that needs such an element?'

'No, I can't.'

'But haven't you noticed that sight and its objects do need one?'

'How?'

'If your eyes have the power of sight and you try to use

them, and if objects have colour, yet you will see nothing and the colours will remain invisible unless a third element is present which is specially constituted for the purpose.'

'What is that?' he asked.

'What you call light,' I answered.

'True.'

'Then the sense of sight and the visibility of objects are connected by something that is by a long way the most valuable of all links – that is, if light is a thing of value.'

'Which it most certainly is.'

'Which, then, of the heavenly bodies [1] do you regard as responsible for it? Whose light would you say it is that makes our eyes see and objects be seen most perfectly?'

'I should say the same as you or anyone else; you mean the sun, of course.'

'Then is the relation of sun and sight such that the sun is identical neither with sight itself nor with the eye in which sight resides, though the eye is the sense-organ most similar to the sun?'

'Yes.'

'So the eye's power of sight is a kind of effusion dispensed to it by the sun.'

'Yes.'

'Then, moreover, though the sun is not itself sight, it is the cause of sight and is seen by the sight it causes.'

'That is so.'

'Well, this is the child of the Good, of which I spoke,' I said. 'The Good has begotten it in its own likeness, and it bears the same relation to sight and visibility in the visible world that the Good bears to intelligence and intelligibility in the intelligible world.'

'Will you explain that a bit further?' he asked.

'You know that when we turn our eyes to objects whose colours are no longer illuminated by daylight, but only by moonlight or starlight, they see dimly and appear to be almost blind, as if they had no clear vision.'

'Yes.'

1. Plato says 'gods'; he believed the heavenly bodies were divine.

508

'But when we turn them on things on which the sun is shining, then they see clearly and their power of vision is restored.'

'Certainly.'

'Apply the analogy to the mind. When the mind's eye rests on objects illuminated by truth and reality, it understands and comprehends them, and functions intelligently; but when it turns to the twilight world of change and decay, it can only form opinions, its vision is confused and its beliefs shifting, and it seems to lack intelligence.'

'That is true.'

'Then what gives the objects of knowledge their truth and the mind the power of knowing is the Form of the Good. It is the cause of knowledge and truth, and you will be right to think of it as being itself known, and yet as being something other than, and even higher than, knowledge and truth. And just as it was right to think of light and sight as being like the sun, but wrong to think of them as being the sun itself, so here again it is right to think of knowledge and truth as being like the Good, but wrong to think of either of them as being the Good, which must be given a still higher place of honour.' 509

'You are making it something remarkably exalted, if it is the source of knowledge and truth, and yet itself higher than they are. For I suppose you can't mean it to be pleasure?' he asked.

'A monstrous suggestion,' I replied. 'Let us pursue our analogy further.'

'Go on.'

'The sun, I think you will agree, not only makes the things we see visible, but causes the processes of generation, growth and nourishment, without itself being such a process.'

'True.'

'The Good therefore may be said to be the source not only of the intelligibility of the objects of knowledge, but also of their existence and reality; yet it is not itself identical with reality, but is beyond reality, and superior to it in dignity and power.'

'It really must be devilish superior,' remarked Glaucon with a grin.

'Now, don't blame me,' I protested; 'it was you who made me say what I thought about it.'

'Yes, and please go on. At any rate finish off the analogy with the Sun, if you haven't finished it.'

'I've not nearly finished it.'

'Then go on and don't leave anything out.'

'I'm afraid I must leave a lot out,' I said. 'But I'll do my best to get in everything I can at the moment.'

'Yes, please do.'

§6. THE DIVIDED LINE

The analogy of the Divided Line is, Plato makes clear, a sequel to the Sun simile, its purpose being to illustrate further the relation between the two orders of reality with which the Sun simile dealt. But it does so from a particular point of view, that of the methods or the states of mind by which we apprehend these two orders or worlds. The purpose of the Line, therefore, is not, primarily, to give a classification of objects. It is made quite clear that both of the two methods of apprehending the intelligible world deal with the same kind of object (the Forms), though each deals with them in a different way; and similarly, though in the physical world there is a difference between physical things and their shadows, that difference is used primarily to illustrate degrees of 'truth' – we know very little about a thing if our knowledge is confined to shadows or images of it. The simile may be set out in the table below (p. 275).

Broadly speaking, the mental operations or states comprised by the four subdivisions are: (A) Intelligence. Pure Philosophy, leading to the vision of ultimate truth. (Plato calls it, among other things, dialectic; a term whose modern associations are quite misleading in interpreting the Republic.) (B) Reason. The procedure of mathematics, purely deductive and uncritical of its assumptions. (C) Belief. Common-sense beliefs on matters both moral and physical; ordinary opinions which are a fair practical guide to life but have not been fully thought out. (Later, in the Timaeus, Plato includes the natural sciences in this sub-section, as they can never reach ultimate truth, being concerned with a changeable world.) (D) Illusion. All the various forms of illusions, 'second-hand impressions and opinions" [1], by which the lives of ordinary people are beset. In this section 'illusion' merely appears as the apprehension

1. J. E. Raven, *Classical Quarterly* (Jan.-April, 1953), p. 28.

of shadows and reflections. But the wider interpretation is demanded by the cave simile, which elaborates in a more graphic form the classification set out in the Line. And it is also clearly implied in Book X (p. 370 below) that all works of poetry and art are to be included in this sub-section.

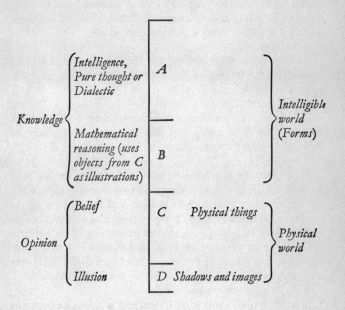

'You must suppose, then,' I went on, 'that there are these two powers of which I have spoken, and that one of them is supreme over everything in the intelligible world, the other over everything in the visible world – I won't say in the physical universe or you will think I'm playing with words.[2] At any rate you understand there are these two orders of things, the visible and the intelligible?'

2. The Greek words for 'visible' and for 'physical universe' (or more literally 'heaven') bear some resemblance to each other, and it had been suggested that there was some connection between them.

'Yes, I understand.'

'Well, take a line divided into two unequal parts, corresponding to the visible and the intelligible worlds, and then divide the two parts again in the same ratio, to represent degrees of clarity and obscurity. In the visible world one section stands for images: by "images" I mean first shadows, then reflections in water and other close-grained, polished surfaces, and all that sort of thing if you understand me.'

'I understand.'

'Let the other section stand for the objects which are the originals of the images – animals, plants and manufactured objects of all kinds.'

'Very good.'

'Would you be prepared to admit that these sections differ in their degree of truth, and that the relation of image to original is the same as that of opinion to knowledge?'

'I would.'

'Then consider next how the intelligible part of the line is to be divided. In one section the mind uses the originals of the visible world in their turn as images, and has to base its inquiries on assumptions and proceed from them to its conclusions instead of going back to first principles: in the other it proceeds from assumption back to self-sufficient first principle, making no use of the images employed in the other section, but pursuing its inquiry solely by means of Forms.'

'I don't quite understand.'

'I will try again; and what I have just said will help you to understand. I think you know that students of geometry and similar forms of reasoning begin by taking for granted odd and even numbers, geometrical figures and the three kinds of angle, and other kindred data in their various subjects; these they regard as known, and treat as basic assumptions which it is quite unnecessary to explain to themselves or anyone else because they are self-evident. Starting from them, they proceed through a series of consistent steps to the propositions which they set out to examine.'

'Yes, I know that.'

'You know too that they make use of and reason about visible figures, though they are not really thinking about them at all, but about the originals which they resemble; they are arguing not about the square or diagonal which they have drawn but about the absolute square or diagonal, or whatever the figure may be. The figures they draw or model, which again have their shadows and reflections in water, they treat as illustrations only, the real subjects of their investigation being invisible except to the eye of the mind.'

511

'That is quite true.'

'This sort of reality I described as intelligible, but said that the mind was forced to use assumptions in investigating it, and because it was unable to ascend from these assumptions to a first principle, used as illustrations objects which in turn have their images on a lower plane, in comparison with which they are themselves thought to have a superior clarity and value.'

'I understand,' he said. 'You are referring to what happens in geometry and kindred sciences.'

'Then when I speak of the other section of the intelligible part of the line you will understand that I mean that which reason apprehends directly by the power of pure thought; it treats assumptions not as principles, but as assumptions in the true sense, that is, as starting points and steps in the ascent to the universal, self-sufficient first principle; when it has reached that principle it can again descend, by keeping to the consequences that follow from it, to a final conclusion. The whole procedure involves nothing in the sensible world, but deals throughout with Forms and finishes with Forms.'

'I understand,' he said; 'though not entirely, because what you describe sounds like a long job. But you want to distinguish the section of intelligible reality which is studied by the activity of pure thought, as having greater clarity and certainty than the section studied by the mathematical sciences; in these sciences assumptions serve as principles and their subject-matter must be reasoned about and not directly perceived, and because they proceed *from* assumptions and not *to* first principles they can never finally understand their subject-matter, even though it can be understood with the help of a first principle. And I think that you call the state of mind of geometers and the like Reason but not Intelligence, meaning by Reason something midway between opinion and intelligence.'

'You have understood me well enough,' I said. 'And you may assume that there are, corresponding to the four sections of the line, four states of mind: to the top section Intelligence, to the second Reason, to the third Opinion, and to the fourth Illusion. And you may arrange them in a scale, and assume that they have degrees of clarity corresponding to the degree of truth and reality possessed by their subject-matter.

'I understand,' he replied, 'and agree with your proposed arrangement.'

§7. THE SIMILE OF THE CAVE

This is a more graphic presentation of the truths presented in the analogy of the Line; in particular, it tells us more about the two states of mind called in the Line analogy Belief and Illusion. We are shown the ascent of the mind from illusion to pure philosophy, and the difficulties which accompany its progress. And the philosopher, when he has achieved the supreme vision, is required to return to the cave and serve his fellows, his very unwillingness to do so being his chief qualification.

As Cornford pointed out, the best way to understand the simile is to replace 'the clumsier apparatus' of the cave by the cinema. It is the moral and intellectual condition of the average man from which Plato starts; and though clearly the ordinary man knows the difference between substance and shadow in the physical world, the simile suggests that his moral and intellectual opinions often bear as little relation to the truth as the average film does to real life.

BK
VII

'I want you to go on to picture the enlightenment or ignorance of our human conditions somewhat as follows. Imagine an underground chamber, like a cave with an entrance open to the daylight and running a long way underground. In this chamber are men who have been prisoners there since they were children, their legs and necks being so fastened that they can only look straight ahead of them and cannot turn their heads. Behind them and above them a fire is burning, and between the fire and the prisoners runs a road, in front of which a curtain-wall has been built, like the screen at puppet shows between the operators and their audience, above which they show their puppets.'

'I see.'

'Imagine further that there are men carrying all sorts of gear 515 along behind the curtain-wall, including figures of men and animals made of wood and stone and other materials, and that some of these men, as is natural, are talking and some not.'

'An odd picture and an odd sort of prisoner.'

'They are drawn from life,' I replied. 'For, tell me, do you think our prisoners could see anything of themselves or their fellows except the shadows thrown by the fire on the wall of the cave opposite them?'

'How could they see anything else if they were prevented from moving their heads all their lives?'

'And would they see anything more of the objects carried along the road?'

'Of course not.'

'Then if they were able to talk to each other, would they not assume that the shadows they saw were real things?'

'Inevitably.'

'And if the wall of their prison opposite them reflected sound, don't you think that they would suppose, whenever one of the passers-by on the road spoke, that the voice belonged to the shadow passing before them?'

'They would be bound to think so.'

'And so they would believe that the shadows of the objects we mentioned were in all respects real.'

'Yes, inevitably.'

'Then think what would naturally happen to them if they were released from their bonds and cured of their delusions. Suppose one of them were let loose, and suddenly compelled to stand up and turn his head and look and walk towards the fire; all these actions would be painful and he would be too dazzled to see properly the objects of which he used to see the shadows. So if he was told that what he used to see was mere illusion and that he was now nearer reality and seeing more correctly, because he was turned towards objects that were more real, and if on top of that he were compelled to say what each of the passing objects was when it was pointed out to him, don't you think he would be at a loss, and think that what he used to see was more real than the objects now being pointed out to him?'

'Much more real.'

'And if he were made to look directly at the light of the fire, it would hurt his eyes and he would turn back and take refuge in the things which he could see, which he would think really far clearer than the things being shown him.'

'Yes.'

'And if,' I went on, 'he were forcibly dragged up the steep and rocky ascent and not let go till he had been dragged out into the sunlight, the process would be a painful one, to which he would much object, and when he emerged into the light his eyes would be so overwhelmed by the brightness of it that he wouldn't be able to see a single one of the things he was now told were real.'

'Certainly not at first,' he agreed.

'Because he would need to grow accustomed to the light before he could see things in the world outside the cave. First he would find it easiest to look at shadows, next at the reflections of men and other objects in water, and later on at the objects themselves. After that he would find it easier to observe the heavenly bodies and the sky at night than by day, and to look at the light of the moon and stars, rather than at the sun and its light.'

'Of course.'

'The thing he would be able to do last would be to look directly at the sun, and observe its nature without using reflections in water or any other medium, but just as it is.'

'That must come last.'

'Later on he would come to the conclusion that it is the sun that produces the changing seasons and years and controls everything in the visible world, and is in a sense responsible for everything that he and his fellow-prisoners used to see.'

'That is the conclusion which he would obviously reach.'

516

'And when he thought of his first home and what passed for wisdom there, and of his fellow-prisoners, don't you think he would congratulate himself on his good fortune and be sorry for them?'

'Very much so.'

'There was probably a certain amount of honour and glory to be won among the prisoners, and prizes for keen-sightedness for anyone who could remember the order of sequence among the passing shadows and so be best able to predict their future appearances. Will our released prisoner hanker after these prizes or envy this power or honour? Won't he be more likely to feel, as Homer says, that he would far rather be "a serf in the house of some landless man",[1] or indeed anything else in the world, than live and think as they do?'

'Yes,' he replied, 'he would prefer anything to a life like theirs.'

'Then what do you think would happen,' I asked, 'if he went back to sit in his old seat in the cave? Wouldn't his eyes be blinded by the darkness, because he had come in suddenly out of the daylight?'

'Certainly.'

'And if he had to discriminate between the shadows, in competition with the other prisoners, while he was still blinded 517 and before his eyes got used to the darkness – a process that might take some time – wouldn't he be likely to make a fool of himself? And they would say that his visit to the upper world had ruined his sight, and that the ascent was not worth even attempting. And if anyone tried to release them and lead them up, they would kill him if they could lay hands on him.'

'They certainly would.'

'Now, my dear Glaucon,' I went on, 'this simile must be connected, throughout, with what preceded it.[2] The visible

1. *Odyssey*, XI, 489.
2. i.e. the simile of the Sun and the analogy of the Line. The detailed relations between the three figures have been much disputed. The translation assumes the following main correspondences:

| Tied prisoner in the cave | Illusion |
| Freed prisoner in the cave | Belief |

realm corresponds to the prison, and the light of the fire in the prison to the power of the sun. And you won't go wrong if you connect the ascent into the upper world and the sight of the objects there with the upward progress of the mind into the intelligible realm – that's my guess, which is what you are anxious to hear. The truth of the matter is, after all, known only to God. But in my opinion, for what it is worth, the final thing to be perceived in the intelligible realm, and perceived only with difficulty, is the absolute form of Good; once seen, it is inferred to be responsible for everything right and good, producing in the visible realm light and the source of light, and being, in the intelligible realm itself, controlling source of reality and intelligence. And anyone who is going to act rationally either in public or private must perceive it.'

'I agree,' he said, 'so far as I am able to understand you.'

'Then you will perhaps also agree with me that it won't be surprising if those who get so far are unwilling to return to mundane affairs, and if their minds long to remain among higher things. That's what we should expect if our simile is to be trusted.'

'Yes, that's to be expected.'

'Nor will you think it strange that anyone who descends from contemplation of the divine to the imperfections of human life should blunder and make a fool of himself, if, while still blinded and unaccustomed to the surrounding darkness, he's forcibly put on trial in the law-courts or elsewhere about the images of justice or their shadows, and made to dispute about the conceptions of justice held by men who have never seen absolute justice.'

'There's nothing strange in that.'

518 'But anyone with any sense,' I said, 'will remember that the

Looking at shadows in the world outside the cave	Reason
Looking at real things in the world outside the cave	Intelligence
Looking at the sun	Vision of the Form of Good.

Mr J. E. Raven's 'Sun, Divided Line and Cave' (*Classical Quarterly*, Jan.-April 1953) is the best recent discussion of the subject.

eyes may be unsighted in two ways, by a transition either from light to darkness or from darkness to light, and that the same distinction applies to the mind. So when he sees a mind confused and unable to see clearly he will not laugh without thinking, but will ask himself whether it has come from a clearer world and is confused by the unaccustomed darkness, or whether it is dazzled by the stronger light of the clearer world to which it has escaped from its previous ignorance. The first state is a reason for congratulation, the second for sympathy, though if one wants to laugh at it one can do so with less absurdity than at the mind that has descended from the daylight of the upper world.'

'You put it very reasonably.'

'If this is true,' I continued, 'we must reject the conception of education professed by those who say that they can put into the mind knowledge that was not there before – rather as if they could put sight into blind eyes.'

'It is a claim that is certainly made,' he said.

'But our argument indicates that this is a capacity which is innate in each man's mind, and that the faculty by which he learns is like an eye which cannot be turned from darkness to light unless the whole body is turned; in the same way the mind as a whole must be turned away from the world of change until its eye can bear to look straight at reality, and at the brightest of all realities which is what we call the Good. Isn't that so?'

'Yes.'

'Then this business of turning the mind round might be made a subject of professional skill, which would effect the conversion as easily and effectively as possible. It would not be concerned to implant sight, but to ensure that some one who had it already was turned in the right direction and looking the right way.'

'That may well be so.'

'The rest, therefore, of what are commonly called qualities of the mind perhaps resemble those of the body, in that they are not innate, but are implanted by training and practice; but the power of knowing, it seems, belongs to some diviner faculty, which never loses its power, but whose effects are good or bad

519

according to the direction in which it is turned. Have you never noticed how shrewd is the glance of the type of men commonly called bad but clever? Their intelligence is limited, but their sight is sharp enough in matters that concern them; it's not that their sight is weak, but that they put it to bad use, so that the keener it is the worse its effects.'

'That's true.'

'But suppose,' I said, 'that such natures were cut loose, when they were still children, from the dead weight of worldliness, fastened on them by sensual indulgences like gluttony, which distorts their minds' vision to lower things, and suppose that when so freed they were turned towards the truth, then the same faculty in them would have as keen a vision of truth as it has of the objects on which it is at present turned.'

'Very likely.'

'And is it not also likely, and indeed a necessary consequence of that we have said, that society will never be properly governed either by the uneducated, who have no knowledge of the truth, or by those who are allowed to spend all their lives in purely intellectual pursuits? The uneducated have no single aim in life to which all their actions, public and private, are directed, the intellectuals will take no practical action of their own accord, fancying themselves to be no longer of this world.'

'True.'

'Then our job as Lawgivers is to compel the best minds to attain what we have called the highest form of knowledge, and to ascend to the vision of the Good as we have described, and when they have achieved this and seen enough, prevent them behaving as they now do.'

'What do you mean by that?'

'Remaining in the upper world, and refusing to return again to the prisoners in the cave below and share their labours and rewards, whether they are worth having or not.'

'But surely,' he protested, 'that will not be fair. We shall be compelling them to live a poorer life than they might live.'

'The object of our legislation,' I reminded him again, 'is not the welfare of any particular class, but of the whole community. It uses persuasion or force to unite all citizens and 520 make them share together the benefits which each individually can confer on the community; and its purpose in fostering this attitude is not to enable everyone to please himself, but to make each man a link in the unity of the whole.'

'You are right; I had forgotten,' he said.

'You see, then, Glaucon,' I went on, 'we shan't be unfair to our philosophers, but shall be quite justified in compelling them to have some care and responsibility for others. We shall tell them that philosophers in other states can reasonably refuse to take part in the hard work of politics; for society produces them quite involuntarily and unintentionally, and it is only just that anything that grows up on its own should feel it has nothing to repay for an upbringing which it owes to no one. "But you," we shall say, "have been bred to rule to your own advantage and that of the whole community, like king-bees in a hive; you are better educated than the rest and better qualified to combine the practice of philosophy and politics. You must therefore each descend in turn and live with your fellows in the cave and get used to seeing in the dark; once you get used to it you will see a thousand times better than they do and will recognize the various shadows, and know what they are shadows of, because you have seen the truth about things right and just and good. And so our state and yours will be really awake, and not merely dreaming like most societies to-day, with their shadow battles and their struggles for political power, which they treat as some great prize. The truth is quite different: the state whose rulers come to their duties with least enthusiasm is bound to have the best and most tranquil government, and the state whose rulers are eager to rule the worst."

'I quite agree.'

'Then will our pupils, when they hear what we say, refuse to take their share of the hard work of government, though spending the greater part of their time together in the pure air of philosophy?'

'They cannot refuse, for we are making a just demand of just men. But of course, unlike present rulers, they will approach the business of government as an unavoidable necessity.'

'Yes, of course,' I agreed. 'The truth is that if you want a well-governed state you must find for your future rulers some career they like better than government; for only then will you have government by the truly rich, those, that is, whose riches consist not of money, but of the happiness of a right and rational life. If you get, in public affairs, men who are so morally impoverished that they have nothing they can contribute themselves, but who hope to snatch some compensation for their own inadequacy from a political career, there can never be good government. They start fighting for power, and the consequent internal and domestic conflicts ruin both them and society.'

'True indeed.'

'Is there any other life except that of true philosophy which looks down on political power?'

'None that I know of.'

'And yet the only men to get power should be men who do not love it, otherwise we shall have rivals' quarrels.'

'That is certain.'

'Who else, then, are we to compel to undertake the responsibilities of ruling, if it is not to be those who know most about good government and who yet value other things more highly than politics and its rewards?'

'There is no one else.'

PART EIGHT

EDUCATION OF THE PHILOSOPHER

*

Having described the Philosopher Ruler, Plato proceeds to the further education, beyond that described in Part III, necessary to produce him. This further education consists of five mathematical disciplines – arithmetic, plane and solid geometry, astronomy, and harmonics – followed by a training in pure philosophy or 'Dialectic' in Plato's sense. Though some concessions are made to utilitarianism, the main stress throughout is on the training of the mind, with the vision of the Good as its ultimate objective; and mathematics is to be studied without any immediate practical or scientific aim in view.

§I. PRELIMINARY

The type of study required must be one that will provoke the mind to thought.

'THEN would you like us to consider how men of this kind are to be produced, and how they are to be led up to the light, like the men in stories who are said to have risen from the underworld to heaven?'

'I should like it very much.'

'It's not a thing we can settle by spinning a coin,' I said. 'What is at issue is the conversion of the mind from the twilight of error to the truth, that climb up into the real world which we shall call true philosophy.'

'Yes, of course.'

'So we must try to find out what sort of studies have this effect.'

'Yes.'

'Well, Glaucon,' I asked, 'what should men study if their minds are to be drawn from the world of change to reality? Now it occurs to me that we said our rulers must be trained for war when they were young.'

'We did.'

'Then the subject we're looking for must be relevant in war too.'

'How do you mean?'

'It mustn't be useless to soldiers.'

'Not if we can avoid it.'

'Well, we've already arranged for their physical training and their education in literature and music. And of these two, physical training is concerned with the world of change and decay, for the body, which it looks after, grows and declines.'

'Yes, clearly.'

522 'So it won't be the study we are looking for.'

'No.'

'Then what about the literary education which we described earlier on?'

'That,' he reminded me, 'was the complement of their physical education. It gave them a moral training, and used music and rhythm to produce a certain harmony and balance of character rather than knowledge; and its literature, whether fabulous or factual, had a similar ethical content. There was nothing in it to produce the effect you are seeking.'

'Your memory's quite correct,' I said, 'we shan't find what we want there. But where shall we find it, Glaucon? The more practical forms of skill don't seem very elevating –'

'Certainly not. But if we exclude them, as well as physical and literary education, what else is there left?'

'Well, if we can't think of anything outside them, we must find some feature they all share.'

'What do you mean?'

'For example, there is one thing that all occupations, practical, intellectual, or scientific, make use of – one of the first things we must all learn.'

'What?'

'Something quite ordinary – to tell the difference between one, two and three; in a word, to count and calculate. Must not every practical or scientific activity be able to do that?'

'Yes, it must,' he agreed.

'And war as much as any other?'

'Very much so.'

'I wonder if you have noticed what a silly sort of general Agamemnon is made to look on the stage when Palamedes claims to have invented number, and so organized the army at Troy and counted the ships and everything else. It implies that nothing had been counted before and that Agamemnon, apparently, did not know how many feet he had, if he couldn't count. He must have been a funny sort of general!'

'He must indeed,' he said, 'if it's really true.'

'So soldiers must learn, as well as other things, how to calculate and count.'

'Yes, of course, if they're to be able to organize an army, indeed if they are to be human at all.'

'I wonder, then,' I asked, 'if you would agree with me that 52) this is probably one of the subjects we are looking for, which naturally stimulates thought, though no one makes proper use of its power to draw men to the truth.'

'How do you mean?'

'I'll try to explain what I have in mind,' I said, 'and show you how I distinguish in my own mind between things that have the effect I mean and things that have not. If you will tell me where you agree and disagree, we can then see more clearly whether I have the right idea.'

'Explain.'

'Right,' I said. 'You see, there are some perceptions which don't call for any further exercise of thought, because sensation can judge them adequately, but others which demand the exercise of thought because sensation cannot give a sure result.'

'You obviously mean things seen at a distance, or drawn in perspective.'

'No, you haven't quite got my meaning,' I replied.

'Then what do you mean?' he asked.

'By perceptions that don't call for thought I mean those that don't lead to contradiction; those that do call for thought are those that lead to contradiction in the sense that in them sensation is ambiguous between two contraries, irrespective of distance. But you will understand more clearly if I put it as follows. Here, we say, are three fingers, the middle, third and little one.'

'Yes.'

'And you've got what I call a close view of them. But there's a further point.'

'What is it?'

'Each of them looks as much a finger as any other, and it makes no difference whether it's in the middle or at either end, whether it's white or black, fat or thin, and so on. There is nothing here to force the mind of the ordinary man to stop and think what a finger is; for at no stage has sight presented the finger to it as being also the opposite of a finger.'

'No, it hasn't.'

'So there's nothing in this sort of perception likely to call for or stimulate thought.'

'No.'

'But what about the size of the fingers? Can sight distinguish their differences of size properly? Does it matter which one is in the middle or at the end? And can touch distinguish differences of thickness or degrees of hardness and softness? Aren't all the senses in fact deficient in their perception of such 524 qualities? Don't they operate as follows – touch, for example, which is concerned with hardness must also be concerned with softness, and reports to the mind that the same object is both hard and soft.'

'Yes.'

'Then must not the mind find it difficult in such cases to understand what this sense means by hard, if it says the same thing is soft as well? Or again, what light and heavy mean, if the sense concerned indicates that what is heavy is light and what is light is heavy?'

'Yes; this sort of message puzzles the mind and needs investigation.'

'It's probably in this sort of case, then,' I said, 'that the mind calls in reason and thought, and tries to investigate whether one object has been reported to it or two.'

'I suppose so.'

'And if the answer is two, each of the pair is a separate entity.'

'Yes.'

'And if each is a separate entity, and between them they make up two, then the mind will perceive two separate entities; for if they weren't separate it wouldn't perceive two but one.'

'That is correct.'

'But sight, we said, perceives large and small as qualities which are not distinct but run into each other.'

'Yes, so we said.'

'And to clear the matter up thought must adopt the opposite approach and look at large and small as distinct and separate qualities. And from that there follows the question, what is meant by large and small?'

'That's perfectly true.'

'And that is how we came to distinguish the intelligible and the visible.'

'Correct.'

'This was what I was trying to say just now, when I said that we are called on to think when our senses receive opposite impressions, but that otherwise thought remains dormant.'

'Yes, I understand now,' he said, 'and agree with you.'

§2. THE FIVE MATHEMATICAL STUDIES

Mathematics has, pre-eminently, the characteristics required in § 1, and Plato proceeds to list five mathematical disciplines which the Philosopher Ruler must study.

1. *Arithmetic*

'Then in which category do you think the unit and number fall?'

'I don't know.'

'You can work it out from what we have said,' I told him. 'If our perception of the unit, by sight or any other sense, is quite unambiguous, then it provides no more stimulus to seek for truth than did our perception of a finger. But if it is always combined with the perception of its opposite, and seems to involve plurality as much as unity, then it calls for the exercise of judgement and forces the mind into a quandary in which it must stir itself to think, and ask what unity in its absolute sense means; and if that is so, the study of the unit is among those that provoke the mind and turn it to the vision of reality.'

'Well, the perception of unity by sight most certainly has these characteristics; for we see the same thing both as a unit and as an unlimited plurality.'

'And if that's true of the unit,' I said, 'it must be true of number as a whole.'

'It must.'

'And number is the medium of counting and calculation.'

'Of course.'

'So both will lead the mind on to search for truth.'

'Yes, they are extraordinarily effective for the purpose.'

'And so they should be included among the studies we are looking for. Soldiers must study them so that they can organize their armies, and philosophers because they cannot escape from this transient world to ultimate reality unless they can reason.[1] And our Guardians are both soldiers and philosophers.'

'That is true.'

'We can, then, properly lay it down that arithmetic shall be a subject for study by those who are to hold positions of responsibility in our state; and we shall ask them not to be amateurish in their approach to it, but to pursue it till they come to understand, by pure thought, the nature of numbers – they aren't concerned with its usefulness for mere commercial calculation, but for war and for the easier conversion of the soul from the world of becoming to that of reality and truth.'

'Excellent.'

'You know,' I said, 'now that we have mentioned arithmetic, it occurs to me what a subtle and useful instrument it is for our purpose, if one studies it for the sake of knowledge and not for commercial ends.'

1. The Greek word can mean both 'reason' and 'calculate arithmetically'.

'How is that?' he asked.

'As we have just said, it draws the mind upwards and forces it to argue about pure numbers, and will not be put off by attempts to confine the argument to collections of visible or tangible objects. You must know how the experts in the subject, if one tries to argue that the unit is divisible, won't have it, but make you look absurd by multiplying it if you try to divide it, to make sure that their unit is never shown to contain a multiplicity of parts.'

'Yes, that's quite true.'

'What do you think they would say, Glaucon, if one were to 526 say to them, "This is very extraordinary – what are these numbers you are arguing about, in which you claim that every unit is exactly equal to every other, and at the same time not divisible into parts?" What do you think their answer would be to that?'

'I suppose they would say that the numbers they mean can be apprehended by thought, but that there is no other way of grasping them.'

'You see therefore,' I pointed out to him, 'that this study looks as if it were really necessary to us, since it so obviously compels the mind to think in order to get at the truth.'

'It certainly does have that effect,' he agreed.

'Another point – have you noticed how those who are naturally good at calculation are nearly always quick at learning anything else, and how the slow-witted, if trained and practised in calculation, always improve in speed even if they get no other benefit? Yet I suppose there's hardly any form of study which comes harder to those who learn or practise it.'

'That is true.'

'For all these reasons, then, we must retain this subject and use it to train our ablest citizens.'

'I agree.'

11. *Plane Geometry*

'That's one subject settled, then. Next let us see if the one that follows it is of any use to us.'

'Do you mean geometry?' he asked.

'Exactly.'

'It's obviously useful in war,' he said. 'If a man knows geometry it will make all the difference to him when it comes to pitching camp or taking up a position, or concentrating or deploying an army, or any other military manoeuvre in battle or on the march.'

'For that sort of purpose,' I replied, 'the amount of geometry or calculation needed is small. What we want to find out is whether the subject is on the whole one which, when taken further, has the effect of making it easier to see the Form of the Good. And that, we say, is the tendency of everything which compels the mind to turn to the blessedness of the ultimate reality which it must somehow contrive to see.'

'I agree,' he said.

'So if it compels us to contemplate reality, it will be useful, but otherwise not.'

'That's our view.'

527 'Well, then, no one with even an elementary knowledge of geometry will dispute that it's a science quite the reverse of what is implied by the terms its practitioners use.'

'Explain.'

'The terms are quite absurd, but they are hard put to it to find others. They talk about "squaring" and "applying" and "adding" and so on, as if they were *doing* something and their reasoning had a practical end, and the subject were not, in fact, pursued for the sake of knowledge.'

'Yes, that's true.'

'And what is more, it must, I think, be admitted that the objects of that knowledge are eternal and not liable to change and decay.'

'Yes, there's no question of that: the objects of geometrical knowledge are eternal.'

'Then it will tend to draw the mind to the truth and direct the philosophers' thought upwards, instead of to our present mundane affairs.'

'It is sure to.'

'Then you must be sure to require the citizens of your ideal

294

state not to neglect geometry. It has considerable incidental advantages too.'

'What are they?' he asked.

'Its usefulness for war, which you have already mentioned,' I replied; 'and there is a certain facility for learning all other subjects in which we know that those who have studied geometry lead the field.'

'They are miles ahead,' he agreed.

'So shall we make this the second subject our young men must study?'

'Yes.'

III. *Solid Geometry*

It is clear from the way in which Plato speaks of it that this branch of mathematics was little developed in his day.

'And the third should be astronomy. Or don't you agree?'

'Yes, I certainly agree. A degree of skill in telling the seasons, months and years is useful not only to the farmer and sailor but also to the soldier.'

'You amuse me,' I said, 'with your obvious fear that the public will disapprove if the subjects you prescribe aren't thought useful. But it is in fact very difficult for people to believe that there is a faculty in the mind of each of us which these studies purify and rekindle after it has been ruined and blinded by other pursuits, though it is more worth preserving than any eye since it is the only organ by which we perceive the truth. Those who agree will think your proposals admirable; but those who have never realized it will probably think you are talking nonsense, as they won't see what other benefit is to be expected from such studies. Make up your mind which party you 528 are going to argue with – or will you ignore both and pursue the argument for your own satisfaction, though without grudging anyone else any benefit he may get from it?'

'That's what I'll do,' he replied; 'I'll go on with the discussion chiefly for my own satisfaction.'

'Then you must go back a bit,' I said, 'as we made a wrong choice of subject to put next to geometry.'

'How was that?'

'We proceeded straight from plane geometry to solid bodies in motion without considering solid bodies first on their own. The right thing is to proceed from second dimension to third, which brings us to cubes and other three-dimensional figures.'

'That's true enough,' he agreed, 'but the subject is one which doesn't seem to have been much investigated yet, Socrates.'

'For two reasons,' I replied. 'There is no state which sets any value on it, and so, being difficult, it is not pursued with energy; and research is not likely to progress without a director, who is difficult to find and, even if found, is unlikely to be obeyed in the present intolerant mood of those who study the subject. But under the general direction of a state that set a value on it, their obedience would be assured, and research pressed forward continuously and energetically till the problems were solved. Even now, with all the neglect and inadequate treatment it has suffered from students who do not understand its real uses, the subject is so attractive that it makes progress in spite of all handicaps, and it would not be surprising if its problems were solved.'

'Yes, it has very great attractions,' he said. 'But explain more clearly what you said just now. You said geometry dealt with plane surfaces.'

'Yes.'

'Then you first said astronomy came next, but subsequently went back on what you had said.'

'More haste less speed,' I said. 'In my hurry I overlooked solid geometry, because it's so absurdly undeveloped, and put astronomy, which is concerned with solids in motion, after plane geometry.'

'Yes that's what you did,' he agreed.

'Then let us put astronomy fourth, and assume that the neglect of solid geometry would be made good under state encouragement.'

IV. *Astronomy*

In reading Plato's disparagement of observation here two things should be remembered.

(1) 'Plato's primary purpose here is not to advance physical science, but to train the mind to think abstractly' (Cornford, p. 241). (2) Mathematical astronomy was still only just beginning, and until the astronomer has his mathematical tools he can make no progress; it was the insistence, in the Academy, on the essentially mathematical nature of the problems that led to the rapid progress of astronomy in the two hundred years after Plato's death. Plato himself later gave a higher place to observation in the Laws *and* Epinomis.

'That is fair enough,' he said. 'And since you have just been attacking me for approving of astronomy for low motives, let me approve of it now on your principles; for it must be ob-vious to everyone that it, of all subjects, compels the mind to look upwards and leads it from earth to heaven.' 529

'Perhaps I'm an exception,' I said, ' for I don't agree. I think that, as it's at present handled by those who use it as an introduction to philosophy, it makes us look down, not up.'

'What do you mean?' he asked.

'I think you've a really splendid idea of the study of "higher things",' I replied. 'Perhaps you think that anyone who puts his head back and studies a painted ceiling is using his mind and not his eyes. You may be right, and I may be just simple minded, but I can't believe that the mind is made to look up-wards except by studying the ultimate unseen reality. If anyone tries to learn anything about the world of sense whether by gaping upwards or blinking downwards, I don't reckon that the result is *knowledge* – there is no knowledge to be had of such things – nor do I reckon his mind is directed upwards, even if he's lying on his back or floating on the sea.'

'I'm guilty,' he said, 'and deserve to be scolded. But how else do you mean that astronomy ought to be studied if it's to serve our purpose?'

'Like this,' I said. 'The stars in the sky, though we rightly regard them as the finest and most perfect of visible things, are far inferior, just because they are visible, to the true realities; that is, to the movements and bodies in movement whose true relative speeds are to be found in terms of pure numbers and perfect figures, and which are perceptible to reason and thought but not visible to the eye. Do you agree?'

'Yes.'

'Well, then,' I went on, 'we ought to treat the visible splendours of the sky as illustrations to our study of the true realities, just as one might treat a wonderful and carefully drawn design by Daedalus or any other artist or draughtsman. Anyone who knew anything about geometry, and saw such a design, would admire the skill with which it was done, but would think it absurd to study it in the serious hope of learning the truth about proportions such as double or half.'

530

'It would be absurd to hope for that,' he agreed.

'Isn't the true astronomer in the same position when he watches the movements of the stars?' I asked. 'He will think that the sky and the heavenly bodies have been put together by their maker as well as such things can be; but he will also think it absurd to suppose that there is anything constant or invariable about the relation of day to night, or of day and night to month, or month to year, or, again, of the periods of the other stars to them and to each other. They are all visible and material, and it's absurd to look for exact truth in them.'

'I agree now you put it like that,' he said.

'We shall therefore treat astronomy, like geometry, as setting us problems for solution,' I said, 'and ignore the visible heavens, if we want to make a genuine study of the subject and use it to put the mind's native wit to a useful purpose.'

'You are demanding a lot more work than astronomy at present involves,' he said.

'We shall make other demands like it, I think, if we are to be any use as lawgivers. But,' I asked, 'can you think of any other suitable study?'

'Not at the moment.'

v. *Harmonics*

Which is to be treated on the same principles as Astronomy.

'All the same, there are several species of motion,' I said. 'I suppose that an expert could enumerate them all; but even I can distinguish two of them.'

'What are they?'

'The one we've been talking about and its counterpart.'

'What's that?'

'I think we may say that, just as our eyes are made for astronomy, so our ears are made for harmony, and that the two are, as the Pythagoreans say, and as we should agree, sister sciences. Isn't that so?'

'Yes.'

'And as the work involved is considerable we will consult them on the subject, and perhaps on others too. But all through we must maintain the principle we laid down when dealing with astronomy, that our pupils must not leave their studies incomplete or stop short of the final objective. They can do this just as much in harmonics as they could in astronomy, by wasting their time on measuring audible concords and notes.' 531

'Lord, yes, and pretty silly they look,' he said. 'They talk about "intervals" of sound, and listen as carefully as if they were trying to hear a conversation next door. And some say they can distinguish a note between two others, which gives them a minimum unit of measurement, while others maintain that there's no difference between the notes in question. They are all using their ears instead of their minds.'

'You mean those people who torment catgut, and try to wring the truth out of it by twisting it on pegs. I might continue the metaphor [1] and talk about strokes of the bow, and accusations against the strings and their shameless denials – but I'll drop it, because I'm not thinking so much of these people as of the Pythagoreans, who we said would tell us about harmonics. For they do just what the astronomers do;

1. Greek law allowed the torture of slaves for the purpose of extracting evidence from them.

they look for numerical relationships in audible concords, and never get as far as formulating problems and asking which numerical relations are concordant and why.'

'But that would be a fearsome job,' he protested.

'A useful one, none the less,' I said, 'when the object is to discover what is right and good; though not otherwise.'

'That may well be.'

§3. DIALECTIC

The mathematical studies are only the preliminary to Dialectic. We are reminded of the Line and Cave (Part VII, §§ 6 and 7). Dialectic is the exercise of pure thought or intelligence, the highest section of the Line; its object is the vision of the Good, the last stage in the ascent from the Cave, when the eye can look at the sun itself. Exactly what Plato meant by Dialectic has been much disputed. It is clearly concerned with both mathematics and morals, in each bringing a coherence and certainty lacking at an earlier stage; but Plato deliberately avoids detail and precision, and if we say that Dialectic is a purely philosophic activity, that it gives coherence to the whole of a man's knowledge, and leads finally to a vision of ultimate reality, we have, perhaps, said as much as can be said with certainty.

'Yes,' I said, 'for it's only if we can pursue all these studies until we see their kinship and common ground, and can work out their relationship, that they contribute to our purpose and are worth the trouble we spend on them.'

'So I should imagine. But it means a great deal of work.'

'And you don't suppose it's more than a beginning, do you?' I asked. 'The subjects we've described are only a prelude to our main theme. For you don't think that people who are good at them are trained philosophers, do you?'

'Heavens, no, with very few exceptions.'

'And can they ever acquire the knowledge we regard as essential if they can't argue logically?'

'No, they can't.'

532 'But isn't this just the note which Dialectic must strike? It is an intellectual process, but is paralleled in the visible world, as

we said, by the progress of sight from shadows to real creatures, and then to the stars, and finally to the sun itself. So when one tries to reach ultimate realities by the exercise of pure reason, without any aid from the senses, and refuses to give up until the mind has grasped what the Good is, one is at the end of an intellectual progress parallel to the visual progress we described.'

'That's perfectly true.'

'And isn't this progress what we call "dialectic"?'

'Yes.'

'The prisoners in our cave,' I went on, 'were released and turned round from the shadows to the images which cast them and to the fire, and then climbed up into the sunlight; there they were unable to look at animals and plants and at the light of the sun, but turned to [1] reflections in water and shadows of things (real things, that is, and not mere images throwing shadows in the light of a fire itself derivative compared with the sun). Well, the whole study of the subjects we have described has the effect of leading the best element in the mind up towards the vision of the highest reality, just as the body's most perceptive organ was led to see the brightest of all things in the material and visible world.'

'I quite agree with all you've said myself,' said Glaucon; 'I think it's very difficult to accept in some ways, but as hard to deny in others. However, as this isn't the only occasion on which we shall hear about it and there will be plenty of opportunities to return to it in the future, let us suppose it is so for the present and go on to deal with the main course as thoroughly as we have dealt with the prelude. Tell us what sort of power Dialectic has, and how many kinds of it there are and how they are pursued; for they seem to lead to our destination, where we shall get some rest at the end of our journey.'

'My dear Glaucon,' I said, 'you won't be able to follow me 533 further, not because of any unwillingness on my part, but be-

---

1. I prefer Ast's θέα to the O.C.T. θεῖα, but if Adam's explanation of θεῖα is correct (a 'Platonic phrase for reflections of natural objects'), my translation is still, I think, accurate.

cause what you'd see would no longer be an image but truth itself, that is, so far as I can see it; I wouldn't like to be sure my vision is true, but I'm quite sure there is something for us to see, aren't you?'

'Of course.'

'And you agree that dialectic ability can only be acquired after the course of study we have described, and in no other way?'

'I'm quite sure of that.'

'And it can't be denied that it's the only activity which systematically sets about the definition of the essential nature of things. Of other activities some are concerned with human opinions or desires, or with growing or making things and looking after them when they are grown or made; others, geometry and the like, though, as we have said, concerned with reality, can only see it in a kind of dream, and never clearly, so long as they leave their assumptions unquestioned and cannot account for them. For how can any chain of reasoning result in knowledge if it starts from a premiss it does not really know and proceeds to a conclusion and through steps which it does not know either?'

'It can't possibly.'

'Dialectic, in fact, is the only activity whose method is to challenge its own assumptions so that it may rest firmly on first principles. When the eye of the mind gets really bogged down in a morass of ignorance, dialectic gently pulls it out and leads it up, using the studies we have described to convert and help it. These studies we have often, through force of habit, referred to as branches of *knowledge,* but we really need another term, to indicate a greater degree of clarity than opinion but a lesser degree than knowledge – we called it Reasoning earlier on. But I don't think we shall quarrel about a word, the subject of our inquiry is too important for that.'

'It is indeed.'

'So we shall be content to use any term that will indicate clearly the faculty we mean.'

'Yes.'

'Then let us be content with the terms we used earlier on for the four divisions of our line – knowledge, reason, belief, and illusion. The last two we class together as opinion, the first two as intelligence, opinion being concerned with the world of becoming, knowledge with the world of reality. Knowledge stands to opinion as the world of reality does to that of becoming, and intelligence stands to belief and reason to illusion as knowledge stands to opinion. The relation of the realities corresponding to intelligence and opinion and the twofold divisions into which they fall we had better omit if we're not to land ourselves in an argument even longer than we've already had.'

'Yes,' said Glaucon; 'I agree about all that, so far as I can follow you.'

'So you agree in calling the ability to give an account of the essential nature of each particular thing Dialectic; and in saying that anyone who is unable to give such an account of things either to himself or to other people has to that extent failed to understand them.'

'I can hardly do otherwise.'

'Then doesn't the same apply to the Good? If a man can't define the Form of the Good and distinguish it clearly from everything else, and then defend it against all comers, not merely as a matter of opinion but in strict logic, and come through with his argument unshaken, you wouldn't say he knew what Absolute Good was, or indeed any other good. Any notion such a man has is based on opinion rather than knowledge, and he's living in a dream from which he's unlikely to awake this side of the grave, where he will finally sleep for ever.'

'With all that I agree emphatically.'

'Well, then, if you ever really had the job of bringing up and educating these imaginary children of yours, you would not, I imagine, let them reach positions of high responsibility in society without having their ideas put in order?'

'No.'

'So you will lay it down that their powers of argument must be developed by an appropriate education.'

'With your help I will.'

'Then we can regard Dialectic as the coping-stone of our
535 educational system, which completes the course of studies and
needs no further addition.'

'Yes.'

§4. SELECTION AND CURRICULUM

*Plato first emphasizes the moral and, more particularly, intellectual
virtues necessary in those who are to embark on the course outlined. He
then specifies the length of time needed for each stage and the age at
which it should be started. The first stage, described in Part III, lasts
till the age of eighteen. From eighteen to twenty there are two years of
physical training and military service. Then, between the ages of twenty
and thirty, selected candidates are put through the mathematical disciplines; that stage is followed (after further selection) by five years' Dialectic, any earlier introduction to which is, we are reminded, very dangerous; then follow fifteen years' practical experience in subordinate
offices, after which those who survive all these tests are fully qualified
Philosopher Rulers and divide their time between philosophy (which
they prefer) and ruling.*

'All you have to do now, then,' I went on, 'is to decide who
should study these subjects and how.'

'Yes, that's all.'

'Do you remember the kind of people we picked when you
were choosing our Rulers?'[1]

'Of course I do.'

'In most respects we should pick them again – we should
prefer the steadiest and bravest and, so far as possible, the best-
looking. But we shall also look not only for moral integrity
and toughness, but for natural aptitude for this kind of education.'

'And how would you define that?'

'Well, my dear chap,' I said, 'they need intellectual eagerness, and must learn easily. For the mind shirks mental effort
more than physical, in which it can share the hard work with
the body.'

1. P. 156.

'True.'

'They must have good memories, determination and a fondness for hard work. How, otherwise, will they be ready to go through with such an elaborate course of study on top of their physical training?'

'They won't unless they have every natural advantage.'

'Which explains what is wrong with philosophy to-day and why it has a bad reputation; as we said before,[1] it isn't taken seriously enough, and the people who take it up aren't genuine about it as they should be.'

'How do you mean?' he asked.

'First of all,' I said, 'anyone who takes it up must have no inhibitions about hard work. He mustn't be only half inclined to work, and half not – for instance, a man who is very fond of hunting and athletics and all kinds of physical exercise, but has no inclination to learn and dislikes intellectual effort of any kind. And there are people just as one-sided in the opposite way.'

'That's very true.'

'We shall regard as equally crippled for the pursuit of truth a mind which, while it detests deliberate lying, and will not abide it in itself and is indignant to find it in others, cheerfully acquiesces in conventional misrepresentations and feels no indignation when its own ignorance is shown up, but wallows in it like a pig in a sty.' 536

'I entirely agree.'

'We must be as careful to distinguish genuine and bogus in dealing with all the virtues – discipline, courage, broadmindedness and the rest. Failure to make the distinction on the part of an individual or a community merely leads to the unwitting employment of people who are unsound and bogus in some way whether as friends or rulers.'

'That is very true.'

'We must avoid these mistakes,' I went on. 'If we pick those who are sound in body and mind and then put them through our long course of instruction and training, Justice herself can't blame us and we shall preserve the constitution of our

1. P. 259 ff.

society; if we make any other choice the effect will be precisely the opposite, and we shall plunge philosophy even deeper in ridicule than it is at present.'

'Which would be a shameful thing to do.'

'It would,' I agreed. 'But I'm not sure I'm not being slightly ridiculous at the moment myself.'

'How?'

'I was forgetting that we are amusing ourselves with an imaginary sketch, and got too worked up. I had in mind as I spoke the unjust criticisms that are made of philosophy, which annoyed me, and my anger at the critics made me speak more seriously than I should.'

'Oh, come!' he said, 'I didn't think you were too serious.'

'Well, I felt I was. However, don't let's forget that when we were making our earlier choice,[1] we chose elderly men; but that won't do now. We mustn't let Solon persuade us that as one grows old one's capacity for learning increases, any more than one's ability to run; the time for all serious effort is when we are young.'

'Undoubtedly.'

'Arithmetic and geometry and the other studies leading to Dialectic should be introduced in childhood, though we mustn't exercise any form of compulsion.'

'Why?' he asked.

'Because a free man ought not to learn anything under duress. Compulsory physical exercise does no harm to the body, but compulsory learning never sticks in the mind.'

'True.'

'Then don't use compulsion,' I said to him, 'but let your children's lessons take the form of play. You will learn more about their natural abilities that way.'

'There's something in what you say.'

'Do you remember,' I reminded him, 'that we said that our children ought to be taken on horseback to watch fighting, and, if it was safe, taken close up and given their taste of blood, like your hounds?'

'Yes, I remember.'

1. P. 157.

'Well, we must enrol in a select number those who show themselves most at home in all these exercises and studies and dangers.'

'At what age?' he asked.

'As soon as their necessary physical training is over. During that time, whether it be two or three years, they won't be able to do anything else; physical fatigue and sleep are unfavourable to study. And one of the most important tests is to see how they show up in their physical training.'

'True.'

'After that time, then, at the age of twenty, some of them will be selected for promotion, and will have to bring together the disconnected subjects they studied in childhood and take a comprehensive view of their relationship with each other and with reality.'

'That is the only way to make knowledge permanent.'

'And also the best test of aptitude for Dialectic, which is the ability to take the comprehensive view.'

'I agree.'

'You will have to keep all this in view and make a further choice among your selected candidates when they pass the age of thirty. Those who show the required perseverance in their studies, in war, and in their other duties, will be promoted to higher privileges, and their ability to follow truth into the realm of pure reality, without the use of sight or any other sense, tested by means of Dialectic. And here, my friend, you will have to go to work very carefully."

'Why particularly?'

'Haven't you noticed the appalling harm done by Dialectic at present?'

'What harm?'

'It fills people with indiscipline.'

'Oh, yes, I've noticed that.'

'And does it surprise you?' I asked. 'Aren't you sorry for the victims?'

'Why should I be?'

'Well, imagine a child who has been brought up in a large, 538 rich, and powerful family, with many hangers-on; when he grows up he discovers that he is not the child of his so-called parents, but can't discover who his real parents are. Can you imagine how he will feel towards the hangers-on and his supposed parents, first while he still doesn't know they aren't his real parents, and then when he does? Shall I tell you what I should expect?'

'Yes, do.'

'Well, I should expect that, so long as he didn't know they weren't his real parents, he would respect his mother and father and supposed relations more than the hangers-on, be more concerned with their needs, and less inclined to do or say anything outrageous to them, or to disobey them in matters of importance.'

'Very likely.'

'But when he discovered the truth, I should expect him to give up respecting them seriously and devote himself to the hangers-on; their influence with him would increase, he'd associate with them openly and live by their standards, and, unless his natural instincts were particularly decent, he'd pay no more attention to his reputed parents and relations.'

'That's all very likely. But,' he asked, 'what bearing has the illustration on philosophic discussions?'

'This. There are certain opinions about what is right and fair in which we are brought up from childhood, and whose authority we respect like that of our parents.'

'True.'

'And there are certain habits of an opposite kind, which have a deceitful attraction because of the pleasures they offer, but which no one of any decency gives in to, because he respects the authority of tradition.'

'True again.'

'Yes,' I said, 'but what happens when he is confronted with the question, "What do you mean by 'fair'?" When he gives the answer tradition has taught him, he is refuted in argument, and when that has happened many times and on many different grounds, he is driven to think that there's no difference between fair and foul, and so on with all the other moral values, like right and good, that he used to revere. What sort of respect for their authority do you think he'll feel at the end of it all?'

'He's bound to feel quite differently.'

'Then when he's lost any respect or feeling for his former beliefs but not yet found the truth, where is he likely to turn? Won't it be to the deceitful attractions of pleasure?'

'Yes, it will.'

'And so we see indiscipline supplanting tradition.'

'Inevitably.'

'Yet all this is a natural consequence of starting on philosophic discussions in this way, and, as I've just said, there's every reason for us to excuse it.'

'Yes, and be sorry about it,' he agreed.

'Then if you want to avoid being sorry for your thirty-year-olders, you must be very careful how you introduce them to such discussions.'

'Very careful.'

'And there's one great precaution you can take, which is to stop their getting a taste of them too young. You must have noticed how young men, after their first taste of argument, are always contradicting people just for the fun of it; someone proves them wrong, and they follow his lead and argue that other people are wrong, like puppies who love to pull and tear at anyone within reach.'

'They like nothing better,' he said.

'So when they've proved a lot of people wrong and been proved wrong often themselves, they soon slip into the belief that nothing they believed before was true; with the result that they discredit themselves and the whole business of philosophy in the eyes of the world.'

'That's perfectly true,' he said.

'But someone who's a bit older,' I went on, 'will refuse to have anything to do with this sort of idiocy; he won't contradict just for the fun of the thing but will be more likely to follow the lead of someone whose arguments are aimed at finding the truth. He's a more reasonable person and will get philosophy a better reputation.'

'True.'

'In fact all we've been saying has been said in the attempt to ensure that only men of steady and disciplined character shall be admitted to philosophic discussions, and not anyone, however unqualified, as happens at present.'

'I entirely agree.'

'Then suppose twice as long is spent on a continuous and intensive study of philosophy as we proposed should be spent on physical training, will that be enough?'

'Do you mean six years or four?'

'It doesn't matter,' said I; 'make it five. After that they must be sent down again into the Cave we spoke of, and compelled to hold any military or other office suitable for the young, so that they may have as much practical experience as their fellows. And here again they must be tested to see if they stand up to the temptations of all kinds or give way to them.'

'And how long do you allow for this stage?'

'Fifteen years. And when they are fifty, those who have come through all our practical and intellectual tests with success must be brought to their final trial, and made to lift their mind's eye to look at the source of all light, and see the Good itself, which they can take as a pattern for ordering their own life as well as that of society and the individual. For the rest of their lives they will spend most of their time in philosophy, but when their turn comes they will turn to the weary business of politics and do their duty as Rulers, not for the honour they get by it but as a matter of necessity. And so, when they have brought up successors like themselves, they will depart this life, and the state will set up a public memorial to them and sacrifice to them, if the Pythian Oracle approves, as divinities, or at any rate as saints.'

'It's a fine picture you have drawn of our Rulers, Socrates.'

'And some of them will be women,' I reminded him. 'All I have said about men applies equally to women, if they have the necessary qualifications.'

'Of course,' he agreed, 'if they are to share equally in everything with the men, as we described.'

'Well, then, do you agree that the society and constitution we have sketched is not merely an idle dream, difficult though its realization may be? The indispensable condition is that political power should be in the hands of one or more true philosophers. They would despise all present honours as mean and worthless, and care most for doing right and any rewards it may bring; and – most important and essential of all – they would, throughout their reorganization of society, serve and forward the interests of justice.'

'How would they proceed?'

'They would begin by sending away into the country all citizens over the age of ten; having thus removed the children 541 from the influence of their parents' present way of life, they would bring them up on their own methods and rules, which we have described. This is the best and quickest way to establish our society and constitution, and for it to succeed and bring its benefits to any people among which it is established.'

'Yes, that's much the best way; and I think, Socrates,' he added, 'that you have explained very well how such a society would come into existence, if ever it did.'

'Then haven't we said enough about this state of ours and the corresponding type of man? For it's surely obvious what type we shall want.'

'Perfectly obvious,' he agreed. 'And I agree with you that there's no more to be said.'

PART NINE

IMPERFECT SOCIETIES

*

Plato now returns to the point at which he broke off to describe the provisions for women and children and the training of the Philosopher Ruler (p. 200), and proceeds to describe four imperfect types of society – Timarchy, Oligarchy, Democracy, and Tyranny. They are described as if they occurred in that order in a historical series; but Plato is concerned with a moral degeneration, and the historical framework should not be taken too literally. To each society there corresponds a type of individual, whose description follows immediately after that of the society. The origin and character of these individual types and of the society to which they correspond are described quite independently (the origin of democracy, for example, is different from that of the 'democratic man'), and not all individuals in each society can be of the type corresponding to it (there can, for example, strictly speaking only be one 'tyrant' in a tyranny); but the traits in the individual will be those admired in the society to which he corresponds, he will be its ideal man, and the description of this ideal serves to throw further light on the society.

§1. RECAPITULATION

Enumeration of the four imperfect societies to be described.

BK
VIII
543 'WELL, that's that. What we have agreed, Glaucon, is that in the perfect state women and children should be held in common, that men and women should share the same education and the same occupations both in peace and war, and that they should be governed by those of their number who are best at philosophy and war.'

'That is what we have agreed.'

'We have agreed too that, when our Rulers are appointed, they will take the soldiers and settle them in accommodation where there are no private quarters but everything is common to all; and besides that you will remember what we said about property.'

'Yes,' he said, 'it was that they should possess none of the things other men now do; they were to train for war and act as Guardians over the community as a whole, in return for which they were to get their keep as their annual wage.'

'That is right,' I said. 'But now we've dealt with all that, tell me, where were we when we started off on it? Let us pick up the track again.'

'That's easy. You were talking, as you were just now, as if you had finished your description of the state, and were saying that the state you had described and the individual corresponding to it were what you would call good – though as we have now seen you could do something much better in the way of a description of them. Anyhow, you were saying that if this was the right kind of state, the others must be wrong. And, I remember, you said that the others were four in number, and that it was worth discussing how they and the characters corresponding to them had gone wrong, so that, having examined the various types of character and ranged them in order of goodness and badness, we could then consider whether the best was the happiest, and the worst the most miserable, or not. I was just asking what the four kinds of society were when Polemarchus and Adeimantus interrupted, and your reply to them has brought us to where we now are.' 544

'You've a very good memory,' I said.

'Well, let's go back, like a wrestler practising the same hold again, and I will ask you the same question and you try to give me the answer you were going to give.'

'I will if I can.'

'Well, I'm particularly anxious myself to hear what these four kinds of society are.'

'There's no difficulty about that,' I replied. 'The ones I mean have names in common use. There is the much admired Cretan or Spartan type; secondly, and second in common estimation, though it's burdened with many evils, there is the type called oligarchy; thirdly, and by contrast, follows democracy; and finally comes tyranny, often thought the finest and most famous, but really the most diseased society of all. Do you know of any other type of society which can be reckoned a distinct species? There are hereditary monarchies, and states where office is bought, but these and other similar examples are really crosses between our four types, and are to be found as frequently among barbarians as Greeks.'

'Yes, there are many odd variations.'

'You realize, I suppose,' I went on, 'that there must be as many types of individual as of society? Societies aren't made of sticks and stones, but of men whose individual characters, by turning the scale one way or another, determine the direction of the whole.'

'Yes; society must be formed of individuals.'

'Then, if there are five types of society, there must presumably be five types of individual character.'

'Yes.'

'But we have already described as truly just and good the type corresponding to our ideal society.'

'Yes, we have.'

145 'What we must do next, then, is to go through the inferior types, the competitive and ambitious man who corresponds to the Spartan form of society, and then the other three, the oligarchic and democratic and tyrannic. Thus we can contrast the worst type of man with the best, and complete our inquiry into the relative happiness and unhappiness which pure justice and pure injustice bring, and know whether we are to pursue injustice with Thrasymachus, or justice with the argument we are examining.'

'That is just what we want to do.'

'We began our discussion of moral qualities by examining them in society before we examined them in the individual, because it made for greater clarity. Shall we do the same thing now? We will take first the ambitious society – I know no current name for it; let us call it "timarchy" or "timocracy" – we will examine it and then look at the corresponding individual beside it; we will then deal similarly with oligarchy and the oligarchic man, and again with democracy and the democratic man, and finally come to the society governed by a tyranny, and take a look at it and the tyrannical character. We can then try to form a proper judgement on the whole matter.'

'Yes; that would be the logical order in which to look at them and reach a decision.'

§2. TIMARCHY

In this description Plato has Sparta in mind; it is not easy to relate it to anything in our experience. The Spartans were, in effect, a military aristocracy living in a serf-population.

The section opens with an account of how Timarchy originates from the ideal state. The details are explained in the footnotes; the principle is that the change is due to social strife, however that may start.

'Then let us try,' I said, 'to describe how our ideal state turns into a timocracy. The answer is perhaps simple. Change in any society starts with disagreement among the ruling class; as long as the ruling class remains united, even if it is quite small, no change is possible.'

'That is true.'

'Then how will change take place in our state? How will Auxiliaries and Rulers come to fall out with each other or among themselves? Shall we invoke the Muses, like Homer, and ask them to tell us "how the quarrel first began?" Let us imagine that they are talking to us in a rather dramatic, high-flown fashion, pretending to be very much in earnest, though they are really only teasing us as if we were children.'

'How?'

'Like this. – It will be difficult to bring about any change for the worse in a state so constituted; but since all created things must decay, even a social order of this kind cannot last for ever, but will decline. And it will break up as follows. Not only for plants that grow in the earth, but for animals that live on it, there are seasons when mind and body are productive, seasons which come when a certain period is completed,[1] of

1. The meaning of the following passage is briefly this: There is a period of gestation in all plants and animals, fixed by nature; this applies to the 'divine creature', i.e. the universe as a whole, as much as it does to man. As we have seen above (Part VI, §2), the Rulers have to arrange for the breeding of citizens, and the decline of the ideal society originates from their making mistakes in so doing. This is here expressed in an elaborate, and perhaps only half-serious, mathematical form, in which a 'number' is said to 'control' the whole process.

546

longer duration for the long-lived, shorter for the short-lived. And though the Rulers you have trained for your city are wise, reason and perception will not always enable them to hit on the right and wrong times for breeding; some time they will miss them and then children will be begotten amiss. For the divine creature there is a period defined by a perfect number; for the human creature the number is the first in which root and square multiplications (comprising three dimensions and four limits) of basic numbers, which make like and unlike, and which increase and decrease, produce a final result in completely commensurate terms; [1] of these basic numbers four and three, coupled with five, yield two harmonies when raised to the power of four, of which one is a square with side a multiple of a hundred, the other a rectangle of which one side is one hundred squares of diameters of a square of side five, each diminished by one if the diameters are irrational, or by two if the diameters are rational, the other side of one hundred cubes of three. [2]

'This number, which thus measures and controls the earth, is responsible for the quality of births, and when the Guardians forget this and mate brides and bridegrooms inopportunely, the resulting children will be neither gifted nor lucky.

---

1. $3^3 + 4^3 + 5^3 = 216$. The number of days in the period of gestation of a seven-months child, the minimum period of gestation, so the Greeks believed. The normal period was arrived at by adding to 216 the product of 3, 4, and 5; $3 \times 4 \times 5 = 60 + 216 = 276$.

2. $(3 \times 4 \times 5)^4 = 3,600^2$, and $4,800 \times 2,700$ which again $= 3,600^2$. The second figure is arrived at by taking a square of side 5. The diameter of this is $\sqrt{50}$. This, to the nearest whole ('rational') number is 7: $7^2 \times 100 = 4,900$, diminished by 1 for each 7^2, i.e. by $1 \times 100 = 100$, $= 4,800$. Alternatively, the 'irrational' diameter is $\sqrt{50}$; square this and it is 50; multiply by 100 and it is 5,000, diminish by 2 for each 50, i.e. by $2 \times 100 = 200$, and again you have 4,800. $3,600^2$ is the number of days in a 'Great Year' (the time it takes the heavenly bodies to return to the same relative positions), which is supposed to be the 'period' of the universe as a whole (the 'divine creature'). Plato does not tell us how the two numbers (216 and 3,600) are to be related, and if there is a serious meaning to be found in them it is that microcosm (man) and macrocosm (universe) are related and governed by principles that are, basically, mathematical.

This is Adam's explanation and the reader is referred to him for detail.

The best of them will be appointed to office by their elders, but won't really be worthy of it, and so when they come to hold the posts their fathers held will start neglecting us, though they are Guardians, and under-value education, first intellectual and then physical, with the result that your young men will be worse educated. In the next generation Rulers will be appointed who have lost the true Guardian's capacity to distinguish the metals from which the different classes of your citizens, like Hesiod's, are made – gold, silver, bronze, and iron; and when iron and silver or bronze or gold are mixed, an inconsistent and uneven material is produced, whose irregularities, wherever they occur, must engender war and hatred. That, then, is the pedigree of strife, wherever it happens.'

547

'And we shall assume their answer is right,' he said.

'As indeed it must be, coming from the Muses,' I replied.

'And what will the Muses say next?' he asked.

'Once internal strife has started, the two elements [1] pull in different directions; the iron and bronze towards private profit and property in land and houses and gold and silver, the other two, the silver and gold, having true riches in their own hearts, towards virtue and the traditional order of things. The violence of their opposition is resolved in a compromise under which they distribute land and houses to private ownership, while the subjects whom they once ruled as freemen and friends, and to whom they owed their maintenance, are reduced to the status of serfs and menials, and they devote themselves to war and holding the population in subjection.'

'I agree; that is the origin of the change.'

'And will not the resultant society,' I asked, 'lie between the ideal and oligarchy?'

1. We are concerned at this stage with a dissension between two elements in the governing class, i.e. the Guardians (Rulers plus Auxiliaries), who have become corrupted and into the gold and silver of whose composition (cf. the allegory on p. 160) iron and bronze has entered, with the result that they no longer maintain their former way of life or relation to the third class.

'Yes."

'So much for the change. What will be its results? Isn't it clear that a constitution midway between our earlier society and oligarchy will have some of the features of each as well as certain peculiarities of its own?'

'Yes.'

'Then do you think it will resemble our earlier society in features such as these – respect for authority, the soldier-class abstaining from agriculture, industry, or business, the maintenance of the common messes, and the attention paid to physical and military training?'

'Yes.'

'Its own peculiar characteristics, on the other hand, will be, for example, a fear of admitting intelligent people to office, because intelligence is no longer combined with simplicity and sincerity; it will prefer simpler and more hearty types, who prefer war to peace. It will admire the tricks and stratagems which are needed in war, which will be its constant occupation.'

'Yes.'

'A feature it will share with oligarchy,' I went on, 'will be its love of money. There will be a fierce and secret passion for gold and silver, now that there are private strong rooms to hide it in, and now that there are the four walls of their private houses – expensive nests in which they can spend what they like on their wives and anyone else they choose.'

'That is very true.'

'They will also be mean about money, because though they love it they may not acquire it openly; but they will be ready enough to spend other people's money for their own satisfaction. They will enjoy their pleasures in secret, avoiding the law like truant children; the reason being that they have been educated by force rather than persuasion, owing to neglect of the true principles of a philosophic education and an over-emphasis on physical at the expense of intellectual training.'

'The society you are describing is very much of a mixture of good and evil,' he said.

'Yes, it is,' I agreed. 'But it has one salient feature, due to its emphasis on the strenuous element in us [1] – ambition and the competitive spirit.'

'Very true.'

'So much, then, for the origin and nature of this kind of society,' I said. 'We have only sketched it in outline without filling in the details, because an outline is enough to enable us to distinguish the types of just and unjust men, and because it would be an interminable labour to go through all types of society and their corresponding individuals in detail.'

'You are quite right.'

§3. THE TIMARCHIC CHARACTER

'Then what about the individual corresponding to the society we have just sketched? What is he like and how is he produced?'

'I suspect,' said Adeimantus, 'that he's rather like Glaucon here as far as the competitive spirit goes.'

'Yes, perhaps he is,' I replied. 'But there are other features in which he's not so like him.'

'What are they?'

'He must be rather more self-willed, and rather less well-read, though not without intelligent interests; ready to listen, but quite incapable of expressing himself. He will be harsh to his slaves, because his imperfect education has left him uncertain of his superiority to them; he will be polite to his equals and obey his superior readily. He will be ambitious to hold office himself, regarding as qualifications for it not the ability to speak or anything like that, but military achievements and soldierly qualities, and he'll be fond of exercise and hunting.'

'That's the spirit of the society he's living in.'

'When he's young,' I continued, 'he will despise money, but the older he grows the keener he will get about it. His nature has a touch of avarice and there are flaws in his character because he has lost his best safeguard.'

'And what is that?' asked Adeimantus.

549

1. Cf. p. 183.

'A properly trained mind,'[1] I said. 'That is the only thing that will preserve the character of its possessor intact through life.'

'A fair answer.'

'Well, then, that's the type of young man corresponding to the timocratic society.'

'Agreed.'

'And this is roughly how he's produced. Suppose a young man, whose father is a good man but lives in a badly-run state and avoids office and honours and law-suits and all the bother attached to them, being quite content with a back seat to save himself trouble –'

'How does that produce our type?'

'When he hears his mother complaining that *her* husband isn't one of the bosses, and being slighted by other women because of it; she sees that her husband is not very keen on making money, but avoids the wranglings and bickerings of politics and the law, which he treats very lightly, and keeps his own counsel, while he doesn't take her unduly seriously, though he does not neglect her. All this annoys her and she says that the boy's father isn't a real man and is far too easy-going, and goes on with all the usual complaints women make in the circumstances.'

'And a dreary lot of them there are too,' said Adeimantus.

'And, as you know,' I went on, 'servants who seem quite loyal will sometimes repeat the same sort of thing to the children behind their master's back. And if they see the father failing to prosecute someone who owes him money or has done him some wrong, they tell the son that when he grows up he must have his rights and be more of a man than his father. The boy hears the same sort of thing outside and sees how those who mind their own business are called silly and not thought much of, while those who don't get all the honour and glory. He hears and sees all this, and on the other hand listens to what his father has to say and sees his way of life from close to and contrasts it with other people's; as a result he is torn in

1. A very difficult phrase to translate. Cornford has 'a thoughtful and cultivated mind'.

two directions, his father's influence fostering his rational nature, and that of the others his desire and his ambition.[1] And since he's not really at heart a bad chap, but has merely got into bad company, he takes a middle course between the two, and resigns control of himself to the middle element and its competitive spirit, and so becomes an arrogant and ambitious man.'

'You seem to me to have given a very complete account of his genesis,' he said.

'In that case,' I replied, 'the description of our second society and individual is done.'

'It is.'

§4. OLIGARCHY

A society in which wealth is the criterion of merit and the wealthy are in control. The appearance of a 'drone' class of criminals and malcontents.

'We must go on, as Aeschylus says, to "another man matched with another state," or rather, if we are to follow our plan, to the state first.'

'Proceed.'

'Well, I suppose that the next kind of society is an oligarchy.'

'And what exactly do you mean by an oligarchy?'

'A society where it is wealth that counts,' I said, 'and in which political power is in the hands of the rich and the poor have no share of it.'

'I understand.'

'We must first describe how oligarchy originates from timocracy – though heaven knows it's obvious enough even to a blind man.'

'Tell us how.'

'The accumulation of wealth in private hands is what destroys timarchy. The men become extravagant, and for this

1. The three 'parts' of the mind, p. 183 ff.

reason pervert the law and disobey it, and the women follow their example.'

'That's all likely enough.'

'And mutual jealousy spreads the disease throughout the ruling class.'

'Likely again.'

'The further they go in the process of accumulating wealth, the more they value it and the less they value goodness. For aren't wealth and goodness related like two objects in a balance, so that when one rises the other must fall?'

'Emphatically yes.'

551   'So the higher the prestige of wealth, the lower that of goodness will be.'

'Obviously.'

'And so, since we practise what we admire and neglect what we despise, there is a transition from the ambitious, competitive type of man to the money-loving businessman, honour and admiration and office are reserved for the rich, and the poor are despised.'

'That is so.'

'At this stage they introduce legislation to define a certain minimum amount of property – greater or less according to the narrowness of the oligarchy – as a necessary qualification for office, a measure they force through by armed violence, if they have not already got their way by terrorism. Do you agree?'

'Yes.'

'Then that is, briefly, how an oligarchy is set up.'

'Yes, but what sort of a society is it?' he asked. 'What are its characteristic faults?'

'In the first place,' I replied, 'its whole basis is unsound. For consider, if one chose ships' captains on grounds of wealth, and never gave a poor man a command, even if he was the better sailor –'

'You would have some pretty bad navigation.'

'And isn't the same true of any other form of authority?'

'Personally I should agree.'

'Except politics?' I asked. 'Or is it true in politics too?'

'It is truest of all about politics,' he replied, 'for political authority is the most difficult and the most important.'

'That, then, is one very serious fault in oligarchy. But there is another hardly less serious.'

'What?'

'That it inevitably splits society into two factions, the rich and the poor, who live in the same state and are always plotting against each other.'

'Heaven knows that's just as serious.'

'Its inability to wage war is another discreditable feature. The oligarchs can't do this because they must either arm the people, whom they fear worse than the enemy, or, if they don't, have the thinness of their ranks shown up by the stress of battle; and they are too grasping to want to pay the expenses of a war.'

'Yes, that's another bad feature.'

'Then what about the fact that the same people engage in many different occupations, farming, business, and war? We condemned this once; do we think it right now?' 552

'Certainly not.'

'Then we come to the worst defect of all, which makes its first appearance in this form of society.'

'What is it?'

'That a man can sell all he has to another and live on as a member of society without any real function; he's neither businessman nor craftsman nor soldier, but merely one of the so-called indigent poor. This is allowed to happen in oligarchies; otherwise you would not get the sharp division between rich and poor.'

'True.'

'There's another point. When our pauper was rich, did he perform any of the useful social functions we've just mentioned simply by spending his money? Though he may have appeared to belong to the ruling class, surely in fact he was neither ruling, nor serving society in any other way; he was merely a consumer of goods.'

'That is all he was,' he agreed, 'a mere consumer, whatever he seemed to be.'

'Don't you think we can fairly call him a drone? He grows up in his own home to be a plague to the community, just as a drone grows in its cell to be a plague to the hive.'

'An apt comparison, Socrates.'

'Then would you agree, Adeimantus, that all winged drones have been created without stings, but that our two-footed ones vary, and some have stings and some not; and that the stingless type end their days as beggars, the stinging type as what we call criminals?'

'Yes, entirely.'

'Obviously, then,' I went on, 'in any state where there are beggars there are also, hidden away somewhere, thieves and pick-pockets and temple robbers and all such practitioners of crime.'

'Obviously.'

'And do you find beggars in an oligarchy?'

'Most people are beggars except the ruling class.'

'Then we may suppose there are also plenty of stinging drones, in the shape of criminals whom the government is careful to hold in restraint.'

'Yes,' he agreed.

'And the reason for their existence is lack of education, bad training and a bad form of government.'

'It is.'

'That, then, is what the oligarchic society is like, and those, 553 more or less, are its faults,' I said; 'and we may regard our account of this type of constitution, in which power is linked with property, and of which oligarchy is the common name, as complete. Let us proceed to the corresponding individual, his origin and character.'

'Yes, let us.'

§5. THE OLIGARCHIC CHARACTER

His sole object is to make money.

'The transition from timarchic to oligarchic man takes place, I think, as follows. The timarchic man has a son who at first admires his father and follows in his footsteps; then he sees him suddenly wrecked in some political disaster – he has, perhaps, spent all his substance and energy in some military command or other position of authority, only to be brought into court on false charges and put to death, or exiled, or deprived of his rights and property.'

'That might well happen.'

'The son sees all this,' I continued, 'and, frightened by his sufferings and the loss of his property, incontinently dethrones courage and ambition from the place they have held in his heart. Reduced to poverty, and forced to earn his living, by slow and painful economy and hard work he succeeds in amassing a fortune; so won't he proceed to elevate the profit-motive to the throne, and let it govern like an oriental despot with tiara, chain, and sword?'

'Yes.'

'While reason and ambition squat in servitude at its feet, reason forbidden to make any calculation or inquiry but how to make more money, ambition forbidden to admire or value anything but wealth and the wealthy, or to compete for anything but cash or cash-value.'

'There's no transition quicker or more violent than that from ambition to avarice,' he said.

'And isn't the man we have described our oligarchic type?' I asked.

'He certainly developed from the type corresponding to the society from which oligarchy developed,' he replied.

'Then let's see if he has similar characteristics.'

'Go on.'

554

'The first similarity is in the overriding importance he gives to money.'

'Of course.'

'Again, he is economical and hard-working, satisfying only his necessary wants and indulging in no other expenses, but repressing his other desires as pointless.'

'True again.'

'Yes, he's rather a squalid character,' I said, 'always on the make and putting something by – a type commonly much admired. And again, surely, we see the similarity to our oligarchic society.'

'I agree,' he said; 'money is the chief motive for both.'

'Yes, because I don't suppose he was ever properly educated.'

'I should think not; otherwise he wouldn't have promoted a blind [1] actor to play his chief part.'

'A good point. Now, tell me,' I went on, 'I suppose that his lack of education will breed desires in him, like the pauper and criminal drones, which his general carefulness will keep under restraint.'

'Yes, certainly.'

'And do you know where these criminal desires will show themselves?'

'Where?'

'In his handling of the guardianship of orphans, or of any other matter where he has plenty of scope for dishonesty. There it becomes quite clear that the high reputation for honesty which he has in other business transactions is due merely to a certain respectable constraint which he exercises over his evil impulses, for fear of their effect on his concerns as a whole. There's no moral conviction, no taming of desire by reason, but only the compulsion of fear.'

'Very true.'

'And what is more, you are pretty sure to find evidence of these drone desires when a man of this kind is spending other people's money.'

'Oh, very much so.'

'This sort of man, then, is never at peace in himself, but has a kind of dual personality, in which the better desires on the whole master the worse.'

'True.'

'He therefore has a certain degree of respectability, but comes nowhere near the real goodness of an integrated and united character.'

'I agree.'

'And, being a mean fellow, he's a poor competitor for any

1. Wealth was proverbially a blind god to the Greeks.

personal success or high ambition in public life; he's unwilling 555
to spend money in the struggle for distinction, and scared of
stirring up a whole lot of expensive desires to fight on the side
of his ambition. So, like a true oligarch, he fights with only
part of himself, suppressing the rest, and though he loses the
battle he saves his money.'

'Yes, that's true.'

'Then need we hesitate any longer to say that the grasping
money-maker corresponds to the oligarchic society?'

'No.'

§6. DEMOCRACY

*Equality of political opportunity and freedom for the individual to do
as he likes are, for Plato and Aristotle, the salient characteristics of
democracy. Plato is writing, of course, about democracy in the ancient
city-state, and has Athens particularly in mind (cf. Introduction,
p. 22f.); but translation into terms of modern experience is not
difficult.*

'Our next subject, I suppose, is democracy. When we know
how it originates, and what it is like, we can again identify and
pass judgement on the corresponding individual.'

'That would be consistent with the procedure we've been
following.'

'Then doesn't oligarchy change into democracy because of
lack of restraint in the pursuit of its objective of getting as rich
as possible?'

'How does that happen?'

'Because the Rulers, owing their power to wealth as they do,
are unwilling to curtail by law the extravagance of the young,
and prevent them squandering their money and ruining themselves; for it is by loans to such spendthrifts or by buying up
their property that they hope to increase their own wealth and
influence.'

'That's just what they want.'

'It should then be clear that love of money and adequate
self-discipline in its citizens are two things that can't co-exist in
any society; one or the other must be neglected.'

'That's pretty clear.'

'This failure to curb extravagance in an oligarchy often reduces to poverty men born for better things.'

'Yes, often.'

'Some of them are in debt, some disfranchised, some both, and they settle down, armed with their stings, and with hatred in their hearts, to plot against those who have deprived them of their property and against the rest of society, and to long for revolution.'

'Yes, they do.'

'Meanwhile the money-makers, bent on their business, don't appear to notice them, but continue to inject their poisoned loans wherever they can, and to demand their high rates of interest, with the result that the drones and beggars multiply.'

'A result that's bound to follow.'

'Yet even when the evil becomes flagrant they will do nothing to quench it, either by preventing men from disposing of their property as they like, or by other suitable legislation.'

'What legislation?'

'It's only a second best, but it does compel some respect for decent behaviour. If contracts for a loan were, in general, made at the lender's risk, there would be a good deal less shameless money-making and a good deal less of the evils I have been describing.'

'Much less.'

'But as it is the oligarchs oppress their subjects as we have said, while as for themselves and their dependants – their young men live in luxury and idleness, physical and mental, and lose all their energy and ability to resist pain or pleasure; and they themselves care for nothing but making money, and have no higher moral standards than the poor.'

'True.'

'Such being the state of rulers and ruled, what will happen when they come up against each other in the streets or in the course of business, at a festival or on a campaign, serving in the navy or army? When they see each other in moments of danger, the rich man will no longer be able to despise the poor man; the poor man will be lean and sunburnt, and find himself fighting next to some rich man whose sheltered life and super-fluous flesh make him puff and blow and quite unable to cope. Won't he conclude that people like this are rich because their subjects are cowards, and won't he say to his fellows, when he meets them in private, "This lot are no good; they've had it"?'

'I'm quite sure he will.'

'When a person's unhealthy, it takes very little to upset him and make him ill; there may even be an internal cause for disorder. The same is true of an unhealthy society. It will fall into sickness and dissension at the slightest external provocation, when one party or the other calls in help from a neighbouring oligarchy or democracy; while sometimes faction fights will start without any external stimulus at all.'

'Very true.'

557

'Then democracy originates when the poor win, kill or exile their opponents, and give the rest equal rights and opportunities of office, appointment to office being as a rule by lot.'

'Yes,' he agreed, 'that is how a democracy is established, whether it's done by force of arms or by frightening its opponents into retreat.'

'What sort of a society will it be?' I asked, 'and how will it be run? The answer, obviously, will show us the character of the democratic man.'

'Obviously.'

'Would you agree, first, that people will be free? There is liberty and freedom of speech in plenty, and every individual is free to do as he likes.'

'That's what they say.'

'That being so, won't everyone arrange his life as pleases him best?'

'Obviously.'

'And so there will be the greatest variety of individual character?'

'There's bound to be.'

'I dare say that a democracy is the most attractive of all societies,' I said. 'The diversity of its characters, like the different colours in a patterned dress, make it look very attractive. Indeed,' I added, 'perhaps most people would, for this reason, judge it to be the best form of society, like women and children who judge by appearances.'

'Very likely.'

'And, you know, it's just the place to go constitution-hunting. It contains every possible type, because of the wide freedom it allows, and anyone engaged in founding a state, as we are doing, should perhaps be made to pay a visit to a democracy and make his choice from the variety of models it displays, before he proceeds to make his own foundation.'

'It's a shop in which he'd find plenty of models on show.'

'Then in democracy,' I went on, 'there's no compulsion either to exercise authority if you are capable of it, or to submit to authority if you don't want to; you needn't fight if there's a war, or you can wage a private war in peacetime if you don't like peace; and if there's any law that debars you from political or judicial office, you will none the less take either if they come your way. It's a wonderfully pleasant way of carrying on in the short run, isn't it?'

'In the short run perhaps.'

'And isn't there something rather charming about the good-temper of those who've been sentenced in court? You must have noticed that in a democracy men sentenced to death or exile continue, none the less, to go about among their fellows, who take no more notice of them than if they were invisible spirits.'

'I've often seen that.'

'Then they're very considerate in applying the high principles we laid down when founding our state; so far from interpreting them strictly, they really look down on them. We said that no one who had not exceptional gifts could grow into a good man unless he were brought up from childhood in a good environment and given a good training; democracy with a grandiose gesture sweeps all this away and doesn't mind what the habits and background of its politicians are, provided they profess themselves the people's friends.'

'All very splendid.'

'These, then, and similar characteristics are those of democracy. It's an agreeable, anarchic form of society, with plenty of variety, which treats all men as equal, whether they are equal or not.'

'The picture is easy to recognize.'

§7. THE DEMOCRATIC CHARACTER

Versatile but lacking in principle.

'Then let us look at the democratic individual. And first we should look at his origin, as we did with the society. It is this. Our mean oligarchic character may have a son, whom he will bring up in his own ways.'

'So far, so good.'

'He will forcibly restrain himself from those pleasures that lead to expense rather than profit, the "unnecessary" pleasures as they have been called.'

'Yes, obviously.'

'Then do you think that, if we are to avoid arguing in the dark, we had better define the difference between necessary and unnecessary desires?'

'Yes, I think so.'

'Desires we can't avoid, or whose satisfaction benefits us, can fairly be called necessary, I think. We are bound by our very nature to want to satisfy both, and so may surely with 559 justice use the term "necessary" to describe them.'

'Yes.'

'But we can describe as unnecessary all desires which can be got rid of with practice, if we start young, and whose presence either does us no good or positive harm. Isn't that fair enough?'

'Fair enough.'

'Shall we give examples of each, to get a general idea of what we mean?'

'I think we should.'

'Would you say that the desire to eat enough for health and strength, and the desire for the plain food requisite for the purpose, was necessary?'

331

'Yes, I think so.'

'And of this plain food some is necessary for mere survival as well as for good health, some for good health only.'

'Certainly.'

'But the desire for a more varied and luxurious diet is one which, with discipline and training from an early age, can normally be got rid of, and which is physically harmful and damaging to the intelligence and self-control. May it not therefore rightly be called unnecessary?'

'Undoubtedly.'

'The first kind of desire we could also call economical, because of its practical usefulness, the second kind wasteful.'

'True.'

'And does not the same hold good of sex and the other desires?'

'Yes.'

'Then what we called the drone type must be swayed by a mass of unnecessary pleasures and desires, the mean oligarchic type by necessary ones.'

'Yes.'

'Let's go back to the question how the democratic man originates from the oligarchic. This generally happens when a young man, brought up in the narrow economical way we have described, gets a taste of the drones' honey and gets into wild and dangerous company, where he can be provided with every variety and refinement of pleasure, with the result that his internal oligarchy starts turning into a democracy.'

'That's bound to happen.'

'In society the change took place when one party brought in sympathizers from outside to help it. Will the change in our young men be brought about when one or other type of desire in him gets assistance from similar passions outside him?'

'Yes, certainly.'

'Thus, if the oligarchic element in him gets support and assistance from the remonstrances and criticisms of his father

and other members of his family, the result is a conflict of fac- 560
tions and a self divided against itself. And sometimes the
democratic element gives way to the oligarchic, and some of
his desires are destroyed and some driven out; and a certain
sense of decency is produced in the young man's mind and internal order restored.'

'Sometimes.'

'Alternatively the exiled desires are succeeded by others like
them, produced by his father's ignorance of how to bring him
up properly; and these grow in number and strength, lead him
back to his old associates, and breed and multiply in secret.'

'That often happens.'

'In the end they capture the seat of government, having discovered that the young man's mind is devoid of knowledge,
principle and truth, the most effective safeguards the mind of
man can be blessed with.'

'Far the most effective.'

'The vacant place is filled instead by an invasion of pretentious fallacies, and back he goes to live with the Lotus-eaters.
If his family send help to the economical element in him, the
pretentious invaders shut the gates of the citadel, and will not
admit it; nor will they listen to the individual representations
of old and trusted friends. They make themselves masters by
force, they call shame silliness and drive it into disgrace and
exile; they call self-control cowardice and expel it with abuse;
and they call on a lot of useless desires to help them banish
economy and moderation, which they regard as provincial
parsimony.'

'All very true.'

'They expel the lot and leave the soul of their victim swept
and garnished, ready for the great initiation which follows,
when they lead in a triumphal torchlight procession of insolence, licence, extravagance, and shamelessness. They praise
them all extravagantly and call insolence good breeding, licence liberty, extravagance generosity, and shamelessness
courage. Do you agree that that's how a young man brought 561
up in the necessary desires comes to throw off all inhibitions
and indulge desires that are unnecessary and useless?'

'A very clear description.'

'For the rest of his life he spends as much money, time and trouble on the unnecessary desires as on the necessary. If he's lucky and doesn't get carried to extremes, the tumult will subside as he gets older, some of the exiles will return, and the invaders won't have it all their own way. He'll establish a kind of equality of pleasures, and will give the pleasure of the moment complete control till it is satisfied, and then move on to another, so that all have their fair share and none is underprivileged.'

'That's true.'

'If anyone tells him that some pleasures, because they spring from good desires, are to be encouraged and approved, and others, springing from evil desires, to be disciplined and controlled, he won't listen or open his doors to the truth, but shakes his head and says all pleasures are equal and should have equal rights.'

'Yes, that's just what he does.'

'In fact,' I said, 'he lives for the pleasure of the moment. One day it's wine, women, and song, the next bread and water; one day it's hard physical training, the next indolence and ease, and then a period of philosophic study. Next he takes to politics and is always on his feet saying or doing whatever comes into his head. Sometimes all his ambitions are military, sometimes they are all directed to success in business. There's no order or restraint in his life, and he reckons his way of living is pleasant, free and happy.'

'A very good description of one who believes in liberty and equality,' he commented.

'Yes,' I said, 'and I think that the versatility of the individual, and the attractiveness of his combination of diverse characteristics, match the variety of the democratic society. It's a life which many men and women would envy, it has so many possibilities.'

'It has indeed.'

562 'This, then, is the individual corresponding to the democratic society, and we can fairly call him the democratic man.'

'Agreed.'

334

§8. TYRANNY[1]

The conflict of rich and poor in democracy, and the tyrant's rise as popular champion; his private army and the growth of oppression.

'We've still got the most splendid society and individual of all to describe,' I said, 'tyranny and the tyrant.'

'Yes, we have.'

'Well, my dear Glaucon, what is the nature of tyranny? It's obvious, I suppose, that it arises out of democracy.'

'Yes.'

'Then isn't it true that tyranny arises out of democracy in the same sort of way that democracy arises out of oligarchy?'

'How do you mean?'

'The main objective of oligarchy, for the sake of which it was established, was, I think we agreed, wealth.'

'Yes.'

'And its fall was due to the excessive desire for wealth, which led to the neglect of all other considerations.'

'True.'

'Then does not democracy set itself an objective, and is not excessive desire for this its downfall?'

'And what is this objective?'

'Liberty,' I said. 'You must have heard it said that this is the greatest merit of a democratic society, and that for that reason it's the only society fit for a free man to live in.'

'It's certainly what they often say.'

'Then, as I was just saying, an excessive desire for liberty at the expense of everything else is what undermines democracy and leads to the demand for tyranny.'

'Explain.'

'A democratic society in its thirst for liberty may fall under

---

1. I have used the traditional 'tyrant' and 'tyranny' to translate the Greek words of which they are, in fact, transliterations. As Cornford points out, the essential feature of the Greek 'tyrant' was that he was an absolute and sole ruler, and he accordingly uses the more neutral word 'despot'. But already in Plato's day the use of the word implied a certain moral disapproval, and tyrant is therefore a suitable translation.

the influence of bad leaders, who intoxicate it with the neat spirit; and then, unless the authorities are very mild and give it a lot of liberty, it will curse them for oligarchs and punish them.'

'That is just what a democracy does.'

'It goes on to abuse as servile and contemptible those who obey the authorities and reserves its approval, in private life as well as public, for rulers who behave like subjects and subjects who behave like rulers. In such a society the principle of liberty is bound to go to extremes – it will permeate private life and in the end infect even the domestic animals with anarchy.'

'How do you mean?'

'Well,' I said, 'it becomes the thing for father and son to change places, the father standing in awe of his son, and the son neither respecting nor fearing his parents, in order to assert his independence; and there's no distinction between citizen and alien and foreigner. And there are other more trivial things. The teacher fears and panders to his pupils, who in turn despise their teachers and attendants; and the young as a whole imitate their elders, argue with them and set themselves up against them, while their elders try to avoid the reputation of being disagreeable or strict by aping the young and mixing with them on terms of easy good fellowship. The extreme of popular liberty is reached when slaves – male and female – have the same liberty as their owners – not to mention the complete equality and liberty in the relations between the sexes generally.'

'Let's have the whole story while we're at it, as Aeschylus says.'

'Right,' I said; 'you shall. You would never believe – unless you had seen it for yourself – how much more liberty the domestic animals have in a democracy. Love me love my dog, as the proverb has it,[1] and the same is true of the horses and donkeys as well. They walk about the streets with a fine freedom, and bump into people they meet if they don't get out of their way. Everything is full of this spirit of liberty.'

1. The Greek proverb is 'like mistress, like dog' (cf. 'like mistress, like maid').

'You're telling me!' he said. 'I've often suffered from it on my way out of town.'

'What it all comes to is this,' I said, 'that the minds of the citizens become so sensitive that the least vestige of restraint is resented as intolerable, till finally, as you know, in their determination to have no master they disregard all laws, written or unwritten.'

'Yes, I know.'

'Well, this is the root from which tyranny springs,' I said; 'a promising beginning.'

'Yes, but what happens next?' he asked.

'The same disease which afflicted and finally destroyed oligarchy, afflicts democracy, in which it has more scope, still more virulently and enslaves it. Indeed, any extreme is liable to produce a violent reaction; this is as true of the weather and 564 plants and animals as of political societies.'

'It's what one would expect.'

'So from an extreme of liberty one is likely to get, in the individual and in society, a reaction to an extreme of subjection. And if that is so, we should expect tyranny to result from democracy, the most savage subjection from an excess of liberty.'

'That's quite logical.'

'But I haven't answered your question, which was, what is the disease which enslaves democracy and oligarchy alike? You remember me talking about a class of thriftless idlers, whom I compared to drones, their energetic leaders to drones with stings, the more inert mass of followers to drones without stings.'

'An apt comparison too.'

'Whenever these two elements appear in society they cause trouble,' I said, 'as phlegm and bile do in the body. The good doctor and the good law-giver must make provision against both in advance, just as the bee-keeper who knows his job will try to prevent drones being bred at all, and if they are bred cut them out at once, cells and all.'

'A very necessary operation.'

'Then, in order that we may be in a better position to judge, let us proceed as follows. Let us suppose a democratic society falls into three groups, as indeed it does. First comes the group we have mentioned, larger than in an oligarchy because of the freedom it gets, and a good deal more energetic.'

'How is that?'

'In an oligarchy it is despised and kept from power, and so lacks practice and strength. In a democracy practically all the leaders are drawn from it. Its more energetic elements do the talking and acting, the remainder sit buzzing on the benches and won't let anyone else speak, so that all public business, with trifling exceptions, is in their hands.'

'Quite true.'

'Then there's a second group which emerges from the mass; everyone's on the make, but the steadiest characters will be most successful in making money.'

'Very likely.'

'And the drones find them a most convenient source to squeeze honey from.'

'It's not much use squeezing poor men.'

'And so this group, on which the drones batten, are called the Rich.'

'That's it.'

565 'The third group is the mass of the people, who earn their own living, take little interest in politics, and aren't very well off. They are the largest class in a democracy, and once assembled are supreme.'

'Yes,' he said, 'but they won't assemble often unless they are given their share of honey.'

'They get their share all right,' I replied. 'Their leaders rob the rich, keep most of the proceeds for themselves, and distribute the rest to the people.'

'Yes, that's how they get their share.'

'Those whom they've plundered are forced to defend themselves, in the Assembly and elsewhere, as best they can, and are then accused of plotting against the people and being reactionaries and oligarchs, even though in fact they may have no revolutionary intentions.'

'That's true.'

'In the end, when they see the people trying to wrong them, not out of malice, but out of ignorance and because they've been misled by the spite of their leaders, they've no choice but to turn reactionaries in earnest, not because they want to, but because the drones' stings have poisoned them.'

'Perfectly true.'

'There follow impeachments and trials in which the two parties bring each other to court.'

'There do indeed.'

'In this struggle don't the people normally look to a single popular leader, whom they nurse to greatness?'

'Yes, as a rule.'

'Then it should be clear,' I said, 'that this is the root from which tyranny invariably springs.'

'Perfectly clear.'

'Then how does the popular leader turn into a tyrant? Isn't it, clearly, when he starts doing what we hear about in the story about the shrine of Zeus Lykaeus in Arcadia?'

'What is the story?'

'That the man who tastes a single piece of human flesh, mixed in with the rest of the sacrifice, is fated to become a wolf. Surely you've heard the tale?'

'Yes, I have.'

'The same thing happens with the popular leader. The mob will do anything he tells them, and the temptation to shed a brother's blood is too strong. He brings the usual unjust charges against him, takes him to court and murders him, thus destroying a human life, and getting an unholy taste of the blood of his fellows. Exiles, executions, hints of cancellation 566 of debts and redistribution of land follow, till their instigator is fatally bound either to be destroyed by his enemies, or to change from man to wolf and make himself tyrant.'

'That is an inevitable necessity.'

'It is he who leads the class war against the owners of property. And if he's exiled, and then returns in spite of his enemies, he returns a finished tyrant.'

'Obviously.'

'And if they are unable to banish him, or set the citizens

against him and kill him, they form a conspiracy to assassinate him.'

'That's what usually happens,' he agreed.

'Then follows the notorious gambit which all tyrants produce at this stage of their career, the demand for a personal bodyguard to preserve the champion of the people; and this the people grant him without misgiving, because they fear for his safety.'

'Yes, that is so.'

'Then it's time for anyone who is rich, and under suspicion of being an enemy of the people as well, to act on the oracle given to Croesus, and

> flee by Hermus' pebbled shore,
> nor fear the shame of coward more.'[1]

'He certainly won't get a second chance to be ashamed.'

'No,' I agreed, 'it'll be death if he's caught. Meanwhile there's no question of our champion "measuring his length in the dust" [2]; he overthrows all opposition and grasps the reins of state, and stands, no longer champion, but the complete tyrant.'

'That's the inevitable conclusion,' he agreed.

'Then shall we describe the happy condition of this man, and of the state in which a creature like him is bred?'

'Yes, please, let us.'

'In his early days he has a smile and a kind word for everyone; he says he's no tyrant, makes large promises, public and private, frees debtors, distributes land to the people and to his own followers, and puts on a generally mild and lenient air.'

'He has to.'

'But I think we shall find that when he has disposed of his foreign enemies by treaty or destruction, and has no more to fear from them, he will continue to make trouble abroad in order that the people may continue to need a leader, and in order that high taxation may reduce them to poverty and force

567

---

1. Herodotus, 1, 55.   2. *Iliad*, XVI, 776.

them to attend to earning their living rather than to plotting against him.'

'Clearly.'

'And if he suspects anyone of having ideas of freedom and not submitting to his rule, he will find an excuse to get rid of them by handing them over to the enemy. For all these reasons a tyrant must always be provoking war.'

'Yes, he must.'

'But all this lays him open to unpopularity.'

'Inevitably.'

'So won't some of the stronger characters among those who helped him to power, and now hold positions of influence, begin to speak pretty freely to him and to each other, and blame him for what is happening?'

'Very probably.'

'Then he must root them out, all of them, till there's not a man of any consequence left, whether friend or foe. He must keep a sharp eye out for men of courage or vision or intelligence or wealth; for, whether he likes it or not, it is his happy fate to be their constant enemy and to find a way to purge them from the state.'

'A remarkable kind of purge,' he remarked.

'Yes,' I returned, 'and the reverse of a purge in the medical sense. For the doctor removes the poison and leaves the healthy elements in the body, while the tyrant does the opposite.'

'Yet it seems inevitable, if he's to remain in power.'

'He has the happy choice,' I said, 'between a life with companions most of whom are worthless and all of whom hate him, and an inevitable death.'

'That is his fate.'

'And the greater the unpopularity of this policy, the larger and the more trustworthy must his bodyguard be.'

'Inevitably.'

'Where will he look for men on whom he can rely?' I asked.

'They will flock to him of their own accord,' he answered, 'if he pays them.'

'Goodness!' I exclaimed, 'do you mean another swarm of drones from abroad?'

'That's what I mean.'

'But won't he also want to recruit on the spot?'

'How will he do that?'

'By robbing the citizens of their slaves, freeing them, and enrolling them in his bodyguard.'

'That's true; and very faithful members of it they will be.'

'What an enviable lot the tyrant's is,' I exclaimed, 'if these 568 are the trusty friends he's left with after his earlier purges.'

'Well, there it is,' he said.

'And I suppose these newly-made citizens, whose company he enjoys, admire him very much, though all decent men detest and avoid him.'

'Of course.'

'No wonder, then, that tragedy in general and Euripides in particular among tragedians have such a reputation for wisdom.'

'How so?'

'Because of that profound remark of his about tyrants being "wise because they keep company with the wise." He meant, no doubt, by the wise the companions we've described.'

'Yes, and what is more he calls tyranny godlike, and praises it in many other ways. But so do the other poets.'

'And therefore,' I said, 'the tragic poets will perhaps, in their wisdom, forgive us and states whose constitution is like ours, if we refuse to admit them because they sing the praises of tyranny.'

'I think those who have any wits will forgive us,' he said.

'Yes, and I expect they will make a tour of other states, where they will hire actors, with their persuasive voices, to play their works to large audiences, and sway them over to tyranny or democracy.'

'I expect so.'

'They will, of course, get money for their services and make a great reputation, particularly with tyrants, but also, though to a lesser degree, with democracies. But the higher up our series of constitutions they go, the more their reputation fails them, as if it were short of breath and couldn't climb higher.'

'Very true.'

'But we are digressing,' I said. 'We must go back to our tyrant's private army. How is he to maintain the changing ranks of this splendid and motley gang?'

'Obviously he'll use any temple treasures there are, so long as they last, and the property of his victims.[1] That will enable him to tax the people less.'

'And when these sources fail?'

'Then he and his boy-friends and girl-friends will live on his parents' estate.'

'I see,' I said. 'You mean that the people who have bred him will have to maintain him and his crew.'

'They will have no option.'

'No option?' I said. 'But what if they get annoyed and say that it's not right for a father to keep his son when he's grown up – it's the son should keep the father: and that they never intended, when they bred him and set him up, that when he grew great *they* should be *his* slaves, and have to keep him and his servile rabble; on the contrary, *he* was to be *their* champion and free them from the power of the wealthy and so-called privileged classes? What if they then order him and his partisans to leave the country, like a father ordering his son out of the house with his riotous friends?' 569

'Then the people will find out quick enough what sort of a beast they've bred and groomed for greatness. He'll be too strong for them to turn out.'

'What?' I exclaimed. 'Do you mean that the tyrant will dare to use violence against the people who fathered him, if they oppose him?'

'Yes,' he said, 'when he has disarmed them.'

'So the tyrant is a parricide,' said I, 'and little comfort to his old parent. In fact, here we have real tyranny and no mistake, and the people find, as the saying is, that they've jumped out of the frying-pan of subjection to free men into the fire of subjection to slaves, and exchanged their excessive and unlimited

1. Reading καὶ τὰ τῶν ἀπολομένων with Adam.

freedom for the harshest and bitterest of servitudes, where the slave is master.'

'That is exactly what happens.'

'Well,' I said, 'I think we can fairly claim to have given an adequate description of how democracy turns to tyranny and what tyranny is like.'

'I think we can.'

§9. THE TYRANNICAL CHARACTER

Its essential similarity to the criminal type.[1]

'We've still to describe the individual of tyrannical character and see how he develops from the democratic man, what he's like, and whether his life is a happy or miserable one.'

'Yes, we're still left with him.'

'There's something else I want to do too.'

'What?'

'I don't think our classification of the desires is complete. And as long as that's incomplete the object of our investigation will remain obscure.'

'Well, now's your chance.'

'Good. What I want to get clear about is this. I think that some of the unnecessary pleasures and desires are immoral. Perhaps we are all born with them, but they are disciplined by law and by a combination of reason and the better desires till in some people they are got rid of altogether, or rendered few and feeble, though in some they retain their numbers and strength.'

'But what are the desires you mean?'

'The sort that emerge in our dreams, when the reasonable and humane part of us is asleep and its control relaxed, and our bestial nature, full of food and drink, wakes and has its fling and tries to secure its own kind of satisfaction. As you know, there's nothing too bad for it and it's completely lost to all sense and shame. It doesn't shrink at the thought of intercourse with a mother or anyone else, man, beast or god, or

1. Cf. Fielding, *Jonathan Wild.*

344

from murder or sacrilege. There is, in fact, no folly or shamelessness it will not commit.'

'That's perfectly true.'

'But a man of sound and disciplined character, before he goes to sleep, has wakened his reason and given it its fill of intellectual argument and meditation; his desires he has neither starved nor indulged, so that they sink to rest and don't plague the highest part of him with their joys and sorrows, but let it alone to pursue unhampered its quest for knowledge of past, present or future; the third part of him [1] he calms and keeps from quarrels so that he sleeps with an untroubled temper. Thus he goes to rest with the other two parts of him quietened, and his reasoning element stimulated, and is in a state to grasp the truth undisturbed by visions of wrong-doing.'

'That's exactly what happens.'

'We've been digressing, I know, but my point is this – that even in the most respectable of us there is a terribly bestial and immoral type of desire, which manifests itself particularly in dreams. Do you think I'm talking sense, and do you agree?'

'Yes, I agree.'

'Then let's go back to our democratic man. He was produced, you remember, by an upbringing under an economical father, whose desires centred entirely on business, and who had no use for the "unnecessary" desires for amusement or elegance.'

'Yes, I remember.'

'But he got into the company of men with more sophisticated tastes and desires of the kind we described, took to their ways, and was driven by his dislike of his father's meanness to all sorts of excesses; yet at heart he was a better man than his corrupters, and so effected what he thought was a very reasonable compromise between the two lives, getting the best of both and avoiding both meanness and extravagance – in fact, he turned into a democratic character from an oligarchic.'

'Yes, I still think that's true.'

'Suppose, then,' I went on, 'he has in due course a son whom he brings up in his own ways. Suppose, further, that the same

1. Cf. p. 183 ff. above.

thing happens to the son as to the father; he's drawn towards complete licence (which his tempters call complete liberty), his father and family support moderation, and his tempters come in on the other side. And when the wicked wizards who want to make him a tyrant despair of keeping their hold on the young man by other means, they contrive to implant a master passion in him to control the idle desires that divide his time between them, like a great winged drone – unless you can think of a better description for such a passion?'

'No – that describes it very well.'

'The other desires buzz round it, loading it with incense and perfume, flowers and wine, and all the pleasures of a dissolute life, on which they feed and fatten it until at last they produce in it the sting of mania. Then the master passion runs wild and takes madness into its service; any decent opinions or desires and any feelings of shame still left are killed or thrown out, until all discipline is swept away, and madness usurps its place.'

'A very complete description of the genesis of the tyrannical man.'

'Isn't this the reason,' I asked, 'why the passion of sex has for so long been called a tyrant?'

'Maybe.'

'And isn't there also a touch of the tyrant about a man who's drunk?'

'Yes.'

'And the madman whose mind is unhinged imagines he can control gods and men and is quite ready to try.'

'That's certainly true.'

'Then a precise definition of a tyrannical man is one who, either by birth or habit or both, combines the characteristics of drunkenness, lust, and madness.'

'Certainly.'

'So much, then, for his origin. And how does he live?'

'I must pass the ball back to you; you tell me.'

'I will,' I said. 'When a master-passion has absolute control of a man's mind, I suppose life is a round of holidays and dinners and parties and girl-friends and so on.'

'It's bound to be.'

'And there will be a formidable extra crop of desires growing all the time and needing satisfaction.'

'There will indeed.'

'So whatever income he has will soon be expended, and he'll
start borrowing and drawing on capital.'

'Yes.'

'When these sources fail, his large brood of desires will
howl aloud, and he will inevitably be stung to madness by
them, and still more by the master passion under which they
all serve, and will cast about to find someone to rob by force 574
or fraud. He *must* get something from somewhere or his life
will be torment and agony.'

'He must.'

'In his own life it's always been the later pleasure that has
had the better of it at the expense of the earlier, and so he considers that his mother and father, as the older generation,
should take second place to him and that, when his share of
the family estate is exhausted, he should help himself to their
property. If they don't give in to him, I suppose he'll try first
to get his way by fraud and deceit.'

'I suppose so.'

'And if he can't, will he stop short of robbery and violence?'

'I don't think so.'

'And if his old mother and father put up a resistance and
show fight, will he feel any hesitation about playing the tyrant
to them?'

'I wouldn't give much for his parents' chances,' said Adeimantus.

'Do you really mean that he will strike his own mother and
his poor old father, his nearest and dearest, and, if they're all
under the same roof, subordinate them to his latest mistress or
his latest young favourite, who have no claims on him at all?'

'That is just what I mean.'

'What a lucky thing it is,' I said, 'to have a tyrant for a son!'

'A real bit of luck,' he agreed.

'And I suppose that when he comes to the end of his father'
and mother's resources, having by now a pretty considerable
swarm of pleasures collected in himself, he'll start by burgling

a house or holding someone up at night, and go on to clean out a temple. Meanwhile the old, accepted beliefs about right and wrong, on which he was brought up, will be overcome by others, once held in restraint but now freed to become the bodyguard of his master-passion. When he was still democratically-minded and under the influence of the laws and his father, they only appeared in his dreams; but under the tyranny of the master-passion he becomes in reality what he was once only occasionally in his dreams, and there's nothing, no taboo, no murder, however terrible, from which he will shrink. His passion tyrannizes over him, a despot without restraint or law, and drives him (as a tyrant drives a state) into any venture that will profit itself and its gang, a gang collected partly from the evil company he keeps and partly from the impulses which these evil practices have freed within himself. Do you think that's the sort of life he will lead?'

'Yes, I think so.'

'And if there are only a few characters of this kind in a state and the bulk of the people are law-abiding, they will emigrate and take service with a tyrant elsewhere, or else fight as mercenaries in any war there is going on. In times of complete peace, they stay at home and commit a lot of minor crimes.'

'Such as?'

'They become thieves, burglars, pick-pockets, footpads, temple robbers, and kidnappers; or, if they have a ready tongue, they turn informers and false witnesses or take bribes.'

'I suppose you call all these minor crimes so long as the criminals are few.'

'Minor is a relative term,' I replied, 'and so far as the welfare or wickedness of the community goes, crimes like these don't come within miles of tyranny. But when the criminals and their followers increase in numbers and become aware of their strength, the folly of the people helps them to produce a tyrant, and they pick the man in whose heart passion is most tyrannical.'

'Yes, that is what best fits a man to be a tyrant.'

'And if the people submit to him, well and good. If not, he'll punish his country, if he can, just as he punished his parents, and the land which has borne and bred him, his motherland as the Cretans call it, will have to slave to maintain his upstart gang of followers. Which was the object of all his ambitions, was it not?'

'Yes, it was.'

'Men of his kind behave the same sort of way in private life, before they have gained power. Their companions are subservient parasites, and they are themselves always prepared to give way and put on the most extravagant act of friendship if 576 it suits their purpose, though once that purpose is achieved their tune changes.'

'It does indeed.'

'So they pass their lives without a friend in the world; for tyrannical characters must always be either master or slave, and never taste true friendship or freedom.'

'True.'

'So we shall be right to call them untrustworthy and, if our definition of justice was correct, the perfect specimen of injustice.'

'Quite right.'

'We can sum it all up by saying that the worst type of man behaves as badly in real life as we said some men do in their dreams; which is just what happens when a natural tyrant gains absolute power, and the longer he holds it the greater his corruption.'

'That is inevitable,' said Glaucon, who took up the argument at this point.

§10. THE TYPES OF CHARACTER AND THEIR DEGREES OF HAPPINESS

Having sketched the four types of imperfect society and the four corresponding types of character, Plato proceeds to rank them in order of happiness, and in particular to contrast the perfectly just man, the Philosopher Ruler, with the completely unjust man, the Tyrant, thereby answering the original question asked by Glaucon and Adeimantus.

1. On the evidence provided by the descriptions given it is shown that they rank in happiness in the order in which they were discussed, with the tyrant as the most unhappy.

'Now isn't it clear,' I asked, 'that the wickedest men are also the unhappiest? and that therefore, in fact, the longer and more extensive a tyrant's power, the greater his unhappiness, whatever most people may think?'

'It must be so.'

'And does not the tyrannical man correspond to the state governed by a tyranny, the democratic man to a democratic state, and so on?'

'Yes.'

'And so in goodness and happiness the relations between the different types of individual will correspond to the relations between the different types of state?'

'Of course.'

'Then what is the relation between a state governed by a tyrant and one governed by philosopher kings as we first described?'

'They are opposite extremes,' he replied; 'one is the best and one the worst possible.'

'I won't ask you which is which,' I said, 'as I think that is obvious. But would you make the same judgement about their relative happiness and unhappiness? And we must not be overawed by the sight of the tyrant himself and his immediate following, but have a thorough look round and examine the whole society before giving our answer.'

'That's a fair request. And it is obvious that there is no more unhappy society than that ruled by a tyrant, and none happier than our philosopher kingship.'

'We should, I think, be right to make the same request when dealing with the corresponding individuals. We should expect the true judge to see below the surface into the man's character, and not be overawed like a child by the pomp and circumstance of the tyrant's life, but see through them. He will then be competent to form a judgement, to which we should listen, particularly if he has lived with a tyrant and seen how he behaves in his own house and with his own family – the best place to catch him stripped of all his dramatic paraphernalia – as well as seeing him in the emergencies of public life. So should we ask him to tell us about the relative happiness

577

and unhappiness of the tyrant's life compared with the others?'

'That's a very fair request too.'

'Then shall we pretend that we ourselves have the necessary judgement and experience, so that we may have someone to answer our questions?'

'All right.'

'Let us approach the question by dealing with the characteristics of the individual one by one, in the light of the analogy between state and individual.'

'What characteristics?'

'To begin with the state, is a state ruled by a tyrant in a condition of freedom or slavery?'

'It is in complete slavery.'

'And yet it contains masters who are free men.'

'Yes, but they are a minority. The mass of the people and the best elements in it are miserable slaves without rights.'

'Well, then,' I said, 'if the individual is analogous to the state, he must be similarly placed. He will hardly be able to call his soul his own because the best elements in him will be enslaved and completely controlled by a minority of lower and lunatic impulses.'

'Yes, that must be so.'

'Then is such a man in a condition of freedom or slavery?'

'Of slavery, obviously.'

'And is not the state enslaved to a tyrant least able to do as it wishes?'

'Yes.'

'So the mind in which there is a tyranny will also be least 578 able to do what, as a whole, it wishes, because it is in the grip of madness, and so full of confusion and remorse.'

'Of course.'

'Is a state under a tyranny rich or poor?'

'Poor.'

'So the corresponding character must be poverty-stricken and unsatisfied.'

'Yes.'

'Both state and individual, again, will be haunted by fear.

And just as you will find the state full of complaints and sorrow and mourning and pain, so the individual is in the same straits under the mad tyranny of his desires and passions.'

'Very true.'

'For all these reasons and for many others you decided that the state ruled by a tyrant was the unhappiest of all.'

'And wasn't I right?' he asked.

'Perfectly right,' I answered. 'And with all these reasons in mind, what have you to say about the tyrannical man?'

'He's clearly the unhappiest of all men.'

'There,' I said, 'you are wrong.'

'Why?' he asked.

'Because there's someone still unhappier,' I said.

'Who is it?'

'I think,' I said, 'that you will perhaps agree that the tyrannical individual is even unhappier if he's not left to live as a private citizen, but has the misfortune to be thrust by circumstance to supreme power.'

'I should guess from what we've already said that that is true.'

'Yes,' I said, 'but we are concerned with the most important issue in life, the choice of good and evil, and guessing isn't good enough; we must see what the arguments are.'

'Yes, you're quite right.'

'I think we ought to start from the following considerations.'

'Well, what are they?'

'Let us consider a wealthy private slave-owner with a large number of slaves. The control of large numbers is a first step to tyranny; the difference is one of degree.'

'Yes.'

'These slave-owners, as you know, don't live in fear of their slaves.'

'Why should they?'

'There's no reason at all; but do you know why?'

'Because the individual has the support of society as a whole.'

'Exactly,' I said. 'But imagine now that some god were to take a single man who owned fifty or more slaves and were to transport him and his wife and children, his goods and chattels and his slaves, to some desert place where there would be no other free man to help him; wouldn't he be very much afraid that he and his wife and children would be done away with by the slaves?'

'Very much afraid.'

'So he'd have to curry favour with some of these very slaves, make them large promises, and give them their freedom, much against his will, till he became the parasite of his own servants.' 579

'It would be his only alternative to destruction,' he said.

'Then suppose god surrounded him with neighbours who would not tolerate the claims of any man to control another, and would punish fiercely anyone attempting to do so.'

'That would make his predicament still worse, because he would be surrounded by enemies on all sides.'

'Yet this is just the sort of predicament in which the tyrant is caught. He is naturally a prey to fears and passions of every sort, as we have described; and he's the only person in the state who can't travel abroad or see the things the ordinary citizens like to see, much as he really wants to, but must stay in the shelter of his home, like a woman, and envy the freedom with which other men can travel and see things worth seeing.'

'Very true.'

'The tyrannical character, therefore, whom you judged to be the most wretched of men because of the disorder prevailing within him, is in all these ways still worse off when he ceases to be a private citizen, and is compelled by fate to become a real tyrant and to control others though he cannot control himself. It's just as if you compelled an invalid or cripple to spend his life on military service or in athletic competitions instead of living quietly at home.'

'Yes, that's a very apt comparison, Socrates.'

'And so, my dear Glaucon, will you agree that the actual tyrant's condition is utterly wretched, and his life harder than the one you thought hardest?'

'I entirely agree.'

'So, whatever people may think, the truth is that the real

tyrant is a slave and a parasite, dependent on scoundrels. He can never satisfy his desires, and behind his multitudinous wants you can see, if you look at it as a whole, the real impoverishment of his character; his life is haunted by fear and – if the condition of the state he rules is any guide, as we know
580 it is – torn by suffering and misery. Add to all that what we said before, that his power will make him still more envious, untrustworthy, unjust, friendless, and godless, a real sink of every iniquity, and you can see that he's a source of unmitigated misery both to himself and his neighbours.'

'No one who has any sense could deny it.'

'Come on, then,' I said, 'you must act as final judge for us, and give us your verdict how these five types – the philosopher king, the timocratic, the oligarchic, the democratic and the tyrannical man – stand in order of happiness.'

'The verdict is easy,' he replied. 'I rank the competitors in the order of their appearance, not only in happiness but also in moral worth.'

'Then shall we hire a herald,' I asked, 'or shall I proclaim the judgement of the son of Ariston myself – that the supremely happy man is the justest and the best, that is, the philosopher king who can govern himself, and that the supremely wretched man is the wickedest and worst, that is, again, the man who is a tyrant at heart and a tyrant in fact in his own country?'

'You may proclaim it,' he said.

'And may I add that the judgement remains true whether their true characters are known to men and gods or not?'

'You may.'

2. *On the basis of the threefold classification of the elements in the human mind made earlier (p. 183 f.), it is shown that the life of the just man and the philosopher is pleasanter than any other.*

'Well, there is one of our proofs,' I said. 'Let us see what you make of the second one.'

'What is it?'

'We divided the mind of the individual into three elements,

corresponding to the three classes in the state. Our further proof starts from that.'

'And how does it proceed?'

'As follows. Each of the three elements has its own pleasures, its own desires, and its own governing principles.'

'How do you mean?'

'We saw,' I said, 'that one element in a man gives him understanding, another spirit and enterprise, while the third shows itself in too many forms for us to be able to describe it in a single word. We accordingly called it after its most salient characteristics, "desire", because of the violence of the desires for food and drink and sex and the like, or "acquisitiveness", because wealth is the means of satisfying desires of this kind.'

'As indeed it is,' he said.

581

'Now would it be a fair summary of this third element to say that its pleasures and motives were entirely centred in gain, so that we could describe it by saying that its motive was profit or gain?'

'I think it would.'

'Similarly the element of spirit is entirely devoted to the achievement of success and reputation; could we not therefore appropriately say that its motive is honour or ambition?'

'Very appropriately.'

'And of course it is obvious that the element of understanding is solely directed to the discovery of the truth, and is least concerned with wealth or reputation; and so we may say that the corresponding motives here are knowledge and wisdom.'

'I agree.'

'Then in the human mind must not one or other of these three sets of motives predominate?'

'It must.'

'That is why we divide men into three basic types, according to whether their motive is knowledge, success or gain; and each type, of course, has its appropriate pleasures.'

'Yes, certainly.'

'If you asked each of these three types in turn which of the three lives was the pleasantest, he would, of course, put his own first. Will the money-maker set any value on the pleasures of success or knowledge compared with his profits, unless they have a cash value?'

'None at all.'

'And what about the man of ambition?' I asked. 'Doesn't he think the pleasures of money-making rather vulgar, and those of learning, unless they bring fame, mere idle nonsense?'

'True.'

'And what are we to suppose the philosopher thinks of other pleasures compared with that of knowing the truth and being always engaged in the pursuit of it? Won't he rank them far lower, regarding them as "necessary" in the strict sense, things he'd do without if they weren't unavoidable?'

'There can be no doubt of that.'

'When therefore the three types of pleasure and three types of life are being compared, simply on the grounds of the pleasure they give and without any reference to their moral quality, how are we to find out the truth?'

'I'm sure I don't know,' he said.

'Look at it in this way. What do we need if we are to judge fairly? Can you suggest any better standards than experience, intelligence, and reason?'

'Certainly not.'

'Then look. Which of the three men we have described has the greatest experience of all three types of pleasure? Is the money-maker's knowledge of the truth such that you would rank his experience of the pleasures of knowledge above the philosopher's experience of the pleasures of gain?'

'Far from it,' he said. 'The philosopher cannot help tasting the pleasures of gain from his earliest years; but the money-maker is under no necessity to taste or experience the intensity of the pleasure of knowing the truth – indeed, he would find it difficult to do so even if he wished.'

'Then the philosopher has the advantage over the money-maker in his experience of both kinds of pleasure.'

'A very considerable advantage.'

'And how does he compare with the man of ambition? Has

he less experience of the pleasures of honour than the ambitious man of the pleasures of knowledge?'

'No. Honour comes to each, if he attains his object; for the rich man and the brave man and the wise man are all widely respected. All three therefore know what the pleasures of honour are; but only the philosopher can taste the pleasure of contemplating the truth.'

'As far as experience goes, then,' I said, 'the philosopher is in the best position to judge.'

'Much the best.'

'And he is the only one in whom intelligence is joined with experience.'

'True.'

'And besides, it is the philosopher, and not either of the other two, who has the necessary tools.'

'What do you mean?'

'We said our judgement must be reached through reason, and rational argument is the philosopher's special tool.'

'That's true.'

'Now, if wealth and profit were our criterion, the value-judgements of the money-maker would inevitably contain the highest degree of truth.'

'Inevitably.'

'And if our criterion were honour, success and courage, the same would be true of the man of ambition.'

'Obviously.'

'But since we are judging by experience, intelligence and reason ... ?'

'It follows that truth is to be found in the judgements of the philosopher and man of reason.'

'Of the three types of pleasure, therefore, the pleasantest is 583 that which belongs to the element in us which brings us knowledge, and the man in whom that element is in control will live the pleasantest life.'

'It must be so,' he agreed. 'The wise man speaks with authority when he prefers his own life.'

'And which life and which type of pleasure will he rank second?'

'Obviously that of the ambitious, soldierly type. It is nearer his own than the money-maker's is.'

'So the pleasures of gain come last, I suppose.'

'Of course they do.'

3. *The philosopher's pleasures are the most real of all pleasures: all others are to some extent mixed with pain and therefore illusory, particularly the pleasures of the tyrant.*

'Well, the just man has beaten the unjust in the first two rounds; now for the third, before which wrestlers at the Olympic Games invoke Olympian Zeus the Saviour. I think I've heard some wise man say that only the pleasures of the intelligence are entirely true and unadulterated, and all others illusory. A fall in this round should finally settle the matter.'

'It should. But explain what you mean.'

'I will,' I said, 'but you must help by answering my questions.'

'You have only to ask them.'

'Tell me, then,' I asked, 'is not pleasure the opposite of pain?'

'Very much so.'

'And is there not a state in which we feel neither enjoyment, nor pain?'

'There is.'

'It will lie between the two, I suppose, giving the mind rest from both. Do you agree?'

'Yes.'

'Do you remember,' I went on to ask, 'what patients always say when they are ill?'

'What?'

'That there is nothing pleasanter than health, though they had not realized it till they were ill.'

'Yes, I remember.'

'And haven't you heard people in pain saying that there is no greater pleasure than relief from pain?'

'I have.'

'You must, in fact, have noticed many similar cases in which the pain we suffer makes us glorify freedom and rest from pain as the highest pleasure, rather than any positive enjoyment.'

'Perhaps,' he suggested, 'it is because in those circumstances rest is welcomed as definitely pleasurable.'

'Then when enjoyment ceases,' I replied, 'the rest from pleasure will be painful.'

'Maybe.'

'In that case rest, which we said was our intermediate state between pleasure and pain, will itself be both pleasure and pain.'

'Apparently.'

'But can something which is neither of two things be both of them?'

'I think not.'

'What is more, both pleasure and pain are psychological processes, are they not?'

'Yes.'

'But didn't we see just now that to feel neither pleasure nor 584 pain is to be in a state of rest between the two?'

'We did.'

'Then can it be right to suppose that absence of pain is pleasure or absence of enjoyment pain?'

'No, it can't.'

'It cannot therefore, in fact, be so. The state of rest must seem pleasant by contrast with previous pain or painful by contrast with previous pleasure; but, judged by the standard of real pleasure, neither experience can be genuine, but must be some sort of illusion.'

'That is what the argument implies.'

'To rid your mind of any idea you may still have that pleasure really is the cessation of pain, and pain the cessation of pleasure, look at pleasures that don't follow pain.'

'Where do I look for them and what are they?' he asked.

'There are a lot of them,' I answered, 'but the best example is the pleasures of smell. These are very intense, come quite suddenly without any previous pain, and leave no pain behind when they cease.'

'True.'

'So we must not let ourselves believe that pure pleasure is the same as relief from pain, or pure pain the same as the cessation of pleasure.'

'Agreed.'

'And yet,' I went on, 'the majority of the intensest pleasures, so called, which we experience through the body, are of this kind and involve relief from pain.' [1]

'Yes, that's true.'

'And the same applies, does it not, to the pleasures and pains of anticipation that precede them?'

'Yes.'

'Do you know what I think is the best analogy to them?'

'No, tell me.'

'Do you agree that in the natural world there is a top, a bottom, and a middle?'

'Yes.'

'Then won't anyone who rises from the bottom to the middle think he has risen towards the top? And as he stands in the middle and looks down to where he came from, won't he think he's at the top, never having seen the real top?'

'I don't see how he could think anything else.'

'And suppose he then went down again, he would suppose he was going down to the bottom, and would be right.'

'Yes.'

'And all his judgements would be made in ignorance of what top, middle, and bottom really were.'

'Obviously.'

'Then is it surprising that the views of men who are ignorant of the truth should be as unsound about pleasure and pain and the neutral state between them as they are about a good many other things? When they are subjected to pain, they will think they are in pain and their pain will be real. But they will be convinced that the transition from pain to the neutral state brings satisfaction and pleasure, whereas in fact their ignorance of true pleasure leads them to make a false contrast between pain and the absence of pain, just as someone who had never seen white might similarly contrast grey with black.'

585

1. e.g. the pleasure of eating is preceded by the pain of hunger.

'That's none of it in the least surprising,' he said. 'In fact, I don't see how it could be otherwise.'

'Then consider; aren't hunger and thirst and the like states of physical depletion?'

'Of course.'

'And ignorance and empty-headedness states of mental depletion?'

'Certainly.'

'And they can be satisfied by replenishing the body with food and the mind with understanding?'

'They can.'

'And don't we get more satisfaction from replenishing what is more rather than what is less real?'

'Much more, obviously.'

'Then which is more truly real, things like bread, meat and drink and food generally, or things like judgement, knowledge, understanding and other qualities of mind? Put the question this way – which do you think is more truly real, something belongs to the realm of unchanging and external truth, exists in it and shares its nature, or something which belongs to the realm of change and mortality, exists in it and shares its nature?'

'That which belongs to the eternal realm is much more real.'

'And are not knowledge and truth as much features of the eternal realm as reality?'

'Yes.'

'And a lesser degree of truth means a lesser degree of reality?'

'Necessarily.'

'So in general the sort of thing that supplies the needs of the body is less true and less real than the sort of thing that supplies the needs of the mind.'

'Much less.'

'And isn't the same true of the body itself as compared with the mind?'

'Yes.'

'But the more real the means of satisfaction and the thing satisfied, the greater, presumably, the reality of the satisfaction.'

'I agree.'

'It follows that, if we experience pleasure when we are appropriately satisfied, the more real our satisfaction and its source, the more genuine and completely real the consequent enjoyment and pleasure; whereas the less real the means of satisfaction the less truly and certainly we are satisfied and the less reliable and less genuine our pleasure.'

'That is inevitable.'

586 'Those, therefore, who have no experience of wisdom and goodness, and do nothing but have a good time, spend their life straying between the bottom and middle in our illustration, and never rise higher to see or reach the true top, nor achieve any real satisfaction or sure and unadulterated pleasure. They bend over their tables, like sheep with heads bent over their pasture and eyes on the ground, they stuff themselves and copulate, and in their greed for more they kick and butt each other with hooves and horns of steel, and kill each other because they are not satisfied, as they cannot be while they feed on unreality a part of themselves which is itself unreal and insatiable.'

'My dear Socrates,' said Glaucon, 'you sound as if you were preaching a sermon on the life of the common man.'

'And are not the pleasures of such a life inevitably mixed with pain, and mere images and shadows of true pleasure? They owe their intensity to contrast, and breed mad desires in the hearts of fools, who fight about them as Stesichorus said the heroes fought in ignorance at Troy about a mere image of Helen.'[1]

'Something of the sort is inevitable.'

'Then what about the element of spirit? Isn't it inevitably the same story again, when a man pursues honour or success or ambition to the bitter end, without sense or reason, and they make him envious, violent, and impatient?'

'Yes, inevitably again.'

1. In Euripides' *Helen*, 'Helen relates that Hera gave Paris a phantom in place of the true Helen. While Greeks and Trojans fought for a wraith, she herself has lived in Egypt, waiting for Menelaus': Norwood, *Greek Tragedy*, p. 259.

'I think, then,' I said, 'that we may venture to conclude that if our desire for gain and our ambition will follow the guidance of knowledge and reason, and choose to pursue only such pleasures as wisdom indicates, the pleasures they achieve will be the truest of which they are capable, because truth is their guide, and also those proper to them – for isn't what is proper to a thing what is best for it?'

'Yes, that's certainly so.'

'Then if the mind as a whole will follow the lead of its philosophic element, without internal division, each element will be rightly performing its own function, and in addition will enjoy its own particular pleasures, which are the best and 587 truest available to it.'

'Absolutely true.'

'But when either of the other two elements is in control, it cannot achieve its own proper pleasure, and compels the other two to pursue a false pleasure that is not their own.'

'True.'

'And won't this effect be produced most markedly by the elements furthest removed from philosophy and reason?'

'Very much so.'

'And is not what is furthest removed from reason furthest removed also from law and order?'

'Obviously.'

'And didn't we see that the passionate and tyrannical desires were the furthest from law and order, the orderly and philosophic desires the nearest?'

'Yes.'

'So the tyrant is furthest removed from man's true and proper pleasure, the philosopher king nearest it; and the tyrant leads the most unpleasant, the philosopher king the most pleasant of lives.'

'All that necessarily follows.'

4. *Finally, it is shown that the tyrant is* 729 *times more unhappy than the philosopher king.*

'Do you know,' I asked, 'exactly how much unhappier the tyrant is than the philosopher king?'

'No, tell me.'

'There are three types of pleasure,' I replied, 'one genuine, two spurious.[1] The tyrant, in his flight from law and reason, sinks even below the spurious type, surrounding himself with an armed gang of slavish pleasures, and his degradation is not easy to describe. One might do it as follows. The tyrant was third in order from the oligarch, the democratic type intervening between them.'

'Yes.'

'So (if our argument is correct) his pleasure will be a phantom three times further from reality than the oligarch's.'

'True.'

'The oligarch, again, was third in order from the philosopher king or ideal type.'

'He was.'

'So the distance of the tyrant's pleasure from true pleasure can be expressed numerically as three times three.'

'So it seems.'

'The tyrant's phantom pleasure is, therefore, in simple numerical terms a plane number.'[2]

'Exactly.'

'Square this and then cube it and it becomes obvious how great the distance is.'[3]

'Obvious to a mathematician anyway!'

'Conversely, you will find, if you work out the cube, that the measure of difference between the two is that the philosopher king lives seven hundred and twenty-nine times more happily than the tyrant, and the tyrant the same amount more unhappily than the philosopher king.'

'What a terrific great calculation,' he exclaimed, 'to show 588 how much difference there is between the just and unjust man and their pleasures and pains!'

1. Corresponding to the three elements in the mind and to the first three political types – philosopher-king, timocrat, and oligarch.

2. The Greeks often represented numbers spatially, and a 'plane' number is one that can be represented by a plane figure the product of whose sides yields the number in question; here, $3 \times 3 = 9$.

3. We are given no reason why 9 should be cubed, but Adam notes 'the calculations are inspired by a desire to reach the total 729': see p. 365 note 1.

'But it's quite correct,' I replied, 'and fits human life, if human life is measured by days and nights and months and years.'[1]

'As of course it is.'

'And if the good and just man is so much superior to the bad and unjust man in terms of pleasure, will not his superiority be infinitely greater in terms of moral beauty and value?'

'Infinitely greater,' he replied emphatically.

§11. CONCLUSION

Wrongdoing and injustice therefore cannot pay, and goodness brings its own reward. But it is doubtful if the ideal society described, where goodness would have full scope, will ever exist on earth.

'So far so good,' I said. 'Having got so far, let us recall what it was that started us off. It was, I think, the assertion that wrongdoing paid the man who combined complete injustice with a reputation for justice.'

'That was it.'

'Well, now that we have agreed what the effects of justice and injustice are, we can have a word with its author.'

'What shall we say?' he asked.

'Let us show him what his assertion really implies, by comparing the human personality to one of those composite beasts in the old myths, Chimaera and Scylla and Cerberus and all the rest.'

'I know the stories.'

'Imagine a very complicated, many-headed sort of beast, with heads of wild and tame animals all round it, which it can produce and change at will.'

'Quite a feat of modelling,' he replied; 'but fortunately it's easier to imagine than it would be to make.'

'Imagine next a lion, and next a man. And let the many-

---

1. The precise meaning is uncertain. But Philolaus, the Pythagorean, held that there were $364\frac{1}{2}$ days in the year: there are presumably the same number of nights, and $364\frac{1}{2} \times 2 = 729$. Philolaus also believed in a 'great year' of 729 months.

headed creature be by far the largest, and the lion the next largest.'

'That's rather easier to imagine.'

'Then put the three together and combine them into a single creature.'

'Done.'

'Then give the whole the external appearance of one of the three, the man, so that to anyone unable to penetrate beneath the outer surface it looks like a single creature, a man.'

'That is done too.'

'Then let us point out that to say that it pays the man to do wrong and not to do right, is to say that it pays him to give the many-headed beast a good time, and to strengthen it and the lion and all its qualities, while starving the man till he becomes so weak that the other two can do what they like with him; and that he should make no attempt to reconcile the three and make them friends, but leave them to snarl and wrangle and devour each other.'

'That is just what it means to approve injustice and wrong-doing.'

'On the other hand, to say that it pays to be just is to say that we ought to say and do all we can to strengthen the man within us, so that he can look after the many-headed beast like a farmer, encouraging the growth of its tamer elements and preventing the wilder ones growing, while he makes an ally of the lion and looks after the interests of all three by reconciling the other two with each other and with himself.'

'That, again, is exactly what it means to approve of justice.'

'The glorification of injustice is therefore wrong on all counts, and the glorification of justice right. For, whether you look to pleasure or profit or reputation, to praise justice is to tell the truth, to disparage it to talk ignorant nonsense, and not to know what you are talking about.'

'Yes, I agree.'

'But let us deal gently with our opponent; his mistake isn't his fault. "My dear chap," let us say to him, "what is the purpose of conventional morality? Does not right conduct aim at subjecting the beast in us to our human, or perhaps I should

366

say our divine, element; while wrongdoing enslaves our humaner nature to the beast?" He's bound to agree with that, isn't he?'

'Yes, if he listens to me.'

'Then on this reckoning,' I asked, 'can it possibly pay anyone to make money by doing wrong, if the result of his so doing is to enslave the best part of himself to the worst? No one would say it paid to sell his son or daughter as a slave to harsh and wicked masters, however high the price; if one ruthlessly enslaves the divinest part of oneself to the most godless and abominable, is it not a miserable piece of bribery, with results far more fatal than Eriphyle's sale of her husband's life for a necklace?'   590

'If I may answer for him,' said Glaucon, 'I should say it was far more fatal.'

'And why has self-indulgence always been censured? Isn't it because it gives too much freedom to the monstrous multiform creature within us?'

'Obviously.'

'And are not obstinacy and bad temper censured for tuning up the strength of the lion and dragon in us too far; whereas luxury and effeminacy are censured for relaxing it till it grows slack and cowardly?'

'Yes.'

'And we blame flattery and meanness when they subordinate the spirited element in us to the unruliness of the beast, and when, to gratify the beast's greed and love of money, they school the lion to put up with insults and turn it into an ape.'

'True.'

'And why do we despise manual work? Isn't it because it indicates a certain weakness in our higher nature, which is unable to control the animal part of us, and can only serve and pander to it?'

'Yes, I think so.'

'To ensure that people of this type are under the same authority as the highest type, we have said that they should be subjected to that highest type, which is governed by its divine element; but this control is not exercised, as Thrasymachus thought, to the detriment of the subject, but because it is better for every creature to be under the control of divine wisdom. That wisdom and control should, if possible, come from within; failing that it must be imposed from without, in order that, being subject to the same guidance, we may all be brothers and equals.'

'That is all very right.'

'And this is plainly the intention of the law, in the support it gives to all citizens, and of the control we exercise over children, not letting them run free till we have established some kind of self-government in them, and have educated the best in them to take over from the best in us.'

591

'That is clearly so.'

'Then how, my dear Glaucon,' I asked, ' can we possibly argue that it pays a man to be unjust or self-indulgent or do anything base that will bring him more money and power but make him a worse man?'

'We can't possibly.'

'And how can it pay him to escape the punishment of wrongdoing by not being found out? If he escapes doesn't he merely become worse? And if he's caught and punished isn't the beast in him calmed and tamed, and his humaner part set free? And doesn't that mean that he is making the best of his natural gifts, and, by forming a character in which self-control and fair-mindedness are combined, getting something worth more than physical strength and health and good looks, just as the mind is worth more than the body?'

'Perfectly true.'

'This, then, will be the object of the intelligent man's life. The only studies he will value will be those that form his mind and character accordingly. And as for his physical condition and training – he won't live merely with brutish and irrational pleasures in view, indeed he won't even make health his primary concern; strength and health and good looks will mean nothing to him unless self-control goes with them, and we shall always find him keeping physical values in tune with moral and intellectual.'

'He must if he's to be in tune with reality.'

'And won't he observe the same principle of harmony and order in acquiring wealth? He won't be misled, will he, by popular ideas of happiness and make endless troubles for himself by piling up a fortune?'

'I should think not.'

'Because, whether he saves or spends, it will be under the guidance of the principles of self-government in his own heart; and his only concern will be to prevent them being upset either because he's too rich or too poor.'

'Exactly.'

'He will follow the same principles over honours, private or public. If he thinks they will make him a better man he will take and enjoy them, if he thinks they will destroy the order within him, he will avoid them.' 592

'If that is his object, he won't enter politics,' he said.

'Oh yes, he will,' I replied, 'very much so, in the society where he really belongs; but not, I think, in the society where he's born, unless something very extraordinary happens.'

'I see what you mean,' he said. 'You mean that he will do so in the society which we have been describing and which we have theoretically founded; but I doubt if it will ever exist on earth.'

'Perhaps,' I said, 'it is laid up as a pattern in heaven, where those who wish can see it and found it in their own hearts. But it doesn't matter whether it exists or ever will exist; it's the only state in whose politics he can take part.'

'I expect you are right.'

PART TEN

THEORY OF ART

*

This part has the appearance of an appendix, written to justify against anticipated or actual criticism the attack on the poets in Books II and III (Part III). It has been suggested that it should not be taken too seriously, and should be read as an attack on the extravagant claims made for the poets by Greek opinion, rather than as a serious attempt to state a philosophy of art. It is true that the Greeks treated the works of Homer and the poets as their Bible, and true also, as we see from Plato's Ion, where Homer is claimed as a teacher of everything from carpentry to morals and generalship, that extravagant claims were made for them. But there is nothing to suggest that Plato is not serious, though he is often characteristically ironical; and the general contention in §1 that poetry is illusion fits well into the scheme of the Divided Line (p. 274, above).

§1. ART AND ILLUSION

The Greek word mimesis, *'representation', used in Part III to describe dramatic as opposed to narrative poetry, is now used to describe artistic creation as a whole, and interpreted to mean a rather unintelligent imitation.[1] The productions both of the painter and the poet are imitations of a life which has itself only secondary reality, and neither painter nor poet have any knowledge of what they imitate. Pictures and poems are second-hand, unreal, and tell us nothing about life.*

BK
X
595

'YOU know,' I said, 'among all the excellent features of our ideal state, there's none I rank higher than its treatment of poetry.'

'Why exactly?'

'Because it excluded all dramatic representation. Now that

---

1. In visual terms what we should call an extreme photographic realism. Such extreme realism, both in theory and practice, was not uncommon in the early fourth century, and is effectively criticized by Aristotle in the *Poetics*.

we have distinguished the various elements in the mind, we can see even more clearly how essential it is to exclude it.'

'What do you mean?'

'Between ourselves – and you mustn't give me away to the tragedians and other dramatists – such representations definitely harm the minds of their audiences, unless they're inoculated against them by knowing their real nature.'

'What exactly have you in mind?'

'I must tell you, I suppose; yet the love and respect I've always had from a boy for Homer makes me hesitate – for I think he's the original master and guide of all the great tragic poets. But one must not respect an individual more than the truth, and so, as I say, I must tell you.'

'You must,' he said.

'Listen, then; or, rather, answer my questions.'

'Ask away.'

'Can you give me a general definition of representation? I'm not sure that I know, myself, exactly what it is.'

'Then it's not very likely I shall!'

'Oh, I don't know,' I said. 'Short sight is sometimes quicker 596 than long sight.'

'True enough,' he replied. 'But with you here, if I did see anything, I shouldn't much want to say so. You must use your own eyes.'

'Then shall we start where we always do? You know that we always assume that there is a single essential Form corresponding to each class of particular things to which we apply the same name?'

'Yes, I know.'

'Then let us take an instance. For example, there are many particular beds and tables.'

'Yes.'

'But there are only two Forms, one of Bed and one of Table.'

'Yes.'

'Then we normally say that the maker of either of these kinds of furniture has his eye on the appropriate Form; and similarly with other things. For no one could possibly make the Form itself, could he?'

371

'No.'

'I wonder what you would call a man who could make all the objects produced by individual craftsmen?'

'He would be a remarkably clever man.'

'Just a minute, and you'll be more surprised still. For this same craftsman can not only make all artificial objects, but also create all plants and animals, himself included, and, in addition, earth and sky and gods, the heavenly bodies and the underworld.'

'An astonishing bit of craftsmanship!' he exclaimed.

'You don't believe me?' I asked. 'Tell me, do you think that a craftsman of this sort couldn't exist, or (in one sense, if not in another) create all these things? Do you know that there's a sense in which you could create them yourself?'

'What sense?'

'It's not difficult, and can be done in various ways quite quickly. The quickest way is to take a mirror and turn it round in all directions; before long you will create sun and stars and earth, yourself and all other animals and plants, and all the other objects we mentioned just now.'

'Yes, but they would only be reflections,' he said, 'not real things.'

'Quite right,' I replied, 'and very much to the point. For a painter is a craftsman of just this kind, I think. Do you agree?'

'Yes.'

'You may perhaps object that the things he creates are not real; and yet there *is* a sense in which the painter creates a bed, isn't there?'

'Yes,' he agreed, 'he produces an appearance of one.'

597 'And what about the carpenter? Didn't you agree that what he produces is not the essential Form of Bed, the ultimate reality, but a particular bed?'

'I did.'

'If so, then what he makes is not the ultimate reality, but something that resembles that reality. And anyone who says that the products of the carpenter or any other craftsman are ultimate realities can hardly be telling the truth, can he?'

'No one familiar with the sort of arguments we're using could suppose so.'

'So we shan't be surprised if the bed the carpenter makes lacks the precision of reality?'

'No.'

'Then shall we try to define representation now, in the light of this illustration?'

'Yes, please.'

'We have seen that there are three sorts of bed. The first exists in the ultimate nature of things, and if it was made by anyone it must, I suppose, have been made by God. The second is made by the carpenter, the third by the painter.'

'Yes, that is so.'

'So painter, carpenter, and God are each responsible for one kind of bed.'

'Yes.'

'God created only one essential Form of Bed in the ultimate nature of things, either because he wanted to or because some necessity prevented him from making more than one; at any rate he didn't produce more than one, and more than one could not possibly be produced.'

'Why?'

'Because, suppose he created two only, you would find that they both shared a common character or form, and this common character would be the ultimate reality.'

'That's true.'

'And I suppose that God knew it, and as he wanted to be the real creator of a real Bed, and not just a carpenter making a particular bed, decided to make the ultimate reality unique.'

'I suppose so.'

'Then do you think we might call him author of the nature of things or some such name?'

'We could do so with justice; for all his creations are ultimate realities.'

'And what about the carpenter? Doesn't he manufacture the bed?'

'Yes.'

'And what about the artist? Does he make or manufacture?'

'No.'

'Then what does he do?'

'I think that we may fairly say that he represents what the other two make.'

'Good,' said I. 'Then the artist's representation stands at third remove from reality?'

'It does.'

'So the tragic poet, whose art is representation, is third in succession to the throne of truth; and the same is true of all other artists.'

'So it seems.'

598 'We are agreed about representation, then. But, tell me, which does the painter try to represent? The ultimate reality or the things the craftsman makes?'

'The things the craftsman makes.'

'As they are, or as they appear? There is still that distinction to make.'

'I don't understand,' he said.

'What I mean is this. If you look at a bed, or anything else, sideways or endways or from some other angle, does it make any difference to the bed? Isn't it merely that it looks different?'

'Yes, it's the same bed, but it looks different.'

'Then consider – does the painter try to represent the bed or other object as it is, or as it appears? Does he represent it as it is, or as it looks?'

'As it looks.'

'The artist's representation is therefore a long way removed from truth, and he is able to reproduce everything because he never penetrates beneath the superficial appearance of anything. For example, a painter can paint a portrait of a shoemaker or a carpenter or any other craftsman without knowing anything about their crafts at all; yet, if he is skilful enough, his portrait of a carpenter may, at a distance, deceive children or simple people into thinking it is a real carpenter.'

'Yes, it may.'

'In all such cases,' I went on, 'we should be on our guard. When someone tells us that he has met someone who is a master of every craft and knows better than all the experts, we must tell him not to be silly, and not to let himself be taken in by a charlatan, whose apparent omniscience is due entirely to his own inability to distinguish knowledge and ignorance, reality and representation.'

'Very true.'

'We must go on to examine the claims of the tragedians and their chief, Homer. We are told that they are masters of all forms of skill, and know all about morality and religion; for – so the argument runs – a good poet must, if he's to write well, know all about his subject, otherwise he can't write about it. We must ask ourselves whether those who have met the poets, and read their works, have failed to perceive that these are representations at the third remove from reality, and easy to produce without any knowledge of the truth, because they are shadows and not realities; or are they right, and do good poets really know about the subjects on which the public thinks they speak so well?' 599

'It's a question we should certainly examine.'

'Suppose, then, a man could produce both the original and the representation. Do you think he would devote himself to the manufacture of representations and make it the highest object in life?'

'No, I don't.'

'Of course not. If he really knew about the things he repre-sented, he would devote himself to them and not to their representations; he would try to leave behind him the memory of things well done, and be more anxious to be praised for his actions than to write poems in praise of those of others.'

'I agree; the rewards and the reputation would both be greater.'

'We won't, then, expect Homer or any of the poets to ex-plain medicine or any similar skilled activity to us; for ex-ample, if they claim to be real doctors and not merely to imi-tate doctors' talk, we won't ask them to name any poet, ancient or modern, who has performed cures like Aesculapius, or founded a school of medicine as he did. But we *have* a right to cross-question Homer when he tries to deal with matters of such supreme importance as military strategy, political administration and education. "My dear Homer," we shall say, " if our definition is wrong and you are not merely manufacturing shadows at third remove from reality, but are a stage nearer the truth about human excellence, and really capable of judging what kind of conduct will make the individual or the community better or worse, tell us any state whose constitution you have reformed, as Lycurgus did at Sparta and others have done elsewhere on a larger or smaller scale. What city owes the benefit of its legal system to you? Italy and Sicily owe theirs to Charondas, we owe ours to Solon. Tell us who is similarly indebted to you?"'

'I don't think,' said Glaucon, 'that Homer's most devoted admirers could claim there was anyone.'

600   'Well, then, is there any record of a successful war being fought in Homer's day either under his command or with his advice?'

'No.'

'Then had he any practical skill? Did he invent any ingenious practical devices like Thales of Miletus or Anacharsis the Scythian?'

'He did nothing of that sort.'

'Well, if he did no public service, did he found a school of his own, where enthusiastic pupils came to hear him while he lived and to hand on a Homeric way of life to their successors? That was how Pythagoras got his great reputation, and his successors still talk of a Pythagorean way of life which distinguishes them in the eyes of the world from other people.'

'We hear nothing of that sort about Homer. Indeed, if the stories about Homer are true, his friend Creophylus is an even more absurd example of education than his name [1] suggests, as he is said to have paid very little attention to Homer in his own day, when he was still alive.'

'Yes, that's the story,' I said. 'But do you think, Glaucon, that if Homer had really had the knowledge to bring men the benefits of education, instead of merely representing it at

---

1. Beefeater is perhaps the nearest rendering in English. Adam quotes 'I am a great eater of beef, and I believe that does harm to my wits' (*Twelfth Night*, I, 3.90).

second-hand, he would not have had many enthusiastic followers and admirers? Protagoras of Abdera and Prodicus of Ceos and a whole lot of other individual teachers have managed to persuade their contemporaries that no one who has not studied under *them* is fit to manage either private or public affairs; and they are so admired for this expert knowledge that their pupils are almost ready to carry them about shoulderhigh. Would the contemporaries of Homer and Hesiod have let them continue as wandering minstrels, if they had really been able to make them better men? Wouldn't they have clung to them like solid gold and tried to keep them at home, and if they wouldn't stay, gone to school with them wherever they were till they had learnt what they could from them?'

'I think that's perfectly true, Socrates.'

'We may assume, then, that all the poets from Homer downwards have no grasp of reality but merely give us a superficial representation of any subject they treat, including human goodness. For example, as we said just now, the painter paints what looks like a shoemaker, though neither he nor his public 601 know anything about shoemaking, but judge merely by colour and form.'

'True.'

'In the same way the poet can use words as a medium to paint a picture of any craftsman, though he knows nothing except how to represent him, and the metre and rhythm and music will persuade people who are as ignorant as he is, and who judge merely from his words, that he really has something to say about shoemaking or generalship or whatever it may be. So great is the natural magic of poetry. Strip it of its poetic colouring, reduce it to plain prose, and I think you know how little it amounts to.'

'Yes, I've noticed that.'

'Like a face which relied on the bloom of youth for its charm, and had no real beauty.'

'Yes.'

'Here's another point. The artist who makes an image of a thing, knows nothing about the reality but only about the appearance – that was what we said, wasn't it?'

'Yes.'

'But that only takes us half-way.'

'Go on.'

'The painter may paint a picture of bit and bridle.'

'Yes.'

'But aren't they made by the harness-maker and smith?'

'Yes.'

'Then does the painter know what the bit and bridle ought to be like? Isn't this something that even the makers – the harness-maker and the smith – don't know, but only the horseman who knows how to use them?'

'True.'

'Isn't the same thing always true? You always have the three techniques – use, manufacture, and representation.'

'Yes.'

'And isn't the quality, beauty and fitness of any implement or creature or action judged by reference to the use for which man or nature intended it?'

'Yes.'

'It follows that the user must know about a thing and be able to tell the maker how well it has performed its function in use. For example, the flute player reports to the flute-maker on the performance of his flutes, and will give specifications for their manufacture which the flute-maker will follow.'

'Of course.'

'The player, in fact, knows about the merits and defects of his instruments, and the manufacturer will rely on the player's judgement?'

'Yes.'

'The user of an implement is therefore the man who knows about it; the manufacturer is compelled to take instructions from him and rely on his knowledge, and is so able to form a correct opinion [1] about its merits and defects.'

'That is so.'

'What about the artist and his representations? Has he the direct experience of the things he paints to enable him to know whether they are right or wrong? Or has he the correct

1. Cf. the Divided Line, p. 274 above.

opinion that springs from enforced reliance on the orders of someone who knows what he ought to paint?'

'He has neither.'

'So the artist has neither knowledge nor correct opinion about the goodness or badness of the things he represents.'

'Apparently not.'

'So the poet too, as artist, will be pretty ignorant about the subjects of his poetry.'

'Completely ignorant.'

'But he'll go on writing poetry, in spite of his ignorance of all he writes about, and will represent anything that pleases the ignorant multitude.'

'What else can he do?'

'Well,' I concluded, 'we seem to be pretty well agreed that the artist knows little or nothing about the subjects he represents and that his art is something that has no serious value; and that this applies to all tragic poetry, epic or dramatic.'

'Yes, entirely agreed.'

§2. THE APPEAL OF ART AND POETRY

Art and poetry appeal to, and represent, the lower, less rational part of our nature.

'Now, look here,' I said; 'we have said that this process of representation deals with something at third remove from reality, haven't we?'

'Yes.'

'Then what part of the human being does it affect?'

'What do you mean by part?'

'Something like this. The apparent size of an object, as you know, varies with its distance from our eye.'

'Yes.'

'So also a stick will look bent if you put it in the water, straight when you take it out, and differences of shading can make the same surface seem to the eye concave or convex; and it's clearly all a matter of our mind being confused. It is on this natural weakness of ours that the scene-painter and conjuror and their fellows rely when they deceive us with their tricks.'

'True.'

'Measuring, counting, and weighing were invented to help us out of these difficulties, and to ensure that we should not be guided by apparent differences of size, quantity and heaviness, but by proper calculations of number, measurement, and weight – calculations which can only be performed by the element of reason in the mind.'

'Yes, that's true.'

'Yet when reason informs us, as the result of frequent measurements, that one thing is greater than or less than or equal to another, it may be contradicted by appearances.'

'It may be.'

'Yet we said that the same part of us cannot hold different opinions about the same thing at the same time.'

'And we were quite right.'

603 'So the part of the mind which contradicts the measurements cannot be the same as the part which agrees with them.'

'No.'

'But the part which relies on measurement and calculation must be the best part of us, and the part which contradicts them an inferior one.'

'Inevitably.'

'That was the conclusion I had in mind when I said that the work of the painter and of all other artists was far removed from reality, and appealed to an element in us equally far removed from reason, a thoroughly unsound combination.'

'Thoroughly unsound.'

'So art is a poor child born of poor parents.'

'I suppose so.'

'And does this apply to the visual arts only, or also to the art which appeals to the ear, that is, poetry?'

'I should think it probably applies to poetry too.'

'We mustn't rely on probabilities drawn from painting,' I said, 'but consider the part of the mind to which dramatic poetry appeals, and ask how good or bad it is.'

'Yes, that's what we should do,' he agreed.

'Then let us put it like this,' I went on: 'drama represents human beings in action, either voluntary or compulsory; in that action they fare, as they think, well or ill, and experience joy or sorrow. Is that a fair summary?'

'Yes.'

'And does a man remain at unity in himself in all these experiences? We saw that there could be conflict and contradiction in the realm of vision; isn't there a similar conflict and contradiction in the realm of action? There is really no need to ask the question, because, as I remember, we have already agreed that our mind is full of innumerable conflicts of this sort.'

'We were quite right about that.'

'Yes, but there's an omission we ought to make good.'

'What is it?'

'Didn't we say [1] that a good man who loses his son, or anything else dear to him, will bear the misfortune more equably than other people?'

'Yes.'

'Now consider: is it because he will feel no grief? or is that impossible, and is it because he will moderate his sorrow?'

'The second alternative is nearer the truth.'

'Then tell me, will he be more inclined to resist and fight 604 against his grief when his fellows can see him, or when he is alone by himself?'

'Much more inclined when he's with others.'

'On the other hand, when he is alone he will not mind saying and doing things which he would be ashamed to let other people hear or see.'

'That is true.'

'His reason and his principles demand restraint, while his feeling of sorrow prompts him to give way to grief.'

'True.'

'And the simultaneous presence of opposite impulses implies that there are two elements in his nature.'

'Of course.'

'One of these is law-abiding, and ready to submit to the principles of conduct, which say that it is best, so far as we can, to bear misfortune patiently and without bitterness; for it

1. Cf. p. 124.

may prove a blessing in disguise, and nothing is gained by impatience, nor is anything in human life of great consequence; besides, grief prevents us getting just the help we need.'

'And what is that?'

'The help of our reason,' I said, 'which reflects on what has happened and then chooses the best move that the fall of the dice allows. We must learn not to hold our hurts and waste our time crying, like children who've bumped themselves, but to train our mind to banish grief by curing our hurts and rectifying our mistakes as soon as it can.'

'That is the right way to deal with misfortune.'

'And the highest part of us is ready to proceed accordingly.'

'Yes, obviously.'

'The other part of us, which remembers our sufferings and is never tired of bemoaning them, we may, I think, call irrational and lazy and cowardly.'

'Yes, we may.'

'And this recalcitrant element in us gives plenty of material for dramatic representation; but the reasonable element and its unvarying calm are difficult to represent, and difficult to understand if represented, particularly by the motley audience in a theatre, who have no experience of it.'

605 'Very true.'

'The dramatic poet will not therefore naturally turn to this element, nor will his skill be directed to please it, if he wants to win a popular reputation; he will find material for his dramas in the character that is unstable and irritable.'

'Obviously.'

'Then we can fairly take the poet and set him beside the painter. He resembles him both because his works have a low degree of truth and because he appeals to a low element in the mind. We are therefore quite right to refuse to admit him to a properly run state, because he stirs up and encourages and strengthens the lower elements in the mind at the expense of reason, which is like giving power and political control to the worst elements in a state and ruining the better elements. The dramatic poet produces a similar state of affairs in the mind of the individual, by encouraging the unreasoning part of it, which cannot make distinctions of size and confuses large and small, and by creating images far removed from reality.'

'I agree.'

§3. THE EFFECTS OF POETRY AND DRAMA

Poetry, dramatic poetry in particular, has a bad moral effect on its audiences, who learn to admire and imitate the faults it represents. We cannot, therefore, allow poetry in our ideal state.

'The gravest charge against poetry still remains. It has a terrible power to corrupt even the best characters, with very few exceptions.'

'It is indeed terrible if it can do that.'

'Then listen. When we hear Homer or one of the tragic poets representing the sufferings of a great man and making him bewail them at length with every expression of tragic grief, you know how even the best of us enjoy it and let ourselves be carried away by our feelings; and are full of praises for the merits of the poet who can most powerfully affect us in this way.'

'Yes, I know.'

'Yet in our private griefs we pride ourselves on just the opposite, that is, on our ability to bear them in silence like men, and we regard the behaviour we admired on the stage as womanish.'

'Yes, I'm aware of that.'

'Then is it really right,' I asked, 'to admire, when we see him on the stage, a man we should ourselves be ashamed to resemble? Is it reasonable to feel enjoyment and admiration rather than disgust?'

'It seems most unreasonable,' he said.

'Particularly,' I added, 'if you look at it in this way.'   606

'How?'

'If you consider that the poet gratifies and indulges the natural instinct for tears and the desire to give full vent to our sorrows, both of which we restrain in our private misfortunes. Our better nature, being without adequate moral or intellectual training, relaxes its control, on the grounds that it is someone else's sufferings it is watching and that there's nothing wrong in praising and pitying another man with some claim to goodness, even though his grief is excessive; besides, it reckons the pleasure it gets as sheer gain, and would certainly not consent to be deprived of it by condemning the whole poem. For very few people are capable of realizing that our feelings for other people must influence ourselves, and that if we let ourselves feel excessively for the misfortunes of others it will be difficult to restrain our feelings in our own.'

'That is very true.'

'The same argument applies to laughter. For the effect is similar when you enjoy on the stage – or even in ordinary life – jokes that you would be ashamed to make yourself, instead of detesting their vulgarity. You are giving rein to your comic instinct, which your reason has restrained for fear you may seem to be playing the fool, and bad taste in the theatre may insensibly lead you into becoming a buffoon at home.'

'It may indeed.'

'Poetry has the same effect on us when it represents sex and anger, and the other desires and feelings of pleasure and pain which normally accompany our actions. It feeds them when they ought to be starved, and makes them control us when we ought, in the interests of our own welfare and happiness, to control them.'

'I can't deny it,' he said.

'And so, Glaucon,' I continued, 'when you meet people who admire Homer as the educator of Greece, and who say that in social and educational matters we should study him and 607 model our lives on his advice, you must feel kindly towards them as good men within their limits, and you may agree with them that Homer is the best of poets and first of tragedians. But you will know that the only poetry that should be allowed in a state is hymns to the gods and paeans in praise of good men; once you go beyond that and admit the sweet lyric or epic muse, pleasure and pain become your rulers instead of law and the principles commonly accepted as best.'

'Quite true.'

'Our defence, then, when we are reminded that we banished poetry from our state, must be that reason demands it. But in case we are condemned for being insensitive and bad mannered, let us add that there is an old quarrel between philosophy and poetry. One can quote many examples of this ancient antagonism: remarks about the "bitch that growls and snarls at her master", and "a reputation among empty-headed fools", or "the crowd of heads that know too much" and the "subtle thinkers" who are "beggars" none the less.[1] However, let us freely admit that if drama and poetry written for pleasure can prove to us that they have a place in a well-run society, we will gladly admit them, for we know their fascination only too well; but it would be wicked to abandon what we believe to be the truth. I expect you feel the fascination of poetry yourself, don't you,' I asked, 'especially when it's Homer exercising it?'

'I do indeed.'

'It is only fair, then, that poetry should return, if she can make her defence in lyric or other metre.'

'Yes.'

'And we should give her defenders, men who aren't poets themselves but who love poetry, a chance of defending her in prose and proving that she doesn't only give pleasure but brings lasting benefit to human life and human society. And we will listen favourably, as we shall gain much if we find her a source of profit as well as pleasure.'

'Yes, we shall gain a lot.'

'But if they fail to make their case, then we shall have to follow the example of the lover who renounces a passion that is doing him no good, however hard it may be to do so. Brought 608 up as we have been, we are bound to love poetry, and we shall be glad if it proves to have a real value; but in the absence of such proof we shall, whenever we listen to it, recite this argument of ours to ourselves as a charm to prevent us falling under the spell of a passion most men have never outgrown. Our theme shall be that such poetry has no serious value or claim to truth, and we shall warn people against it for fear of its

1. The sources of these quotations are unknown.

effects on their character, and tell them to adopt the view of poetry we have described.'

'I entirely agree.'

'Yes, my dear Glaucon,' I said, 'because the issues at stake, the choice of good and evil, are even greater than they appear, and neither honour nor wealth nor power, nor poetry itself, should tempt us to neglect the claims of justice and goodness.'

'I agree,' he said; 'your argument convinces me, as I think it would anyone else.'

PART ELEVEN

THE IMMORTALITY OF THE SOUL AND THE REWARDS OF GOODNESS

*

§1. THE SOUL IMMORTAL

The soul is immortal because its own specific fault, moral wickedness, cannot destroy it.

'YET, you know,' I said, 'we haven't yet described the chief rewards and prizes that goodness can win.'

'If they're greater than those we've described already, they must be enormous.'

'Can anything grow really great in a short time?' I asked. 'For the span from youth to old age is short compared to the whole of time.'

'A mere nothing,' he agreed.

'Then ought not a thing that is immortal to concern itself with the whole of time rather than with so short a span?'

'I suppose so,' he replied, 'but what of it?'

'Don't you know,' I asked, 'that our soul is immortal and never dies?'

He looked at me in astonishment, and exclaimed, 'Good Lord, no! Do you believe it is?'

'I'd be wrong to deny it,' I said. 'There's nothing difficult about it, as I think you should see.'

'I don't see; but I should like to hear you explain it if it's so easy.'

'I will.'

'Go on.'

'I wonder if you would distinguish between good and evil in the same way that I do.'

'How is that?'

'I call anything that harms or destroys a thing evil, and anything that preserves and benefits it good.'

'I agree.'

'Then hasn't each individual thing its own particular good 609 and evil? So most things are subject to a specific form of evil or disease; for example, the eyes to ophthalmia and the body generally to illness, grain to mildew, timber to rot, bronze and iron to rust, and so on.'

'Yes.'

'And is not their effect to make what is subject to them deteriorate, and finally to destroy it altogether?'

'Yes.'

'A thing's specific evil or fault is therefore what destroys it, and nothing else will do so. For what is good is not destructive, nor what is neutral.'

'That is true.'

'Anything, therefore, whose specific evil can make it deteriorate, but cannot finally destroy it, must surely by its very constitution be indestructible.'

'So it would seem.'

'Then, is the soul subject to any evil which makes it deteriorate?'

'Yes, it certainly is – to all the wickednesses we have been describing, injustice, indiscipline, cowardice, and ignorance.'

'Do any of them finally destroy it? We must not make the mistake of thinking that, because wickedness is the fault of the soul, the wicked or foolish man, when he is caught doing wrong, is destroyed by his wickedness. We must rather look at it like this. The body's specific evil is disease, which weakens and destroys it, till finally it ceases to be a body at all; and the result of the destructive presence of their specific evil is, in all the other instances we quoted, annihilation, is it not?'

'Yes.'

'Let us examine the soul in the same way. Does the presence of injustice and other forms of evil in it destroy and weaken it, till it finally dies and leaves the body?'

'No, certainly not.'

'But it would be quite illogical to suppose that anything

could be destroyed by the specific evil of something else, but not by its own.'

'Quite illogical.'

'For you know of course, Glaucon,' I went on, 'that it would not be right to suppose that the death of the body was due to the badness of its food, which might be old or rotten or have any other characteristic defect; if any such defect in the food set up a process of deterioration in the body, we should say that the body had been killed by one of its own characteristic illnesses of which the bad food was the occasion. But we ought not ever to say that the body, which is one kind 610 of thing, has been killed by the badness of its food, which is another kind of thing, unless the bad food has produced the body's own specific kind of evil.'

'That is quite true,' he agreed.

'It follows by the same reasoning,' I continued, 'that unless bodily evil can produce in the soul the soul's own specific evil, we cannot suppose that it will destroy it, as that would imply that the specific evil of one thing could destroy another quite different thing.'

'Yes, that follows.'

'Until we refute this argument, therefore, we must maintain that the soul remains quite unaffected by fever or disease or injury, or even by the body being blown to fragments – unless, that is, someone can prove to us that any of these experiences make the soul more unjust or wicked than it was. We cannot admit that either the soul or anything else can be destroyed by the presence in another thing of that thing's specific evil in the absence of its own.'

'At any rate no one will ever prove that death makes the soul worse morally.'

'But even if anyone is brave enough to tackle our argument,' I said, 'and, in an attempt to avoid admitting the immortality of the soul, maintains that men become worse and wickeder when they die, we shall still claim that, if it is true, it is their wickedness which kills them; it's like a fatal disease which sooner or later kills from within those who suffer from it, rather than the execution of a criminal by the external forces of the law.'

'If wickedness really is fatal to its possessor,' Glaucon exclaimed emphatically, 'there's nothing very terrible about it; a fatal attack would merely end his troubles. The truth is surely just the opposite. It's other people that wickedness kills, if it can, while, so far from being fatal to its possessor, it makes him full of life and tirelessly energetic.'

'You are quite right,' I agreed. 'And if its own particular fault and its own particular evil has no power to destroy or kill the soul, it is not likely to be an exception to the general rule that nothing can be destroyed by an evil designed to destroy something else, but only by one designed to destroy itself.'

'No, that's hardly likely, I should think.'

611 'Then if there's no evil that can destroy it, either its own or another's, it must exist for ever; that is to say, it must be immortal.'

'It must be.'

'We can take that, then, as proved,' I said. 'And if so, it follows that the same souls have always existed. Their number cannot be decreased, because no soul can die, nor can it increase; any increase in the immortal must be at the expense of mortality, and if that were possible, everything would in the end be immortal.'

'True.'

'But that is something which our argument forbids us to believe. Nor should we believe, either, that in its essential nature the soul is variable and unstable and full of internal conflicts.'

'Why do you say that?' he asked.

'Because it would be difficult for anything made up of many ill-assorted parts to be eternal, as we have just supposed the soul to be.'

'I suppose it would.'

'Our recent argument, then, and the others, prove conclusively that the soul is immortal; but if we want to see it as it really is, we should look at it, not as we do now, when it is deformed by its association with the body and other evils, but in its original purity which reason reveals to us. We shall then find that it is a thing of far greater beauty, and shall be able to distinguish far more clearly justice and injustice and all the other qualities we have talked about. We have described the soul as we at present see it. But it's really in the same state as Glaucus the sea-god, and its original nature as difficult to see as his was after long immersion had broken and worn away and deformed it, and covered it with shells and seaweed and rock, till he looked more like a monster than what he once was. That is the sort of state we see the soul reduced to by countless evils. For the truth we must look elsewhere.'

'Where?' Glaucon asked.

'To the soul's love of truth,' I said. 'Think how its kinship with the divine and immortal and eternal makes it long for them and try to grasp them; think what it might become if it followed this impulse whole-heartedly and was lifted by it out of the sea in which it is now submerged, and if it shed all the rocks and shells which, because it feeds on the earthly things 612 that men think bring happiness, encrust it with a strange and earthy shell. Then one really could see its true nature, composite or single or whatever it may be. However, as it is, we have, I think, described well enough its character and experience in this mortal life.'

'Quite well enough,' he agreed.

§2. THE REWARDS OF GOODNESS IN THIS LIFE

The purpose of the whole argument has been to show that goodness is its own reward, irrespective of consequences. But, now that has been proved, we may add that in fact the good man is rewarded by society in this life.

'And now,' I said, 'I think our argument has fulfilled the conditions you laid down,[1] and, in particular, has avoided mentioning rewards and reputation, as you said Homer and Hesiod do. We have found that goodness is its own reward, and that it pays us to act justly whether or not we have Gyges' ring, and a cap of invisibility into the bargain.'

'That's perfectly true.'

'That being so, Glaucon,' I asked, 'can there be any objec-

[1]. P. 98.

tion if we go on and describe the rewards which justice and goodness bring at the hands of men and gods, in this life and the next?'

'No objection at all.'

'Then you must give up the concession I made.'

'What was that?'

'I agreed, for the sake of argument, that the good man should have a reputation for wickedness and the wicked man for goodness; you said that, though it might in fact be impossible for either men or gods to be so deceived, yet you wanted the concession so that we could judge between goodness and wickedness in themselves, without their consequences. Don't you remember?'

'I can hardly deny it,' he said.

'Then, now that judgement has been given,' I said, 'I want to ask that we should agree to restore Justice her good name with gods and men; she can then reward the reputation for justice as faithfully as we have seen her reward the reality.'

'That's a fair request.'

'Then will you first grant that neither the good nor the wicked man's character is hidden from the gods?'

'Yes.'

'If so, then, as we agreed at the beginning,[1] they will love one and hate the other.'

'That's true.'

'And the man they love may expect, may he not, all the
613 blessings heaven can give him, except in so far as punishment is due to him for offences committed in a former life?'

'Yes.'

'So we must assume that, if the just man is poor or ill or suffering from any other apparent misfortune, it is for his ultimate good in this life or the next. For the gods will never neglect the man whose heart is set on justice and who is ready, by pursuing goodness, to become as like god as man is able.'

'If he is like them they are not likely to neglect him.'

'On the other hand, we may suppose that the reverse of all this is true of the unjust man.'

1. P. 83.

'Most certainly.'

'These, therefore, are the rewards the just man receives from the gods.'

'I should certainly agree.'

'And what about men?' I asked. 'If the truth be told, isn't it this – that the clever rogue is rather like a runner who does well over the first half of the course, but cannot stay it out? He is very quick off the mark, but in the end is humiliated and slinks off with his tail between his legs without any prize. The real runner stays the course and carries off the prize in triumph. Isn't the same thing true in general of the just man? In any action, in dealings with others, or in life itself, isn't he the man who gets both the rewards and the good name among his fellows?'

'Yes.'

'Then will you allow me to say about him all that you said about the unjust man? That is, that the just man, when he grows old, will, if he wishes, hold positions of authority in the state, marry whom he likes and marry his children to whom he likes, and so on, as you said of the unjust man. Conversely the unjust man will, in general, even if he gets away with it when he is young, be caught at the end of the course and humiliated; his old age will be miserable, he will be an object of contempt to citizen and foreigner alike, and will suffer all those punishments you so rightly called barbarous – whipping, torture, branding; there is no need for me to repeat them. May I say all this?'

'Yes, you may fairly say it.'

§3. THE MYTH OF ER

The Good Man's rewards in the life after death. The responsibility of the individual and the doctrine of transmigration. This concluding section of the dialogue is cast in the form of a myth, as is Plato's habit when he wishes to convey religious or moral truths for which plain prose is inadequate. Much of the detail is borrowed from contemporary sources, probably Orphic.

'These, then,' said I, 'are the prizes and rewards which the

614 just man receives from gods and men while he is still alive, over and above the reward of his own virtue.'

'And very sure and splendid they are,' he replied.

'Yet they are nothing in number and quality when compared to the things that await the just man and unjust man after death; you must hear about these too, so that our discussion may pay them both off in full.'

'There are few things I would hear more gladly.'

'It's no Alcinous' tale I have to tell,' I continued, 'but the story of a brave man, Er, son of Armenius, a native of Pamphylia. He was killed in battle, and when the dead were taken up on the tenth day the rest were already decomposing, but he was still quite sound; he was taken home and was to be buried on the twelfth day, and was already lying on the funeral pyre, when he came to life again and told the story of what he had seen in the other world. He said that when his soul left his body it travelled in company with many others till they came to a wonderfully strange place, where there were, close to each other, two gaping chasms in the earth, and opposite and above them two other chasms in the sky. Between the chasms sat Judges, who, having delivered judgement, ordered the just to take the right-hand road that led up through the sky, and fastened the badge of their judgement in front of them, while they ordered the unjust, who carried the badges of all that they had done behind them, to take the left-hand road that led downwards. When Er came before them, they said that he was to be a messenger to men about the other world, and ordered him to listen to and watch all that went on in that place. He then saw the souls, when judgement had been passed on them, departing some by one of the heavenly and some by one of the earthly chasms; while by the other two chasms some souls rose out of the earth, stained with the dust of travel, and others descended from heaven, pure and clean. And the throng of souls arriving seemed to have come from a long journey, and turned aside gladly into the meadow and encamped there as for a festival; acquaintances exchanged greetings, and those from earth and those from heaven inquired each other's ex-
615 periences. And those from earth told theirs with sorrow and

tears as they recalled all they had suffered and seen on their journey, which lasted a thousand years, while the others told of the delights of heaven and of the wonderful beauty of what they had seen. It would take a long time to tell you the whole story, Glaucon, but the sum of it is this. For every wrong he has committed a man must pay the penalty in turn, ten times for each, that is to say, once every hundred years, this being reckoned as the span of a man's life. He pays, therefore, tenfold retribution for each crime, and so for instance those who have been responsible for many deaths, or have betrayed state or army, or have cast others into slavery, or had a hand in any other crime, must pay tenfold in suffering for each offence. And those who have done good and been just and god-fearing are rewarded in the same proportion. He told me too about infants who died as soon as they were born or who lived only a short time, but what he said is not worth recalling. And he described the even greater penalties and rewards of those who had honoured or dishonoured gods or parents or committed murder. For he said that he heard one soul ask another where Ardiaeus the Great was. (This Ardiaeus was the tyrant of a city in Pamphylia some thousand years ago, who had killed his old father and elder brother and done many other wicked things, according to the story.) "He has not come, and he never will," was the reply. "For this was one of the terrible things we saw. We were near the mouth of the chasm and about to go up through it after all our sufferings when we suddenly saw him and others, most of them tyrants, though there were a few who had behaved very wickedly in private life, whom the mouth would not receive when they thought they were going to pass through; for whenever anyone incurably wicked like this, or anyone who had not paid the full penalty, tried to pass, it bellowed. There were some fierce and fiery-looking men standing by, who understood the sound, and thereupon seized some and led them away, while others 616 like Ardiaeus they bound hand and foot and neck, flung them down and flayed them, and then impaled them on thorns by the roadside; and they told the passers-by the reason why this was done and said they were to be flung into Tartarus." And

395

Er said that the fear that the voice would sound for them as they went up was the worst of all the many fears they experienced; and when they were allowed to pass in silence their joy was great.

'These, then, are the punishments and penalties and the corresponding rewards of the other world.'

The paragraph which follows gives, in brief and allusive form, a picture of the structure of the universe, in which the rings on the spindle-whorl are the orbits of the planets and the sphere of the fixed stars. A brief note on the details is given in the appendix on p. 402.

'After seven days spent in the meadow the souls set out again and came on the fourth day to a place from which they could see a shaft of light running straight through earth and heaven, like a pillar, in colour most nearly resembling a rainbow, only brighter and clearer; after a further day's journey they entered this light and could then look down its axis and see the ends of it stretching from the heaven, to which they were tied; for this light is the tie-rod of heaven which holds its whole circumference together like the braces of a trireme. And to these ends is fastened the spindle of Necessity, which causes all the orbits to revolve; its shaft and its hook are of adamant, and its whorl a mixture of adamant and other substances. And the whorl is made in the following way. Its shape is like the ones we know; but from the description Er gave me we must suppose it to consist of a large whorl hollowed out, with a second fitting exactly into it, the second being hollowed out to hold a third, the third a fourth, and so on up to a total of eight, like a nest of bowls. For there were in all eight whorls, fitting one inside the other, with their rims showing as circles from above and forming the continuous surface of a single whorl round the shaft, which was driven straight through the middle of the eighth. The first and outermost whorl had the broadest rim; next broadest was the sixth, next the fourth, next the eighth, next the seventh, next the fifth, next the third and last of all the second. And the rim of the largest and outermost was many-coloured, that of the seventh was the brightest, the eighth was illuminated by the seventh, from which it takes its colour, the second and fifth were similar to each other and yellower than the others, the third was the whitest, the fourth reddish and the sixth second in whiteness. The whole spindle revolved with a single motion, but within the movement of the whole the seven inner circles revolved slowly in the opposite direction to that of the whole, and of them the eighth moved fastest, and next fastest the seventh, sixth and fifth, which moved at the same speed; third in speed was the fourth, moving as it appeared to them with a counter-revolution; fourth was the third, and fifth the second. And the whole spindle turns in the lap of Necessity. And on the top of each circle stands a siren, which is carried round with it and utters a note of constant pitch, and the eight notes together make up a single scale. And round about at equal distances sit three figures, each on a throne, the three Fates, daughters of Necessity, Lachesis, Clotho, and Atropos; their robes are white and their heads garlanded, and they sing to the sirens' music, Lachesis of things past, Clotho of things present, Atropos of things to come. And Clotho from time to time takes hold of the outermost rim of the spindle and helps to turn it, and in the same way Atropos turns the inner rims with her left hand, while Lachesis takes inner and outer rims with left and right hand alternately.

'On their arrival the souls had to go straight before Lachesis. And an Interpreter first marshalled them in order and then took from the lap of Lachesis a number of lots and types of life and, mounting on a high rostrum, proclaimed: "This is the word of Lachesis, Daughter of Necessity. Souls of a day, here you must begin another round of mortal life. No Guardian Angel will be allotted to you; you shall choose your own. And he on whom the lot falls first shall be the first to choose the life which then shall of necessity be his. Goodness knows no master; a man shall have more or less of her according to the value he sets on her. The fault lies not with God, but with the soul that makes the choice." With these words he threw the lots among them, and each picked up that which fell beside him, all except Er himself, who was forbidden to do so. 618

And when each had taken up his lot he knew what number he had drawn. Then the Interpreter set before them on the ground the different types of life, far more in number than the souls who were to choose them. They were of every conceivable kind, animal and human. For there were tyrannies among them, some life-long, some falling in mid-career and ending in poverty, exile and beggary; there were lives of men famed for their good looks or athletic prowess, or for their good birth and family connexions, there were lives of men with none of these claims to fame. And there was a similar choice of lives for women. There was no choice of types of character since of necessity each soul must assume a character appropriate to its choice; but wealth and poverty, health and disease were all mixed in varying degrees in the lives to be chosen.

'Then comes the moment, my dear Glaucon, when everything is at stake. And that is why it should be our first care to abandon all other forms of knowledge, and seek merely for that which will show us how to find the man who will teach us how to tell a good life from a bad one and always choose the better course so far as we can; we must reckon up all that we have said in this discussion of ours, weighing the arguments together and apart to find out how they affect the good life, and see what effects, good or ill, good looks have when accompanied by poverty or wealth or by different types of character, and what again are the effects of the various blends of birth and rank, strength and weakness, cleverness and stupidity, and all other qualities inborn or acquired. If we take all this into account and remember how the soul is constituted, we can choose between the worse life and the better, calling the one that leads us to become more unjust the worse, and the one that leads us to become more just the better. Everything else we can let go, for we have seen that this is the best choice both for living and dead. This belief we must retain unshaken when 619 we enter the other world, so that we may be unmoved there by the temptation of wealth or other evils, and avoid falling into the life of a tyrant or other evil-doer and perpetrating unbearable evil and suffering worse, but may rather know how to choose the middle course, and avoid so far as we can, in this life and the next, the extremes on either hand. For this is the surest way to human happiness.

'But to return. Er told us that the Interpreter then spoke as follows: "Even for the last comer, if he chooses wisely and lives strenuously, there is left a life with which he may be well content. Let him who chooses first look to his choice, and him who chooses last not despair." When he had spoken, the man with the first lot came forward and chose the greatest tyranny he could find. In his folly and greed he chose it without examining it fully, and so did not see that it was his fate to eat his children and suffer other horrors; when he examined it at leisure, he beat his breast and bewailed his choice, and forgot the Interpreter's warning that the fault for his misfortunes was his own, blaming fate and heaven and anything but himself. He was one of the souls who had come from heaven, having lived his previous life in a well-governed state, but having owed his goodness to habit and custom and not to knowledge; and indeed, broadly speaking, the greater part of those who came from heaven, being untried by suffering, were caught in this way, while those who came from earth had suffered themselves and seen others suffer and were not so hasty in their choice. For this reason and because of the luck of the draw there was a general change of good for evil and evil for good. Yet it is true also that anyone who, during his earthly life, faithfully seeks wisdom and whose lot does not fall among the last may hope, if we may believe Er's tale, not only for happiness in this life but for a journey from this world to the next and back again that will not lie over the stony ground of the underworld but along the smooth road of heaven.

'And to see the souls choosing their lives was indeed a sight, 620 Er said, a sight to move pity and laughter and wonder. For the most part they followed the habits of their former life. And so he saw the soul that had once been Orpheus choose the life of a swan; it was unwilling to be born of a woman because it hated all women after its death at their hands. The soul of Thamyris chose the life of a nightingale, and he saw a swan and other singing birds choose the life of a man. The twentieth soul to choose chose a lion's life; it was the soul of Ajax, son of Telamon, which did not want to become a man, because it remembered the judgement of the arms. It was followed by Agamemnon, who also because of his sufferings hated humanity and chose to be an eagle. And Atalanta's turn came somewhere about the middle, and when she saw the great honours of an athlete's life the attraction was too great and she chose it. After her he saw Epeius, son of Panopeus, turning into a skilled craftswoman, and right among the last the buffoon Thersites putting on the form of an ape. And it so happened that it fell to the soul of Odysseus to choose last of all. The memory of his former sufferings had cured him of all ambition and he looked round for a long time to find the uneventful life of an ordinary man; at last he found it lying neglected by the others, and when he saw it he chose it with joy and said that had his lot fallen first he would have made the same choice. And there were many other changes from beast to man and beast to beast, the unjust becoming wild animals and the just tame in every kind of interchange.

'And when all the souls had made their choice they went before Lachesis in the order of their lots, and she allotted to each its chosen Guardian Angel, to guide it through life and fulfil its choice. And the Guardian Angel first led it to Clotho, thus ratifying beneath her hand and whirling spindle the lot it had chosen; and after saluting her he led it next to where Atropos spins, so making the threads of its destiny irreversible; and then, without turning back, each soul came before the throne of Necessity and passing before it waited till all the others had done the same, when they proceeded together to the plain of Lethe through a terrible and stifling heat; for the land was without trees or any vegetation.

'In the evening they encamped by the Forgetful River, whose water no pitcher can hold. And all were compelled to drink a certain measure of its water; and those who had no wisdom to save them drank more than the measure. And as each man drank he forgot everything. They then went to sleep and when midnight came there was an earthquake and thunder, and like shooting stars they were all swept suddenly up and away to be born. Er himself was forbidden to drink, and could not tell by what manner of means he returned to his body; but suddenly he opened his eyes and it was dawn and he was lying on the pyre.

'And so, my dear Glaucon, his tale was preserved from perishing, and, if we remember it, may well preserve us in turn, and we shall cross the river of Lethe safely and shall not defile our souls. This at any rate is my advice, that we should believe the soul to be immortal, capable of enduring all evil and all good, and always keep our feet on the upward way and pursue justice and wisdom. So we shall be at peace with God and with ourselves, both in our life here and when, like the victors in the games collecting their prizes, we receive our reward, and both in this life and in the thousand-year journey which I have described all will be well with us.'

THE SPINDLE OF NECESSITY

THIS passage has been much discussed, but the following points are generally agreed:

(1) The 'Spindle of Necessity' is intended, however imperfectly, to give a picture of the working of the Universe.

(2) Plato thought that the universe was geocentric, with the fixed stars on a sphere or band at the outside, the earth at the centre, and the orbits of the sun, moon, and planets between earth and stars.

(3) The rims of the whorl are intended to represent these orbits, and have the following equivalences:

1. The fixed stars	5. Mercury
2. Saturn	6. Venus
3. Jupiter	7. Sun
4. Mars	8. Moon

Thus, for example, we are told that 'the fourth (Mars) was reddish', and 'the eighth (Moon) was illuminated by the seventh (Sun)'.

(4) The breadth and relative motion of the rims represent the distances and relative speeds of the planets, though it is difficult to be certain about details (cf. Cornford, *Plato's Cosmology*, p. 88).

(5) The singing sirens are Plato's version of the Pythagorean doctrine of the 'harmony of the spheres', which Aristotle describes as follows:

'It seems to some thinkers that bodies so great must inevitably produce a sound by their movement: even bodies on the earth do so, although they are neither so great in bulk nor moving at so high a speed, and as for the sun and the moon, and the stars, so many in number and enormous in size, all moving at a tremendous speed, it is incredible that they should fail to produce a noise of surpassing loudness. Taking this as their hypothesis, and also that the speeds of the stars, judged by their distances, are in the ratios of the musical consonances, they affirm that the sound of the stars as they revolve is concordant. To meet the difficulty that none of us is aware of this sound, they account for it by saying that the sound is with us right from birth and has thus no contrasting silence to show it up; for voice and silence are perceived by contrast with each other, and so all mankind is undergoing an experience

like that of a coppersmith, who becomes by long habit indifferent to the din around him' (*De Caelo*, II, 9, trans. Guthrie
LOEB edition).

In the more detailed interpretation of the passage there is much
uncertainty: the Greek itself is far from unambiguous, and the exact
meaning of the word translated 'braces' is not known. The interpretation on which the translation given is based starts from the
assumption that the governing factor in the passage is the spindle
analogy. Most interpretations start with the pillar-like light and
try to determine what exactly it is, and what exactly is fastened to
what. But this particular sentence is full of difficulties, and we don't
really know at all what a 'brace' was. But we do know what a Greek
spindle was like, and as Plato is using it as an analogy to explain
the arrangement of the stars and planets, it seems best to start not
with the light and the 'braces' but with the spindle. The picture it
gives us, if astronomically somewhat inadequate even by fourth
century standards, is clear enough. The earth lies at the centre, the
planets revolve in rings round it, with the fixed stars on the outermost ring; and the shaft of the spindle is the axis of revolution.
The picture is an imperfect one: for the only thing that matters
astronomically about the elaborately described whorl are the rings
on it, a ring is not a very adequate description of the sphere of the
fixed stars, though it does well enough for the orbits of the planets,
and nothing is said about the shape of the earth, which gets rather
left out of the picture anyway, or about the obliquity of the ecliptic.
But it should be remembered that Plato wrote in a world that was
virtually without machines and that a suitable analogy would have
been hard to find.

If we now go back to the light we notice two things. First, that
it is compared to a pillar and appears (the precise meaning of the
Greek is elusive) to run like an axis through the earth. Second, that
it is not a feature of the universe visible from our part of the earth.
The souls' journey takes place on the earth's surface, as in the
comparable myth in the *Phaedo*. The meadow is, however, clearly in
some distant part of the earth, and it is only after four days' journey
from it that the souls see the light, and only after another day's
journey that they reach it. Any attempt to relate it to any visible
astronomical feature (e.g. the Milky Way) therefore appears to be
mistaken. Besides, if we suppose the earth to be spherical, as it is
in the *Phaedo*, then if we lived at either pole, we should presumably
see the planets circling *round* the horizon: we could only see them
circling overhead, as we in fact do, if we were living towards the

equator, in which case we can reasonably be supposed *not* to be able to see the axial light passing through the poles. It seems best therefore to suppose that the light is a shaft passing through the poles of a spherical earth, and suggested by the spindle-analogy which Plato already had in mind. That analogy also suggested the rather obscure remarks about 'tying' the light to the sky. The spindle shaft has a hook by which it is suspended [1] from the thread which it is spinning; and so we may suppose the axis to be in some way fastened to the heaven which spins round with it. But the analogy is weak here, as we have seen, because the sky, i.e. the *sphere* of the fixed stars, appears as the outermost *rim* of the whorl; and this very weakness may account for the obscurity of the Greek, because Plato was trying to combine two pictures, a dome and a rim, that are incompatible.

The fact that Plato goes on to say the spindle 'revolves on the knees of Necessity', who is herself on the earth's surface where the souls are, supports the view that the spindle is the governing analogy in the passage. Cornford says that we are not concerned with the universe itself, but with a model of it. The spindle is, of course, a model or analogy; but there is no denying that Plato speaks of the spindle of necessity being fastened to the heavens, and it is something of a shock to find that the spindle is 'on the knees of Necessity' because until that point there has been no suggestion that he has been describing anything but the physical universe. But he has used the spindle as an analogy in that description, and so when he starts to talk about the Fates, whose traditional occupation was spinning, he can talk of the spindle as being in the lap of Necessity, even though it is strictly illogical to do so. Necessity can't both sit on the earth, and have the universe, including the earth, on her lap. But it is good symbolism to put the Universe 'on the lap of Necessity', and so the illogicality is overlooked.

---

1. The Greek word translated 'stretching' and 'fastening' (p. 396) could equally mean 'suspended' and may have been suggested by the analogy.

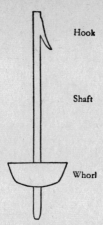

Hook

Shaft

Whorl

Fig. 1 Greek Spindle

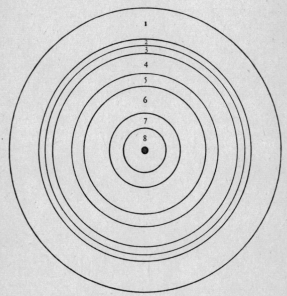

Fig. 2 The Rims on the Whorl (*after Adam*)

MORE ABOUT PENGUINS

If you have enjoyed reading this book you may wish to know that *Penguin Book News* appears every month. It is an attractively illustrated magazine containing a complete list of books published by Penguins and still in print, together with details of the month's new books. A specimen copy will be sent free on request.

Penguin Book News is obtainable from most bookshops; but you may prefer to become a regular subscriber at 3s. for twelve issues. Just write to Dept EP, Penguin Books Ltd, Harmondsworth, Middlesex, enclosing a cheque or postal order, and you will be put on the mailing list.

Some other books published by Penguins are described on the following pages.

Note: *Penguin Book News* is not
available in the U.S.A.

PLATO

THE LAST DAYS OF SOCRATES

Translated by Hugh Tredennick

The trial and condemnation of Socrates (469–399 B.C.), on charges of heresy and corrupting the minds of the young, forms one of the most tragic episodes in the history of Athens in decline. In the four works which compose this volume – *Euthyphro*, *The Apology*, *Crito*, and *Phaedo* – Plato, his most devoted disciple, has preserved for us the essence of his teaching and the logical system of question and answer he perfected in order to define the nature of virtue and knowledge. The vindication of Socrates and the pathos of his death are admirably conveyed in Hugh Tredennick's modern translation.

HOMER
THE ODYSSEY
Translated by E. V. Rieu

Homer's *Odyssey*, composed some three thousand years ago, is still among the very pinnacles of all literature. The story of Odysseus's epic voyage home from Troy to his kingdom of Ithaca brims, like some splendid novel, with a fathomless humanity.

In his introduction to this famous edition Dr Rieu states: 'I have done my best to make Homer easy reading for those who are unfamiliar with the Greek world.' This is too modest. His inspired translations of *The Odyssey* and *The Iliad* have made Homer a modern best-seller.

HOMER
THE ILIAD

Translated by E. V. Rieu

The Greeks considered *The Iliad* their greatest literary achievement, and no epic poem in any language has ever rivalled it. Out of a single episode in the Tale of Troy, Achilles' withdrawal from the fighting and his return to kill the Trojan hero Hector, Homer created a timeless, dramatic tragedy. His characters are heroic but their passions and problems are human and universal, and he presents them with compassion, understanding, and humour against the harsh background of war.

E. V. Rieu's prose translation has the same direct simplicity and subtle elegance which distinguishes his *Odyssey*; it moves swiftly and confidently through the greater complexity of *The Iliad* and never falls short of the nobility of Homer's theme.

EURIPIDES
MEDEA AND OTHER PLAYS

Translated by Philip Vellacott

Four more plays by Euripides (484–407 B.C.) are presented
in this volume in modern English by Philip Vellacott,
who has already translated many of the great Greek
dramas for the Penguin Classics.

Medea, the story of that princess's horrible revenge for
the infidelity of Jason, the hero of the Argonauts, is
Euripides' earliest surviving tragedy, whilst *Heracles* is
among his latest plays. In *Hecabe* and *Electra* he again
underlines the wickedness of revenge. An outspoken
critic of society and the gods, Euripides was at his most
eloquent on the theme of human suffering, and among the
most lyrical of all poets.

Also available
THE BACCHAE AND OTHER PLAYS
ALCESTIS AND OTHER PLAYS

SOPHOCLES
THE THEBAN PLAYS

Translated by E. F. Watling

'The translator is not only a good scholar but also a sensitive producer and actor, so that the theatrical values are much clearer than usual. The dignity of the great orchestra-theatre is maintained, yet the lines will come easily from the lips of a modern and the plays are revealed as containing many unexpected twists of character and even of humour. . . . A trilogy eminently playable' – E. Martin Browne in *Drama*

'Mr Watling's translation of the dialogue into a "much resolved" form of iambic line and the choruses into rhyming verse is extremely successful; its great beauty and extreme speakability far outweigh the few mistakes. Mr Watling has interesting things to say in his introduction about the plays themselves, his methods of translation, and the problems of production' – *Journal of Hellenic Studies*

Also available
ELECTRA AND OTHER PLAYS

PLATO
PROTAGORAS AND MENO
Translated by W. K. C. Guthrie

Plato (427–347 B.C.), the most brilliant of Socrates' pupils, held that philosophy must be a product of living contact between mind and mind, and his dialogues afforded him the means of reaching a wide audience. *Protagoras*, possibly his dramatic masterpiece, deals, like *Meno,* with the problem of teaching the art of successful living and good citizenship. While *Protagoras* keeps to the level of practical commonsense, *Meno* leads on into the heart of Plato's philosophy, the immortality of the soul, and the doctrine that learning is knowledge acquired before birth.